HIKING TRAILS
of South Africa

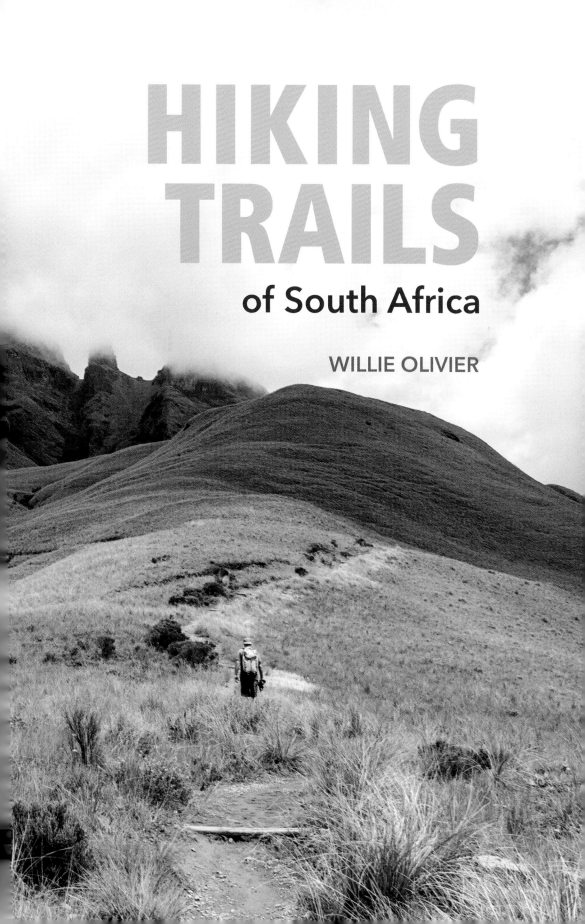

HIKING
TRAILS
of South Africa

WILLIE OLIVIER

Published by Struik Travel & Heritage
(an imprint of Penguin Random House South Africa (Pty) Ltd)
Company Reg. No. 1953/000441/07

The Estuaries No. 4, Oxbow Crescent, Century Avenue, Century City, 7441
PO Box 1144, Cape Town, 8000 South Africa

Visit **www.penguinrandomhouse.co.za**

First published in 2003; Second edition published in 2007, Reprinted in 2007;
Third edition published in 2010, Reprinted in 2010, 2012, 2014; Fourth edition published in 2017, Reprinted in 2019;
Fifth edition published in 2022

Print: 978 1 77584 829 5
ePub: 978 1 77584 788 5

1 3 5 7 9 10 8 6 4 2

Publishing manager: Pippa Parker
Managing editor: Roelien Theron
Senior editor: Colette Alves
Designer: Neil Bester
Typesetter: Deirdré Geldenhuys
Cartographers: John Hall; Genené Hart
Illustrator: Dr Jack
Proofreader: Thea Grobbelaar

Reproduction by Hirt & Carter Cape (Pty) Ltd and Studio Repro
Printed and bound by ABC Press, Parow, Cape Town

While every effort has been made to ensure the accuracy of the information provided, some information will
become outdated during this edition's lifespan. Readers are advised to check information regarding trail facilities,
etc. with the relevant trail authority, especially when making reservations for overnight hiking trails.
The publishers would appreciate information relating to new, upgraded or defunct trails for
incorporation into subsequent editions.

Picture credits
AS = stock.adobe.com; IOA = Images of Africa
Front cover: Matthew Schnetler; back cover: Villiers – AS; half-title page: Roelien Theron; full title page: Nadine – AS;
p. 8: Christian B. – AS; p. 73: Nina du Plessis; p. 74 middle: Lanz von Hörsten/IOA; p. 75 top: Hein von Hörsten/IOA; bottom: Nadine –
AS; p. 78 top: Hein von Hörsten/IOA; p. 80: Richard – AS; bottom: Gerhard Dreyer/IOA; p. 113 bottom: Balarka Robinson – AS;
p. 115 top: Ian Duckels; p. 116 top: Shaen Adey/IOA; p. 117 bottom: Walter Knirr/IOA; p. 118 top: Shaen Adey/IOA; bottom: Peter
Pickford/IOA; p. 119 top: Roger de la Harpe – AS; bottom: Dave Southwood; p. 142: alice – AS; p. 143: Zoomtraveller – AS;
p. 153 top: Justin Klusener – AS; bottom: Shaen Adey/IOA; p. 154: Thomas – AS; p. 155 both: Shaen Adey/IOA; p. 157 top: sara_winter
– AS, bottom: Tony Camacho/IOA; p. 158 bottom: Keith Young/IOA; p. 159 top: Jürgen Bochynek – AS; bottom: Le Roux van Schalkwyk;
pp. 188–9: Shaen Adey/IOA; pp 226–7: Alexandre ROSA – AS; p. 228 top: Christian B. – AS; p. 229 top left and right: Nigel Dennis/
IOA, bottom: Lanz von Hörsten/IOA; pp. 230–1: Olaf Holland – AS; p. 232 top: Dawid de Wet; bottom: Rudi – AS; p. 255: Krause &
Johansen; pp. 270–1: Walter Knirr/IOA; pp. 288–9: Krause & Johansen; p. 295: Fokke Baarssen

AUTHOR'S ACKNOWLEDGEMENTS
The publication of this revised and updated edition would not have been possible
without the support of the various trail authorities, officials and owners who assisted with
the updating of the information. I'm reluctant to single out individuals, as I truly appreciate
all the responses to my telephone and email enquiries; so, a big thank you to everyone who assisted.
I also wish to thank the Penguin Random House staff, especially Roelien Theron for her guidance,
patience and thorough editing and cross-checking. Thank you also to Pippa Parker,
Neil Bester and Deirdré Geldenhuys for their support and assistance.

CONTENTS

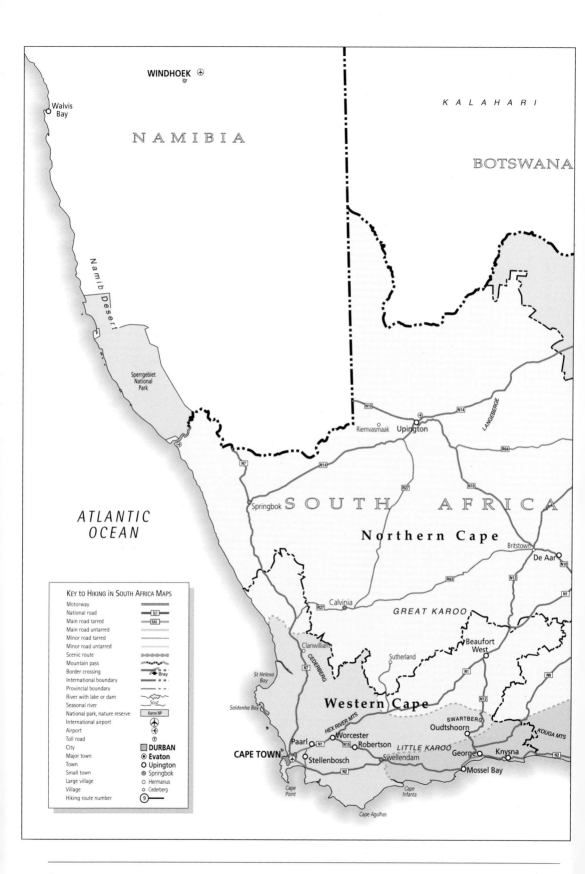

KEY to HIKING IN SOUTH AFRICA MAPS

Motorway	
National road	N1
Main road tarred	R44
Main road untarred	
Minor road tarred	
Minor road untarred	
Scenic route	
Mountain pass	
Border crossing	Bray
International boundary	
Provincial boundary	
River with lake or dam	
Seasonal river	Sout
National park, nature reserve	Karoo NP
International airport	✈
Airport	⊕
Toll road	
City	DURBAN
Major town	⊙ Evaton
Town	O Upington
Small town	⊚ Springbok
Large village	○ Hermanus
Village	∘ Cederberg
Hiking route number	⑨

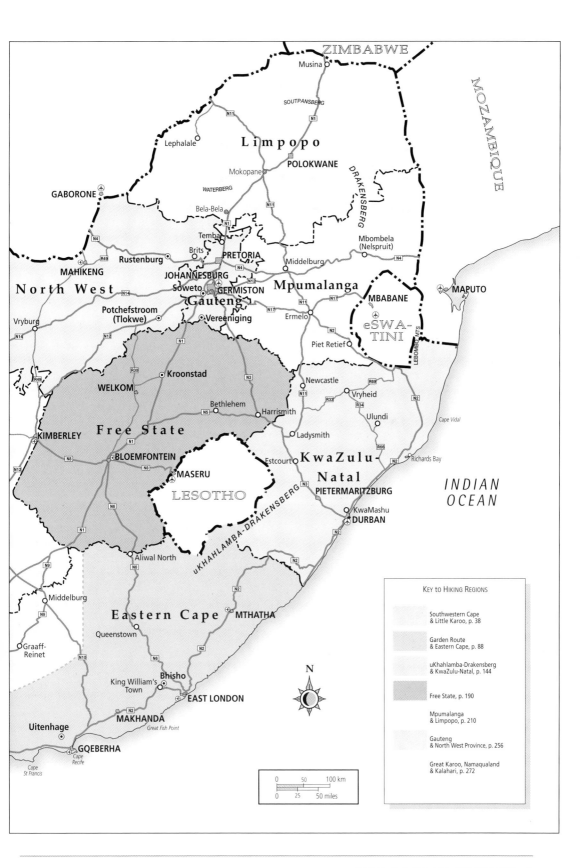

KEY TO HIKING REGIONS

Southwestern Cape
& Little Karoo, p. 38

Garden Route
& Eastern Cape, p. 88

uKhahlamba-Drakensberg
& KwaZulu-Natal, p. 144

Free State, p. 190

Mpumalanga
& Limpopo, p. 210

Gauteng
& North West Province, p. 256

Great Karoo, Namaqualand
& Kalahari, p. 272

SOUTHWESTERN CAPE & LITTLE KAROO

GARDEN ROUTE & EASTERN CAPE

UKHAHLAMBA-DRAKENSBERG & KWAZULU-NATAL

FREE STATE

MPUMALANGA & LIMPOPO

GAUTENG & NORTH WEST

GREAT KAROO, NAMAQUALAND & KALAHARI

INTRODUCTION

Get the most out of this guide by taking time to familiarise yourself with the headings and terminology used, and study the information on planning and preparation for your hike to maximise your enjoyment of the trail and avoid common hiking injuries.

USING THE BOOK

Given the number of walks and overnight trails in South Africa, it is not possible to include every one, and so only those of one hour and longer are listed in this guide. However, a few exceptional walks of under an hour have been included.

The walks and trails in this book have been grouped into broad geographic areas. Not only are these areas commonly used in promoting tourism, but in many instances the fauna, flora, climate and geological features are essentially similar in geographical regions. In some instances, however, the geographical regions overlap with political regions.

For each region a brief overview of the flora, fauna, geology, climate and other relevant aspects is given. By reading this section you will enhance your appreciation and enjoyment of each area's natural highlights.

As a general rule all day walks have been listed under the name of the attraction, conservation area (nature reserve, national park or botanical garden) or city/town where they are located. This will enable readers to easily locate walks and trails in a particular area.

However, where a hike, particularly an overnight hiking trail, is well known by its own name it is listed under that name, rather than that of the nature reserve or park in which it is located. Cross-references are provided to other walks within the same conservation area.

The information provided should assist you in choosing a walk or overnight trail to suit your interest, level of fitness, and the time you have available. Each trail or group of trails has its own entry, with a shaded box at the start that provides information about the hike(s) under the following headings:

Trails For entries with just one walk or trail, the distance in kilometres, time required (hours or number of days) and the trail design are given. Where there are several walk or trail options, the number of walks in a specific reserve or park, city or town, the distance and duration of the shortest and longest walks and the trail designs are provided at the start of the entry. In these instances, the distance, duration and trail design of each individual trail is provided at the end of that trail's description.

The term **open-ended** denotes a trail that has different starting and ending points. The starting point of a **circular** trail is the same as its ending point. A **network** denotes several different trail options, which are often interlinked, while **network from base camp** denotes a trail design that, usually, forms a figure eight. Trails like this can typically be done with only a daypack. **Out-and-return** describes a trail that follows the same outward and return route (i.e. you hike to the end of the trail and then turn around and retrace your steps).

Permits are generally not required for day hikes in local authority nature reserves, wildflower gardens and botanical gardens, but entrance fees are charged in most cases. Conservation fees payable to SANParks parks and reserves managed by provincial conservation authorities do not include guided walks, and in the case of the Eastern Cape Parks and Tourism Agency there is also a charge for walks. Some trails and walks on private properties are open to overnight guests only. It is advisable to always establish whether a permit or advanced booking is required before setting off. Where no address or booking details are provided under **Permits**, a permit is not required. When booking, you should enquire about the minimum number of hikers and, in the case of groups, the maximum number.

Maps Information is provided on the type of map (e.g. sketch map, trail pamphlet with map, downloadable map) available.

Facilities/Activities Facilities, amenities and recreational activities are briefly described.

Pertinent information Here you will find any important information pertaining to the walk or trail. In each regional description there is also a section on important information relating to that region.

The main body of each entry provides a brief description of the type of walk or trail, and also things such as the flora, fauna and landscape along the route, followed by a description of the trail itself.

All trees mentioned in the text follow the names of the National List of Indigenous Trees. For any other flora the scientific name is provided in brackets so as to avoid confusion, since there are no standardised common names for most non-tree species.

Trail terminology

With the proliferation of walks and trails in South Africa, trail terminology has unfortunately gone out of the window. In addition, low-budget travellers are referred to as backpackers, confusing the terminology even further.

Hiking trail is a continuous well-defined route through a natural or human-made environment on which the user carries equipment and food in a backpack. Specific overnight stops are provided at the end of each day's hike.

Backpacking trails are not along designated footpaths and you are free to blaze your own trail. No overnight facilities are provided and sleeping is mainly in the open, in caves or in a tent carried by the backpacker.

Wilderness trails are conducted by a trails officer, in natural and wild areas such as national parks and game reserves. The primary aim of these trails is to give trailists an understanding of and appreciation for nature.

Interpretative trails are usually no more than a few kilometres long, and emphasise education and the interpretation of the environment. A trail pamphlet is supplied to guide you, and at intervals along the route numbered markers indicate features that are explained in the brochure.

Day walks are ideal for those who want to stretch their legs without having to don a heavy backpack. They range in duration from 30 minutes to a full day.

BEFORE YOU GO

Planning

Without proper planning a walk or overnight trail could easily end in disaster, so do remember to spend time on planning your trip. After all, half the fun is in the planning and preparation!

If you are not a seasoned hiker, one of the best ways to familiarise yourself with this very rewarding activity is to join a hiking club. This will enable you to learn from those with years of experience and to join club outings. An internet search for hiking clubs in South Africa will be useful if you are thinking of joining a club.

The South African magazine *Getaway* regularly features articles on hiking trails and equipment and new developments. There are several books with detailed descriptions of day walks and overnight hikes.

Most walks, and just about every hiking and backpacking trail, involve physical exertion, and it stands to reason that, the fitter you are, the more enjoyable you will find your walk or hike. Regular physical exercise is, therefore, essential, and if you intend doing a difficult trail you would be well advised to increase your exercise levels for some time before you attempt it.

When planning a walk or hike, keep the following important points in mind:
- Choose a walk or trail to suit your fitness level. Begin with a few day walks, and then progress to an easy weekend trail, before attempting something too demanding. Always bear the weakest member of the party in mind and ensure that everyone is fit.
- Taking the climate into consideration is of vital importance and will determine what clothing and equipment you need to take. Far too many

day outings on Table Mountain and in the Drakensberg have turned into disaster because of rapid weather changes, inexperience and inadequate preparation.

- Obtain maps and make sure you know how to read and navigate with them. This is especially important when backpacking in wilderness areas. Here, 1:50,000 topographical maps obtained from the Surveyor-General's office will be useful.
- One of the golden rules is never to set off alone, especially on long day walks and hiking trails. On hiking trails, the minimum number of people you should consider walking with is three, but four is safer.
- Check your equipment beforehand and ensure that it is serviceable, especially your boots.
- Before setting off, check the weather forecast and, if necessary, call off your walk or hike.
- Always inform someone of your intended route and expected time of return. In backpacking areas where there is a mountain register, it should be completed correctly and in detail.

Food

Whether on a day walk or a long hiking trail, it is important to replace the energy your body has used by eating healthily. On day walks, snacks like peanuts and raisins, energy bars, dried fruit and snacks with a high nutritional value will suffice. It is important, though, to eat at regular intervals to ensure you keep your energy levels up.

Fortunately for overnight hikers, the days of lugging tins of bully beef and the rather unpalatable old-style soya protein meals up the mountain are long gone. A wide range of new, instant, dehydrated soya protein meals, vegetables, mashed potatoes, instant soups and desserts are available. And with a bit of imagination, and a few fresh ingredients and herbs, the taste of soya protein meals can be even further improved.

If you are prepared to pay quite a bit more for food, specialist outdoor stores usually carry a range of lightweight meals. They are not only very palatable, but are also extremely light and often require little cooking. On the downside, you might find the portions too small if you have a healthy appetite.

Kilojoule intake varies from person to person, but men on average burn up 17,000 to 21,000 kJ (4,000 to 5,000 cal) and women 13,000 to 17,000 kJ (3,000 to 4,000 cal) a day. About 4,185 kJ (1,000 cal) a day should be added for a trail averaging 15 km a day, or when hiking in cold weather. Also, you need about two and a half times as many kilojoules to gain 300 m in altitude as you would if you were walking on level terrain.

The following points are a rough guide to the average person's daily nutritional requirements:

- Two servings of milk or milk products; one serving is 250 ml milk, 60 ml milk powder (dry), 45 g cheese.
- Two servings of protein-rich food; one serving is 80 to 250 ml nuts, 60 ml peanut butter.
- Four servings of fruit and vegetables; one serving is a piece of fruit, 125 ml cooked dehydrated vegetables.
- Four or more servings of carbohydrates; one serving is one slice of bread, 125 ml cooked cereal, 125 ml cooked pasta or rice.

Also remember the following:

- When planning your menu, cater for a maximum of 1 kg of food per person per day, bearing in mind that in cold weather you will have a bigger appetite.
- When hiking in arid areas, take fresh vegetables like cucumber, tomatoes and carrots. They are worth the extra weight.
- Each person should have some snacks, like glucose sweets, nuts, dried fruit, biltong and energy bars.
- Decant the contents of glass bottles into plastic containers. If carrying a foil bag, ensure that it won't be pierced by a sharp object!
- Always carry an extra day's emergency rations of high-energy food (chocolate, nuts and raisins, glucose sweets and energy bars). Don't be tempted to tuck into the rations before completing the trail!
- Pack utensils and food so that they are easily accessible for tea and lunch stops.

Equipment

First-time hikers are confronted by a wide range of scientifically designed, lightweight equipment and deciding what to buy can be a daunting task. The following are some guidelines on buying equipment. Since designs and features are changing continuously, only the general features and principles are discussed.

THREE-DAY SAMPLE MENU

This menu, which caters for three hikers, can be adapted to your group's tastes and the conditions of the particular trail you are hiking. Always consider the facilities at the overnight stops when planning a menu. If wood is available, you can vacuum-pack fresh meat for a braai on the first night.

	Breakfast		Lunch		Supper	
DAY 1	muesli	300 g	6 slices rye bread	375 g	dehydrated beans	90 g
	3 rusks	60 g	6 cheese wedges	100 g	bacon (vacuum-pack)	150 g
	1 orange	300 g	1 small salami	200 g	2 carrots	125 g
	3 sheets crispbread	95 g	1 packet dried figs	125 g	dehydrated onion	25 g
			peanuts and raisins	150 g	tomato	25 g
			3 apples	500 g	1 cube chicken stock	10 g
	If starting from base camp,		1 isotonic drink	80 g	rice	150 g
	replace this meal with usual				1 packet instant	
	breakfast fare.				pudding	100 g
DAY 2	oats	150 g	6 sheets crispbread	190 g	3 cups instant soup	35 g
	3 rusks	60 g	3 hard-boiled eggs	190 g	instant mashed potato	112 g
	1 grapefruit	300 g	1 tin sardines	106 g	1 tin tuna	185 g
	3 slices rye bread	188 g	cucumber	150 g	1 small green pepper	100 g
			1 fruit roll	80 g	dehydrated onion	25 g
			1 isotonic drink	80 g	dehydrated peas	50 g
					1 chicken stock cube	10 g
					instant custard powder	100 g
DAY 3	muesli	300 g	6 sheets crispbread	190 g	3 cups instant soup	35 g
	3 rusks	60 g	6 cheese wedges	100 g	pasta	250 g
	stewed fruit	200 g	1 tomato	200 g	instant pasta sauce	50 g
			1 small tin pâté	100 g	parmesan cheese	120 g
			1 packet dried dates	125 g	1 slab chocolate	200 g
			peanuts and raisins	150 g		
			3 naartjies	500 g	*Black olives or smoked mussels*	
			1 isotonic drink	80 g	*can be added to sauce*	

MISCELLANEOUS

peanut butter	250 g	18 tea bags	54 g	sugar	500 g
jam	300 g	hot chocolate	100 g	6 coffee sachets	75 g
milk powder (4 sachets)	400 g	3 packets biscuits	600 g	salt, pepper, herbs	25 g

Weights given are average and will vary according to the product brand.

Golden rules when buying equipment

- Before buying equipment, spend some time talking to fellow backpackers, browse through manufacturers' catalogues, and consult the literature on equipment.
- Carefully consider your personal requirements. It would serve little purpose, for instance, to buy a lightweight sleeping bag suitable for caravanning if you're planning to hike in the Drakensberg in winter.
- Shop assistants in specialist backpacking stores are an invaluable source of information.
- Don't be tempted to buy specialist equipment from supermarkets. It might be cheaper, but in most cases the staff simply do not have the expertise to advise you.
- Always buy equipment with a reputable brand name. This does not, however, mean that you must buy the most expensive equipment in the store.
- Think of comfort and functionality, not fashion. Personal requirements and taste should ultimately dictate what you buy.
- Decide what price you are prepared to pay. Be realistic, but never compromise on quality for a lower price.

Footwear

Few things can spoil a hike as much as blistered and aching feet, and on any trail comfort begins at ground level, with your feet. Trailing footwear can be divided into four broad categories:
- Lightweight boots or hiking shoes for day walks over easy terrain.
- Medium-weight boots for hiking and backpacking along well-defined trails.
- Mountaineering boots for hiking and backpacking in rugged mountainous terrain and snow.
- Specialist rock-climbing boots.

Worldwide there has been a trend towards light- and medium-weight footwear, and in South Africa the use of Alpine-type mountaineering boots – once the norm – has to a large extent become restricted to winter backpacking trips in the Drakensberg.

This trend was brought about mainly by the lower quality and poorer performance of leather boots, the soaring cost of leather, and also because of environmental considerations.

Taking general trail conditions in South Africa into consideration, lightweight footwear is suitable for most day walks and rambles, while medium-weight boots are suitable for most hiking and backpacking trails.

When buying boots the most important considerations are size, comfort and protection. To ensure a good fit you should wear your hiking socks when fitting boots. Before tying up the laces, push your foot as far forward as possible, until your toes rub against the toe cap. If you can still squeeze a finger down the inside of your heel, you have the right fit. The extra room is necessary to allow your feet to expand and to prevent your toes from rubbing against the toe of the boot when you are walking downhill. Do the laces up firmly, but not too tightly, and ensure that the boots don't constrict the broad part of your feet and that there is sufficient room for your toes to move freely. Walk around the shop and check that your heels are held firmly in the back of the boots. If they lift more than about 6 mm you should try a smaller size.

Always try boots on both your feet. In most people, one foot is slightly bigger than the other and although a boot might fit one foot perfectly, you could find that a boot of the same size is either too big or too small on the other foot.

Once you have the right pair of boots it is important to give them a chance to adjust to the shape of your feet before embarking on your first trip – be it a day walk or an overnight hike. The time it will take to break in your boots will depend on the material (leather or fabric) and the flexibility of the sole. Begin by wearing the boots around the house and on walks over easy terrain, until you are satisfied that they have been properly worn in.

Good-quality boots are expensive and should, therefore, be cared for properly. One of the most common mistakes is to dry wet boots in front of a fire. This causes shrinkage, which can in turn cause the sole to separate from the uppers. Wet boots should be aired as much as possible and then worn until they are dry.

In the course of your travels your boots may be subjected to a great deal of hard wear, rain and sunshine. After every trip, brush the uppers lightly to remove any mud, grime or dust, especially in the seams, and ensure that they are dry. Stuff them with newspaper and store in a dry place. If you opted for leather boots, you should apply polish after every trip and treat them occasionally with Dubbin. This will revitalise the leather and help it to retain its unique qualities – breathability, suppleness, strength and durability – and will also waterproof the boots without affecting their breathability. And, contrary to popular belief, Dubbin does not cause stitch-rot.

Packs

After footwear, your pack is the piece of equipment most crucial to your enjoyment of an outing. Comfort is once again of the utmost importance.

Daypacks range in capacity from 18 to 42 litres, with an average of around 35 litres. Well-padded back and shoulder straps are important features, and a waist strap is useful on larger volume packs.

Backpacks In South Africa most packs are internal frame packs, although external frame packs are still very popular in Europe and the United States.

As with footwear it is important to select the correct length of pack or frame. This is not as simple as it sounds. For example, if you are tall this does not mean a long-frame backpack will necessarily be the right fit. What is important is that the size of the frame/pack is correctly related to your torso size. Most good-quality internal frame packs have a self-adjusting system, enabling people of different heights to use the same pack.

One of the most important features of a backpack is a well-padded hip belt, which helps to transfer up to 70 per cent of the weight from your shoulders to your hips. Load the pack with a few heavy items and fasten the hip belt so that its top edge is just above your hip bone. Adjust the shoulder straps until the pack fits snugly against your back, ensuring that the top harness point is not more than 5 cm below your high prominent neck bone. Ask a shop assistant or friend to help you gauge this position correctly. Because the sizes of packs and frames vary, you might have to try several times before finding the correct fit.

Check that the back of the pack is well padded, and that there is sufficient room between the pack and your back for air ventilation. Remember the old adage: 'If it's a large pack, fill it up. If it's a small pack, it won't fit in.' Considering general weather and other conditions in South Africa, packs with a capacity of 50 to 55 litres and 60 litres are sufficient for women and men respectively, for a weekend trail. For longer trails (e.g. five-day hikes) women will need a pack with a capacity of 55 to 60 litres and men 60 to 75 litres.

Ensure that the fabric is strong, waterproof and abrasion resistant. Backpacks are manufactured from a variety of fabrics, with guarantees ranging from five years to a lifetime, if you're investing in a good-quality pack.

Ask yourself these questions when buying a backpack:
- Are the hip belt and shoulder straps well padded?
- Are the shoulder straps easily adjustable?
- Does the hip belt have a quick-release buckle?
- How many side pockets are there?
- Is there a sack extension (an extension of the backpack's inner fabric enabling you to use the space under the pack's top flap)?
- Are the zips covered with flaps in order to make them more waterproof?

Sleeping bag

When choosing a sleeping bag, your most important choice will be between down and artificial fibre. Once again, there are several factors to consider: weight, warmth, size when packed up, design and price. Your final choice will be determined by how well these suit the intended use of the bag.

Down sleeping bags have the advantage of being light, compact and warm. However, they lose their insulating properties when wet, require special care during washing, and are expensive. In recent years the quality of artificial-fibre sleeping bags has improved tremendously, and they are proving to be viable options to down. They are warm, retain their insulating properties when wet, are easy to wash, and their price is competitive. In addition, the disadvantage of years gone by, bulk, is no longer a factor, and they compare favourably with down sleeping bags in this respect.

Two basic styles of sleeping bag are available: rectangular and cowl top, or mummy-shaped. If you are likely to spend extended periods in cold weather climates, a cowl top makes good sense, as the body-contoured shape provides the best warmth-to-weight ratio.

The bag should have a well-shaped cowl and draw cords, so it can cover your head in cold weather, leaving just a breathing hole open, to reduce heat loss. Some cowl top bags have short zips, but the First Ascent range has 'foot friendly zips' (a South African registered design), so you can use it as a duvet, or zip two bags together.

Rectangular bags are the most popular sleeping bags in South Africa. They usually come with a full zip, which offers the advantage that you can control the temperature inside the bag. On warm evenings the bag can be unzipped to reduce the temperature and in cold weather two bags can be zipped together for extra warmth. At home, the bag can be used as a duvet.

Ensure that the bag you buy has a draught tube (a thin down-filled baffle sewn along the inside of the zip and the face area of the cowl) to prevent heat loss.

Caring for your sleeping bag

- Keep your bag dry. If it does get wet, dry it out in the open as soon as possible. Gently squeeze out excess water, but do not wring the bag. Take care not to damage the draught tube when zipping up or unzipping the bag.
- Never expose your bag to excessive heat, such as direct sunlight or a fire. In down sleeping bags this could cause the down to harden.
- Store your bag loosely – preferably by hanging it up when not in use. If down bags are compressed for extended periods, the natural resilience of the filling will be strained.
- Keep your sleeping bag as clean as possible, both inside and outside. The use of a sleeping bag inner sheet and a sleeping bag cover will not only keep your bag clean, but will also give added warmth; although you'll add about 1 kg in weight.
- Down sleeping bags should always be hand-washed. Fill a bath tub with lukewarm water (40 °C) and add special down soap. Gently wash the bag, avoiding harsh twisting or wringing. Drain the tub, and rinse in fresh water, repeating the process until all the soap is removed. Gently squeeze as much water as possible out of the bag before lifting it out; supporting it from underneath. Dry the bag carefully in a warm place, away from direct heat. Gently massage down lumps into individual plumules.

Closed-cell ground pad

On trails where there are no overnight huts with bunks and mattresses, a closed-cell ground pad (a thin, 6 to 10 mm, high-density foam mattress with excellent insulating properties) is essential to prevent the cold from creeping up from the ground. First time out, you might find the ground pad a bit hard, but remember: it's a lot more comfortable than just sleeping on a ground sheet! In terms of comfort, weight and size (rolled up) it is far superior to open foam and airbeds. High-quality closed-cell groundpads with a thickness of 9 mm are suitable for temperatures as low as -10 °C.

When investing in a ground pad, don't compromise on quality. Cheap products are available, but their durability and the density of the foam are far inferior to a good-quality closed-cell ground pad.

For backpackers prepared to increase the weight of their packs for comfort, a self-inflating mattress is an option. These ingenious mattresses are ideal for backpacking – they are lighter than airbeds, more compact and you just unroll them. Their disadvantages are that they are heavier than ground pads, more expensive, and tend to puncture easily.

Ground sheet

When sleeping out in the open, a ground sheet is useful to keep the area around your sleeping bag clean. The choice here is between a light plastic ground sheet or a sportsman's blanket, which is lined with aluminium foil on the one side and weighs about 310 g. In cold conditions it can be wrapped around you to preserve heat and it can also be used as a makeshift shelter.

The emergency blanket is a very light (70 g) sheet of aluminium foil, one side of which is highly reflective. It takes up hardly any space, is relatively inexpensive, but does not stand up to rough handling and should, therefore, be used only in emergencies for extra insulation, or as an emergency shelter against rain or sun.

Rain gear

Selecting rain gear is bound to be difficult, unless you're prepared to delve deep into your pocket to buy a high-quality product made from outer fabrics such as K-Tech® or Goretex®, which are waterproof and breathable.

Casual rain jackets are usually either water-repellent or waterproof. Water-repellent garments have the advantage of breathability and perform satisfactorily in light rain. However, when adverse weather conditions set in for prolonged periods, they are totally inadequate.

Waterproof garments made from PVC-coated nylon, on the other hand, provide a sealed shell that is unable to breathe. Warm, humid air released by the body is unable to escape through the waterproof material and water vapour is formed inside the shell. This results in an excessive heat build-up and condensation and you end up being soaked inside the garment.

The answer to these problems is garments made from K-Tech® and Goretex®, which are 100 per cent waterproof, but breathable, and virtually impenetrable to wind. These fabrics are expensive, but in inclement weather you will regret not having invested in a high-quality garment.

Backpacking stove

A backpacking stove (a lightweight, portable stove that uses gas – a butane/propane mixture – methylated spirits, benzene or alcohol as a source of fuel) is not only convenient for a quick mug of tea along the trail, but also if you find firewood stocks depleted at overnight huts. In addition, because of the danger of open fires, the negative environmental impact of burning wood, and the cost of providing it, firewood is no longer supplied on many trails.

In years gone by, mountaineers relied heavily on their often temperamental benzene stoves, but nowadays gas seems to be the most popular choice. Other options include methylated spirits (alcohol) and pressurised multi-fuel stoves.

Lightweight gas stoves are clean burning and reasonably efficient when shielded from the wind. Some models have a wider base and an improved burning ring – a great step up from the rather unstable early models, with their high centre of gravity. In windy conditions, at high altitudes and in cold weather, however, cannister gas stoves perform poorly. Empty gas canisters have, unfortunately, become a major source of pollution.

Methylated spirits stoves, commonly known as storm cookers, are easy to operate and reasonably efficient. They perform well in windy conditions, and their wide base makes them stable. A kit consisting of two pots, a frying pan, potgrip, wind shield, burner, and (with some models) a kettle, packs into a compact unit. On the negative side, they have a low fuel to heat ratio, requiring you to carry a large supply of fuel on long trips. This not only takes up space, but also adds to the weight of your pack. In addition, you'll have to invest in some lightweight metal bottles into which to decant the meths. Another negative factor is that this stove will blacken the pots during cooking.

Pressurised multi-fuel stoves are quite expensive, but in terms of performance are far superior to any other stoves, especially at high altitudes and low temperatures. Some models use any type of fuel, from paraffin to aviation fuel.

Tent

On some trails you might have to be self-sufficient, right down to accommodation, and you should never rely on finding caves, or basic shelters, unoccupied.

Mercifully, lighter fabrics have long replaced the trusty old canvas tents of early mountaineers. Not only were they bulky and heavy, but if you happened to touch the inside of the tent accidentally during rain, water would seep through and you would later get a shower of water caused by condensation.

This problem was largely solved by the invention of the double-skinned tent, consisting of an inner tent and a flysheet. The inner tent is made of either an absorbent cotton or a breathable nylon fabric, and is suspended from the tent poles in such a way that it does not touch the flysheet or outer tent. Vapour passes through the breathable fabric of the inner tent and condenses when it comes into contact with the cold flysheet. At the same time, the air trapped between the inner tent and the flysheet acts as an effective insulator.

Features to look for in a quality backpacking tent are a waterproof, sewn-in groundsheet with fairly high side-walls, mosquito-netting at the doors and a bell on either side. A bell is a triangular extension of the flysheet at either end of an A-framed tent, designed to cover the entrances. It reduces wind resistance and creates more space, which can be used for storing equipment.

Tents come in a variety of styles, from the conventional A-frame to a bewildering selection of dome-shaped models. The advantages of dome tents are that they are easy to erect, more spacious, and their streamlined shapes can withstand high winds.

Clothing

Keeping a cool head in hot temperatures is important, so a wide-brimmed hat is preferable to a peak cap. Your hat should provide adequate shade for your face and neck. If you are trailing in an area where cold temperatures can be expected, bear in mind that about 30 per cent of the body's heat is lost from the head. Pack a balaclava or a woollen cap that can be pulled over your ears.

In summer, short-sleeved shirts or blouses are more suitable than T-shirts, which provide little ventilation and tend to cling to one's body. Cotton shirts are more airy and have the added advantage of a collar that can be turned up to protect your neck against the sun.

In winter, it is advisable to pack a long-sleeved, woollen shirt for extra warmth. You'll also need a warm jersey, or a densely knitted, fleece-lined tracksuit top and trousers. Wool is, in all cases, preferable to other fabrics, on account of its excellent insulating qualities. For cold-weather conditions you'll need to invest in something more substantial, like a Polartec® or down jacket.

Even in cold, wet conditions, shorts are preferable to trousers, which can cause discomfort and chafing once they are wet. Never wear jeans – they are heavy (even more so when wet) and take ages to dry.

Your normal underwear should do for a hike, although cotton garments are more comfortable. For cold-weather trailing, thermal underwear is highly recommended. On a hike of a few days you don't need to take a change of underwear for every day, as it's usually possible to wash or rinse underwear on the trail.

A general rule to prevent loss of body heat is to cover the body with three layers of clothing rather than a single, thick layer. This is because heat is prevented from escaping by the dry air trapped between the different layers of clothing.

When it comes to socks, there is no substitute for wool, and although a wool/fibre mixture is acceptable, you must ensure that the percentage of wool is larger than that of the artificial fibre. Avoid nylon socks, as they will overheat your feet and cause blisters. Many hikers prefer to wear two pairs of socks – a thin inner pair of either wool or cotton, and a thick woollen outer pair. This reduces the likelihood of blisters considerably, as the inner socks absorb the chafing that would normally occur on your skin.

Miscellaneous items

I use a Maglite® torch as they last forever, but Petzl® head-torches are also excellent and very popular for hiking. The well-organised hiker will, however, have little need for a torch, and a small torch is usually adequate for cooking and finding your way to the toilet at night. Not only do they take up little space, but they are also light, as are the spare batteries.

A 2-litre water bottle or two 1-litre bottles are essential on any trail. Plastic water bottles are most commonly used, but have the disadvantage of giving water an unpleasant flavour when it is warm. Some plastic water bottles have a felt covering, which helps to keep water cool as long as the felt is kept damp.

A plastic, dish-shaped bowl, or a plate with a rim, is preferable to a flat plate as porridge and saucy food tend to spill over the edge of the plate. Clip-together cutlery sets are useful, but a sharp knife from your kitchen drawer will also prove invaluable. Beware of aluminium mugs; although they retain heat for a long time, they can cause some nasty blistered lips when you are over-eager to begin drinking hot drinks.

Packing your backpack

Here are some hints to assist you when you are packing your backpack:

- Limit the weight of your pack as far as possible. Your pack should never exceed a third of your body weight. Ideally it should weigh 20 per cent of the body weight of women and children, and 25 per cent of the body weight of men. Don't end up stumbling along a trail, burdened by a heavy backpack filled with lightweight equipment.
- Before packing, line your backpack with a large garbage bag or a sac liner (a heavy-duty plastic bag manufactured specifically to line the inside

of packs). This will keep the contents dry if you're caught in the rain during your hike. Although most good quality packs do stand up to their claim of being waterproof, water does sometimes seep through seams and zips, while older packs can lose their waterproof coating.

- Pack systematically to ensure that unnecessary items are not included, and that essential items are not left out. There is nothing as frustrating as discovering that you have forgotten to pack something when you are already on a trail!
- Items you are likely to use often during the day should be easily accessible.
- The bulk of the weight in your pack should be in line with your centre of gravity. Heavy items should be packed in the top half of the pack, closest to your back, so that the lower half of the pack is left for lighter items.
- The kit list overleaf is for a five-day trail. You do not need to follow it religiously – rather adapt it to suit the type of trail you are going on, its length, and your personal needs.

Hiking hints

Few things can be as frustrating as arriving at the end of a hard day's hike in the rain only to discover that your matches are soaked, or that the batteries of your torch have run down. As you gain more experience of the outdoors, you will learn how to avoid these annoying mishaps and turn a good trip into a memorable one. Here are a few basic common-sense hints:

- To avoid the feeling of despair when you switch on your **torch** and nothing happens, turn one of the batteries the wrong way around when not in use to avoid them running down if the torch is accidentally switched on. And always remember to pack **spare batteries** and a **spare bulb**.
- **Waterproof matches** can be bought at speciality backpacking stores, but are expensive and sometimes even these matches do not work when wet. Take a **cigarette lighter**, some matches, and a small piece of striker from a match box in an empty film cannister; it's 100 per cent waterproof when closed properly.

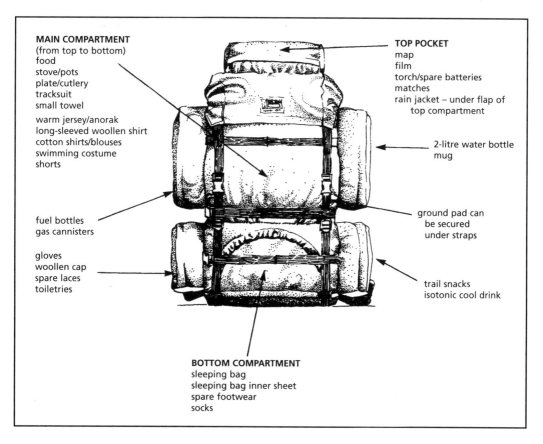

MAIN COMPARTMENT
(from top to bottom)
food
stove/pots
plate/cutlery
tracksuit
small towel

warm jersey/anorak
long-sleeved woollen shirt
cotton shirts/blouses
swimming costume
shorts

fuel bottles
gas cannisters

gloves
woollen cap
spare laces
toiletries

TOP POCKET
map
film
torch/spare batteries
matches
rain jacket – under flap of
    top compartment

2-litre water bottle
mug

ground pad can
    be secured
    under straps

trail snacks
isotonic cool drink

BOTTOM COMPARTMENT
sleeping bag
sleeping bag inner sheet
spare footwear
socks

KIT LIST

Item	Mass in grams	E = Essential O = Optional C = Check facilities	Item	Mass in grams	E = Essential O = Optional C = Check facilities
Backpack			detergent (biodegradable)	50	E
65-litre backpack	1,800	E	dishcloth	80	E
pack cover	25	O	trail snacks	500	E
			trail food (5 days)	5,000	E
Sleeping gear			emergency rations	500	E
sleeping bag	1,800	E	2-litre water bottle (full)	2,075	E
inner sheet	500	O			
pillow	100	O	**Toiletries**		
mattress/ground pad	400	C	tissues	10	O
ground sheet	720	C	toilet paper and trowel	250	E
mosquito net	250	O	towel (small)	250	E
tent, poles and pegs	3,000	C	soap (biodegradable)	50	E
			face cloth/sponge	35	O
Footwear			shaving kit	65	O
boots/walking shoes	1,800	E	toothbrush and -paste	45	E
spare bootlaces	50	E	comb	15	O
spare footwear	750	E	sunscreen cream	120	E
warm, thick socks (2 pairs)	400	E	lip balm	20	E
light, breathable socks (2 pairs)	200	E	foot powder	50	O
gaiters	150	O	insect repellent	50	E
			moisturiser, body lotion	150	O
Clothing					
woollen cap/balaclava	125	C	**Miscellaneous**		
sun hat	75	E	first-aid kit (see p. 31)	300	E
cool hiking shirt/T-shirt x 2	400	E	emergency blanket	70	E
warm long-sleeved shirt	250	E	water purification tablets	50	C
jersey	700	E	litter bag	25	E
shorts x 2	300	E	torch, spare batteries/bulb	115	E
underwear x 3	150	E	pocket knife	100	O
thermal underwear	300	C	candle	60	O
sleepwear	300	C	camera and film	1,000	O
tracksuit	700	E	binoculars (compact)	400	O
gloves/mittens	100	C	map	50	E
waterproof rain gear	600	E	compass	100	O
swimming costume	150	O	permit	7	E
			passport/driver's licence	40	C
Cooking and food			waterproofing bags	50	E
cutlery	50	E	survival bag	240	C
plate and mug	110	E	cord (5 m, thin nylon)	50	E
can opener	20	E	notebook and pencil	50	O
stove, pots, potgrip, fuel	2,000	E	whistle	10	E
matches (waterproofed)	15	E	field guides	variable	O
pot-scourer	20	E	walking stick	variable	O

- A **potgrip** will prevent you from getting your fingers burnt when you move pots or, even worse, seeing your meal end up on the ground. Also very useful is a **long-handled spoon** for stirring food when cooking over an open fire.
- Avoid glass bottles – they are heavier than plastic and can break. Decant liquids into screw-top **plastic bottles** or **aluminium containers**. Some aluminium containers are available in different colours, to ensure that you do not confuse water and fuel bottles. Don't use aluminium containers for acidic liquids as the acids will corrode the aluminium.
- A **squeeze tube** is handy for honey, jam, peanut butter and condensed milk. It is filled from the lower end, which is then sealed with a sliding clamp. It is reusable, but remember not to turn the screw top too tightly, or it may crack.
- If you will be crossing wide rivers during the course of your trail, take along a **survival bag** (a large red or orange heavy-duty plastic bag) to float equipment across. In emergencies it can also be used as a cover for your sleeping bag, although excessive heat build-up and condensation inside the survival bag can be a problem.
- Although each group should have a well-equipped first-aid kit, each person should carry a few **plasters**.
- A very common complaint on trails is sore feet. You should take along an extra pair of **light footwear** (running shoes or sandals), which will give your feet a much-needed rest after a hard day of hiking.
- A 5-m length of thin **nylon rope** can be useful for emergency situations, repairs, and as a washing line.
- Always remember to take **precautions against the sun** – wear a sun hat, use sunscreen, and so on.
- Remember to **pack food away** before going to sleep, or you might discover in the morning that mice or small predators have ruined, or made off with, some of your provisions.
- A **pocket knife** or **multi-tool** is useful on a trail. It is light and compact, and most models have all the gadgets needed: can opener, knife, tweezers and scissors. Attach it to your pack with a piece of string.

TRAIL ETHICS

In view of the increasing number of people using the great outdoors, it has become vitally important to adhere to trail ethics. By doing so you will help to conserve the natural environment for your own enjoyment, and for future generations.

Land
- Don't litter. Tissues tucked into sleeves or under watchstraps inevitably fall out and are one of the most common forms of trailside litter. Cigarette ends, sweet wrappers, toilet paper and empty gas canisters are also a nuisance and should never be left along a trail. Even orange peels, commonly regarded as biodegradable, should not be discarded, as they can take months to decompose.
- Carry a refuse bag and pick up litter along the way.
- Never bury litter. In most cases it will be uncovered by the elements or animals, such as baboons. This is not only unsightly, but broken glass and tins with sharp edges can injure fellow trailists and animals. Remember: carry out what you carry in.
- Avoid shortcuts, as the trail gradient and the potential for erosion increases. It also demands greater exertion.
- Step over erosion bars, barriers or rock, not on them, and avoid dislodging stones.
- Avoid areas with little or no vegetation. They are extremely susceptible to erosion, and can take years to recover from damage.
- Likewise, avoid scree slopes. Hiking on them causes miniature rockfalls, which destroy vegetation that has established itself under difficult conditions.
- Never roll rocks down slopes or over cliffs. This may injure other people, cause fires or erosion, and it destroys vegetation.
- When camping in the wilds, you must make sure that the area is disturbed as little as possible. Set up your camp on level ground, not only for your own comfort, but also because sloping ground erodes easily once the vegetation on it is compacted.
- Keep your backpack as light as possible. This will not only lighten your burden and increase

your enjoyment of the outdoors, but will also reduce erosion and compaction, as the lighter the total load, the less the compaction you will cause.

Water

Many of South Africa's streams and rivers are the habitat of rare and endangered aquatic life, which can easily be destroyed by carelessness. Keep the following in mind:

- Avoid camping closer than 60 m to any body of water, wherever possible.
- Do not use soap in streams or rivers – a good swim is normally sufficient to clean up – and don't brush your teeth directly in streams or rivers. Cooking and eating utensils should be washed away from the water.

Air

One of the main reasons people go trailing is to seek solitude. Noise pollution is as objectionable as littering, so bear these points in mind:

- Avoid shouting, yelling and whistling – it decreases your chances of seeing wildlife.
- If you smoke, take care, especially in dry grasslands. Never smoke while you are hiking. Stop, sit down and relax. Use a flat rock as an ashtray and remember to put the filter in your litter bag.
- Smoke from campfires causes air pollution. Where fires are permitted, keep them small.

Flora and fauna

- Don't pick flowers (they will only wilt) or uproot bulbs.
- Avoid shortcuts as they could destroy sensitive and endangered vegetation.
- Where fires are permitted, remember the following:
- Use existing fireplaces instead of making new ones.
- Choose a level spot where the fire will be well protected from the wind.
- Don't make fires under trees, near vegetation or on the roots of trees; clear the area around the fireplace of all leaves and humus.
- Keep your fire small; that way it's more comfortable to cook over, more intimate, easier to control and you will conserve wood.

- Where the collection of firewood is permissible, use only fallen wood and do not break seemingly dead branches off trees; it is not only unsightly, but often the branches are merely dormant.
- Never leave your fire unattended, and always make sure you keep some water handy.
- Extinguish your fire properly before going to bed or breaking up camp. If the wood hasn't burnt to ash, douse the coals thoroughly with water.
- Don't cut nearby vegetation to sleep on – rather carry a ground pad with you.
- Disturb animals and birds that you come across as little as possible, particularly those with young or in nests, as well as seemingly lost or injured animals or birds. Some animals hide their young during the day, and birds will often not associate with nestlings once they have been handled by humans. In most cases there is little one can do to help an injured animal or bird.
- Don't feed animals or birds. Some animals, especially baboons, soon learn to associate humans with food if they are fed, and can become aggressive scavengers. In addition, you might well pass on harmful bacteria to the animals.

General

- Where toilets are not provided, human waste should be disposed of by the 'cat method'. Select a flat, screened spot at least 60 m from the footpath and open water. Dig a hole no deeper than 20 to 25 cm to keep within the biological layer, where active decomposition takes place, and after use fill the hole with loose soil and trample lightly over it. Toilet paper and sanitary towels should be burned, but take care not to set the veld alight.
- Don't sleep in caves with rock paintings, except where this is expressly permitted, and never tamper with or spray water over rock paintings. Archaeological sites should not be disturbed, nor should artefacts be removed. It is an offence under the National Heritage Act.
- Your enjoyment and appreciation of the outdoors will be considerably enhanced if you read more about the area beforehand. There are numerous pocket-sized field guides on flora and fauna that can be taken along on walks and trails.

HIKING SAFETY

On any walk or trail, safety is always of the utmost importance. Most of the common fatal or serious injuries that occur while hiking can be avoided if you make sure that you observe a few common-sense rules.

Bear the following points in mind – they will not only ensure pleasant hiking, but could also help you to avoid a disaster:

- The group should always be led by the most experienced person among you.
- Plan the day's hike carefully and make an early start if there's a long hike ahead, if the terrain is difficult or unfamiliar to you, or if the weather is hot or will be later in the day.
- Keep in mind that there are considerably fewer daylight hours in winter than in summer.
- Hike at a steady pace. Three kilometres an hour is a good average. For every 300 m gain in altitude an hour can be added to your total walking time. On steep sections it is advisable to shorten your stride and carry on walking. Avoid long breaks; rather have short rest stops and use the opportunity to appreciate your surroundings. It is best to stop for a five-minute break every hour. In between, breaks should be limited to taking just a 'breather', except for tea and lunch breaks. During extended breaks your muscles cool down and it takes quite an effort to get going again.
- Keep the group together. A member lagging behind is an almost sure sign of trouble, exhaustion or exposure. Establish the cause of the problem, assist the person by spreading the weight of their pack among other members of the group and keep them company. In large groups it is advisable to appoint someone to bring up the rear; you'll always know who the last person is.
- Always carry a whistle. It can be used to attract attention should you get lost. Remember the morse code for the international SOS – three short, three long and three short whistles.

Energy and water

- Keep your energy levels up by eating snacks – peanuts and raisins, glucose sweets, chocolate (not in hot weather, as it melts) and dried fruit – between meals.
- Always carry a 2-litre water bottle and fill it up wherever you can. Remember that smaller streams are often dry during the winter months in summer rainfall areas and during the summer in winter rainfall areas.
- Make sure that you keep your water intake up, especially in hot weather, to prevent dehydration, and always keep a reserve supply for emergencies. It is also worth carrying along a rehydration solution.
- Water bottles should always be filled from safe, fast-running streams above any areas of human habitation. Water from any part of the river below an area of human habitation should be regarded as unsafe, and should not be drunk before it has been thoroughly boiled.
- Water that may be infested with bilharzia, cholera or other waterborne diseases should be boiled for at least five minutes. This method is preferable to using commercially available chemicals. Strain water through a handkerchief to remove debris before boiling it.

Inclement weather

- If you encounter bad weather, or if the route proves physically too demanding, do not hesitate to turn back if you have not reached the halfway mark of the day's hike by midday.
- Most of South Africa receives rain in the summer, and thunderstorms are common in the afternoon. Try to reach your destination before the storm sets in.
- Avoid the dangers of lightning by staying clear of prominent features such as trees, ridges, summits, shallow caves and large boulders. Find an open slope; sit on a ground pad or a backpack (preferably on a clean, dry rock), with your knees drawn up, feet together and hands in your lap. If you are in a tent during an electric storm, sit in a crouching position and avoid touching the sides.
- Mist often occurs at high altitudes. If mist does set in, seek a suitable shelter and stay put until it lifts.
- If you are caught in a snowfall, seek shelter and move to a lower altitude at the earliest opportunity, to avoid being trapped if conditions deteriorate.

River crossings

Be aware of the dangers of flash floods and never cross a flooding river. Fortunately, most South African rivers soon return to their normal level after flooding. Either wait until the flood has subsided or make a detour.

- Never camp in riverbeds or valleys. Rainfall in the upper reaches of the river can cause unexpected flash floods with disastrous consequences.
- Some routes necessitate frequent river crossings. At times it might be possible to boulder-hop across, but avoid long jumps with a heavy pack, which could result in a slip, and not only a soaking, but also injury.
- If you're not sure about a river's depth always probe it without your pack. Even if a river is shallow (i.e. knee-deep) you can lose your balance if there are rocks under the water, in which case you will need to discard your pack quickly, as there is a danger of being pinned down underwater by a heavy pack. Undo the pack's hip belt and loosen the shoulder straps, so that you can offload it quickly, if necessary.
- Float packs across deeper rivers – a survival bag is ideal for keeping your pack dry.
- Avoid crossing rivers near the mouth, unless there is a sand bar. If the mouth is open, cross further upstream, where the flow is slower and the river is often shallower. Avoid bends, where the flow is usually stronger and the river deeper.
- When crossing a strong-flowing river, start swimming at a point much higher up than the one you're aiming for. Swim diagonally across, with the flow, and not straight to the other side.

Veld fires

- In the event of a veld fire, try to find shelter in a kloof or ravine rather than going up a slope. Avoid waterfalls, to prevent being trapped below or above the falls by the fire, and make sure that you take care and time to minimise unnecessary risks.

First aid

Most emergency situations are either related to extremes of weather, a physical injury or disability. It is, therefore, essential for every hiker to understand the principles of preventative measures and first aid. It is strongly advisable to read some of the many authoritative publications available on this subject or to enrol for a first-aid course.

Unless you are medically trained, you can give only emergency first aid, which will, hopefully, prevent any deterioration in the condition of the patient until help arrives.

The three most serious physical problems you may encounter are: cessation of breathing, bleeding and shock. All these situations call for immediate action and the following general directions should be followed:

Take control The leader of the group must take control of the situation immediately. If the leader is injured, the next most experienced member must take control. Remain calm, assess the situation and direct the other members of the group to improvise equipment or a shelter.

Approach safely In the event of a serious fall on difficult terrain, care should be taken not to cause rockfalls or to endanger the lives of others. If the casualty cannot be reached safely or the necessary equipment is unavailable, help should be summoned without delay.

Apply emergency first-aid procedures If the casualty can be reached, assess their condition and, if the injury appears to be related in any way to the spinal column, avoid any movement.

Check for breathing Lick your fingers and hold them in front of the injured person's nose, or mouth; put your hand on the chest, or stomach. If you cannot feel breathing, or movement, apply artificial respiration, first removing any obstruction to the air passages.

Check the pulse If the casualty does not have a pulse, begin cardiopulmonary resuscitation (CPR).

Check for serious bleeding Internal bleeding may be indicated if the person is pale, clammy and restless. This can be fatal and medical assistance must be sought immediately. Try to stop fast or heavy external bleeding by applying direct pressure, using a pad of folded cloth and, if possible, elevating the wound.

Treat for shock After any major injury, be on the lookout for signs of shock, which can cause

FIRST-AID KIT

A well-equipped first-aid kit should always accompany a hiking party, even on a day walk or short weekend outing. When putting together your kit, remember that space is limited and that it is always possible to improvise. Trailists suffering from chronic ailments, such as diabetes, asthma, allergies, or weak ankles or knees should ensure that they have sufficient medicine or equipment to take care of themselves.

- ☐ antibiotics
- ☐ anti-diarrhoea pills
- ☐ anti-histamine: cream and tablets
- ☐ anti-inflammatory gel
- ☐ antiseptic: cream and solution
- ☐ bandages: wide crepe & narrow gauze
- ☐ cotton wool
- ☐ eardrops: antiseptic, analgesic
- ☐ eye bath
- ☐ yedrops
- ☐ isotonic drink
- ☐ mosquito repellent
- ☐ nail scissors

- ☐ needle and thread
- ☐ painkillers
- ☐ plasters: zinc oxide and sealed individual plasters
- ☐ safety pins
- ☐ sulphacetimide eye ointment
- ☐ surgical gloves (for use when there is any bleeding, to avoid the transmission of any blood-borne diseases, such as HIV or hepatitis)
- ☐ thermometer
- ☐ throat lozenges
- ☐ tweezers
- ☐ wound dressing

paleness, clammy skin, a fast, weak heartbeat, quick breathing, dizziness or weakness.

After loosening tight clothing, lay the person down, with their feet higher than their head. Reassure and keep the patient comfortable and warm, covering them, without allowing them to get too hot. If possible, give them small sips of warm, sweet tea or sugar water.

Check for other injuries and give first-aid treatment. Start with the neck and work your way down systematically, examining the body for bleeding, sensitivity, fractures, pain or swelling.

Plan what to do Your plan of action depends on whether the casualty can carry on unassisted, if evacuation by the group is possible, or whether outside help is required.

Take the following into account: the nature of the injuries, the time of day, weather conditions, the terrain, the availability of shelter and water, the size and physical condition of the group, and the availability of outside help.

Execute the plan of action If the situation requires evacuation with outside help, at least two members of your group should be sent. They should preferably be stronger members of the group, and they must follow a predetermined route, from which they should not deviate at any point, if at all possible. They should have the following information:

- Where, when and how the accident occurred.
- The number of casualties, as well as the nature and seriousness of the injuries.
- What first aid has been administered, what supplies are still available to those who have remained behind and the condition of the casualties.
- The distance between the casualties and the closest roads and the nature of the terrain.
- The number of people at the evacuation scene.
- What type of equipment might be necessary.
- While waiting for help to arrive, the remaining members of the group can make shelters and prepare hot meals and drinks for the casualty and themselves.

Prevention and cure

About 90 per cent of all ailments on trails are foot and leg problems. The best solution is prevention and avoidance. Make early decisions and treat any ailments or wounds as soon as they occur. Common injuries and health hazards that trailists should be aware of are discussed briefly below. (For ease of reference they are listed alphabetically.)

Bilharzia This disease, which is fairly common in the rural areas of the east coast and the northeast of South Africa, is caused by a snail-borne parasite that attacks the intestines, bladder and other organs of its hosts. Bilharzia is unlikely to occur in streams and rivers above 1,200 m in altitude, because of the unsuitability of fast-flowing water as a habitat for the snail hosts. (High-altitude rivers are typically fast-flowing, as they are usually at quite a steep gradient.) It is also less likely to be found in any body of water that is mixed with sea water. Water temperatures of 0 °C, for three or four nights, are sufficient to kill the snail hosts, while water temperatures of over 28 °C are poorly tolerated by the hosts.

Bilharzia is usually associated with human habitation; so avoid drinking, swimming or washing in water downstream from any human settlement, especially in rural areas. If bilharzia is suspected, boil the water for at least five minutes before use.

Bites and stings With the majority of spider bites, as well as bee, scorpion and wasp stings, discomfort can be relieved by applying an anti-histamine lotion and taking anti-histamine medication. If the patient has an allergic reaction to a sting, arrange for evacuation. Thick-tailed *Parabuthus* scorpion stings and button spider bites could be dangerous, in which case urgent medical assistance is essential.

Blisters Blisters are the most common cause of discomfort and should be treated before they form. If certain spots on your feet are prone to blisters, cover them with a dressing and a broad strip of plaster before putting on your boots. A potential blister can usually be detected when a tender 'hot spot' starts to develop. Cover the affected area immediately with a dressing and zinc oxide plaster.

If a blister forms and you have not completed your trip, it is best to lance the blister with a sterilised needle. Gently press out the liquid, dab the blister with antiseptic and then cover it with a dressing and zinc oxide plaster. This should, ideally, be done once the day's backpacking is over. Check the affected spot regularly for infection. If you have completed your trip, it should preferably not be lanced, but rather left uncovered to heal by itself.

Bruises Swelling from a bad bruise can be reduced by holding the affected area in cold running water, such as a stream, and keeping it elevated and still.

Burns Besides blisters, sunburn (a first-degree burn) is probably the most common ailment suffered on trails. Prevention is better than cure, so wear a sun hat and apply sunscreen lotion frequently, especially on the nose and face. Turn up the collar of your shirt (one of the reasons why a button-up shirt is preferable to a T-shirt) to prevent sunburn to your neck.

Scalds and minor burns should be treated by holding the affected area in cold water until the pain subsides. Do not apply greasy ointments and do not lance burn blisters. If available, cover the burn lightly with a gauze dressing, held in place with a plaster; burns heal better if left exposed to the air.

Burns of a more serious nature should not be immersed in water. Instead, cover the area with a sterile dressing or clean cloth. If clothing sticks to the burn, leave it on. Treat for shock and give the patient plenty of water and an isotonic drink. Help should be summoned as soon as possible.

Cramps Muscular cramps are caused by a shortage of salt or water, or both, combined with physical exertion. Allow the patient to rest, keep the affected area warm and massage gently. Give the patient an isotonic drink and avoid further strenuous exercise until they recover fully.

Diarrhoea and vomiting Diarrhoea and vomiting are natural body mechanisms to dispose of bacteria and should preferably not be treated with commercial medication, unless continuing the hike is unavoidable. For both complaints the patient should be rested and given frequent doses of isotonic drink mixed to half strength.

Stomach pains and biliousness, without diarrhoea and vomiting, could be serious if they are accompanied by a persistent fever. The patient should rest, keep warm and maintain a high fluid intake. Evacuation might be necessary.

Dislocation The symptoms of dislocation are visible deformity and severe pain. It is important to get skilled help quickly, because the dislocated joint will soon begin to swell. Do not attempt to push it back into place unless you are medically trained, as this can damage blood vessels and nerves or cause fractures. Wrap the joint in wet cloths, immobilise with splints if necessary and get the injured person to a doctor as soon as you can.

Ear infections Earaches can be treated with an oily, antiseptic, analgesic eardrop, such as Aurone®. Middle ear infections are far more serious and can affect balance. If you are more than 12 hours from help and the person has a temperature, a wide-spectrum oral antibiotic should be administered.

Foreign bodies, such as insects, in the ear can usually be floated out with warm water or oil. Heat a little oil in a teaspoon (test a drop on the back of your hand to ensure that it's not too hot), pour into the ear and leave for five minutes before letting it run out. Take care not to push the object, especially smooth, hard objects, deeper into the ear in an attempt to get it out.

Exhaustion Prevent exhaustion by avoiding over-exertion, eating trail snacks between meals, and drinking water regularly. If exhaustion does set in, the patient should be allowed to rest at a comfortable temperature, and given food and water with a high glucose content.

Eye injuries and infections Foreign bodies should only be removed if you are able to take them out easily. Any object that is partially embedded in the eyeball should not be removed; cover the eye with a doughnut-shaped bandage held in place with another bandage and evacuate the patient.

In most cases, however, the natural watering of the eye will dislodge and wash away small objects. Bring the upper lid down over the lower eyelid for a second or two; the tears caused by this might wash the object away. If this does not work, let the person blink their eye in an eye bath (a small plastic container that can be held over the eye) and apply eyedrops into the inner corner of the eye. Carefully lift the eyelid by the lashes and let the drops run over the eyeball. Blinking during irrigation might help. You could also try lifting the object out with the corner of a piece of sterile gauze.

Eye infections should be treated with a sulphacetimide eye ointment and covered with a light bandage.

Fever Normal human oral temperature is 37 °C. A temperature which drops below 35 °C should be regarded as serious, whereas up to 39 °C indicates a mild fever and over 40 °C a high fever. Rest and a large fluid intake are essential. Cool the patient down by removing any hot clothing or bedding and wipe them with a wet cloth. Fanning them and giving them aspirin will also help. If there is no obvious cause and the fever persists, evacuation should be considered. Check for malaria symptoms.

Heat exhaustion This condition is caused either by exposure to a hot environment or overheating caused by physical exertion. Symptoms are nausea, dizziness, thirst, profuse sweating and headaches. Lie the patient down in a cool, shady place with their feet higher than their head, loosen their clothing and cover them lightly. Give them frequent isotonic drinks.

Heatstroke or sunstroke Heatstroke is more serious than heat exhaustion as it affects the nervous centre that controls body temperature. It can set in very rapidly, and occurs when the sweating process and other body temperature regulatory mechanisms fail.

Symptoms are an excessive high body temperature, red, dry skin, headaches, irrational behaviour, shivering, cramps, dilated pupils, and, finally, collapse and unconsciousness. Cool the patient down immediately by moving them into the shade, taking off any tight clothing, pouring water over them and wiping them down with wet cloths, and fanning. If the patient is conscious, give them fast-acting aspirin and lots of isotonic drink. Get medical help urgently.

Hypothermia The lowering of the body's core temperature to the point where the heat loss exceeds the heat the body is able to generate results in hypothermia. It is usually caused by a combination of very cold weather, inadequate food intake and unsuitable clothing, as well as over-exertion. One or more of the following symptoms may be present: weakness, slowing of pace, shivering, lack of co-ordination, irrationality, a blue skin colour, difficulty in speaking, decreased heart and respiratory rate, dilated pupils and unconsciousness.

Prevent further heat loss and keep the patient moving, while looking for a suitable shelter. If a suitable shelter is not found within a few minutes, erect the best possible shelter. Remove wet clothing and immediately replace with warm, dry clothes. The patient should then be zipped into a pre-warmed sleeping bag, or warmed up between two people, well covered with sleeping bags. If the patient is able to eat, warm food and drink (sugar/glucose water, chocolate and soup) should be taken. Do not give them alcohol, coffee or any other stimulants. Do not rub the victim to restore circulation, or put them near a fire; direct heat is dangerous.

Lung and throat infections A sore throat without fever can be treated by gargling with salt water or an antiseptic solution, or by sucking throat lozenges. A sore throat with fever will require antibiotics, and the patient should be kept warm and rested.

Bronchitis (symptoms include a bad cough, phlegm, fever/chills, sore/tight chest and some shortness of breath) can be serious and the patient will need rest, warmth and a wide-spectrum antibiotic. If the fever persists, the patient should be evacuated.

Malaria A bite by an infected *Anopheles* mosquito can transmit microscopic blood parasites, resulting in malaria. In areas where malaria is endemic there is always a risk of contracting the disease, while in areas where it is epidemic the risk is generally confined to the rainy months. However, it is advisable to take anti-malaria precautions when visiting any malaria area, even if you are only in transit. Consult your doctor to find out which prophylaxis should be taken.

Taking a few simple preventative measures can reduce the chances of being bitten. After sunset, wear long trousers, a long-sleeved shirt and socks. Apply a mosquito repellent to areas of bare skin (remember to reapply the repellent every few hours, as it loses its effectiveness after a while) and burn mosquito coils indoors.

In its early stages malaria is easily cured, so it is essential to consult a doctor immediately should you develop any flu-like symptoms. These are: a general body ache, severe fever, headache, nausea and diarrhoea. Inform your doctor that you visited a malaria area.

Nosebleeds Change in altitude, increased activity and cold temperatures are the main causes of nosebleeds. Fortunately, most nosebleeds are minor and can be stopped by applying direct pressure firmly against the nostril or pinching the tip of the nose for 5 to 10 minutes. If bleeding persists, pack the nostril with gauze, or cotton wool, pinch for 10 more minutes, and leave the dressing in for two hours or so. Remove carefully. Do not blow your nose for at least four hours after a nosebleed.

Pain Treat general pain with the painkillers in your first- aid kit, taken with plenty of fluid. If the pain persists and there is no obvious cause, seek medical treatment.

Snakebite Chances of being bitten by a snake are extremely remote and only about 16 of the 160-odd South African snake species are deadly. Once again, it is wise to take preventative measures. Keep your eyes open, especially when the path is overgrown. If you carry a stick, swish it in the grass in front of you. Considering that 75 per cent of all bites are below the knee, wear stout boots and gaiters when bundu-bashing. About 15 per cent of bites are inflicted on the hand and finger and, therefore, it is wise to look before placing your hand behind a rock. Similarly, look under and around a rock or log before sitting down on it. Do not overturn logs or rocks; step onto them, not over them.

Except in unusual circumstances, the life of a snakebite victim will seldom be in immediate danger. The venom of a puff adder, which is responsible for most bites, is seldom life-threatening within 10 hours of the bite, while cobra bites usually take two to four hours to cause distress symptoms. Although mamba bites can seriously affect breathing within one or two hours, it is highly unlikely that the victim will die in five minutes, as is popularly believed. Boomslang venom is extremely poisonous, but bites from this back-fanged snake are extremely rare as it is not an aggressive snake. Berg adder bites are never fatal, with patients showing an improvement within three to four days of being bitten.

The main problem when hiking is that a serious snakebite, such as mamba and cobra bites, require 60 to 80 ml antivenom, while snakebite kits usually only contain 20 ml. In addition, the antivenom should be injected intravenously, as after 12 hours as little as 20 per cent of antivenom injected intra-muscularly may have reached the circulation system.

In the event of a snakebite, the following basic first-aid treatment should be given:

- Immobilise the victim as any unnecessary movement will increase the heart rate and consequently the spread of the venom.
- Examine for fang marks and keep the bite area below the level of the victim's heart.
- Reassure the victim and administer a painkiller (avoid aspirin, as it thins the blood) to them if necessary. Do not allow the intake of alcohol.
- If the snake cannot be identified, clean and disinfect the bite area and wait 10 to 15 minutes to see if symptoms develop. If there are no symptoms, keep the victim immobilised and under observation for two to three hours.
- A suction device can be used immediately after the bite, but care should be taken to ensure that you do not massage the bite area. If a suction device is not available, suction with the mouth can be applied through a thin film of plastic.
- For mamba and cobra bites on a limb, apply a crepe bandage or torn strips of cloth firmly (but not too tightly) from just above the bite to the top of the limb. **Do not use a tourniquet** unless you are medically trained, as improper application could reduce the blood flow, causing harm to body tissue. Cold cloths applied to the bite will further slow down the action of the poison. Monitor the patient's breathing and heart rate and, if either or both cease, apply mouth-to-mouth ventilation and/or external chest compression.
- For adder and boomslang bites, do not use a tourniquet or bandage. Adder bites are cytotoxic, or tissue-damaging, and the reduced flow of blood from a tourniquet may intensify this tissue damage. Immobilise the victim and apply cold water or cold wet cloths to the bite.
- If attacked by a spitting snake (such as a cobra or rinkhals) immediately rinse the eyes out with water for at least 10 minutes. Lift the eyelids up so that the water washes under them as well. If water is not available, improvise; use milk, soft drinks, cold tea, or, in emergencies, even urine, but do not wash the eyes with diluted antivenom.
- Don't make an incision at the site of the bite, as this is likely to damage tissue.
- Don't try to kill the snake for identification; a second person could be bitten.
- If it is a serious snakebite, two members of the group should get help and alert the nearest doctor or hospital, providing them with the identity of the snake, if possible.

Sprains and strains Sprains are caused by either tearing or stretching ligaments, or a separation of muscle tendon from the bone, and are most common in the ankle, knee, wrist and shoulder. The symptoms are extreme pain and severe swelling caused by fluid and blood accumulating in the tissue. Elevate the injured limb, and lightly apply cold water or wet cloths. An anti-inflammatory gel can also be used. This will reduce the swelling and minimise deep bleeding. Give the patient a painkiller and, if you are medically trained, bind the joint with a long crepe bandage. Keep the immobilised joint in a comfortable resting position. After 24 hours, change over to heat treatment: warm the sprained joint in the sun or at a fire, or soak it in hot water three or four times a day.

It is often difficult to differentiate between a sprain and a fracture and, if pain persists, splint the affected limb (improvise a splint) and obtain

medical help. Signs of fractures include severe pain, a floppy foot or hand, or difficulty in moving fingers or toes.

Strains are caused by overextending or tearing muscle fibre and are usually less serious than sprains. Treat these as you would sprains.

Tickbites Do not attempt to remove a tick if it does not pull off easily. Rather, cover it with an oily substance, like Vaseline, as the lack of air will likely cause it to loosen its grip.

Disinfect the area of the tickbite well and, should any signs of infection or fever appear within 10 days, visit a doctor right away.

Exploring the outdoors on foot is a thoroughly enjoyable and rewarding pastime, but it requires thorough planning and is, unfortunately, not without hazards. By following the tried and tested advice and hints in this introductory section you will avoid many of the common mistakes inexperienced hikers are prone to making when they go hiking, and your enjoyment of the trail will be enhanced.

Right: The Cederberg Wilderness contains spectacular rock formations of sandstone and shale, which were deposited between 500 and 345 million years ago.

SOUTHWESTERN CAPE & LITTLE KAROO

The many hikes in these two regions make the most of the spectacular coastal and mountain scenery, and of a floral diversity that is unrivalled worldwide. Whether you are a casual rambler or a serious hiker there is a huge range of options, from short, easy strolls on the slopes of Table Mountain to full-day coastal hikes, and even five-day trails through wild mountains. Adventure-seekers will love the adrenaline-pumping kloofing trips, with jumps over waterfalls, and backpackers can blaze their own trails in the Cederberg and Groot Winterhoek wilderness areas.

The area covered in this section stretches from Africa's southwesternmost point, northwards, to the Cederberg. The boundary of the southwestern Cape is formed by the Breede River to the east, and the Cape Folded Mountains to the north.

One of the region's greatest attractions is its fynbos. 'Fynbos' is the collective term for the area's richly varied, fine-leaved mountain vegetation – especially striking in spring when masses of ericas create a riot of colour on mountain slopes, while many protea species and bulbs flower in winter.

The southwestern Cape lies at the heart of the Cape Floristic Region, which stretches from the Cape Peninsula, northwards, in a 40- to 150-km-wide belt to Nieuwoudtville, and eastwards to Gqeberha, with isolated patches occurring as far east as Makhanda. It contains at least 8,550 species of flowering plants (over 40 per cent of South Africa's plant species), with 1,400 bulb species, more than 500 *Erica* species, some 300 types of protea and a wealth of restios (reeds and rushes). The Cape Peninsula has 2,285 plant species, while Table Mountain alone has 1,470 species. Some 5,800 species are endemic to the region, occurring nowhere else on earth. Sadly, though, more than a third of fynbos species are classified as vulnerable, critically rare or endangered, while 29 have already become extinct.

Although it covers only 0.04 per cent of the earth's land surface, the Cape Floristic Region is three times richer than its nearest 'competitor', with more than 1,300 species per 10,000 ha, compared to 420 species per 10,000 ha in Central America.

In fynbos-rich areas large trees are generally absent, except in relic forest patches in protected kloofs, where yellowwood, assegai, red alder, wild peach, hard pear and candlewood may be found.

Along the West Coast, the coastal plains are transformed into a blaze of colour when Strandveld flowers burst into bloom in August and September. Especially conspicuous are the yellow, orange, red and white flowers of the gousblom (*Arctotis* and *Gazania*) species, nemesias and vygies. During autumn and winter a variety of bulbs such as gladioli and lachenalia can be seen flowering.

The southwestern Cape's bird checklist includes 380 species, about 100 of which occur regularly in fynbos. Species to look out for are the fynbos specials: Cape sugarbird, orange-breasted sunbird, Cape rockjumper, Victorin's warbler and Cape siskin.

Langebaan Lagoon is a wetland of international importance, supporting over 37,000 birds (mainly waders) in summer. The offshore islands are important breeding habitats of African penguin, Cape gannet, Hartlaub's gull and crowned cormorant. African oystercatcher can also be seen.

Animals you are most likely to see are baboon, grey rhebok, klipspringer and rock dassie. Grysbok favour densely bushed areas at lower elevations, while steenbok inhabit open grassland. Also to be seen are common duiker, while discarded quills often betray the presence of porcupines.

The leopard is the most important predator in this area, but as it is secretive and nocturnal it is seldom encountered. Other predators include black-backed jackal, caracal, Cape clawless otter, small grey mongoose, and small- and large-spotted genets.

In many conservation areas, large mammals that used to occur in the region, such as bontebok, eland and Cape mountain zebra, have been reintroduced.

Larger mammals are neither spectacular nor plentiful in this region, but many endemic reptiles and amphibians are found here. Many rivers are home to rare and endangered freshwater fish species; the Olifants River system, for example, has eight endemic fish species.

The cliffs of the southwestern Cape coastline are ideal vantage points to look out for the southern right whales that migrate here to calve. They usually make their appearance in June, and start migrating to the Antarctic in November. The coast between Hermanus and De Hoop Nature Reserve offers some of the world's best land-based whale-watching, and there are many other rewarding sites too, such as False Bay, Kleinmond, Witsand, Mossel Bay and Nature's Valley.

The southwestern Cape's spectacular scenery is another drawcard, with attractions such as Table Mountain and Cape Point. The Cape Folded Mountains' contorted rock strata, deep kloofs, waterfalls and sheer, lichen-encrusted rock faces also provide great scenic beauty, and a dramatic backdrop for a coastline varying from picturesque rocky bays and coves to long expanses of white sandy beach.

A long-standing favourite of outdoor enthusiasts is the Cederberg range, with its open-air gallery of rock formations, sculpted by the elements. Delicate rock paintings in many caves and overhangs are a testimony to the Later Stone Age San who once lived here.

The southwestern Cape enjoys a Mediterranean climate, with cold, wet winters and hot, dry summers. In winter, the high mountain peaks are often covered in snow, causing temperatures to drop to below freezing point, although most of the region does not get this cold. In summer, temperatures are regularly in the high 20s, and often in the 30s. Dense banks of mist, accompanied by strong winds, are common in the high mountains, especially during winter, while the southeasterly wind can reach gale force during summer.

The Little Karoo stretches from Worcester in the west to Uniondale in the east, along a narrow valley, and is bounded to the north by the Witteberg and Swartberg ranges, and in the south by the Langeberg and Outeniqua mountains.

The vegetation of this semi-arid region is characterised by a diversity of hardy, small shrubs, Karoo scrub, bulbs and a great variety of succulents. A visit to the area is especially rewarding between August and October, in many of the plants' peak flowering periods.

Bird species include a variety of larks and chats, Karoo korhaan, Layard's tit-babbler, Karoo eremomela, Namaqua warbler and chat flycatcher. Among the raptors are Verreaux's and booted eagles, black harrier, peregrine falcon and rock kestrel.

Sadly, the vast game herds that once roamed the Little Karoo have long since been exterminated. Animals you may see during a hike include baboon, klipspringer, grey rhebok, steenbok, common duiker, rock dassie, and, if you are very fortunate, leopard. There are, however, many small mammals and other creatures, often overlooked but no less fascinating; for example, the aardwolf, honey badger, Cape clawless otter, small-spotted cat and the African leaf-toed gecko, which is restricted to the northern slopes of the Swartberg Mountains. The Little Karoo's Gamka Mountains are a sanctuary for an isolated population of Cape mountain zebra.

IMPORTANT INFORMATION

➤ The mountains of the southwestern Cape are notorious for sudden weather changes, especially during winter, when high winds, driving rain, mist and snow can result in life-threatening situations for those who are ill-equipped or inexperienced.

➤ Summer weather can also be unpredictable. When the southeaster blows, Table Mountain can be enveloped in its characteristic 'tablecloth' of cloud within an hour or two, and it can snow in the Langeberg in December! So, before setting off, obtain a weather forecast, and, if necessary, cancel your hike.

➤ Fynbos offers no overhead cover, so wear a wide-brimmed hat and take precautions against the sun. Always carry water, as mountain streams may be dry in summer.

➤ Fires are a serious threat to fynbos during the dry summer months. Always carry a backpacking stove and take all possible precautions when smoking or making a fire, where it is permitted (see *Flora and fauna*, p. 28).

➤ Beware of ticks. Try to remove them immediately, and check your body thoroughly at the end of the day's hike (see *Tickbites*, p. 36).

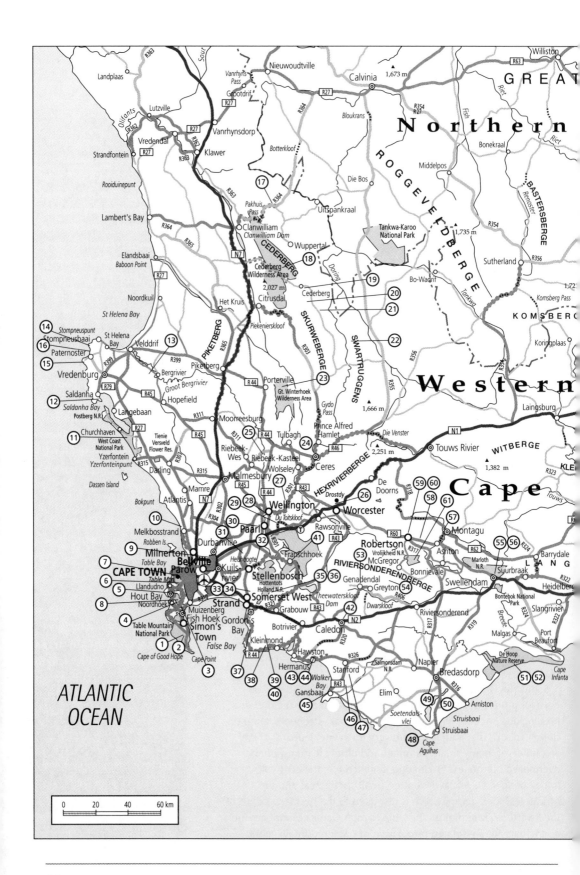

HIKING TRAILS

1. CAPE OF GOOD HOPE

Table Mountain National Park (TMNP)

See no. 2 (p. 43) for hiking trail.

Trails: 8 walks; 1 to 3 hours; circular, open-ended and out-and-return.
Permits: Conservation fee. No booking required for walks.
Maps: *Cape Point and Simon's Town* map by Slingsby Maps. Online orders http://slingsby-maps.myshopify.com.
Facilities/Activities: Angling, snorkelling and scuba diving; braai and picnic sites; tidal pools at Bordjiesrif and Buffels Bay; whale-viewing sites; Visitors' Centre with restaurant, fast-food outlet, information kiosk and curio shop; funicular railway at Cape Point car park.

Established in 1939, as the Cape of Good Hope Nature Reserve, the 7,765-ha reserve now forms one of the focal points of the TMNP. The 250-m-high cliffs at Cape Point are among the highest sea cliffs in the world. From the viewpoint you can enjoy the dramatic vista, and wonder at what Sir Francis Drake described in 1666 as the 'fairest cape and the most stately thing we saw in the whole circumference of the globe'.

The vegetation here is dominated by a wealth of fynbos plants (1,200 species), especially attractive in winter and spring. Mammals to be seen include baboon, bontebok, grey rhebok, red hartebeest, springbok, eland and Cape mountain zebra.

Among the approximately 250 bird species are the rare African (black) oystercatcher and fynbos specials such as the orange-breasted sunbird and Cape sugarbird. The Cape Point cliffs offer unrivalled opportunities for spotting seabirds.

1. Antoniesgat Trail winds along the False Bay coast, from the turning circle south of Buffels Bay to Antoniesgat, one of several caves eroded into the coastal cliffs by the pounding waves. Along the way, trailists will enjoy magnificent views of False Bay and the Hottentots Holland Mountains, the historic Cape Point lighthouse and Vasco da Gama Peak. **3.5 km; 2 hours; out-and-return.**

2. Lighthouse Walks There are two walks: one to the old lighthouse that was operational between 1860 and 1919, and the Spine Walk, which leads to several outlook points with dramatic views over False Bay, Cape Point and the Cape of Good Hope. The Spine Walk is not advisable for those with a fear of heights. Both routes start at the Cape Point car park. **1 hour; out-and-return.**

3. Shipwreck Trail is named after the many ships that foundered here. Among these was the American liberty ship *Thomas T Tucker* that ran aground on her maiden voyage, on the night of 28 November 1942. The outward route follows the coastline past the stern and midship sections of the wreck. A short way on are the remains of the coaster *Nolloth*, which ran onto the rocks at Duikerklip in 1964. From here you can either retrace your steps or return along the Escarpment, which will add another 1.8 km to the distance. **5.2 km; 2 hours; out-and-return or circular.**

4. Gifkommetjie/Platboom Trail meanders from the Gifkommetjie parking area to the coast and then south along the Atlantic shoreline. Beyond Bloubergstrand, the Cape of Good Hope and the old Cape Point lighthouse come into view. The Island, a reef just offshore of Platboom, is a well-known landmark and extensive kelp beds can be seen off Platboom, where the trail ends. **5 km; 1.5 hours; open-ended.**

5. Kanonkop The route gains height steadily to the old signal cannon after which Kanonkop was named. From this vantage point there are fine views of the Da Gama Monument, Buffels Bay and Cape Point. Of interest on the return route, an easy descent, is an old kiln used to burn sea shells for making lime. **4.8 km; 2 hours; circular.**

6. Phyllisia Circuit owes its name to the 452-tonne trawler that ran aground at Hoek van Bobbejaan, just before midnight on 2 May 1968. Starting at the Gifkommetjie parking area, the outward leg of this circuit winds parallel to the coast, while the return leg meanders along the coastline itself. Close to Gifkommetjie there is an optional shortcut, which leads through a bushy area and reduces the total trail distance by 1.3 km. **7 km; 2.5 hours; circular.**

7. Sirkelsvlei From the car park at Olifantsbos, this route meanders through fynbos to the eastern shores of Sirkelsvlei. On the return leg, the trail goes through a sandstone rock arch, past the Eye-of-the-Needle rock formation, and along the short Lumbago Alley rock passage. **7.2 km; 3 hours; circular.**

8. Cape Point to Cape of Good Hope The trail descends through fynbos to the cliffs above Dias Beach (accessible by a wooden staircase) and then continues to the viewpoint at Cape Maclear. Steps have been provided for the descent to the car park at the Cape of Good Hope – the southernmost point of the Cape Peninsula. **3 km; 2 hours (including detour to Dias Beach); out-and-return.**

2. CAPE OF GOOD HOPE HIKING TRAIL
Table Mountain National Park

See no. 1 (p. 42) for walks.

Trail: 33.8 km; 2 days; circular.
Permits: Tel: (021) 712 7471, email: deonese.visser@sanparks.org or musa.makhubele@sanparks.org.
Maps: Pocket guide of trail with map; *Cape Point and Simon's Town* map by Slingsby Maps. Online orders http://slingsby-maps.myshopify.com.
Facilities/Activities: Overnight hut with bunks, mattresses, two-plate gas stove, braai place, solar lighting, shower and toilet.
Pertinent information: Start the first day's hike before 09:00 and collect the hut key from the Access Control Officer.

The first day's hike (23.3 km; 9 hours) starts at the entrance gate to Rooihoogte. It goes around the southern end of Sirkelsvlei, before passing through Blaaubergvlei, which is only open to hikers. From Hoek van Bobbejaan, the coastline is followed closely for 6.7 km to Pegram's Point. From here hikers can either take a shortcut to the hut 19 km from the starting point, or take the 4.5 km longer option, which offers some of the best views of the Cape of Good Hope, Cape Point and False Bay.

The second day's hike (10.5 km; 5 hours) meanders along the Escarpment above Antoniesgat and Rooikrans to the Homestead, and the summit of Kanonkop. The trail skirts the base of Paulsberg, then heads along the edge of the Escarpment to the Smitswinkel Bay viewpoint, close to the end.

3. SILVERMINE
Table Mountain National Park

Trails: 1.5 to 7 hours; network.
Permits: Conservation fee. No booking required.
Maps: *Silvermine and Hout Bay* map by Slingsby Maps. Online orders http://slingsby-maps.myshopify.com.
Facilities/Activities: Picnic sites with water, litter bins and toilets.

Covering more than 2,400 ha of some of the Cape Peninsula's most spectacular scenery, the Silvermine section of the park extends from the lower slopes of the Kalk Bay and Muizenberg mountains in the east to Noordhoek Peak in the west. The area is bisected by Ou Kaapseweg.

The vegetation is dominated by fynbos, and among the nearly 900 plant species known to occur here are 15 endemics, including *Mimetes hirtus*. Patches of indigenous forest are found in the Spes Bona and Echo valleys, and along the Silvermine River. Animals to keep an eye out for include grey rhebok, Cape grysbok and baboon.

1. The Amphitheatre Walk, in the Kalk Bay Mountains east of Ou Kaapseweg, passes through patches of indigenous forests and mountain scenery. Starting at the Kalk Bay end of Boyes Drive, the route climbs to Weary Willy's and then ascends steadily up Echo Valley to a magnificent indigenous forest. About an hour's walk beyond Weary Willy's, the trail emerges into the Amphitheatre, a small basin bounded by sandstone ridges. Continue across the plateau of Ridge Peak and turn right to descend along Spes Bona Valley with its small indigenous forest. On reaching the gravel road, turn right and make your way back to Boyes Drive. **5 km; 2 hours; circular.**

2. Kalk Bay Mountains This route features some of the most spectacular mountain scenery in the Silvermine area. From the Wolfkop parking area, east of Ou Kaapseweg, the route meanders to Junction and Nellie's pools and traverses the twin summits of the Kalk Bay Mountains. It then skirts the head of Spes Bona Valley, and descends to the Amphitheatre. After this it returns to the start along Klein Tuinkloof. **10 km; 4 hours; circular.**

3. Noordhoek Peak, at 754 m the highest point in Silvermine, rewards trailists with spectacular views over Hout Bay and the Sentinel. From the Silvermine Reservoir parking area, west of Ou Kaapseweg, follow a gravel track to the fire lookout. The short detour is worth it for the superb views of Chapman's Peak Mountain. Return to the main track, turn left and continue up until a cairn indicates the turnoff to the summit of Noordhoek Peak, reached after a short climb. From here follow the Panorama Path for about 1 hour to its junction with a gravel road, which you follow back to the car park. **8 km; 3.5 to 4 hours; circular.**

4. ELEPHANT'S EYE CAVE
Silvermine

Trail: 6 km; 3 to 4 hours; out-and-return.
Permits: Conservation fee. No booking required.
Maps: *Silvermine and Hout Bay* map by Slingsby Maps. Online orders http://slingsby-maps.myshopify.com.
Facilities/Activities: Swimming in the Silvermine Dam; picnic areas; braai facilities.
Pertinent information: Do not attempt this route in inclement weather. Follow the cairns where the route is rocky.

Starting at the Silvermine Reservoir car park, make your way up a series of zigzags to Steenberg Ridge, where you will be rewarded with expansive views over the Cape Flats, False Bay and the Hottentots Holland Mountains. Further along you reach the Prinskasteel Waterfall, which plunges in three main falls down the mountain slopes. A short way beyond the waterfall the trail splits off to the left, continuing to the fire lookout; from here it is a short climb to Elephant's Eye Cave just below Constantiaberg peak. The cave is named after the resemblance of the silhouette of Constantiaberg to the back and head of an elephant, with the cave forming the eye. Retrace your tracks to the fire lookout, where you join a sandy track. Follow this track for about 1 km to its junction with a jeep track, then turn left to reach the Silvermine reservoir and the car park about 1.5 km on.

5. HOUT BAY WALKS
Hout Bay

Trails: Several options; 2 to 5 hours.
Permits: No permit required.
Maps: *Silvermine and Hout Bay* map by Slingsby Maps. Online orders http://slingsby-maps.myshopify.com.
Facilities/Activities: None.

The tranquil harbour town of Hout Bay and the mountains surrounding it offer a choice of numerous and interesting walks, ranging from a short historical ramble through the town to a full day's hike for the more energetic.

1. Chapman's Peak Nek to Blackburn Ravine Follow the Chapman's Peak route to Chapman's Peak Nek, but, instead of turning right, turn left and follow the contour path below Noordhoek Peak. The trail winds in and out of several ravines and there are expansive views over Hout Bay harbour and the Sentinel. Blackburn Ravine is reached about 40 minutes' walk beyond Chapman's Peak Nek. After a short descent, follow the gravel track to a parking area on Chapman's Peak Drive, close to East Fort. **5.5 km; 2.5 hours; open-ended.**

2. Chapman's Peak Towering nearly 600 m above the Atlantic Ocean, with precipitous cliffs dropping down to the sea, Chapman's Peak does not present as daunting a challenge as you might think at first glance. Starting at the viewpoint just before Chapman's Peak Drive, you round the peak after which the drive is named. You will find that the first 30 minutes involve a fairly steep climb along a ravine to Chapman's Peak Nek. From here the path rises gently through stands of proteas, traversing the western slopes of Lower Chapman's Peak, before reaching the summit of Chapman's Peak itself. The 360-degree view from the top is simply breathtaking. **5 km; 3.5 hours; out-and-return.**

3. Karbonkelberg and Suther Peak From the end of Bay View Road the trail follows the zigzag gravel road below Kaptein's Peak and Karbonkelberg to the remains of the World War II radar station on Karbonkelberg. As you gain height there are spectacular views of Hout Bay and the Sentinel below, Chapman's Peak at the far side of the bay, the white expanse of Noordhoek Beach, and the Table Mountain chain. A worthwhile 60-minute detour to Suther Peak will be rewarded with breathtaking views of Little Lion's Head and Sandy Bay. **5 km; 3.5 to 4 hours; out-and-return.**

6. KIRSTENBOSCH NATIONAL BOTANICAL GARDEN
Cape Peninsula

See no. 7 (this page) for walks.

Trails: 2 walks; 1.5 to 3 hours. Access to popular Table Mountain walks, such as Skeleton Gorge, is also through Kirstenbosch.
Permits: Entrance fee. No permit required.
Maps: Colour map of walks available at Visitors' Centre.
Facilities/Activities: Visitors' Centre with bookshop, toilets, gift shops, self-service and à la carte restaurants and deli; conservatory; guided walks for groups; Braille Trail and Fragrance Garden for the visually impaired; Sculpture Garden; garden centre; summer concerts; periodic indoor and outdoor art exhibitions; educational centre for school groups; conference centre.

Set against the backdrop of Castle Rock and Fernwood Buttress, Kirstenbosch ranks among the top botanical gardens in the world. It includes 492 ha of natural fynbos and indigenous forest and 36 ha of cultivated gardens, lawns, pathways and water features. Nearly 6,000 plant species indigenous to South Africa have been established in the cultivated garden, while some 900 species occur naturally in this region.

1. Yellowwood Trail This trail passes through splendid indigenous forest on the lower slopes of Table Mountain. After a steady climb to the Contour Path the route continues to Skeleton Gorge Waterfall, from where it is a gentle descent along Smuts' Track to the Fragrance Garden, which is also the starting point. **3 km; 1.5 hours; circular.**

2. Silvertree Trail From Rycroft Gate, the trail ascends to the Contour Path, which you follow past Nursery Ravine and Skeleton Gorge. Beyond Window Stream the path ascends steeply to skirt The Aloes and then descends along the historic Woodcutters' Path (dating back to the 1660s, the era of the Dutch East India Company) to Lubbert's Gift. The route then doubles back, following a path parallel to the Contour Path, but at a lower elevation. The final section makes its way through the protea garden with its abundance of silver trees, a member of the protea family. **7.7 km; 3 hours; circular.**

7. TABLE MOUNTAIN
Table Mountain National Park

Trails: 3 to 20 km; 1 to 8 hours; network.
Permits: Not required at time of writing.
Maps: *Table Mountain* map by Slingsby Maps. Online orders http://slingsby-maps.myshopify.com.
Facilities/Activities: Cableway; self-service restaurant, bistro and shop near Upper Cable Station; abseiling; mountain-bike trails.
Pertinent information: The mountains of the Western Cape are notorious for

One of the world's most famous natural landmarks, Table Mountain forms the focal point of the Table Mountain National Park, proclaimed in May 1998. Flanked by Lion's Head (669 m) and Devil's Peak (1,001 m), the mountain forms an imposing backdrop to the Mother City.

The Peninsula mountain chain has an incredibly rich diversity of fynbos flora, with 1,470 species known to occur on Table Mountain alone. Among its floral splendours are red disa (*Disa uniflora*), drip disa (*Disa longicornis*), silver tree (*Leucadendron argenteum*), proteas, ericas and fields of watsonias. Patches of indigenous yellowwood, assegai and wild peach forest grow in the eastern valleys and sheltered ravines of the mountain.

Among the small mammals you may see are baboon, rock dassie, common duiker and grysbok. The mountain's birdlife includes rock kestrel, Cape sugarbird, southern double-collared and orange-breasted sunbirds, Cape rock-thrush and ground woodpecker.

Since a description of every one of the walks on Table Mountain is impossible, only the most popular routes are described below.

Western Aspect

Overlooking Camps Bay, the western side of Table Mountain is dominated by a series of buttresses, known as the Twelve Apostles. Access to the ascents along the western aspect is along the well-known Pipe Track. **4.5 to 9 km; 3.5 hours; out-and-return.**

Kasteelpoort

The start of this popular ascent is reached by following the Pipe Track from Kloof Nek to the signposted turn-off. The path ascends diagonally under Barrier, Valken and Kasteels buttresses, and then climbs steadily up the left side of the ravine before crossing Kasteelpoort River to emerge on the top. From here it is an easy walk to the Woodhead Reservoir. Alternatively, take the path to the Upper Cable Station via the Valley of the Red Gods, Echo Valley and Fountain Peak. **2.5 hours to top of Kasteelpoort; open-ended.**

Lion's Head

Lion's Head, to the northwest of Table Mountain, is separated from the main table by Kloof Nek and offers a relatively easy ascent with stunning all-round views from its 670-m-high summit.

The route starts about 600 m beyond Kloof Nek, on the Signal Hill road, and initially follows a jeep track before a footpath branches off to the right. The path winds almost around the mountain to the base of the summit cliffs where a ladder provides access to a higher contour path. The final section of the path follows a narrow ridge with a second ladder, which brings you to the summit. The hike to the summit takes about 1.5 hours, with an altitude gain of nearly 400 m. **Approx. 4.5 km; 2.5 hours; out-and-return.**

The North Face

The North Face of Table Mountain forms an amphitheatre, with dramatic sheer cliffs rising up above the centre of Cape Town.

1. Platteklip Gorge, the oldest recorded route up Table Mountain, was ascended in 1503 by the Portuguese navigator Antonio de Saldanha. The gorge, which separates the western and central Tables, provides the most direct ascent up the mountain. However, its steep gradient, stepped rock path, and exposure to the sun make this an exhausting climb. The gorge is signposted along Table Mountain Road, about 1.5 km beyond the Lower Cable Station. From the top of Platteklip, it is a 15-minute walk to the Upper Cable Station, or a 45-minute walk to the 1,085-m-high Maclear's Beacon, the highest point on Table Mountain. **3 hours; open-ended.**

2. Venster-India is a quick way up or down the mountain, but requires some rock scrambling and should be attempted only by experienced hikers. Follow the path from the Lower Cable Station to the Upper Contour Path, then continue along a well-defined track that skirts Venster Buttress, before making your way diagonally across the upper slopes of India Ravine. Some rock scrambling is necessary to get up the buttress between India Ravine and Africa Ravine, and the path then winds below Arrow Face to Kloof Corner Ridge. From here the top is easily reached along Fountain Ledge, where caution should be exercised, as there are some sheer drops at one or two spots. **2.5 to 3 hours; open-ended.**

Devil's Peak

Devil's Peak lies to the northeast of Table Mountain, separated from it by a saddle.

1. Saddle Path From the parking area, which is about 2.5 km beyond the Lower Cable Station on Tafelberg Road, the path zigzags to the Upper Contour Path from where Saddle Path ascends to Saddle Rock. The route then continues along a firebreak to the 1,001-m-high summit of Devil's Peak, where you will be rewarded with spectacular all-round views of Cape Town. The total altitude gain over the course of the hike is about 600 m. **4.5 hours; out-and-return.**

2. Devil's Peak Circuit A delightful alternative, this circuit winds from Newlands Forest to the Contour Path, continuing via King's Blockhouse to Mowbray Ridge. From here the Middle Traverse is followed around the northern and western slopes of Devil's Peak, to Saddle Rock and the firebreak, and up to the summit. The return route is via the Saddle and a steep, winding descent down Newlands Ravine. **5 to 6 hours; circular.**

Eastern Aspect and Constantia Nek

1. Skeleton Gorge is a popular route to Back Table, as the hike is in the shade of the densely wooded gorge. The path follows Smuts' Track to the Contour Path and then ascends steeply up the left of the ravine. Ladders assist trailists in a few steep, rocky sections. Above this section, the gorge opens out, to emerge on Back Table. Here, you can either turn right to Maclear's Beacon (70 minutes one way), or left to return via Castle Rock and descend via Nursery Ravine. **3 to 4 hours; circular via Nursery Ravine.**

2. Constantia Nek to Woodhead Reservoir Also known as the Bridle Path, this is the longest, but easiest, route up Table Mountain. You start the hike at the car park opposite the Constantia

Nek Harbour House restaurant and, after passing through a gate, turn left, to follow a footpath up the slopes of Constantia Corner and Bel Ombre. After a steady climb, the footpath joins the jeep track at a Z-bend. From here, the trail continues along the jeep track past the De Villiers, Alexandria and Victoria reservoirs, to reach Woodhead Dam about 8 km from the beginning of the hike. **5 hours; out-and-return.**

8. HOERIKWAGGO BASE CAMP WALKS
Table Mountain National Park

Trails: Various day walks from tented camps at Smitswinkel, Slangkop and Orange Kloof.
Bookings: SANParks, P O Box 787, Pretoria 0001, tel: (012) 428 9111, fax: (012) 343 0905, email: reservations@sanparks.org.
Maps: *Table Mountain, Silvermine & Hout Bay* and *Cape Point & Simonstown* and the *Digital Hoerikwaggo and Table Mountain National Park* by Slingsby Maps are essential. Online orders http://slingsby-maps.myshopify.com.
Facilities: Tented camps with beds and bedding, communal ablutions (with hot water), equipped communal kitchens and outdoor braai areas. Overnight camps accommodate a maximum of 12 people.
Pertinent information: Sections of the trail are still open to hikers. Incidents of attacks occur sporadically and hikers are advised to walk in groups of four or more people and not to carry any valuables. The section from Smitswinkel to Redhill crosses private land and the consent of the landowners is required to walk in this area. This also applies to the section at the top of Chapmans Peak.

Hoerikwaggo, the Khoikhoi name for Table Mountain, is translated as the 'mountain in the sea'. It is also the name of the trail that was planned to stretch from Cape Point along the spine of Table

Mountain to the Western Table. More than 400 unemployed people from informal settlements were employed to construct and rehabilitate paths and eradicate alien vegetation to boost social development and poverty alleviation. Five overnight stops in tented camps were provided along the 73-km-long trail. The first section between Silvermine, Orange Kloof and Table Mountain was opened in 2006, followed by the other sections. The entire trail is no longer operational, as a result of various unfortunate circumstances, but hikers can use the tented camps as a base for day walks.

1. Smitswinkel Bay

The Smitswinkel Bay tented camp was constructed at the site of the old forestry station, a mere 300 m from the entrance gate to the Cape Point section of the Table Mountain National Park. From here, you can take a short walk to the quaint settlement of Smitswinkel Bay or set off on the path along the eastern slopes of Swartkop Mountains, where you will be rewarded with magnificent views of Kalk Bay. Another option is to explore the numerous walks in Cape Point (conservation fee payable).

2. Slangkop Tented Camp

Nestled among milkwood trees, the Slangkop tented camp is just 100 m from the sea and is an ideal base to explore Noordhoek Beach and Slangkop. The walk from Kommetjie to Noordhoek is an open-ended 8-km ramble along the widest beach in the Cape Peninsula. It can be started either in Kommetjie or Noordhoek, but you will need to make arrangements to be dropped off or collected.

Another option is to hike up Slangkop, where you will be rewarded with stunning views of the Slangkop lighthouse and Kommetjie and explore the ruins of Cobra Camp and the radar station. It was one of five forward operational posts built in the early 1940s to defend the Cape sea route during World War II. From here you can retrace your tracks or explore the paths on Slangkop.

3. Orange Kloof Tented Camp

The delightful Southern Afrotemperate Forest at Orange Kloof, at the southern end of the Table Mountain massif, is one of the largest patches of forest in the Cape Peninsula. The forest with its yellowwood, stinkwood, assegai, red alder and white pear trees was heavily exploited during the early years of the Dutch settlement at the Cape and is a remnant of a much larger forest. It has been protected against fire since 1933 and research has shown that it has more than doubled in size in the past few decades.

Options include walking up Disa Gorge to Hell's Gate, where the stream plunges over a series of natural steps into a pool, or following the contour path on the slopes below the Twelve Apostles. Longer hikes can be undertaken to the Woodhead and Hely-Hutchinson reservoirs built in the late 1800s/early 1900s on the Back Table to supply water to Cape Town. Another option is to set off from Constantia Nek and follow the path to Bel Ombre and Eagles Nest to Constantia Corner, returning via the De Villiers reservoir and the Bridle Path.

9. TYGERBERG NATURE RESERVE
Bellville

Trails: 12 walks; 5 minutes to 4 hours; network. Wheelchair-friendly route: 480 m.
Permits: Obtain at Welgemoed gate, Totius Street, Welgemoed.
Maps: Available at permit offices.
Facilities/Activities: Picnic sites (no fires); environmental education centre, with bookshop and herbarium; educational activities for children.

Set against the western slopes of Tygerberg, this 278-ha nature reserve is an island amid the urban sprawl of the Cape and Tygerberg metropoles. It is one of the few nature reserves that provide protection to West Coast renosterveld, a vegetation type that has virtually been replaced by agriculture and urban development. Among the 160 bird species recorded are the rock kestrel, rufous-breasted sparrowhawk, Cape spurfowl and ground woodpecker.

Trails range from the 210-m-long Wild Olive Trail to the 3.6-km Golden Mole Trail. From a vantage point on the summit of Tygerberg there are views of Paarl Mountain, False Bay and Table Bay.

10. KOEBERG NATURE RESERVE
Melkbosstrand

> **Trails:** 2 walks; 2 and 6 hours, with shorter options.
> **Permits:** Report at Koeberg Visitor Centre.
> **Maps:** Pocket guide with maps available at Visitor Centre.
> **Facilities/Activities:** Picnic site; bird hide.

Set aside by Eskom to protect the fragile environment of the West Coast, the Koeberg Nature Reserve covers 3,000 ha of Strandveld vegetation, dune fields, wetlands and coastal scenery. It is home to herds of bontebok and springbok, Burchell's zebra, grysbok, steenbok and common duiker, as well as a variety of smaller mammals such as caracal and genet. There are good birding possibilities, with a checklist of over 169 species. Points of interest along both trails are numbered and explained in the trail brochure.

1. Grysbok Trail traverses the section of the reserve to the southeast and south of the Koeberg nuclear power station. It alternates between dunes, the coastline, milkwood trees and typical Strandveld vegetation, which is especially attractive in spring. A viewpoint just off the coast provides an ideal vantage point for southern right whales between May and November. **5.7 km; 2 hours with a 2.5-km option; circular.**

2. Dikkop Trail to the north of the power station winds through Strandveld vegetation and restio fields, across dunes and along the beach. A shelter near the halfway mark provides protection against the sun and the wind. Good birding can be enjoyed at the evaporation dams. **19.3 km; 6 hours with 6.5-km and 16.3-km options; circular.**

11. WEST COAST NATIONAL PARK
Saldanha

> **Trails:** 2 hiking trails: 27.3 and 28 km; 2 days; circular. 2 day walks: 4.6 and 13.9 km.

> **Maps:** Full-colour park map.
> **Bookings:** For Strandveld Trail contact Geelbek Information Centre, tel: (022) 707 9902/3. Bookings for Postberg Hiking Trail and Steenbok Day Walk open in June, tel: (022) 707 9902/3.
> **Facilities/Activities:** Restaurant, information centre and education centre at Geelbek; bird hides; cycling routes.
> **Pertinent information:** Postberg is only open in August and September, and trails in this section must be completed before16:00, when the gate closes. It is advisable to apply insect repellent to discourage stinging flies, especially during spring and early summer. Ticks are common, so you should always wear long trousers.

The West Coast National Park covers nearly 28,000 ha, incorporating Langebaan Lagoon and the adjoining land to the east, most of the peninsula to the west of the lagoon, 16 Mile Beach and the four islands. The lagoon is a wetland of immense ecological, intercontinental importance, supporting upwards of 37,000 birds in summer, of which 92 per cent are waders, mainly Palaearctic species. Among the 250 species on the park's bird checklist are flamingo, African marsh harrier, chestnut-banded plover, Cape spurfowl and Cape long-billed lark.

The vegetation is typical Strandveld, characterised by dense low shrubs, succulents, grasses and reeds. Game species include eland, kudu, steenbok, grysbok and common duiker.

Geelbek

Geelbek, at the southern end of the lagoon, is the site of a Cape Dutch manor house built in 1860.

Strandveld Trail On this self-guided interpretative route, trailists are introduced to the many fascinating facets of the West Coast – Strandveld, dunes and the coast. The first day's route covers 14 km (5 hours), while the second day's hike covers 16 km (5 to 6 hours), including a pleasant stretch of coastal walking along 16 Mile Beach. Since hikers set off from the Geelbek Visitors' Centre each day, only a daypack is required. Hikers wanting to overnight in the park can book accommodation at Duinepos, a privately owned facility which operates within the park close to Geelbek. **30 km; 2 days; circular from base camp.**

Postberg Section

Situated on the peninsula to the west of Langebaan Lagoon, this 1,800-ha section of the park is renowned for its annual spring flower display in August and September. During these months the veld is transformed into a blaze of colour by fields of daisies, geophytes and succulents. Adding to its allure are granite outcrops, the rocky coastline and herds of game.

1. Postberg Hiking Trail The first day's hike (13 km; 6 hours) skirts Konstabelkop and winds along the slopes below Postberg and Lookout, from where there are splendid views over the lagoon. The trail then heads southwest to the overnight stop at Plankiesbaai. On the second day's hike (11 km; 3.5 hours) the rocky coastline gives way to the sandy expanses of 16 Mile Beach, which you follow to the wreck of the *Pantelis A. Lemos*. From here the trail doubles back to the starting point. **24 km; 2 days; circular.**

2. Steenbok Day Walk follows the same route as the Postberg Hiking Trail for 2 km and then deviates to the left, heading for the Vingerklippe – granite monoliths pointing skywards like fingers. Still further on, the route links up with the overnight trail, which you follow to Plankiesbaai, and then Kreeftebaai. At Tzaarsbank the trail curves back to the start. **10 km; 4 hours; circular.**

12. *SAS SALDANHA* NATURE TRAIL
Saldanha Bay

Trails: 4 walks; 1.5 to 5 hours; circular.
Permits: Not required, but check with SAS Saldanha whether the reserve is open, tel: (022) 702 3999, fax: (022) 702 3629.
Maps: Colour trail pamphlet indicating walks.
Facilities/Activities: Water and toilets at start of trail.

Pertinent information: Precautions against ticks are advisable. Parking for this trail is only allowed at the North Gate.

The rocky headland embracing the northern side of Saldanha Bay has a long military history and has served as a naval training base since 1948. The entire military area of 1,800 ha has been set aside as a nature reserve, and among the game to be seen are springbok, red hartebeest, grey rhebok and ostrich. The trail network takes trailists past a number of World War II military sites, numerous archaeological sites and many geological features. Hiking is especially rewarding during the spring flower season.

1. Blue Route, the shortest of the four circuits, winds around Malgaskop, the site of the gun batteries of the coastal artillery and the spotlights that lit the bay during World War II. **4 km; 1.5 hours; circular.**

2. Green Route meanders around Malgaskop and Baviaansberg, which can be ascended along a footpath. From the summit there are stunning views of the entrance to Saldanha Bay. The trail then skirts a salt pan as it continues to Long Point before looping back to the start. **9.6 km; 3 hours; circular.**

3. Red Route Starting at the Bomsgat, the trail follows the coastline of North Bay and then meanders between Malgaskop and Baviaansberg. It then skirts a salt pan before reaching Long Point. The return leg leads over the summit of Môresonkop back to the end at West Gate. **14 km; 5 hours; circular.**

4. Yellow Route follows the same course as the Red Route, except that it does not go along North Bay and around Môresonkop. **11 km; 4 hours; circular.**

13. HELDERWATER TRAILS
Hopefield

Trails: 2 walks; 3 and 6 hours; circular.
Bookings: Langrietvlei, cell: 083 286 2457, email: langrietvlei@sandveld.co.za.

Maps: Sketch maps.
Facilities/Activities: Self-catering chalets; braai area on river; canoeing; swimming; water-skiing.
Pertinent information: Middle October to middle May is generally the best time, as the wetlands are difficult to negotiate outside of these months. The summer months can be hot.

Situated along the Lower Berg River, the farm Langrietvlei dates back to 1715. With its tidal, seasonal and permanent pans, river frontage and magnificent fynbos vegetation, it offers trailists a diverse hiking experience and excellent bird-watching opportunities.

1. Helderwater Trail mainly follows the Berg River, offering good birding and the chance to see wild pigs in the reeds during the early mornings and late afternoons. Braai facilities are provided at the 9-km mark, where a rowing boat can be dropped off for those wishing to explore the river. **10 km; 3 hours; circular.**

2. Langrietvlei Trail meanders along the Berg River and past a tidal pan, which attracts a rich diversity of waterbirds. In the vlei areas, trailists might chance upon wild horses, the descendants of horses used by the British military during the South African War (1899–1902). Up to 2,000 flamingoes can be seen at Pink Pan, which normally holds water until January, while the seasonal pans usually begin to dry up from mid-October. **20 km; 6 hours; circular.**

14. STOMPNEUSBAAI TO PATERNOSTER
Stompneusbaai

Trail: 30 km; 10 hours; open-ended.
Permits: Not required.
Maps: Sketch map.
Facilities/Activities: None.
Pertinent information: An early start is essential. Trailists must carry their own water.

This rather long walk follows the coast from Stompneusbaai past Golden Mile, Britannia Bay and Cape St Martin before skirting the Groot Paternoster Private Nature Reserve. The landscape along the trail alternates between the rocky coastline, with a sprinkling of tidal pools, sheltered bays and sweeping white beaches. In spring, the coastal fynbos adds a blaze of colour to the landscape.

15. TIETIESBAAI TO SWARTRIET
Paternoster

Trail: 17 km; 6 hours; open-ended.
Permits: Not required.
Maps: Sketch map.
Facilities/Activities: Camp site with ablutions in Cape Columbine Nature Reserve.
Pertinent information: Carry water.

Featuring rocky beaches, coastal fynbos and dunes, this coastal hike is especially worthwhile during the spring flower season. Among the seabirds to look out for are the African (black) oystercatcher, sanderling, kelp gull, tern, and white-breasted, Cape, bank and crowned cormorants. Rich in marine life, the rocky pools and gullies are well worth exploring. The trail ends at Swartriet, where accommodation is available at Swartriet Chalets.

16. FIVE BAY SLACKPACKING TRAIL
Paternoster to Jacobsbaai

Trail: 2.5 days; 38 km; guided and supported.
Bookings: Cape West Coast Biosphere Reserve, Old Station Building, 64 Main Road, Vredenburg, cell: 083 708 4007, email: trails@capebiosphere.co.za; website: www.capebiosphere.co.za.
Maps: Not required.

Facilities/Activities: 2 nights' accommodation in Paternoster.
Pertinent information: Guided and fully supported hike inclusive of transfers and qualified guide. You only need to carry a daypack with at least two litres of water per person. A sunhat is essential and sunscreen should be applied regularly.

Permits: Obtainable at Traveller's Rest Farm Stall and Restaurant on the farm Traveller's Rest, the site of the trail.
Maps: Trail pamphlet with descriptions of 10 rock art sites available at Traveller's Rest Farm Stall and Restaurant.
Facilities/Activities: Fully equipped self-catering cottages sleeping from 5 to 10 persons; restaurant serving local dishes for groups.

This trail meanders along the West Coast from Paternoster to Jacobsbaai in the Cape West Coast Biosphere Reserve, which was designated by UNESCO as a biosphere reserve in 2000. The biosphere stretches from the mouth of the Diep River at Milnerton to the Berg River in the north, while the eastern boundary is demarcated by the Koeberg-Dassenberg-Swartberg-Karringberg ranges. The trail is one of several initiatives to create jobs and economic opportunities for communities living in the biosphere reserve.

The route takes hikers along wide sandy beaches and rocky shores, and along footpaths where the coast is inaccessible. Along the way the guides will share their intimate knowledge of the history, fauna and flora of the area. A variety of marine birds can be seen along the coast, while the Strandveld vegetation is especially attractive between August and October.

The hike starts with a leisurely sundowner stroll of 5 km along the beach at Paternoster, followed by a 5-km stroll back. **10 km; 3 to 4 hours.**

The second day's hike follows the coast to the 263-ha Cape Columbine Reserve. The hike then continues to Tietiesbaai, Varswaterbaai, Noord-Wesbaai and Trekoskraal, from where hikers are transferred back to Paternoster. **17 km; 8 hours.**

On day three, hikers are transferred to Trekoskraal and follow the coast to Wesbaai, Hospitaalbaai/Gonnemanskraal and Jacobsbaai, from where they are transferred back to Paternoster and the end of the trail. **11 km; 5 hours.**

17. SEVILLA ROCK ART TRAIL
Clanwilliam

Trail: 6 km; 4 hours; circular.

The starting point for this trail on the farm Traveller's Rest is located a short way after crossing the Brandewyn River when approaching from Clanwilliam. The route winds above and below rocky ledges and high cliffs overlooking the Brandewyn River. There are 10 marked rock art sites along the trail, some with rather fascinating paintings. Humans are portrayed in various styles, ranging from recognisable 'normal' figures and 'hook-headed' forms to stick-like shapes, and there are depictions of dancing women with steatopygia and of people in a procession. Animals, too, are a common feature of the rock art found along the trail. Several of these paintings – including one of two large yellow elephants – are about 75 cm long, representing some of the largest works on the trail. Other paintings of animals depict a gemsbok, quaggas (an extinct species, resembling a zebra) and animals that resemble a bat-eared fox and a hartebeest. There are also several handprints on some of the rock surfaces along the trail.

From the ninth rock art site the trail traverses Rooigang and then crosses the Brandewyn River to reach the tenth, and last, site. From here, you can follow the track on the southern side of the river back to the start or continue to the Sevilla cottages. A short detour to Milden's Pool, where you can swim, is especially worthwhile on a hot day.

Another option is to explore the **Olive Tree Walk**, a 45-minute circular route.

Rock Art of the Western Cape, Book 1: The Sevilla Trail & Traveller's Rest by Peter Slingsby is an indispensable guide for anyone doing the trail. The book includes information about each of the rock art sites as well as the plants that occur along the way.

18. CEDERBERG WILDERNESS
Citrusdal, Clanwilliam

Trails: Over 250 km; 1 to several days; network.
Permits: CapeNature Contact Centre, cell: 087 087 8250, email: reservation.alert@capenature.co.za or book online at www.capenature.co.za. The wilderness is divided into three blocks, and there is a limit of 50 people in each block. Groups are limited to a minimum of 3 and a maximum of 12 people. Access to the Maltese Cross and Wolfberg Cracks is through Dwarsrivier. Permits are obtainable from Dwarsrivier, tel: (027) 482 2825, fax: (027) 482 1188, email: sanddrif@cederbergwine.com. For overnight hikes via the Maltese Cross and Wolfberg Arch a permit must be obtained from CapeNature.
Maps: The two-map set *Hike the Cederberg* (1:40,000) by Slingsby Maps (www.slingsbymaps.com) is indispensable.
Facilities/Activities: Algeria has 46 camp sites with powerpoints and ablution blocks and two fully equipped cottages (Garskraal and Rietdak), accommodating 5 and 10 people respectively. Electricity, bed linen and kitchenware are provided, but visitors must bring their own towels. Cottages with solar lights, gas stove, fridge and geyser, bed linen and kitchenware are available at Uitkyk (8 people), Waenhuis (4 people), and Prik-se-Werf, Peerboom and Sas-se-Werf (4 people each). Visitors must bring their own towels. All cottages have outside braai facilities as well as indoor fireplaces. Kliphuis, 20 km east of Clanwilliam, has 10 camp sites with ablution blocks. No electricity is available. Book through CapeNature at the above address (see Permits).
In the wilderness area there are basic mountain huts, without any facilities, at Heuningvlei, Middelberg, Crystal Pool, Sneeukop, Sleepad and Sneeuberg. The huts can be used on a first-come, first-served basis.
Pertinent information: Fires are not allowed in the wilderness area. A closed-cell ground pad, good sleeping bag, warm clothing and waterproof gear are essential, especially between May and September when temperatures plummet and snow can occur.

Extending from the Middelberg Pass at Citrusdal, northwards, to beyond the Pakhuis Pass, the Cederberg Wilderness covers 71,000 ha of spectacular mountainscapes. Over countless aeons the joint forces of nature have eroded the sandstone rock into fascinating natural sculptures. Well-known features include the 15-m-high Wolfberg Arch, the Wolfberg Cracks, a narrow cleft reaching 30 m into the bowels of the Wolfberg, and the Maltese Cross, which stands 20 m high. The Cederberg Wilderness is one of the eight clusters of the Cape Floral Region Protected Areas, which were inscribed as a UNESCO World Heritage Site in 2004.

The vegetation is characterised by fynbos, with relic forest patches in sheltered kloofs. Endemic to the Cederberg, Clanwilliam cedar (*Widdringtonia cedarbergensis*) grows among the rocks and crags at altitudes of over 1,000 m above sea level. The cedar restoration project propagates cedars in a nursery, and annual plantings of saplings into the cedar tree's natural habitat are carried out to ensure the survival of the species.

Another Cederberg endemic, the beautiful snow protea (*Protea cryophila*), grows only above the snowline. It occurs in very few places, among them Sneeuberg and Sneeukop. The northern Cederberg is the habitat of yet another endemic member of the protea family, the rocket pincushion (*Leucospermum reflexum*).

Mammals include baboon, rock dassie, spectacled dormouse (or namtap), grey rhebok, grysbok and common duiker. The Cederberg is an important refuge for leopard, and in 1988 a leopard conservation area was established in conjunction with private landowners. Tracks are often seen in the footpaths, but owing to their nocturnal habits, leopards are seldom encountered.

Among the myriad bird species to be seen are Cape rockjumper, Cape sugarbird, orange-breasted sunbird, protea seedeater, Victorin's warbler, Cape siskin and Verreaux's eagle.

1. Block A covers the northern Cederberg and includes Pakhuis, the Krakadouw range and Skerpioenberg. Although not as popular as the central and southern zones, the rugged scenery of the Krakadouw makes it worthwhile. From Kliphuis a footpath descends along Amon se Kloof to the Jan Dissels River Valley, where a cave near a South African War (1899–1902) blockhouse serves as an overnight stop. From here a footpath ascends along Krakadouw Poort to Heuningvlei. The third day's hike is an easy stroll along a jeep track, back to Pakhuis Pass. **40 km; 3 days; circular.**

2. Block B extends from Skerpioenberg, southwards, to the Wolfberg. A popular two-day hike is the Crystal Pool circuit. From Algeria a footpath ascends steadily along Helsekloof, past a beautiful waterfall, to Middelberg. Continuing from here, you come to the well-known landmark of Cathedral Rocks, with their crenellated spires, before crossing the Grootlandsvlakte. After following Wildehoutdrif the path ascends steeply up Groot Hartseer before reaching Crystal Pool. On the second day the route ascends along Engelsmanskloof to the jeep track, which you follow to Sleepad Hut. After descending to Grootlandsvlakte, you backtrack along the outward route. **26 km; 2 days; circular.**

Other well-known destinations in Block B include Welbedacht Cave, Tafelberg, Wolfberg Arch via Gabriël's Pass, and Wolfberg Cracks (see below).

3. Block C covers the western and southern part of the wilderness, as well as the southwestern end. The most direct access to the Maltese Cross is through Dwarsrivier Farm (see p. 53). The 2,027-m-high Sneeuberg, the highest point in the Cederberg, forms an impressive backdrop, and, as the name 'snow mountain' suggests, is often covered in snow during winter. Also of interest is Duiwelsgat, a remote valley passed when hiking from Sneeuberg Hut to Uitkyk Pass via Noordpoort. **12 km; 5 hours; open-ended.**

19. SANDDRIF HOLIDAY RESORT
Cederberg, Citrusdal

Trails: 4 walks; 35 minutes to 8 hours; circular and out-and-return.
Bookings and Permits: tel: (027) 482 2825, email: sanddrif@cederbergwine. com, web: www.sanddrif.com.
Maps: *Cederberg – The Touring Map* and *Hike the Cederberg*, Slingsby Maps (www.slingsbymaps.com).
Facilities/Activities: Fully equipped self-catering chalets and camp sites with ablution facilities at Sanddrif; mountain-bike trails; rock climbing; observatory; wine-tasting.

Overlooked by the Wolfberg to the east and Sneeuberg to the west, the Dwarsrivier Valley is a magnet for outdoor enthusiasts keen to explore the Cederberg's best-known natural landmarks, such as the Wolfberg Cracks and Arch, and the Maltese Cross.

1. Wolfberg Cracks and Arch Sanddrif is an ideal base for a hike to the Wolfberg Cracks, which dominate the skyline north of the farm and the Wolfberg Arch. From the start it is a strenuous ascent to the spectacular third crack, which ranges in height and width from a tight squeeze to several metres. Of special interest are two enormous rock arches, spanning 29 m and 20 m respectively. A short way on, you have to clamber to a higher level and then squeeze underneath a huge boulder. On emerging from the Cracks, it is an easy walk of about 90 minutes to the Wolfberg Arch. To return, either backtrack or descend along Gabriël's Pass and follow the jeep track back. **Cracks: 4 hours out-an-return; Cracks and Arch: 8 hours; circular.**

2. Maltese Cross From the parking area, about 7 km from Dwarsrivier, a footpath and cairns point the way to the well-known Maltese Cross. The path ascends steadily, and you will reach the formation after a 90-minute walk. **7 km; 3.5 to 4 hours; out-and-return.**

20. CEDERBERG PARK, KROMRIVIER
Cederberg, Citrusdal

Trails: 6 walks; 2 to 8 hours; circular and out-and-return.
Bookings: Cederberg Park, Kromrivier, tel: (027) 482 2807, email: bookings@cederbergpark.com.
Maps: *Cederberg – The Touring Map* and *Hike the Cederberg* by Slingsby Maps (www.slingsbymaps.com).
Facilities/Activities: Self-catering cottages; camp sites; restaurant; mountain biking; rock climbing; 4x4 route; horse-riding.

Kromrivier Farm and the Cederberg Tourist Park are favourites with many outdoor enthusiasts. Adjoining the Cederberg Wilderness and Breekkrans, a property of the Mountain Club of South Africa, Kromrivier is also conveniently close to the Stadsaal Caves.

1. Disa Pool is an easier ascent along the Kromrivier, passing Kromrivier Cave and a waterfall before reaching Disa Pool, where clumps of *Disa tripetaloides* can be seen flowering in profusion between December and February. **3 to 4 hours; out-and-return.**

2. Maltese Cross The outward leg traverses the slopes below Dwarsrivierberg and Sugarloaf Peak, and then curves around the northern slopes of The Pup to reach the Maltese Cross, which lies a short way further on. The return leg heads over Kokspoort and then ascends along the Kromrivier, passing Disa Pool and the Kromrivier Cave on the way. **7 to 8 hours; circular.**

The four other options include an easy ramble from the top of Kromrivier Pass to the Stadsaal Caves, **Truitjieskraal** (3 hours), **Wit-kleigat** (2 to 3 hours), and **Apollo Cave and Lunar Tunnel** (7 to 8 hours).

21. NUWERUST
Cederberg, Citrusdal

Trails: 3 walks; 2 to 7 hours, circular.
Permits: Nuwerust Rest Camp, P O Box 270, Koue Bokkeveld 6836, tel: (027) 482 2813, email: info@cederbergexperience.co.za.
Maps: Brochure of walks with map.
Facilities/Activities: Self-catering cottages.

Nuwerust, in the southeastern Cederberg, nestles amid beautiful surroundings dominated by the deep, narrow kloof of the Brandkraals River and sheer orange sandstone cliffs. As it is situated on the western edge of the Little Karoo, the vegetation is typically renosterveld, with a variety of geophytes, scrub and succulents, as well as fynbos. Mammal species include grey rhebok, grysbok, klipspringer and the nocturnal and ever-elusive leopard.

1. Waterfall Route ascends rather gently along the lower slopes of Klipbokkop to a waterfall in the Klipbokkop River and then loops back. Along the way the trailist can expect to be treated to spectacular views of the Brandkraals River Valley. **6 km; 2 hours; circular.**

2. Rooiberg Trail begins with a steep ascent to the Rooiberg Plateau, north of the Brandkraals River. From the plateau there are spectacular views of the Swartruggens to the east, and the Breekkrans Mountains to the west. The trail then winds down to the deep kloof of the Brandkraals River, which you follow for 3 km to the rest camp. **12 km; 4.5 hours; circular.**

3. Klipbokkop Trail gains over 700 m in altitude to the peak, Klipbokkop, after which the mountain is named (*klipbok* is a colloquial Afrikaans name for the klipspringer). The final ascent involves some rock scrambling, but the stunning views make the climb worthwhile. The first and last sections of the trail follow the Waterfall Route. **15 km; 7 hours; circular.**

22. KAGGA KAMMA PRIVATE NATURE RESERVE
100 km northeast of Ceres

> **Trails:** 3 walks; 2 to 4 hours; circular.
> **Permits:** Kagga Kamma Nature Reserve, tel: (021) 872 4343, fax: 086 500 0800, email: info@kaggakamma.co.za.
> **Maps:** Available at reception.
> **Facilities/Activities:** Luxury huts and 'caves'; restaurant; swimming pool; San cultural tours; sundowner, night and game drives; stargazing at the mini observatory.

> alert@capenature.co.za or book online at www.capenature.co.za Sneeugat: Franz Zeeman, tel: (023) 230 0729. De Hoek: Mr Flip Langenhoven, tel: (023) 240 0339.
> **Maps:** Reserve pamphlet showing trails.
> **Facilities/Activities:** Basic overnight huts (no facilities) at Groot Winterhoek and De Tronk; basic shelters at Perdevlei.
> **Pertinent information:** No fires allowed, except at overnight huts at De Tronk. After heavy rains, the Groot Kliphuis River and other streams can be difficult to cross. Only 6 people per day admitted on the Die Hel to De Hoek route, which is closed during harvest season (1 December to 30 April).

Situated high up in the Swartruggens range, which separates the Karoo from the Koue Bokkeveld, the Kagga Kamma Nature Reserve lies amid rugged, but spectacular, scenery. Weirdly shaped sandstone formations, rock arches and crags form an awesome backdrop to a captivating landscape of valleys, mountains and canyons.

Highlights include rock painting sites dating back as far as 6,000 years. Verreaux's eagle, rock kestrel, double-banded courser, southern black korhaan and African harrier-hawk are among the nearly 245 bird species recorded in this area to date. Game animals to be seen include springbok, gemsbok, bontebok, eland and grey rhebok.

Self-guided Trails The three trails in the Kagga Kamma Private Nature Reserve, Blue (4 km; 1.5 hours), Red (7 km; 2.5 hours) and White (9 km; 4 hours), meander among spectacular sandstone rock formations that have been eroded into fascinating shapes, some of which contain rock art paintings.

23. GROOT WINTERHOEK WILDERNESS AREA
Porterville

> **Trails:** 90 km; 2 or more days; network.
> **Permits:** CapeNature Contact Centre, cell: 087 087 8250, email: reservation.

Proclaimed in 1985, the Groot Winterhoek Wilderness Area covers 19,200 ha of wild countryside and rugged mountains, dominated by the 2,077-m-high Groot Winterhoek peak. Among the profusion of fynbos plants are many proteas, including some exceptionally large waboom (*Protea nitida*), bearded protea (*Protea magnifica*) and *Protea recondita*. There is also a rich diversity of ericas, which are especially attractive during the summer months. Unlikely to escape attention in January and February is the abundance of showy red disas (*Disa uniflora*) gracing the stream and riverbanks. The wilderness forms part of the Cape Floral Region Protected Areas inscribed as a UNESCO World Heritage Site in 2004.

1. De Tronk One of the highlights of Groot Winterhoek is the deep gorge carved by the Vier-en-Twintig Riviere, which plunges over a waterfall into a magnificent pool at Die Hel. From the parking area to the overnight stop at De Tronk (13 km; 3 hours) you follow the course of the Groot Kliphuis River. The hike to Die Hel is 10 km out-and-return. A few rock paintings can be seen in an overhang on the way into Die Hel. **36 km; 2 days; out-and-return.**

2. Perdevlei-De Tronk Circuit A longer circuit leads from the parking area to Groot Kliphuis (16 km; 5 hours), and then to Perdevlei (7 km; 2 hours). From Perdevlei it is a 12-km, 4-hour hike to De Tronk, and a 10-km, 3-hour walk to Die Hel and back. The 13-km return leg along the Kliphuis River to the parking area takes about 4 hours. **58 km; 3 or 4 days; circular.**

Other options include a demanding two-day kloofing trip from Die Hel to De Hoek, and a 14-km out-and-return hike from the farm Rooiland to the Sneeugat River. For both these hikes permission must be obtained from the landowners (see 'Permits').

24. CHRISTIE PRINS HIKING TRAIL
Prince Alfred Hamlet

Trail: 2 walks; 2 to 4 hours; circular.
Permits: Not required.
Maps: Download from https://koelfontein.co.za/what-we-do/stay-explore/.
Facilities/Activities: None.

The Christie Prins Hiking Trail in the Skurweberg mountains, northwest of Prince Alfred Hamlet, starts on the farm Koelfontein, 4 km outside the village. The short route (5 km; 2 hours) meanders through fynbos and rewards hikers with spectacular views. The longer route (3 to 4 hours) climbs steeply for 1 km, then levels off before descending to the old Gydo Pass. Hikers can cool off along the way in a natural swimming pool. The trail is maintained by the DF Conradie Primary School.

25. SILWERFONTEIN HIKING TRAIL
Gouda

Trail: 15 km; 7 to 8 hours or 2-day hike; circular.
Permits: Silwerfontein Guest Farm, P O Box 235, Tulbagh 6820, cell: 079 500 1906, email: info@silwerfontein.co.za.
Maps: Sketch map.
Facilities/Activities: Self-contained guest cottage (sleeps 2); converted double-decker bus (sleeps 10) with shower, toilet

and boma; Ontongs overnight cave (no facilities); angling; swimming; windsurfing; mountain biking.
Pertinent information: Open fires are strictly prohibited.

Situated in the mountains above Voëlvlei Dam, the 1,000-ha Silwerfontein Farm has been declared a natural heritage site and has 35 species of the protea family (10 per cent of the total number of Proteaceae species in South Africa). Among these are 7 red data species, including the only remaining population of 27 plants of *Sorocephalus imbricatus*. Silwerfontein, a member of the 200-km² Voëlvlei Nature Conservancy, is also a sanctuary to 10 per cent of the world's geometric tortoise population. Among the 203 bird species recorded here are blue crane and African fish eagle. Animals you might chance upon include gemsbok, grey rhebok, klipspringer, grysbok and leopard.

The first day of the Silwerfontein Hiking Trail (6 km; 4 hours) leads through eucalyptus and pine plantations, before climbing up through the fynbos on the slopes of the Voëlvlei Mountains to a saddle. The trail then ascends steeply to the Ontongs Cave – just below the summit – a total gain of nearly 700 m in altitude from the start. The cave was named after Jakob Ontong, who gained notoriety as a stock thief two centuries ago. The second day's hike (9 km; 3 hours) starts with a climb up a gully to the summit of Ontongskop Peak (815 m). After descending, the trail makes its way to Beacon Peak (634 m) and on to Corner Peak (622 m). You then follow a kloof to a contour path that takes you back to the start of the trail. On both days trailists can enjoy great views over Voëlvlei Dam and the surrounding winelands.

26. KAROO DESERT NATIONAL BOTANICAL GARDEN
Worcester

Trails: 6 walks; 30 minutes to 5 hours; circular and out-and-return.
Permits: Entrance fee. No permit required.
Maps: Brochure of garden available.

Set against the Brandwag Mountains near Worcester, the Karoo Desert National Botanical Garden is the only true succulent garden in the southern hemisphere and on the African continent. The garden covers 144 ha of natural vegetation (protected as a flora reserve), and 11 ha are under cultivation. It lies at the heart of the succulent Karoo biome and, as well as the 400 plant species that occur here naturally, some 6,000 species, including 300 rare and endangered species, have been established. The cultivated section features group plantings of related species and gardens reflecting the flora from different regions, such as the Richtersveld, the Worcester-Robertson Karoo, Knersvlakte and Namibia. The succulents are most impressive from April to October, while vygies provide a blaze of colour from mid-July to mid-October.

Several short trails traverse the lower reaches of the garden, including the 450-m-long **Karoo Adventure Trail**, which displays some typical Karoo vegetation, the **Braille Trail** of just under 1 km, and the **Shale Trail**, which meanders for 1.7 km among the shale koppies. Three longer trails, ranging from 4 to 7 km, traverse the natural northern section of the garden.

27. BAIN'S KLOOF, LIMIETBERG NATURE RESERVE
Wellington

See no. 29 (p. 59) for walks.

Trails: 3 walks; 3 to 6 hours; out-and-return and open-ended.
Permits: CapeNature Contact Centre, cell: 087 087 8250, email: reservation.alert@capenature.co.za.
Maps: Trail pamphlet with basic maps.
Facilities/Activities: Camp site and picnic site at Tweede Tol.

The Limietberg Nature Reserve stretches over 117,000 ha of mountain slopes, cliff faces and wild river valleys, from Franschhoek in the south to the Groot Drakenstein Mountains in the east and Voëlvlei Mountains in the north. The vegetation is mainly mountain fynbos, with a wide variety of ericas, proteas and restios. Animals to be seen include leopard, klipspringer, grey rhebok, baboon and dassie. The reserve forms part of the Boland Mountain Complex, one of the eight clusters of the Cape Floral Region Protected Areas, which were inscribed as a UNESCO World Heritage Site in 2004.

1. Bobbejaans River Trail winds from the Eerste Tol parking area down to the Wit River. You cross the river, then ascend briefly and take an easy walk along a contour above the Bobbejaans River. After about 3.5 km you turn off to rock pools in the river. The final 750 m of the trail ascends steeply to the three-tiered Bobbejaans River waterfall. **9 km; 3 hours; out-and-return.**

2. Happy Valley Trail follows a jeep track from Eerste Tol, past the ruins of an old house, to Hugo's Rest. From here, it follows the course of the Wit River, with its natural pools, to Junction Pool, one of the best pools for swimming in the Boland Mountains. **9 km; 4 hours; out-and-return.**

3. Rockhopper Trail is a moderate to difficult adventure, where trailists find their own way down the boulder-strewn bed of the Wit River. Starting from Eerste Tol, the trail involves rock-hopping, swimming and walking, and ends at Tweede Tol. Noteworthy among the riverine vegetation is the Breede River yellowwood. As this is a linear route you will need a vehicle at the start and at the end. The route is closed when the level of the river is high. Hazards include adverse weather, flooding rivers after rain, slippery rocks, wind and ticks! **8 km; 6 hours; open-ended.**

28. PATATSKLOOF HIKING TRAILS
Wellington

Trails: 2 walks; 2 to 4 hours; out-and-return and circular from mountain parking area.
Bookings: Patatskloof/Zielenrust, Andries cell: 083 447 0216, email: info@zielenrust.co.za.

Situated on the lower western slopes of the Limietberg against the backdrop of Pic Blanc (849 m), the Patatskloof Hiking Trail owes its name to the wine farm on which it is situated.

Mountain fynbos, dominated by ericas, members of the protea family, restios, as well as a rich diversity of geophytes, covers the mountain slopes. Be on the lookout for endemic fynbos birds such as the protea seed-eater, Victorin's scrub-warbler, Cape rockjumper and Cape sugarbird. Mammals you might chance upon include klipspringer, baboon, rock dassie, grey rhebok, common duiker and Cape grysbok.

1. Hawequa Mirror Trail From the mountain parking area the trail ascends steadily for about 2.5 km to the base of the Seven Sisters cliffs, where a memorial tablet is a reminder of the tragedy that occurred when a young student died on 19 November 1959. Along the way you will enjoy stunning views of the Berg River Valley stretching from Simonsberg in the south to Voëlvlei Dam in the north. **5 km; 2 to 3 hours; out-and-return.**

2. Scouts Trail also starts from the mountain parking area. **12 km; 4 hours; circular.**

29. DU TOITSKLOOF, LIMIETBERG NATURE RESERVE
Paarl

See no. 27 (p. 58) for walks.

1. Krom River From the parking area near the Worcester exit of the Huguenot Tunnel, backtrack for 700 m and turn right. After crossing the Molenaars River, the trail heads upstream for about 10 minutes and then ascends along the right-hand slopes of the Krom River. Just before reaching the first waterfall the path passes through a magnificent patch of indigenous forest. Extreme caution must be exercised when climbing to the second waterfall with its attractive pool. **7 km; 2.5 hours; out-and-return.**

2. Elands River This hike starts immediately to the south of the Worcester exit of the Huguenot Tunnel. After an initial steep climb, the trail levels off to follow the Elands River, with an occasional climb away from the river. The trail then descends to Fisherman's Cave, where an inviting pool awaits the weary hiker. From here, the path continues for another 500 m along the river course, ending at sheer cliffs. **8 km; 3 hours; out-and-return.**

3. Mias Poort Walk begins with a long and steep ascent (about 2 hours) to the ridge of Huguenot Kop. An easy walk along the ridge is followed by another steep climb to the cross, erected in February 1945 by the Italian prisoners of war who built the Du Toitskloof Pass. The unsurpassed views are ample compensation for all the exertion in getting to the 1,318-m-high summit of Huguenot Kop. The trail head is on the Paarl side of the old Du Toitskloof Pass. **8 km; 3 hours; out-and-return.**

30. PAARL MOUNTAIN NATURE RESERVE
Paarl

The huge, shiny granite outcrop that characterises Paarl Mountain dominates the landscape to the west of the Berg River. Covering an area of 50 km², the mountain is 12 km long and up to 5 km wide. The upper elevations fall within the 1,990-ha Paarl Mountain Nature Reserve, which also incorporates the Meulwater Wild Flower Reserve.

1. Klipkershout Trail in the southern part of the reserve winds through fynbos with a profusion of proteas. Wild olive trees, wagon trees and the klipkershout, or rock candlewood (*Maytenus oleoides*), to which the trail owes its name, are conspicuous among the massive granite outcrops. **4.5 km; 1.5 hours; circular.**

2. Bretagne Rock is the highlight of the reserve for most visitors and offers an easy walk up to the summit. There is a chain to assist you with the final ascent to the top, from where there are wonderful 360-degree views of the Berg River Valley, Table Mountain and False Bay. There are also several other footpaths and a number of gravel roads that traverse the reserve.

31. DELVERA TRAILS
Klapmuts

Klapmutskop (522 m) dominates Delvera and the surrounding wine estates. This landmark's upper slopes were cleared of alien vegetation and set aside as the Klapmutskop Conservancy in 2004 to protect the endangered Swartland shale renosterveld vegetation and yellowwood forest.

This trail traverses the vineyards below Klapmutskop. The **Delvera Hiking Trail** (9.75 km; 3 hours) ascends steadily up Klapmutskop and gains nearly 300 m in altitude. But you will be rewarded with spectacular views of the surrounding countryside as the trail makes its way around Klapmutskop (522 m). The less strenuous **Vineyard Walk** (5.25 km; 1.5 hours) leads to the Pepper Tree on the slopes of Klapmutskop and introduces hikers to seven wine cultivars. Permits for a walk to the farm dam, which is home to a variety of birds, can also be bought. All trails start at the Delvera AgriTourism Centre.

32. JONKERSHOEK NATURE RESERVE
Stellenbosch

Situated about 9 km from Stellenbosch, the Jonkershoek Valley ranks among the most beautiful in South Africa. Enclosed by the spectacular Jonkershoek Twins peaks, the three Ridge Peaks, Guardian Peak, Pic-Sans-Nom, and the Stellenbosch Mountain, the upper Jonkershoek Valley lies within the 8,900-ha Jonkershoek Nature Reserve. The reserve forms part of the Boland Mountain Complex – one of the eight clusters of the Cape Floral Region Protected Areas, which were inscribed as a UNESCO World Heritage Site in 2004. The reserve's vegetation is dominated by a rich diversity of fynbos, while riverine forest is typically found in protected kloofs.

1. Swartboskloof-Sosyskloof This easy scenic route ascends along the western slopes of Swartboskloof for about 2 km, passing through a patch of beautiful indigenous forest. It then traverses along a contour to Sosyskloof before winding back to the start. **5.3 km; 2 hours; circular (or, if longer route to lookout is taken, 6.9 km; 2.5 hours; circular).**

2. Tweede Waterval Walk is an easy ramble along the Eerste River past Eerste Waterval (First Waterfall), followed by a steep climb along a gorge to the foot of Tweede Waterval (Second Waterfall). The dangerous ascent to this waterfall is closed. **6.4 km; 2 hours; out-and-return.**

3. Panorama Circuit From the bridge on the hairpin bend of the Circular Drive, there is a steep climb to a contour path just below Third Ridge and Banghoek peaks. Following the contour path you reach Bergriviernek, from where there are spectacular views of Assegaaiboskloof. The path then winds across the Dwarsberg Plateau, with its marshy areas and streams surrounded by disas, to Kurktrekker, at the head of Swartboskloof. There is a short detour to the summit of Guardian Peak (1,227 m) here, with stunning, panoramic views of the Cape Peninsula, from Table Mountain to Cape Point, Robben Island, False Bay, Cape Hangklip and the peaks of the Hottentots Holland range. From Kurktrekker the path descends along Swartboskloof past Second and First waterfalls to the starting point. **17 km; 6 hours; circular.**

4. Swartboskloof Route ascends the steep Swartboskloof, gaining over 900 m in altitude over the first 4.5 km, but the panoramic views are ample reward. The route then traverses fairly level terrain to the top of Kurktrekkernek where there is a steep 2.5-km descent to the Waterfall Route. **18 km; 6 hours; circular.**

33. HELDERBERG NATURE RESERVE
Somerset West

Trails: 35 minutes to 3 hours; network.
Permits: Entrance fee. No permit required.

Maps: Map can be downloaded from www.helderbergnaturereserve.co.za.
Facilities/Activities: Information centre; museum; picnic area (no fires); restaurant.

The Helderberg provides an impressive backdrop to the 245-ha Helderberg Nature Reserve on its lower southern slopes, which are covered in fynbos. It is a very popular birding destination, counting specials, such as the Cape sugarbird, orange-breasted sunbird, Victorin's warbler and protea seedeater, among its 140 bird species. There is also small game, including grysbok, common duiker and steenbok, which trailists may chance upon.

The reserve is traversed by a network of interlinking footpaths, providing options ranging from a short 35-minute amble in the cultivated section to longer hikes higher up the mountain slopes. A highlight of the reserve is Disa Gorge, just below the cliffs, with its remnant indigenous forest of red alder and yellowwood trees. Disas can be seen in bloom here in December and January.

34. HELDERBERG FARM TRAIL
Helderberg

Trails: 5 walks; 40 minutes to 9 hours or overnight trail; network.
Bookings: Entrance fee. No permit required for day walks. For overnight trail, book with Helderberg Farm Trail, P O Box 507, Somerset West 7129, tel. and fax: (021) 855 4308, email: helderbergplaas@mweb.co.za.
Maps: Map can be downloaded from www.helderbergplaas.co.za.
Facilities/Activities: Huts with beds, water and toilets 1 km from start; picnic and braai sites; strawberries are available when in season (September).
Pertinent information: Carry water. No swimming is allowed in streams and pools. Fires are not permitted.

Hugging the western foothills of the Helderberg, the historic Helderberg Farm dates back over three centuries to 1692. The vegetation is typical mountain fynbos, interspersed with patches of rock candlewood, wild peach, wild olive and blossom trees. Close on 100 bird species have been recorded here, and baboon, grysbok and common duiker are among the animals to be seen.

The trail network consists of a number of interlinked colour-coded loops that can be done either individually as day walks, or together as a two-day hiking trail. Highlights include Granny's Forest, with its mix of indigenous and exotic trees and 17 fern species, and a viewpoint with spectacular views over False Bay to the south, the Stellenbosch winelands to the north, and the Cape Peninsula to the west.

35. BOLAND HIKING TRAIL
Hottentots Holland Nature Reserve

See no. 36 (this page) for kloofing routes.

Trails: 2 trails; 18.2 km and 28 km; 2 days; circular and out-and-return.
Permits: CapeNature Contact Centre, cell: 087 087 8250, email: reservation.alert@capenature.co.za or book online at www.capenature.co.za.
Maps: Detailed colour trail map.
Facilities/Activities: Showers, toilets and parking at Nuweberg.
Pertinent information: Trails may be closed temporarily due to flooding and bad weather. Weather conditions can change rapidly and hikers should be prepared for sudden weather changes.

The Hottentots Holland Nature Reserve forms part of the Boland Mountain Complex – one of the eight clusters of the Cape Floral Region Protected Areas, which were inscribed as a UNESCO World Heritage Site in 2004. Over 1,300 plant species have been recorded in the 42,000-ha reserve, including more than 150 erica species, which blanket the slopes during spring and summer. The proteas are seen at their best between July and September.

1. Sphinx Route The first 3.5 km of the trail follows plantation roads through pine plantation before branching off onto a single track which ascends steadily to the Sphinx, a rock outcrop resembling the famous Egyptian sphinx. Continuing its steady ascent, the trail skirts Nuweberg towering about 300 m above to your left. Further along you cross the headwaters of the Palmiet River, where water is available from the streams during the winter months. From the Palmietpad the trail continues to ascend before levelling off. Landdroskop Hut is a stone structure built around a central room with the sleeping quarters leading off. Shamrock Lodge, situated nearby, is a wooden hut, but has better views. The second day's hike is an easy amble down to the start along a jeep track. **18.2 km; 2 days; circular.**

2. Orchard Route Starting at Nuweberg, the trail initially ascends gently before it drops down steeply into the Riviersonderend Kloof, which is crossed by means of a wooden bridge. After a short but steep ascent the trail more or less follows a contour path from where there are wonderful views of the Theewaterskloof Dam and the patchwork of apple and pear orchards in the Vyeboom Valley below. After a short descent, you cross the river in Boesmanskloof by means of a suspension bridge to reach the huts. Aloe Ridge huts are named after the fan aloe, which is restricted to the Franschhoek Mountains in the south and the Roodezand Mountains at Tulbagh. The common name is derived from the strap-shaped leaves which are arranged in an erect flat fan. They grow on rocky slopes and their scarlet flowers are seen at their best between August and October. A short way upstream of the suspension bridge is a refreshing swimming pool where you can cool off. On the second day's hike, you will retrace your tracks of the previous day, but the scenery is no less spectacular. It's an easy day's walk and the only long climb is the one that has to be negotiated after crossing the Riviersonderend. **28 km; 2 days; out-and-return.**

36. KLOOFING ROUTES
Hottentots Holland Nature Reserve

Trails: 2 routes; 7 to 9 hours; circular.

Unlike hiking trails where clear trails are followed, there are no demarcated routes on kloofing trips, which involve boulder-hopping, wading through water, swimming, and jumping over waterfalls. It should not be undertaken by people afraid of heights, and novice groups must be accompanied by an experienced leader. A dry bag, footwear with a good grip, wetsuit, towel and warm clothes are essential as the water is cold throughout the year. Also remember to pack sunscreen and high-energy snacks.

1. Riviersonderend Gorge is an ideal entry-level introduction to kloofing, but should still be regarded as difficult. From the Nuweberg office, a jeep track is followed until you reach a signpost directing you to turn right. You then follow the original section of the Boland Hiking Trail to Boesmanskloof/Aloe Ridge Huts through splendid fynbos vegetation and stunning scenery. The start of the kloofing adventure is reached after a 4.7-km walk and the kloof section is about 6 km long. The route follows the deep gorge carved by the Riviersonderend and alternates between wading through pools, swimming, boulder-hopping and scrambling over rocks. There are a number of small waterfalls to negotiate, but the highest compulsory one is 7 m high. At Junction Pool, a good lunch stop, the Suicide Gorge route joins the Riviersonderend Gorge. From here, the canyon opens up, and you eventually reach the end of the kloof at a weir. After a steep climb out of the kloof

the trail levels off as you head for the Nuweberg office. **14.4 km; 7 to 8 hours; circular.**

2. Suicide Gorge is regarded as very difficult and offers a more extreme adventure for adrenaline junkies, requiring several nerve-wracking compulsory jumps over waterfalls. From Nuweberg, the trail initially follows the same onward route as the Riviersondered Gorge route, but you continue for just short of another 4 km to the entry point. Although the kloofing section is only 1.3 km long, it is physically demanding and you need to be fit. Shortly after descending into the kloof, there's a delightful rock slide into a pool below, and from here the route varies between swimming through pools and jumping over several waterfalls. Shortly before reaching the end of Suicide Gorge two compulsory waterfall jumps have to be negotiated in quick succession, the highest one being 14 m high. The exit trail, at the junction of Suicide Gorge and Riviersonderend, is 200 m upstream in the Riviersonderend Kloof. A 6.5-km walk takes you back to Nuweberg. **16.2 km; 8 to 9 hours; circular.**

37. CRYSTAL POOL HIKE
Gordon's Bay

This trail in the 8,500-ha Steenbras River Nature Reserve is managed by the Cape Town City Council and falls within the Kogelberg Biosphere Reserve. The trailhead is along Faure Marine Drive (R44), just after crossing the bridge over the Steenbras River. The route initially follows a well-defined footpath, but be prepared for lots of boulder-hopping and rock scrambling as you make your way up the deep gorge carved by the Steenbras River to Reed Pool, Deep Pool, Elena's Pool and, finally, Crystal Pool – after which the trail has been named. From here you have to retrace your tracks. **4 km; 3 to 4 hours; out-and-return.**

38. HAROLD PORTER NATIONAL BOTANICAL GARDEN
Betty's Bay

Trails: 4 walks; 1 to 3 hours, out-and-return.
Permits: Entrance fee. No permit required, except for Leopard's Kloof Trail.
Maps: Available at office.
Facilities/Activities: Picnic sites and restaurant.
Pertinent information: Permits for Leopard's Kloof are issued on a first-come, first-served basis from 08:00 to 14:00.

Set between sea and mountains, the Harold Porter National Botanical Garden lies in the heart of the Cape Floristic Region. The garden covers 200 ha of mountain fynbos and forested kloofs, with streams, two waterfalls and natural rock pools. There is also a small area under cultivation, with collections of plant families, and ponds and lawns. One of 10 national botanical gardens, Harold Porter focuses on the flora of the Western Cape winter rainfall region.

1. Zigzag Walk As the name suggests, this trail zigzags up the mountain slopes, gaining some 200 m in altitude, to Bobbejaankop, from where there are spectacular views of the coast and the rugged mountains. A side branch of the trail leads to Disa Pool, beneath a magnificent waterfall. Red disas cling to the moist cliffs and can be seen flowering in January. **2 to 3 hours; out-and-return.**

2. Leopard's Kloof features deep pools, waterfalls, and a lovely patch of forest, with assegai, red alder, yellowwood, wild olive and candlewood trees. The ascent of the gorge to the base of the third waterfall is steep, but there are ladders to help you. **3 km; 2 hours; out-and-return.**

39. KOGELBERG NATURE RESERVE
Kleinmond

See no. 40 (p. 65) for hiking trail.

Trails: 7 walks; 1 to 8 hours; circular, open-ended and out-and-return.
Permits: CapeNature Contact Centre, cell: 087 087 8250, email: reservation.alert@capenature.co.za or book online at www.capenature.co.za.
Maps: Reserve pamphlet with walks indicated available.
Facilities/Activities: Five fully furnished self-catering eco-cabins at Oudebosch; white-water kayaking (1 June to 30 September); mountain biking from Oudebosch office to Stokoe's Bridge and back; swimming; angling at Rooisand (permit required).

Situated in the heart of the Cape Floristic Region, an estimated 1,600 plant species (nearly 20 per cent of all fynbos species) occur in the Kogelberg Nature Reserve. The reserve is a sanctuary for some of the finest examples of fynbos and pristine riverine vegetation. The reserve forms the focal point of the Kogelberg Biosphere which was designated by UNESCO in 1998. It is also part of the Boland Mountain Complex – one of the eight clusters of the Cape Floral Region Protected Areas, which were inscribed as a UNESCO World Heritage Site in 2004.

Among the 150 endemic plant species here is the endangered marsh rose (*Orothamnus zeyheri*), while six of the country's 13 mimetes species also occur here. To date, some 176 erica species have been recorded in the area, which constitutes more than a quarter of the total number of South African erica species.

The reserve consists of an area of 18,000 ha, which forms the core of the Kogelberg Biosphere Reserve, and several smaller fragments. The first official biosphere reserve to be proclaimed in South Africa, its core area is bordered by buffer and transition zones. There are several starting points for the walks:

Oudebosch

1. Oudebosch-Harold Porter initially follows the same route as the Kogelberg Trail, but crosses into the Harold Porter National Botanical Garden. From the watershed the trail follows a contour path along the western slopes of Leopard's Kloof, before descending along the Zigzag Trail to the cultivated section of the garden. This is a one-way route and you will need a vehicle to drop you off at Oudebosch and another to collect you at the Harold Porter National Botanical Garden. **6 km; 3 hours; open-ended.**

2. Palmiet River Trail From the reserve office at Oudebosch the path meanders for about 4.5 km through magnificent fynbos along the Palmiet River. High mountain peaks dominate the scenery and there are several inviting pools with white sandy beaches where hikers can cool off on a hot day – remember to pack a swimming costume. There is a choice of two return routes: either retrace your steps or follow the final stretch of the Kogelberg Trail back to the start. **10 km; 3 hours; circular.**

3. Kogelberg Trail begins at the reserve office and follows the slopes above the Oudebos River, through Oudebosch, a patch of relic indigenous forest, past Platbos. From Platbos the route follows the one remaining spoor of a rehabilitated jeep track to Louwsbos, and then continues on another jeep track along the course of the Louws River. The descent follows the outward section of the Palmiet River Trail, on the eastern slopes of Dwarsberg. **24 km; 8 hours; circular.**

Highlands

The starting point, on the eastern boundary of the reserve, is reached via Highlands Road and the Mountain to Ocean Forest (MTO) Highlands Plantation.

1. Perdeberg Trail From the western boundary of the MTO Highlands Plantation (the area has been rehabilitated to fynbos, in light of the fact that MTO plantations are being phased out in the Western Cape), the trail initially meanders along a jeep track across the plateau of the Palmiet Mountains. It then follows a footpath along the upper slopes of the Perdeberg, with a short detour to the summit of Perdeberg (654 m) from where there are expansive views over the coast and the scenic Palmiet Valley to the north. The trail then doubles back to rejoin the jeep track. **22 km; 7 to 8 hours; out-and-return.**

Kleinmond

1. Three Sisters Walk From the starting point, just beyond Jean's Hill above Kleinmond, the path winds in a clockwise direction along the lower slopes of the Three Sisters before ascending steeply to their 634-m-high summit. From here there are far-reaching views over Kleinmond, Cape Hangklip to the west, and Danger Point to the east. The route then follows a path along the edge of sheer cliffs, and, after skirting around the 479-m-high Sandown Peak, makes its way along the edge of Perdeberg to Jean's Hill, where it descends steeply to the end. **8 km; 4 hours; circular.**

40. HIGHLANDS HIKING TRAIL
Kogelberg Nature Reserve

See no. 39 (p. 64) for walks.

Trail: 37 km; 2 days; circular.
Permits: CapeNature Contact Centre, cell: 087 087 8250, email: reservation. alert@capenature.co.za or book online at www.capenature.co.za.
Maps: A map and trail description.
Facilities/Activities: Overnight hut in Kleinmond Caravan Park, with bunk beds, fireplace and communal ablutions.
Pertinent information: Hikers must make their own arrangements for accommodation in Kleinmond. Pack a swimming costume for the Botrivier Lagoon crossing.

The trail begins on the farm Iona, on Highlands Road, from where it makes its way through orchards, pine plantations and fynbos, before descending steeply to the Botrivier Lagoon. Depending on the time of year, the crossing can be either ankle or waist deep. The trail then follows the sandy coastline to the overnight hut in Kleinmond, 21 km (6 to 7 hours) from the start. On the second day (16 km; 8 hours), the trail skirts the Three Sisters and then ascends steeply up the slopes of the Perdeberg. The last 9 km follows a jeep track back to the start.

41. MONT ROCHELLE NATURE RESERVE
Franschhoek

Trails: 10 trails; 1 to 7 hours; circular, out-and-return and open-ended.
Permits: Obtain at entrance gate from 09:00 to 17:00 daily. No cash accepted, only debit or credit cards, SnapScan, Zapper or Masterpass apps.
Maps: Download from https://montrochellehiking.co.za/plan-your-visit/.
Facilities/Activities: Paragliding.

Situated to the east of historic Franschhoek, Mont Rochelle Nature Reserve covers 1,728 ha of spectacular mountain peaks and wild kloofs, and has a rich diversity of fynbos. The reserve forms part of the Theewaterskloof Conservancy, and game that historically occurred in the area is being reintroduced.

1. Cats' Pass Trail Starting just outside Franschhoek, the first 2.5 km of the trail steeply ascends the original Cats' Pass. Built in 1819, some 400 m in altitude is gained to the intersection with the modern pass, at the summit of this new pass. There are some lovely views of the patchwork of farms in Franschhoek Valley. From the summit of Franschhoek Pass the 8-km descent follows Cats' Pass and then the alternative built by Major Holloway. Historic reminders along the way include Muller's Bridge, Jan Joubertgat Bridge (1825),

the Cats' Toll House, and the old outspan, where travellers and oxen used to rest. **10.5 km; 5 hours; open-ended.**

2. Dutoitskop An ascent of Dutoitskop from the reserve office (near the hairpin bend at the summit of Franschhoek Pass) involves a steady climb along a ridge to the 1,418-m-high Dutoitskop, gaining over 700 m in altitude. From the summit of Dutoitskop there are great views of the Wemmershoek Mountains and Dam to the north, and the Franschhoek Valley to the west. **12 km; 5 hours; out-and-return.**

3. Perdekop From the reserve office (near the hairpin bend at the summit of the Franschhoek Pass) the trail steadily ascends a kloof, to the watershed and the Wemmershoek viewpoint. Follow the watershed to the 1,575-m-high Perdekop, in the northeastern corner of the reserve; great views are ample reward for the climb. **15 km; 6 hours; out-and-return.**

42. CALEDON WILDFLOWER GARDEN
Caledon

Trail: 10 km; 3.5 to 4.5 hours; circular.
Permits: Entrance fee. No permit required.
Maps: Sketch map.
Facilities/Activities: Tea room; public toilets; picnic sites.

The Caledon Nature Reserve and Wildflower Garden was laid out on land granted to the municipality by Queen Victoria, in 1899, for the establishment of a park. The cultivated section of the garden consists of 56 ha of flower beds, lawns, ponds and picnic sites. The remaining 158 ha is pristine natural vegetation.

From the starting point, just beyond the tea room, the trail ascends steeply to the crest of the Swartberg. Along this section trailists are rewarded with extensive views of the Overberg. The trail then winds back along Vensterkloof, past Die Venster (The Window), a rock arch overlooking the garden.

43. FERNKLOOF NATURE RESERVE
Hermanus

Trails: 50 km; 45 minutes to full day; network.
Permits: Entrance fee. No permit required.
Maps: Map available from the Fernkloof Nature Reserve Visitors' Centre.
Facilities/Activities: Visitors' Centre; herbarium; nursery; picnic sites.

Fernkloof Nature Reserve, with its deep ravines, streams and cascades, lies at the western end of the Kleinrivier mountain range above Hermanus. The reserve covers about 1,446 ha. There are several endemics among the reserve's more than 1,050 plant species. The flowers are at their best in September and October, but many of the more than 40 protea species bloom during winter.

The various trails offer breathtaking views across Walker Bay to the south, and the Hemel-en-Aarde Valley and Kleinmond to the west. An ascent of the 842-m-high Aasvoëlkop, the highest point in Fernkloof Nature Reserve, is well worth the effort for the fine views. Other highlights include the ravine of Fernkloof, Boekenhoutbos with its fine specimens of Cape beech trees, and Cave Falls, named after the waterfall that cascades through the roof of the cave.

44. CLIFF PATH
Hermanus

Trail: 12 km; 4 hours; open-ended.
Permits: Not required.
Maps: Obtain from Hermanus Tourism Bureau, tel: (028) 312 2629.
Facilities/Activities: Water points; toilets.

This unique coastal trail is situated in a nature reserve. It traverses the coves and sandy beaches from the new harbour to the mouth of the Klein River in the east. Along the walk hikers will encounter a variety of vegetation types. These range from coastal scrub and dune fynbos to patches of forest. There are various scenic vantage points where benches have been strategically placed for hikers to rest and enjoy the view.

Hermanus offers some of the best land-based whale-watching in the world. For that reason the Cliff Path is especially popular between June and November. During these months large numbers of tourists flock to the town to view the numerous southern right whales that visit the coast to calve. Of historic interest along the trail is the Old Harbour, with its small museum.

45. DUIWELSGAT HIKING TRAIL
Gansbaai

Trail: 7 km; 3 hours; open-ended.
Permits: Permit for Klipgat in Walker Bay Nature Reserve obtainable at the reserve.
Maps: Sketch map from Gansbaai Tourism, tel: (028) 384 1439, email: info@gansbaaiinfo.com.
Facilities/Activities: None.

This scenic trail links several historic sites along the coast of Gansbaai. From the municipal camp site the trail goes through Stanford's Cove, which was used as a harbour from which farm produce was shipped to the Cape in the 1840s.

Further along the coast the trail takes you past De Kelders (The Cellars). This is a cave containing a freshwater swimming pool, which was created by water seepage.

Next along the way is Die Stal (The Stable). Horses from the *Birkenhead*, which struck the Danger Point reef in 1852, were said to have swum ashore here. A short way further on is Duiwelsgat (Devil's Hole), the deep hole in the rocks after which the trail is named. The trail ends at Klipgat, a cave that was inhabited by Stone Age people. There are excellent whale-watching opportunities from the cliffs between June and November.

46. PLATBOS FOREST TRAIL
Gansbaai

Trail: 1 to 2 hours; circular.
Permits: Prior reservation essential. Platbos Hiking Trail, P O Box 1438, Gansbaai 7220, cell: 082 411 0448, email: info@platbos.co.za.
Maps: Sketch map and information brochures on forest environments and trees.
Facilities/Activities: Picnic site and ablution facilities; benches along trail; nursery.
Pertinent information: Guided and self-guided options. Light refreshments are served under the forest canopy on the guided walk.

Covering some 30 ha, the Platbos Forest is the southernmost forest on the African continent. The Platbos Forest Trail is an easy ramble through magnificent indigenous forests of white stinkwood, white pear, hard pear and milkwood, with some specimens being up to a thousand years old. A rare relic of an ancient sand forest, its composition is unlike any other forest in the southwestern Cape. Trees have been marked along the trail and information on the forest environment and the different tree species is provided in brochures.

The forest is alive with birdsong, and flycatchers, cardinal woodpeckers, sombre greenbuls, Cape batis and owls are among the species recorded. Bushbuck, grysbok, grey rhebok, caracal and a variety of small mammals occur in the area. The walk is easily undertaken by young and old and has benches and a waterhole.

47. FYNBOS TRAIL
Stanford/Gansbaai

Trail: 26 km; 3 days. Coastal add-on option: 34 km; 4 days.
Bookings: Fynbos Trail, cell: 082 464

5115, email: info@fynbostrail.co.za or book online at www.fynbostrail.co.za.
Maps: Colour map with contour profiles.
Facilities/Activities: Depends on hiking option selected.
Pertinent information: There are three hiking options: guided slackpacking, self-guided slackpacking, and self-guided, self-catering.

This delightful trail meanders through pristine fynbos and magnificent forests.

Starting at the Growing the Future Sustainable Agriculture and Life Skills College on Grootbos Nature Reserve, the first day's route (6.6 km; 3 hours) meanders through coastal Strandveld to the Steynsbos Milkwood Forest. Some of the milkwood trees in the forest, one of only eight forests of this type in the world, are about a thousand years old. From here you ascend steadily to Pinnacle Viewpoint. After a level stretch, the trail descends steeply to the overnight stop at Fynbos Retreat.

The second day's hike (11 km; 6 hours) descends along a valley to the Witvoetkloof and a delightful waterfall. From here it is a steep climb up the limestone hills of the Agulhas Plain and the route then winds up the slopes of Grootberg before descending into Flower Valley. Here hikers are invited to a picnic lunch in the indigenous Stinkhoutsbos Forest, followed by a tree planting. This initiative supports the rehabilitation of the forest, which was badly damaged by a devastating fire that swept through the area in 2006. The remaining 5 km to the overnight stop at Witkrans is over relatively easy terrain.

The final day's hike (7.8 km; 3 hours) starts with a steady climb before descending to the indigenous forests of Baviaans Fonteyn. After meandering through fynbos, you follow the route through the Grootbos Milkwood Forest before reaching Grootbos Garden Lodge, where you end the trail with a leisurely lunch (guided slackpacking and self-guided slackpacking options). The self-guided, self-catering option ends at Steynsbos, near where the trail started.

Hikers can add an additional day and night to the trail, starting at De Kelders and hiking along Walker Bay to a pick-up point, from where they will be transferred to the start of the main hike at the Sustainable Agriculture and Life Skills College.

48. AGULHAS NATIONAL PARK
Cape Agulhas

Trails: 2 trails; 1 to 3 hours; circular.
Permits: Conservation fee. Permits not required.
Maps: Brochure with map and information about points of interest along the trails can be purchased at the park's reception office opposite the lighthouse.
Facilities: None.
Activities: Visit the southernmost point of Africa and the Agulhas lighthouse.
Pertinent information: The Two Oceans Hiking Trail is open only to overnight visitors in the Agulhas Rest Camp.

The Agulhas National Park protects nearly 22,000 ha of the Agulhas Plain, which is renowned for its exceptional fynbos flora.

1. Rasperpunt Hiking Trail starts and ends at the *Meisho Maru* shipwreck west of the Cape Agulhas lighthouse and follows the coastline to beyond Rasperpunt. A steep ascent to the dune crests awaits hikers on the return route. **5.5 km; 2 hours; circular.**

2. Two Oceans Hiking Trail starts and ends in the Agulhas Rest Camp and meanders through fynbos vegetation. The terrain is reasonably flat except for the ascent to Sandberg, from where hikers have a superb view of the meeting point of the Atlantic and Indian oceans. **10.5 km; 3 hours (shorter options 3 km; 1 hour or 4.5 km; 2 hours); circular.**

49. HEUNINGBERG NATURE RESERVE
Bredasdorp

Trails: 2 walks; 3.5 to 4 hours; circular.
Permits: Entrance fee. No permit required.

Maps: Map can be downloaded from http://heuningbergnaturereserve.yolasite.com.
Facilities/Activities: None.

The nucleus of this reserve on the slopes of Heuningberg was first established as a wildflower garden; it was subsequently incorporated into an 800-ha nature reserve. Among the more than 300 plant species growing here are several endemics, including the rare trident pincushion (*Leucospermum heterophyllum*) and the Bredasdorp lily (*Cyrtanthus gutherieae*), which flowers in March and April.

The trails described below offer wonderful views over Bredasdorp and the Ruggens to the north, the Heuningberg to the west, Struisbaai to the south, and Waenhuiskrans and De Hoop Nature Reserve to the east.

1. Eps Joubert (White) Trail meanders through the southern section of the reserve, ascending the slopes of Drinkwaterkloof to the watershed. The trail then continues above Uitvlugkloof before linking up with the Yellow Route at the 7-km mark. Lot's Wife is a conspicuous rock formation close to the beacon (366 m) on Heuningberg. **10 km; 3.5 hours; circular.**

2. Yellow Route contours around the western and northern slopes of Heuningberg to the Pulpit Rock. From here it is a steady ascent to the plateau, where the route links up with the Eps Joubert Trail, followed by an easy descent. **12 km; 4 hours; circular.**

50. DE MOND NATURE RESERVE
Bredasdorp

Trails: 2 walks; 2 to 4 hours; circular and open-ended.
Permits: CapeNature Contact Centre, cell: 087 087 8250, email: reservation.alert@capenature.co.za.
Maps: Reserve pamphlet with Sterna Trail indicated available from reserve office.

Facilities/Activities: Picnic sites (no fires permitted); freshwater and marine angling (permits required).

Pertinent information: Hikers must keep to paths to avoid damage to sensitive vegetation. The reserve and the coast to Arniston are important breeding habitats for rare bird species; birds should not be disturbed. The unidirectional De Mond to Arniston Trail necessitates transport arrangements.

cell: 087 087 8250, email: reservation.alert@capenature.co.za.

Maps: Available at the reserve office.

Facilities/Activities: Cottages equipped with a stove and fridge, but visitors must provide own bedding, cooking and eating utensils, and food; camp sites; picnic site; mountain-bike trail. Potberg Environmental Education Centre caters for groups of students.

Pertinent information: Water must be carried on all day walks. Trailists can take along snorkelling gear for the Coastal Trail.

Centred on the Heuningnes River mouth, De Mond Reserve covers 954 ha of shifting and stabilised sand dunes, tidal flats, salt marshes and fynbos vegetation.

The reserve is a very important breeding habitat for South Africa's most endangered coastal bird, the Damara tern. The Caspian tern and the wonderful but rare African (black) oystercatcher are also found in this reserve.

1. Sterna Trail Starting at the reserve office, the trail passes through riverine vegetation, as well as dune forest and stabilised dunes, before following the sandy coastline for just over 2 km. After heavy winter storms the wreck of the *Maggie* is visible to the south of the river mouth. The final section of the trail makes its way across tidal flats and skirts the salt marshes. **7 km; 2 hours; circular.**

2. De Mond to Arniston Trail follows the sandy coastline from De Mond to Arniston. Southern right whales can be spotted along the coast between June and November. Stone fishing traps built by Khoisan people and the remains of an old shipping beacon are of historical interest along the trail, which winds past Waenhuiskrans. **8 km; 4 hours; linear.**

51. DE HOOP NATURE RESERVE

East of Bredasdorp

See no. 52 (p. 71) for hiking trail.

Trails: 6 walks; 2 to 4 hours; circular and out-and-return.

Permits: CapeNature Contact Centre,

Covering 36,000 ha, De Hoop Nature Reserve is a mosaic of wetland, coastal fynbos, shifting sand dunes, coastal plains and limestone hills. De Hoop Vlei, a wetland of international importance, forms part of the western boundary, while Potberg dominates the scenery in the north.

Of the reserve's more than 1,500 plant species, 50 are endemic to the Bredasdorp, Agulhas and Infanta area, while 12 species are endemic to Potberg. Among these are a small ground protea (*Protea denticulata*) and *Aspalathus potbergensis*.

Mammals to be seen include bontebok, Cape mountain zebra, eland, grey rhebok, grysbok and baboon. There are over 250 species of bird here, including 12 waterfowl species, 13 species of migrant waders, the African fish eagle, secretarybird and African (black) oystercatcher. The Cape vulture population has increased from about 40 in the 1970s to an estimated 120 birds today.

The coast off De Hoop has the highest density of southern right whales along the whole South African coast, and between June and November up to 50 whales can be seen at a time, some as close as 500 m offshore.

Potberg

The 611-m-high Potberg, which lies in the north of the reserve, is of special importance from a conservation point of view. It is not only home to numerous endemic plant species, but its cliffs provide nesting sites for the largest Cape vulture colony in the Western Cape. Although there is no public access to the colony, these magnificent birds are often seen soaring overhead from the Klipspringer Trail.

1. Klipspringer Trail winds along the lower slopes of Potberg, past pools in the Potberg River, and Black Eagle Cave. Cape vulture are often seen at close range in the mornings as they take off from their roosting and nesting sites in Vulture Kloof. **5 km; 2 hours; circular.**

2. Potberg Trail leads to the summit of Potberg, with panoramic views over the reserve, the Breede River and Witsand. About 400 m in altitude is gained during the course of this trail. **10 km; 4 hours; out-and-return.**

De Hoop

Situated on the eastern edge of the vlei, the historic De Hoop homestead is the focal point of the reserve. The Vlei Trail network consists of a 15-km loop, with two shorter options, and offers magnificent views over De Hoop Vlei. The vlei attracts huge numbers of birds, up to 30,000 at a time. Among the birds found here are flamingo, waterfowl, waders and African fish eagle.

1. Coot Trail 5 km; 2 hours; circular.

2. Heron Trail 8 km; 3 hours; circular.

3. Grebe Trail 15 km; 4 hours; circular.

De Hoop Coast

De Hoop Nature Reserve is bounded to the south by a spectacular, 45-km-long stretch of coastline, ranging from white sandy beaches to rocky coves, and sandstone and limestone cliffs, which have been eroded into peculiar shapes by the wind and waves.

Coastal Trail From Klipkoppie in the west to Koppie Alleen in the east, the coastline is characterised by a sweeping sandy beach, backed by shifting sand dunes, reaching up to 90 m above sea level. East of Koppie Alleen, the rocky coast contains small coves and fascinating weathered rock formations, which give way to the kilometre-long expanse of white beach at Potbergstrand. Along the course of the hike there is ample opportunity to explore the marine life in the rock pools. Klipkoppie and Koppie Alleen are excellent whale-watching points. **Koppie Alleen to Klipkoppie: 8 km; 3 hours; open-ended. Koppie Alleen eastwards: 10 km; 3 hours; out-and-return.**

52. WHALE TRAIL
De Hoop Nature Reserve

See no. 51 (p. 70) for walks.

Trail: 56.7 km; 5 days; circular.
Permits: CapeNature Contact Centre, cell: 087 087 8250, email: reservation. alert@capenature.co.za or book online at www.capenature.co.za.
Maps: Trail map.
Facilities/Activities: Cottages with beds, mattresses, kitchen, living room, hot showers, toilets, fireplace and solar-powered electricity.
Pertinent information: Group bookings of a minimum of 6 people and a maximum of 12. Slackpacking option available. Pack snorkelling gear. Hikers are taken from Koppie Alleen to Potberg by shuttle bus.

The Whale Trail offers trailists an opportunity to explore the diverse landscapes and major habitats of De Hoop Nature Reserve.

The first day's hike (14.7 km; 8 hours) is the most demanding. The trail climbs to the summit of Potberg and then winds along the slopes above Groenkloof, descending to the Cupidoskraal overnight hut.

On day two (14 km; 8 hours), the trail ascends to the crest of Potberg, gaining some 300 m in altitude. Further along, the trail traverses limestone hills, where you are likely to see many Bredasdorp protea (*Protea obtusifolia*) before descending to Noetzie, a delightful bay along the coast.

Day three's hike (8 km; 6 hours) stretches between Noetzie and Hamerkop, and since only a short distance is covered there is ample time to explore the coastline. Stilgat, a natural tidal pool, offers trailists rewarding snorkelling opportunities, and there are also several whale-watching points.

The fourth day's hike to Vaalkrans (11 km; 7 hours) starts with a long stretch along the beach. Beyond Lekkerwater the coast becomes quite rocky. Highlights of this section include rock pools and calcrete formations, eroded into fascinating shapes.

The final day's hike (9 km; 6 hours) makes its way along the rocky coast past Potberg Beach, a white sandy cove. It then continues along the rocky shore past Whalewatch Point to Koppie Alleen, where the trail ends. Along the way there are once again ample opportunities for snorkelling.

53. GENADENDAL HIKING TRAIL
Genadendal

Trail: 25.3 km; 2 days; circular.
Permits: CapeNature Contact Centre, cell: 087 087 8250, email: reservation. alert@capenature.co.za or book online at www.capenature.co.za.
Maps: Trail pamphlet with map.
Facilities/Activities: Overnight facilities are available at the Moravian Mission Church in Genadendal and also at the overnight stop on the farm Die Hoek.
Pertinent information: Groups are limited to 14 people; the maximum number of hikers is 24 per day. Hikers need to carry their own water, especially on the second day of the hike. Fires are only permitted at Die Hoek.

The trail starts and ends in the historic settlement of Genadendal, which dates back some 200 years. In 1783, Moravian missionaries established a mission station at the foot of the Riviersonderend Mountains that would later become the town of Genadendal. From Genadendal the route traverses the 69,500-ha Riviersonderend Conservation Area – surrounded by the towns of Riviersonderend, Villiersdorp, McGregor and Greyton, as well as private land.

The first day's trail (14.3 km; 8 hours) starts with a steep ascent up the eastern slopes of Perdekop, and about 500 m is gained in altitude to Wonderklippe, an ideal rest stop. It then continues to Klein Koffiegat and Groot Koffiegat, where there are cool mountain pools, ideal for swimming in on a hot day. From here the trail gradually descends to the overnight hut at Die Hoek. The initial gentle ascent of the second day's hike (11 km; 7 hours) is followed by a long, steady climb to a nek between Arendkop and Uitkykkop, where the weirdly shaped sandstone formations are particularly striking. The trail then descends along the southern slopes of Uitkykkop to Genadendal.

54. BOESMANSKLOOF
Greyton and McGregor

Trail: 14 km;1 day; open-ended.
Permits: CapeNature Contact Centre, cell: 087 087 8250, email: reservation. alert@capenature.co.za or book online at www.capenature.co.za.
Maps: Trail pamphlet with map.
Facilities/Activities: Private accommodation is available and must be arranged by hikers at Greyton and McGregor, and at Die Galg, where the trail starts and ends.
Pertinent information: The trail has a limit of 50 hikers per day. Trailists need to make arrangements to have a vehicle waiting for them at the end of the trail. Alternatively, the trail can be done as an out-and-return route.

Covering some 69,000 ha of state and private land, the Riviersonderend Conservation Area is managed as a mountain catchment area. This is a unique and beautiful area of mountain peaks, steep cliffs, rugged kloofs and mountain fynbos. Over 50 species of restios are also found here. Of special conservation interest are two endemic *Erica* species: *E. galgebergensis* and *E. parvulisepala*.

This traverse of the Riviersonderend Mountains follows what was once the only direct link between the historic villages of McGregor and Greyton, and can be hiked in either direction. From Greyton the trail gains over 400 m in altitude along a jeep track to a viewpoint below Perdekop. It then descends to Boesmanskloof, where there are a series of deep and refreshing pools at Oakes Falls, wonderful for swimming in on a hot summer's day. The trail starts and ends at Die Galg (The Gallows), about 14 km from McGregor or Greyton.

This page: Hikers can explore the Cape of Good Hope section of the Table Mountain National Park along several delightful day walks, ranging from one to three hours, or set off on a two-day circular walk of just short of 34 km.

This page: Hikes through the Cederberg Wilderness take in famous landmarks like Tafelberg and The Spout (above), and pass many of the cedar trees (left) that are endemic to the area. The overnight shelters (below) along the way may be basic, but they're set in spectacular surroundings.

Right: The Wolfberg Arch is over 15 m high and 18 m wide, and is one of the great highlights of the Cederberg.

Below: Sneeuberg, the highest peak in the Cederberg, forms an impressive backdrop to the 20-m-high Maltese Cross, one of numerous fascinating rock formations in the Cederberg Wilderness Area.

Above: The coastline along the Whale Trail in the De Hoop Nature Reserve alternates between secluded coves, sandy beaches and low cliffs.

Right: Footpaths in the Harold Porter National Botanical Garden, just an hour or so from Cape Town, meander through cultivated areas, as well as natural fynbos and forested kloofs with mountain streams.

This page: The Boland Hiking Trail passes many natural pools (left), which are perfect for a refreshing swim. This hike makes its way through the heart of the Cape Floristic Region – look out for the striking red disa (*Disa uniflora*, above) en route.

This page: It's important for hikers to take precautions against the sun, as there are few trees and little else in the way of overhead cover on the Boland Hiking Trail, which crosses over the Riviersonderend River (below).

Top: Hikers on the Swartberg Trail, in the southwestern Cape, can enjoy incredible views of the Little Karoo.

Left: Goedgeloof Hut is one of two you'll stay in along the Swellendam Hiking Trail, also in the southwestern Cape.

Next page: The Harkerville Coast Hiking Trail takes hikers along a rugged stretch of coastline of the Garden Route.

55. MARLOTH NATURE RESERVE
Swellendam

See no. 56 (this page) for hiking trail.

Trails: 6 walks; 1 to 6 hours; out-and-return; circular; semi-circular.
Permits: CapeNature Contact Centre, cell: 087 087 8250, email: reservation.alert@capenature.co.za or book online at www.capenature.co.za.
Maps: Day trails map available at the reserve office.
Facilities/Activities: Picnic sites intermittently along day walks; braai facilities at Marloth.

The Marloth Nature Reserve was named in honour of the renowned botanist Dr Rudolf Marloth, who demarcated an area of 190 ha for a nature reserve in 1928. In 1981 the reserve was enlarged to 11,000 ha. The Langeberg range lies within the reserve, which protects a rich diversity of fynbos. Isolated patches of remnant indigenous forest occur on the southern slopes of the mountain.

The network of day walks in the Marloth Nature Reserve is for those not wanting to do the Swellendam Hiking Trail. The trails wind through mountain fynbos with proteas, ericas, reeds and rushes, as well as delightful patches of indigenous forest.

1. Duiwelsbos Walk ascends steadily alongside a stream through a delightful patch of indigenous forest. The walk ends at a small waterfall. **2.1 km; 1 hour; out-and-return.**

2. Koloniesbos is a delightful patch of forest consisting of yellowwood, stinkwood, candlewood, Cape beech, red alder and Cape gardenia. The name Koloniesbos dates back to the 1740s, when the district was known as *De Colonie in de Verre Afgeleegene Contreije* (the colony in the remote regions). This is an easy walk through fynbos and a charming forest. **2.5 km; 1 hour; semi-circular.**

3. Plaat Loop ascends to the Plaat and then continues along the contours of the southern slopes of Elfuurkop and Twaalfuurkop. The trail winds through magnificent fynbos above Duiwelsbos and Koloniesbos before making its way back to the start. **12 km; 4 hours; circular.**

4. Twaalfuurkop This trail winds steeply up the slopes of the Langeberg to the summit of Twaalfuurkop (1,428 m), gaining some 1,200 m in elevation. It is a strenuous walk, but your efforts will be rewarded with great views of the wheat fields of the Overberg and Swellendam far below. Hikers should be prepared for sudden weather changes and extreme weather. **12.4 km; 6 hours; out-and-return.**

5. Appelbos Loop owes its name to the Appelbos River which rises below Tienuurkop. The route takes you through mountain fynbos on the Plaat, along the slopes below Tienuurkop, and indigenous forest at Wamakersbos. **21 km; 5 to 6 hours; circular.**

56. SWELLENDAM HIKING TRAIL
Marloth Nature Reserve

See no. 55 (this page) for walks.

Trail: 51.7 km; 5 days; circular.
Permits: CapeNature Contact Centre, cell: 087 087 8250, email: reservation.alert@capenature.co.za.
Maps: Trail map.
Facilities/Activities: Overnight huts with bunk beds and mattresses (no bunk beds or mattresses at Boskloof), toilets and water.
Pertinent information: Groups are limited to a minimum of 3 and a maximum 12. A backpacking stove is essential as fires are only permitted at Wolfkloof, the last hut. Hikers are not allowed to deviate from the trail onto private properties at Goedgeloof and Wolfkloof.

This demanding trail traverses the 11,000-ha Marloth Nature Reserve in the Langeberg range above Swellendam. One of the most outstanding features is the reserve's floral wealth, which changes with the seasons. The trail leads to isolated valleys tucked away in the mountains, across tranquil streams and through patches of indigenous forest. Along the way there are panoramic views of the wheat farms of the Overberg to the south, and the arid plains of the Little Karoo to the north.

The first day's hike (11.8 km; 5 hours) involves a steady ascent to Klipkraal, with an altitude gain of some 800 m. The trail then descends to the overnight hut, which lies at the head of the remote Boskloof.

Day two (10 km; 4 hours) begins with a climb along the Drosterspas to the watershed, with sweeping views of the Little Karoo. A steep descent through fields of yellow conebushes (*Leucadendron*) brings you to the stone huts at Goedgeloof.

The third day's hike (10 km; 4 hours) also starts with a steep ascent, but from Warmwaternek the trail levels out. This section passes above the appropriately named Protea Valley, with its profusion of the plants. Among them are the king protea (*Protea cynaroides*), peach protea (*P. grandiceps*), brown-bearded sugarbush (*P. speciosa*) and the broad-leaved sugarbush.

The 13-km leg of the original trail from Proteavallei Hut to Nooitgedacht and the 21.3-km trail from Nooitgedacht to Wolfkloof have been closed. The Vensterbank route from Proteavallei has also been closed.

From Proteavallei, the Kruispad route (6.2 km) descends for a short distance before ascending slightly to the upper reaches of Wolfkloof. After following a contour, the trail crosses a nek, makes its way up to a ridge and contours around a peak before following a zigzag course downwards. The final leg descends steeply into Wolfkloof Hut.

The hike from Wolfkloof (10.7 km) starts with a steep climb and then levels off before dropping sharply into Hermitagekloof, where another steep ascent has to be negotiated. The last section of the trail is over easy terrain.

57. MONTAGU MOUNTAIN NATURE RESERVE
Montagu

Trails: 2 walks; 6 and 9 hours; circular.
Permits: Obtain at Joubertpark reserve entrance, tel: (023) 614 2471, email: info@montagu-ashton.info.

Maps: Download from www.montagu-ashton.info.
Facilities/Activities: Klipspringer Hut (1.3 km from Old Mill starting point): 6 bunks, mattresses, braai facilities, shower with donkey for hot water and flush toilet.

The northern slopes of the Langeberg, west of Montagu, are protected by the 1,200-ha Montagu Mountain Nature Reserve. The vegetation ranges from dry mountain fynbos and succulents on the lower slopes to more mesic fynbos higher up. Laid out in a figure eight, with the overnight huts at the start/finish, hikers have a choice of hiking one trail or both.

1. Cogmanskloof Trail ascends steadily uphill for the first 2 km and then traverses the slopes above Droogekloof to Cogmanskloof, with its sheer cliffs. Along the way, trailists enjoy expansive views of the lichen-covered cliffs of the Droogekloof and the surrounding mountains. The return leg is a gentle ascent up the slopes above the valley in which Montagu lies. John Montagu, after whom the town is named, was a colonial secretary of the Cape in the 19th century. **12 km; 4 to 6 hours; circular.**

2. Bloupunt Trail winds up Rietkloof and then ascends to the summit of Bloupunt. From the 1,266-m-high summit there are spectacular views, with the towns of Montagu, McGregor, Robertson, Ashton and Bonnievale clearly visible. From here the trail traverses De Drie Bergen (The Three Mountains) and then descends along Donkerkloof, with its three small waterfalls. **15.6 km; 6 to 9 hours; circular.**

58. PAT BUSCH MOUNTAIN RESERVE
Robertson

Trails: 40 km; 30 minutes to 5 hours; network.
Bookings: Email: stay@patbusch.co.za.
Maps: Rough sketch map.

Facilities/Activities: Fully equipped self-catering cottages and houses; trout and bass angling; mountain biking; 4x4 trail; swimming and canoeing in the dam.

Situated on two wine-producing farms, Bergplaas and Berg en Dal, the 2,000-ha Pat Busch Mountain Reserve has been set aside to protect the flora and fauna of the Langeberg foothills. The vegetation is mainly mountain fynbos, with a profusion of proteas and ericas, but a variety of indigenous trees grow in the valleys and along the riverbanks. With a bird checklist of some 150 species, birding can be rewarding. Animals to be seen include gemsbok, grey rhebok, grysbok, steenbok, Cape clawless otter and caracal.

A network of trails runs through valleys and beside two streams, with rock pools, in the undulating foothills of the range. By combining several shorter trails, trailists can follow a 12-km, 5-hour circular route, with longer options to the summit of Tafelberg (742 m) and Olifantskop, further afield in the Langeberg.

59. FISH EAGLE HIKING TRAIL
Van Loveren Family Cellar, Robertson

Trail: Self-guided; 7.5 km; 3 hours circular.
Permits: Van Loveren Family Cellar, P O Box 19, Klaasvoogds, Robertson 6707, tel: (023) 615 1505, fax (023) 615 1336, email: info@vanloveren.co.za.
Maps: Trail is well marked.
Facilities/Activities: Mountain biking (5.7 km family trail and 15 km trail); bike rentals; bistro; cellar tours and wine-tasting.

This easy to moderate trail commences at the winery and initially meanders along the Breede River with its riverine vegetation. Once you have crossed the river, the route ascends through mountain fynbos to Rooikrans. Here trailists are rewarded with spectacular vistas of a mosaic of vineyards, the Robertson Valley and the surrounding mountains. More than 100 bird species have been recorded here, including the iconic African fish eagle (after which the trail has been named). Other interesting species to be on the lookout for include the tambourine dove, ground woodpecker and Cape rock-thrush.

Also of interest is a rare rock formation known as the Klaasvoogds olivine melilitite intrusion, which appears as a dark triangle on the hill to the south of the winery. This fine-grained alkaline igneous rock was first described in 1936. The intrusion occurred some 1.3 million years ago and the only other example can be found at Sutherland.

60. ARANGIESKOP HIKING TRAIL
Dassiehoek Nature Reserve, Robertson

Trail: 21 km; 2 days; circular.
Permits: Langeberg Municipality, tel: (023) 626 8200, email: trailbookings@langeberg.gov.za.
Maps: Sketch map.
Facilities/Activities: Dassiehoek: overnight hut with 35 beds, mattresses, hot-water showers and fireplace. Arangieskop: hut with 23 beds, mattresses, lounge, hot shower, toilets and fireplace.
Pertinent information: This trail is extremely physically demanding and should only be attempted by hikers who are fit and experienced.

The scenery of Dassiehoek Nature Reserve, north of Robertson, is strikingly beautiful. With its sheer cliff faces, deep gorges and high mountain peaks it makes the perfect setting for this magnificent trail.

Traversing the north of the reserve, the first day's hike (9.5 km; 6.5 hours) involves a gruelling ascent of over 1,100 m to the overnight hut, which overlooks the Koo Valley to the north. From here there are breathtaking views of the wild mountain valleys and the mosaic of farms in the Breede River Valley, which make an ample reward for the day's difficult hike.

The second day's hike (11.7 km; 6 hours) begins with a climb to the 1,850-m-high Arangieskop, where hikers are again rewarded with great views. Over the course of the next 2.5 km the trail loses some 650 m in altitude as it makes its way down into a ravine with an inviting swimming hole and enormous red alder trees. Lower down the river, the trail leaves the ravine and, after a fairly level traverse, ascends briefly, before gradually descending to Dassiehoek.

61. VROLIJKHEID NATURE RESERVE
Robertson

Trails: 2 walks; 1 and 7 to 8 hours; circular and out-and-return.
Permit: CapeNature Contact Centre, cell: 087 087 8250, email: reservation.alert@capenature.co.za.
Maps: Pamphlet with walks indicated.
Facilities/Activities: Bird hides; toilets.
Pertinent information: From November to March extremely high temperatures are common and hiking should commence before 09:00.

The vegetation of the Vrolijkheid Nature Reserve, situated 15 km south of Robertson in the Elandsberg Mountains, is characterised by a mixture of succulents, dwarf shrubs and patches of renosterveld. The landscape is especially attractive between August and October, when a rich diversity of plants (over 160 species) can be seen in full bloom. Unlikely to escape attention in spring are huge sheets of gousblomme (*Gazania krebsiana*).

Mammals found in this area include springbok, klipspringer, grysbok, grey rhebok and the caracal (*rooikat* in Afrikaans), after which the Rooikat Trail has been named. Among the 175 bird species are Verreaux's eagle and African fish eagle, jackal buzzard and pale chanting goshawk. A reptile to look out for is the Robertson dwarf chameleon.

1. Heron Trail traverses easy terrain across the plains to two dams, each with its own bird hide. These are ideal for those wanting to observe some of the reserve's waterbirds. Among these are grey and black-headed herons, African rail, red-chested flufftail, African spoonbill, South African shelduck, and several kingfisher species. **3 km; 1 hour; out-and-return.**

2. Rooikat Trail follows an undulating course along river valleys and ridges, gaining 435 m in altitude to Witkrantz, the highest peak in the reserve. The trail then leads over Kranskop and Klein Spitzkop before winding down to the plains. Along the way are beautiful views of the Riviersonderend Mountains to the south, and the Langeberg range to the north. Although caracal do live in the reserve, they are shy animals and are seldom encountered. **19 km; 7 to 8 hours; circular.**

62. ELANDSBERG TRAIL
Ladismith

Trail: 13.9 km; 6 to 8 hours; circular.
Permits: Not required.
Maps: Available from Ladismith Tourism Bureau, tel: (028) 551 1378, email: ladismithvisitorcentre@gmail.com.
Facilities/Activities: None.

This trail ascends the slopes of the Elandsberg, which dominates the skyline above Ladismith. The first 1.5 km follows a firebreak at the foot of the mountain and then climbs steeply to near Stanley de Witt's Light. It then winds along the slopes of Toringberg (2,126 m) before descending steeply back to the start. The total altitude gain is 792 m, so the trail should be attempted only by fit hikers.

63. TOWERSIG TRAIL
Ladismith

Trails: 2.7 to 12.1 km; 45 minutes to 5 hours; network.
Permits: Not required.
Maps: Available from Ladismith Tourism

The lower slopes of the Elandsberg, just north of Ladismith, provide the setting for this trail network, which consists of two interlinked loops of 2.7 and 12 km respectively. Along the course of the various routes you will be rewarded with wonderful scenic views of the Little Karoo and Toringberg, which rises over 1,500 m above Ladismith. The vegetation of the trail's surroundings is characterised by mountain fynbos, and among the noteworthy species that you might chance upon while you are hiking is the particularly striking Ladismith protea.

64. OUKRAAL HIKING TRAIL
Gamka Mountain Nature Reserve, Calitzdorp

Trail: 24.8 km; 2 days; circular.
Permits: CapeNature Contact Centre, cell: 087 087 8250, email: reservation. alert@capenature.co.za or book online at www.capenature.co.za. Only one group allowed on overnight trail.
Maps: Pamphlet with trail map.
Facilities/Activities: Tierkloof: information centre, picnic sites and toilets; base camp with beds, mattresses, gas fridge, stove, fireplace and ablutions. Oukraal: stone shelter, toilet.

Situated at the eastern end of the Gamka-Rooiberg range, this reserve covers 9,428 ha. The north of the mountain is characterised by deep ravines and steep slopes, rising to Bakenkop (1,100 m), the highest point in the reserve. The vegetation is dominated by mountain fynbos, with spekboomveld and mountain renosterveld occurring on the lower slopes.

Animals found in the reserve include Cape mountain zebra, eland, red hartebeest, grey rhebok, klipspringer, common duiker and grysbok. Leopard are also found here. Among the bird species to be seen are the martial eagle, African harrier-hawk, gymnogene, peregrine falcon, acacia pied barbet, Cape rock-thrush and orange-breasted sunbird.

The first day's hike (13.2 km; 6 hours) ascends through riverine vegetation up Tierkloof for about 5 km, to an overhang. A short way further on, the trail splits off to the right, continuing its ascent to Oukraal, with a total altitude gain of some 700 m. From Oukraal there are spectacular views over the Little Karoo, the Outeniqua Mountains to the south, and the Swartberg to the northwest. The second day's hike (11.6 km; 4 hours) loops down the mountain slopes before rejoining the outward leg of the trail.

From the information centre there are also four easy walks, ranging from 700 m (20 minutes) to the Pied Barbet Trail of 4.1 km (2 hours). Some of the plants and trees along the trails have been marked, and can be identified by referring to the list on the permit.

The many interesting bird species occurring in the Gamka Mountain Nature Reserve are also listed on the permit.

65. GAMKASKLOOF
Swartberg Nature Reserve

Trail: 6 km; 3 hours; circular.
Permits: CapeNature Contact Centre, cell: 087 087 8250, email: reservation. alert@capenature.co.za.
Maps: Interpretative pamphlet with map.
Facilities/Activities: Two restored houses (self-catering); bush camp and camp site, with cold shower and braai facilities; angling in the Gamka River.

Also known as Die Hel, Gamkaskloof lies at the western end of the Swartberg Nature Reserve. The first farmers settled in the fertile valley in 1830 and for over a century, until 1963, when it was linked by a road to the Swartberg Pass, it was one of the most remote settlements in South Africa. Hardship forced the people to leave in the 1970s and, after the last farmer left in 1991, the area came under the control of CapeNature Conservation. Among the numerous places of historic interest are an old Norwegian mill, threshing floors, the Middelplaas school, which was built in 1923, and old dwellings.

Grootkloof Interpretative Trail winds up Grootkloof for about 1.5 km and then traverses the surrounding mountain slopes, passing through Kleinkloof to Lemoenkloof, down which the trail descends. Along the trail there are 26 points of interest that are interpreted in the trail brochure. Many of them relate to particular plants of the area and the way in which they were used by the original inhabitants of Gamkaskloof.

The trail brochure also provides a wealth of additional information on topics like the local geology and animals (such as baboon and porcupine), and on some of the old buildings and other structures found in the area.

66. SWARTBERG HIKING TRAIL
Swartberg Nature Reserve

Trails: 33.2 km; 2 days; circular or open-ended. 2 day walks; 7.4 and 8.4 km.
Permits: CapeNature Contact Centre, cell: 087 087 8250, email: reservation.alert@capenature.co.za or book online at www.capenature.co.za.
Maps: Reserve pamphlet with trails indicated.
Facilities: Overnight hut with bunks, mattresses and cooking shelter. Bookings for De Hoek Resort, tel: (044) 272 8214.
Pertinent information: Keys for the Bothashoek hut must be collected from and returned to the CapeNature Oudtshoorn office between 07:30 and 16:00, Monday to Friday. The Crest Route should not be hiked in inclement weather.

This 121,000-ha nature reserve provides protection to the eastern Swartberg range, and stretches from the Gamka River in the west to the Uniondale/Willowmore road in the east. Part of the Cape Folded Mountains, the range is characterised by spectacular folded rock formations. The vegetation is dominated by mountain fynbos. Over 2,000

species grow here, among them the groove-leafed protea (*Protea canaliculata*), water sugarbush (*Protea punctata*) and strap-leaf sugarbush (*Protea lorifolia*). The reserve is part of the Swartberg Complex – one of the eight clusters of the Cape Floral Region Protected Areas, which were inscribed as a UNESCO World Heritage Site in 2004.

The animals here are typical fynbos species: grey rhebok, klipspringer, common duiker, grysbok, steenbok, kudu and baboon. Among the 150 bird species found here are the Verreaux's, martial and booted eagles, Cape rockjumper, Victorin's warbler, Cape sugarbird and sunbirds.

Although CapeNature has closed the Ou Tol hut, hikers can still start or end their hike at Ou Tol, but will have to be dropped off or collected until the facility is reopened.

From Ou Tol, there is a choice of following either the Crest Route (12 km; 4 hours) or the jeep track (12.8 km; 4 hours) to Bothashoek Hut and then returning to Ou Tol. Another option is to continue to the alternative starting or ending point at De Hoek Resort.

The Crest Route winds along the summit of the Swartberg and offers expansive views of the Little and Great Karoo. After crossing the Swartberg Pass, the trail ascends steadily, gaining some 300 m in altitude to Windgathoogte. The trail then descends to Albertsberg and continues along an undulating course to Bothashoek Hut.

From Bothashoek it is a steady climb for 2 km along the jeep track (also used as a 4x4 route), but the remainder of the trail to Ou Tol is easy.

From the starting point at the De Hoek Resort, the trail (8.4 km; 3 to 4 hours) ascends steeply, gaining some 735 m in altitude. As a result of the relentless uphill, this route should only be attempted by very fit hikers.

At Ou Tol there is a choice of two relatively easy day walks.

1. Platberg Circle meanders around Platberg, north of Ou Tol, and after 4 km joins the Swartberg Pass, which is then followed back to the start. **8.4 km; 3 hours; circular.**

2. Ou Tol Circle Route follows a track to Die Top and winds clockwise around Ou Tol. **7.4 km; 2.5 hours; circular.**

67. DE RUST HERITAGE WALK

De Rust

Trails: Self-guided or guided walk through the village.
Contact: Cell: 082 777 1519; website: https://derustheritage.org.za.
Maps: The De Rust Heritage Walking Trail booklet has a map and information on buildings in the village.
Facilities/Activities: Restaurants in village.

Situated between the Swartberg to the north and the Kammanassie Mountains in the south at the southern end of Meiringspoort, De Rust is also known as the 'Gateway to the Little and the Great Karoo'. The village was laid out on the farm De Rust, a Dutch name meaning 'The Rest', in 1900 and many of the Victorian-style buildings dating back to the turn of the 20th century are well preserved.

The Heritage Walk was initiated by De Rust Heritage to promote the town's rich history and buildings to the community and visitors. Guided walks conducted by local residents, an initiative of the Heritage Community Upliftment Programme, can be booked through the De Rust Heritage Trust.

The walk starts at the Old Mill built in the mid-1800s on the original farm Voëlgesang and passes several beautifully restored Victorian-style houses and places of interest. The walk ends at Vredelus farmstead, which was part of the original De Rust farm. Among the buildings to be seen are the Dutch Reformed Church consecrated in 1902, the Ou Koshuis (old boarding school) and many vintage houses.

Snow is common in the Swartberg in winter.

GARDEN ROUTE & EASTERN CAPE

For those keen to explore this fascinating region on foot, there are numerous options, ranging from short walks and easy coastal rambles to overnight trails in the Garden Route and the Drakensberg in the northeastern corner of the Eastern Cape. The Garden Route's mosaic of indigenous forests, lakes, lagoons and long expanses of desolate beach — set against a backdrop of towering mountains that stretch from Heidelberg eastwards to the verdant Tsitsikamma forests — make it a glorious area for walkers and trailists to explore.

One of the focal points of the Garden Route is the magnificent indigenous forest, with its ancient forest monarchs festooned with old man's beard, lush glades of ferns, moss-covered tree trunks and tranquil streams. Covering 60,000 ha, just 0.25 per cent of South Africa's land surface, the forest occurs discontinuously along the narrow coastal strip between Mossel Bay and Humansdorp, and constitutes the largest area of natural forest in South Africa. It is composed of about 87 different indigenous tree species, including real and Outeniqua yellowwoods, stinkwood, assegai, red alder, ironwood, white pear and Cape beech. In addition, there are also 55 woody shrub, 52 fern and 47 vine species, as well as a rich variety of geophytes, epiphytes, grasses and forbs.

The indigenous forests of Knysna and Tsitsikamma are the habitat of some 40 typical forest bird species. Among these are the crowned eagle, Knysna turaco, Narina trogon, Cape and chorister robin-chats, white-starred robin, terrestrial brownbul, and the olive thrush. Other species to look out for include the green wood-hoopoe, tambourine dove and Knysna woodpecker.

Large animals are poorly represented in the indigenous forests. The Knysna forests and the adjoining fynbos areas were once home to a large population of elephants, but sadly their numbers have decreased to just three, or even fewer, and chances of seeing them are extremely remote. Among the animal species you may chance upon are bushbuck, blue duiker and vervet monkey, while tell-tale signs of bushpig, porcupine, caracal and leopard may also be encountered. You are unlikely to see the animals themselves, though, as they are typically shy and nocturnal.

Another feature of the Garden Route is the string of lakes stretching between Wilderness and Sedgefield. Aptly named South Africa's 'Lake District', the five lakes are the habitat of 72 waterbird species and, at times, support up to 24,000 birds a month. Species to look for include the great crested and black-necked grebe, yellow-billed duck, southern pochard, red-chested flufftail and African marsh harrier.

The coastal plains of the Garden Route are bounded by the lofty mountain peaks of the Langeberg, Outeniqua and Tsitsikamma ranges. Here, at the eastern limit of its distribution, the mountain fynbos is considerably poorer than that of the southwestern Cape, but between May and November the mountain slopes are transformed into a blaze of colour when several erica species burst into bloom. Also to be seen is a variety of proteas, reeds, rushes and bulbs, while remnant patches of indigenous forest occur in sheltered kloofs. The usual fynbos mammals and birds occur.

The Garden Route offers a wide range of trails through indigenous forest and fynbos-covered mountains, as well as along the coast, which varies from long sandy beaches to rocky shores backed by steep cliffs. Options range from short day walks to extended overnight hikes.

East of the Tsitsikamma Mountains lie the Groot-winterhoek range and the Amatola Mountains. Steeped in the history of the Eastern Cape frontier wars, the Amatola Mountains are also renowned for their many splendid cascades, natural pools, stunning views and patches of indigenous forests.

Two animal species that occur in the Eastern Cape forests, but not further west, are the tree dassie and the samango monkey. Also found here is the giant *Michrochaetus* earthworm, the largest earthworm in the world (reaching lengths of up to 7 m), and the Pirie Forest, northwest of King William's Town, is the best-known habitat of the endangered giant golden mole. In the forest canopy, look out for flocks of noisy Cape parrots, a species that reaches the western limit of its distribution in the Alexandria forests northeast of Gqeberha. Alexandria Forest is a distinct coastal forest type, named after the area in which it is predominantly found, around the town of Alexandria.

The Wild Coast is one of the most breathtaking stretches of coastline in the world. It extends from just northeast of East London to the Mthamvuna River, the boundary between the Eastern Cape and KwaZulu-Natal provinces. The heart of the Wild Coast, however, extends from the Kei River to the Mthamvuna River. The coastline boasts small sandy coves fringed by wild banana trees, tranquil estuaries with mangrove communities, grassy headlands and fascinating natural features. Well-known formations include the Mzamba petrified trees and other fossils, just south of the Mthamvuna River, and Cathedral Rock. At Waterfall Bluff two waterfalls cascade directly into the sea.

Numerous ships foundered along this stretch of coast with its strong currents and huge waves, among them the HMS *Grosvenor*, which reputedly had the gem-covered Peacock Throne of India, worth over $10 million, on board when it ran aground on the night of 2 August 1782. Other famous shipwrecks include those of the *Santo Alberto* (1593), the *São João* (1552) and the *São Bento* (1554).

In the remote northeastern corner of the Eastern Cape, the southern extremity of the Drakensberg is found. It is characterised by spectacular sandstone outcrops, rugged valleys, clear mountain streams and high mountain peaks, which are often covered in snow during the winter months. Rock paintings on the walls of caves and overhangs are reminders of the early San people who lived here for centuries, possibly thousands of years, until the arrival of white settlers in the nineteenth century.

This area does not support large herds of game, but it does have a rich diversity of birds. Among the species recorded here are the Cape vulture, bearded vulture and grey crowned crane. Noteworthy Drakensberg grassland species that you should look out for include the Drakensberg rockjumper, yellow-breasted pipit and Drakensberg siskin.

The Garden Route and the Eastern Cape lie in an all-year rainfall area. In the west, the rainfall is distributed fairly evenly throughout the year, but in the interior and further east the highest rainfall is recorded between October and March.

Temperatures along the coast are typically moderate during the summer months, but between May and September daily minimum temperatures drop to below 12 °C. In the interior, however, the mountains in the northeast of the Eastern Cape are often covered in snow, and during mid-winter daily minimum temperatures of below 5 °C are not uncommon.

IMPORTANT INFORMATION

➤ Weather conditions in the mountains are often extremely unpredictable, so you should always be prepared for sudden weather changes during your hike. Mist is quite common high up in the mountains, while snow can be expected on the high peaks in winter, especially in the Eastern Cape Drakensberg, which is also known for violent thunderstorms during the summer months.

➤ Trails in the mountains and in the forests can become very slippery after heavy rains, so it is essential to hike in boots that have a good grip.

➤ After heavy rains, rivers in mountainous areas can come down in flood and may be difficult to cross. Either wait until the river can be negotiated safely, or turn back to the overnight hut.

➤ It is advisable to use a good insect repellent and to take precautions against ticks. Try to remove any ticks that you find on yourself right away, if possible, and make sure that you check your body thoroughly when you return from your hike.

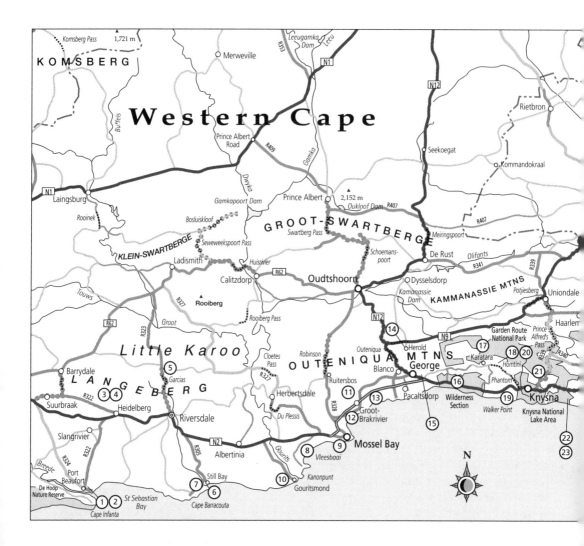

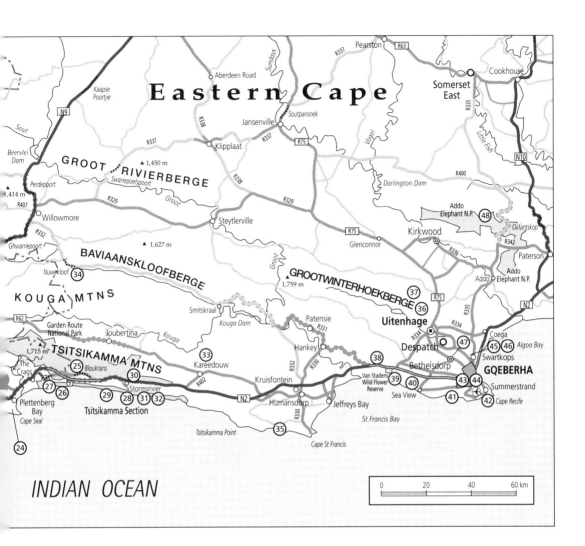

Continued on pp. 92–93

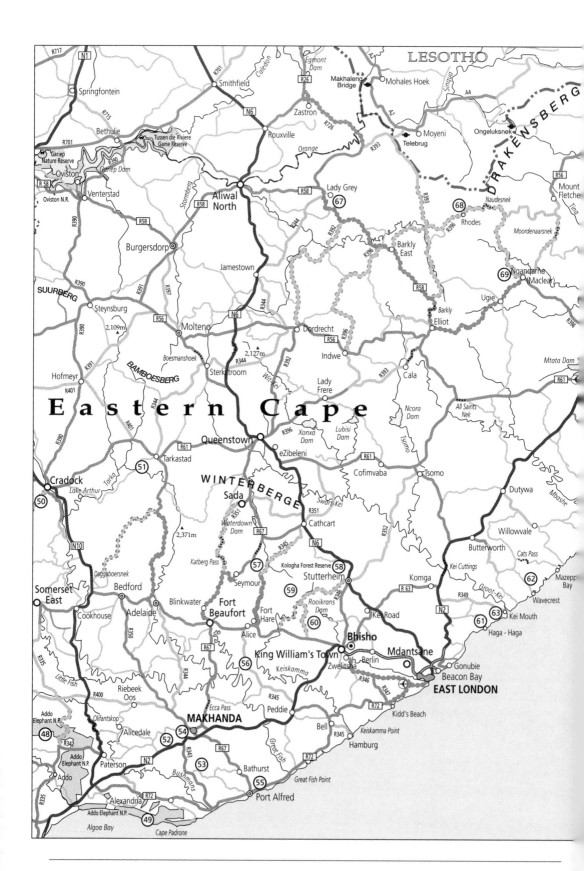

1. WITSAND WALKS
Witsand

> **Trails:** Several walks; 2.5 to 20 km; 1 to 6 hours; open-ended and out-and-return.
> **Permits:** Not required. For information contact Helen & Owen Jarman, tel: (028) 537 1717, email: accom@witsand.co.za, web: www.witsand.co.za.
> **Facilities/Activities:** None.

Situated on the eastern bank of the Breede River, just before it enters the sea, the popular coastal resort of Witsand and historic Port Beaufort, a short way upstream, offer a variety of walks. St Sebastian Bay lies at the eastern end of the stretch of coast where the majority of southern right whale cow and calf pairs congregate between June and November. In 2001 up to 37 sightings were made in the bay, also known as the Whale Nursery of South Africa.

1. Infanta Walk starts at Kontiki on the western bank of the Breede River and follows its sandy shore until it gives way to rocks at Kabeljoubank. Beyond Infanta the route winds up Infanta Hill, an excellent vantage point for whale-watching. **5 km; 2 hours; out-and-return.**

2. Breede River Mouth Walk meanders along the sandspit on the eastern bank of the Breede River. At low tide the walk follows the river's edge and, further along, the sea, but at high tide the route is across soft sand and dunes. **6 km; 2 hours; out-and-return.**

3. Moodies Well Walk follows the sandy eastern sweep of St Sebastian Bay for 4 km. The route will take you to a well dug by a Scotsman in the nineteenth century to store water on camping and fishing trips. The walk should be done at low tide. **8 km; 3 hours; out-and-return.**

Other walks in the area include the River View Walk and the Moddergat Walk. The River View Walk (2.5 km; 1 hour; circular) starts at the Witsand jetty and, as the name suggests, follows the tarred road running alongside the river. Enjoy the stunning views of the Breede River before you join the Port Beaufort/ Witsand road. Follow this road back to the start. The Moddergat Walk (4 km; 1.5 hours; open-ended) on the western side of the Breede River follows the rocky coastline from Infanta to the river's mouth and then meanders along its banks past Kontiki to Moddergat.

2. PUNTJIE WALK
Witsand

> **Trail:** 15 to 20 km; 6 hours; open-ended.
> **Permits:** Not required.
> **Maps:** Not available.
> **Facilities/Activities:** None.
> **Pertinent information:** The walk can only be done at low tide in summer. Transport has to be arranged back to Witsand from Puntjie.

This route follows the sandy shores of San Sebastian Bay for about 4 km to Moodies Well. The coastline becomes more rocky as you approach Voëlklip; further along, the coast is dominated by 20-m-high sandstone cliffs. The walk ends at Puntjie at the mouth of the Duivenhoks River. The settlement with its thatched *kapstyl* houses is a heritage site. For advice on the walk, call Pietie (082 738 2101), a local guide familiar with the area. **15 to 20 km; 6 hours; open-ended.**

3. BOOSMANSBOS WILDERNESS AREA
Heidelberg

See no. 4 (p. 95) for walks.

> **Trail:** 27 km; 2 days or longer; circular.
> **Permits:** CapeNature Contact Centre, cell: 087 087 8250, email: reservation. alert@capenature.co.za or book online at www.capenature.co.za.
> **Maps:** Trail pamphlet with sketch map. It is advisable to obtain the 1:50,000 topographical map 3320DD Warmwaterberg.

Facilities/Activities: Camp site with hot-water ablutions and guest cottage at start of the trail; very basic shelters without facilities at Helderfontein. Carry a small tent.
Pertinent information: The total number of trailists allowed in the wilderness area is 12 per day. No fires are permitted.

The Boosmansbos Wilderness Area (part of the Cape Floral Region Protected Areas World Heritage Site) lies within the Langeberg range. The wilderness area is characterised by imposing mountain peaks, high krantzes, deep ravines and pockets of indigenous forest.

The vegetation is dominated by mountain fynbos, and in spring the southern slopes are blanketed in magnificent pink ericas, while cone bushes create a yellow sea across the northern slopes. Outeniqua and real yellowwoods, stinkwood, Cape holly and candlewood are among the tree species that occur in a handful of secluded forest patches in the mountain. A further approximately 40 species can be found in the Grootvadersbosch Nature Reserve, situated on the southern boundary of the wilderness area. Grootvadersbosch is the largest indigenous forest west of Knysna.

The first day's hike (14 km; 6 hours) steadily ascends the eastern slopes of Dwarsberg, winding in and out of Bobbejaanskloof and Vaalrivierkloof until reaching a nek. From here, the trail follows a fairly easy traverse in an easterly direction to reach Helderfontein.

Not to be missed is a visit to the nearby Boosmansbos, the lovely patch of indigenous forest to which the wilderness area owes its name. Another worthwhile excursion from Helderfontein is an ascent of the 1,637-m-high Grootberg, the highest peak in the area. From the summit there are uninterrupted 360-degree views as far as Cradock Peak in the east, the Riviersonderend Mountains in the west, Towerkop in the north, the patchwork of wheatfields of Heidelberg to the south and the town of Riversdale to the southeast.

The second day's hike (13 km; 5 hours) is a downhill walk along the rough Barend Koen se Pad for about 7 or 8 km until a footpath deviates off to the right. The path descends steeply into the deep

gorge carved by the Duivenhoks River, an ideal resting stop, and then climbs out of the valley to join a reserve management road, which takes you back to the start.

4. GROOTVADERSBOSCH NATURE RESERVE
Heidelberg

See no. 3 (p. 94) for wilderness area.

Trails: 2 walks; 3 and 5 hours, with shorter options; circular.
Permits: CapeNature Contact Centre, cell: 087 087 8250, email: reservation.alert@capenature.co.za.
Maps: Pamphlet of walks with sketch map.
Facilities/Activities: Camp sites with ablutions; bird hide; mountain-bike trail.

Situated about 22 km northwest of Heidelberg, the Grootvadersbosch Nature Reserve lies at the foot of the Langeberg. Covering 250 ha, it is the largest indigenous forest west of Knysna, and consists of dry and moist Knysna forest types. Among the common species found here are the Outeniqua and real yellowwoods, stinkwood, wild peach, assegai, Cape beech and ironwood.

Among the nearly 200 plus bird species that have been recorded here to date are the Knysna turaco, crowned eagle, the elusive Narina trogon, the blue-mantled crested flycatcher, olive bushshrike and Knysna woodpecker.

1. Bushbuck Trail is appropriately named after the bushbuck, which was first described from a specimen collected at Grootvadersbosch over two centuries ago in 1780. You may also spot baboon, as well as the Cape grysbok, which favours the forest margins and fynbos. **10 km; 4 hours; circular, with shorter options.**

2. Grysbok Trail After initially winding through the transitional zone, between the indigenous forest and fynbos, the Grysbok Trail traverses the beautiful fynbos-covered lower southern slopes of the Langeberg range. The Sunbird Loop offers a shorter 3-km option, if you prefer a quicker hike. The fynbos vegetation here is especially attractive between early August and end October. **15 km; 5 hours; circular.**

5. SLEEPING BEAUTY TRAIL
Riversdale

Trail: 12.5 km; 8 hours; out-and-return.
Permits: CapeNature Contact Centre, cell: 087 087 8250, email: reservation. alert@capenature.co.za or book online at www.capenature.co.za.
Maps: None, but route is clearly marked.
Facilities: None.
Pertinent information: Do not ascend Sleeping Beauty in inclement weather, and be prepared for sudden weather changes.

Mountain fynbos dominates the vegetation on the Langeberg's wetter southern slopes, while small patches of indigenous forest occur in the kloofs. Typical trees include yellowwood, stinkwood, red alder, hard pear, Cape beech and candlewood. The northern slopes, by contrast, are dry with characteristic Karoo species.

The range to the north of Riversdale is renowned for its profusion of fynbos plants, including rarities such as the Riversdale heath (*Erica blenna*) and two cone bush species endemic to the Riversdale Mountains: *Leucospermum mundii* and *Leucospermum winterii*. Among the proteas are the king protea (*Protea cynaroides*), peach protea (*Protea grandiceps*), as well as broad-leaved, blue and greenhead sugarbushes. Also to be seen here is the cushion-shaped cliff cushion bush (*Oldenburgia paradoxa*).

Garcia's Pass, which links Riversdale to Ladismith, was designed by the famous road engineer Thomas Bain. Construction started in 1873, but the pass was only opened to traffic on 31 December 1877, after many delays. It was named after the Civil Commissioner of Riversdale at the time, A.H. Garcia.

The old Toll House on Garcia's Pass, where the Sleeping Beauty Trail starts, was first occupied on 1 November 1877. It was rebuilt when the roof was blown off in 1910 and continued to be used until toll fees were abandoned on 31 December 1918. The building was declared a national monument in 1968.

Starting at Ou Tol on Garcia Pass, the Sleeping Beauty Trail owes its name to the mountain peak which resembles the profile of a beautiful woman reclining. The path initially winds through fynbos and then ascends along a kloof, where you cross four mountain streams to a yellowwood forest (fill your water bottle here) before emerging in fynbos again.

The trail then zigzags steeply to a saddle behind Sleeping Beauty, gaining over 300 m in altitude over the final 1.5 km. Towering over the surrounding coastal plains, the 1,343-m-high peak offers spectacular views of Riversdale and the Korentepoort Dam that make the climb worthwhile. **12.5 km; 8 hours; out-and-return.**

6. STILBAAI WALKS
Stilbaai

Trails: 5 walks; 1 to 4 hours; open-ended, circular and out-and-return.
Permits: Not required.
Maps: None.
Facilities/Activities: None.
Pertinent information: For more info contact Stilbaai Tourism Bureau, tel: (028) 754 2602.

Situated at the mouth of an estuary, Stilbaai is a coastal resort popular with holiday-makers and anglers. It has a wealth of archaeological treasures, including intertidal fish-trap complexes built by coastal Khoisan (possibly as far back as 2,000 years ago) and middens. A distinctive variation of Middle Stone Age artefacts, characterised by symmetrical, leaf-shaped (stone) points, was first discovered here. Tame eels and pansy shells are among the many attractions offered by the town's walks.

1. West Bank Route Among the highlights of this trail are views of the estuary, Khoisan fish traps and close-up views of the tame eels. **3 to 6 km; 1 to 2 hours; open-ended.**

2. Pauline Bohnen Route in the eponymously named 150-ha nature reserve passes through coastal fynbos with expansive views of the ocean and the coast. Among the animals you might chance upon are bushbuck, grysbok and common duiker. **4 to 8 km; 1.5 to 3 hours; circular.**

3. Strandloper Route recalls the early Khoikhoi and San inhabitants of the area (known as *strandlopers* in Afrikaans, meaning 'beach walkers'). Starting from the Jagersbosch Community Centre in Stilbaai West, the trail winds along the rocky coastline past Morris Point and Kleinplaatjie before returning to the start. Attractions include views of the estuary, the fishing harbour, historic buildings, Khoisan fish traps and Stilbaai's famous tame eels. **8 km; 3 hours; circular.**

4. Lappiesbaai Route is best hiked during low tide. From Lappiesbaai the route follows the sandy coastline for about 4 km to the Preekstoel, a rock formation reminiscent of a pulpit. Look out for pansy shells on the beach. **8 km; 3 hours; out-and-return.**

5. Southern Right Trail extends along the coastline from Morris Point to Jongensfontein. The first part of the walk is characterised by red sand dunes and, except for sandy coves at Kleinplaatjie, Sandhoek and Koppiesbaai, the coast is rocky. Highlights include ancient Khoikhoi and San fish traps, middens and the coastal cave at Jongensgat, while the variety of sea shells is a conchologist's delight. **11 km; 4 hours; open-ended.**

7. ALIKREUKEL SLACKPACKING TRAIL
Blombos to Stilbaai and further east

Trail: 4-day slackpacking hike; 45 km; and 4-km kayak paddle.
Bookings: info@alikreukeltrail.co.za; contact Derek 076 292 2866 or Clifton 082 457 1135.
Maps: Basic map.
Facilities/Activities: This is a fully inclusive and supported trail. The rates include four nights' accommodation in comfortable overnight establishments, guide fees, all meals (as well as snacks and a lunch pack along the trail), purified water, visit to the Blombos Cave museum, the kayak paddle on the Goukou River, olive tasting with lunch, all local transport during the trip, and luggage portage. A self-catering option is also available.
Pertinent information: The minimum group size is 8 and the maximum is 14. Only two hikes are offered each month. Trail dates coincide with optimum spring tide dates to make the best of the tidal rock pools, seeing the fish traps and appreciating the coastal ecology, as well as limiting soft sand walking.

On this trail, hikers follow in the footsteps of the early Khoikhoi inhabitants, who supplemented their diet with food from the sea. They combed the shores and rock pools for edible seafood – mussels, limpets and alikreukel, to which the trail owes its Afrikaans name. This edible sea snail is also known as the giant periwinkle, ollycrock or turban. The Khoikhoi also built intertidal fishing traps at various places along the southern Cape coast. Southern right whales are regularly seen between July/August and September/October, when they migrate to the southwestern Cape coast to calve and breed. In addition to enjoying the spectacular coastal scenery, hikers will also gain an insight into the fascinating early history, marine life, geology, flora and fauna of the coast from the expert guide leading the trail.

On the first day's hike (16 km; 8 hours), hikers are transported to Blombos Private Nature Reserve. The trail winds through fynbos above the cliffs to Blombos Arch, an archway in the sandstone rock, and past Blombos Cave. Archaeological excavations have provided evidence that the cave was inhabited as far back as 100,000 years ago. The most significant discovery is a rock fragment with nine red lines drawn with ochre crayon. Dated at around 73,000 years old, it is the oldest evidence of rock art in the world. About 7 km from the start the trail descends to the coastline and continues past Heuningnesbaai to Jongensfontein.

The second day's hike (12 km; 5 to 6 hours) follows the rocky coastline with its numerous pools from Jongensfontein past Jongensgat Cave and the Bosbokduin Private Nature Reserve with its collection of thatch-roofed cottages. Beyond Noordkapper Point, which owes its name to the Afrikaans name for the southern right whale, lies a long stretch of sandy beach where the Khoikhoi built fish traps between 2,000 and 3,000 years ago. The final section of the day's hike meanders through the Skulpiesbaai Nature Reserve and a milkwood tree forest.

Day three starts with an easy walk to the Still Bay Museum to view the Blombos Cave exhibition. Hikers are then transported up along the Goukou River for a 60-minute paddle in kayaks to an olive farm, where lunch is enjoyed before they are transported back to Stilbaai.

On day four (11 km; 5 hours), hikers set off from the Preekstoel, a rock which years ago resembled a pulpit, in Stilbaai East. The trail follows the sandy beach to Geelkrans, named after the yellow colour of the cliffs. Highlights along the unspoilt stretch of beach include semi-petrified dunes that have been eroded into cliffs with fascinating textures and shapes, as well as an amazing alikreukel shell midden from the era of the 'Strandloper'.

8. OYSTERCATCHER TRAIL
Mossel Bay

Trails: Two guided and fully catered trails; 32 km, 2 nights/3 days; 42 km, 3 nights/4 days; open-ended, but transport is provided back to the start.
Bookings: Cell: 082 078 1696, email: nature@oystercatchertrail.co.za.
Maps: Colour map.
Facilities/Activities: Luxury guesthouses; lunches and dinners incorporate local traditional meals (fish braais, mussel soup and home-made bread); snorkelling; transport from the finish back to Mossel Bay.
Pertinent information: Trails are conducted for groups of between 6 and 12 people from mid-April to the end of November. The minimum age for participants is 10 years.

These all-inclusive trails along the coast, west of Mossel Bay, are conducted by a local guide and aim to create environmental awareness of the Garden Route. Caves, shell middens and ancient fish traps along the coast are reminders of the early Khoisan people in whose footsteps trailists will be following. There's time to swim and explore the rock pools along the coast. Between July and October hikers can also observe the southern right whale.

There are two options. The first day of the three-night, four-day trail largely follows the St Blaize Trail (this page) to Dana Bay (15 km) with a stop at the Pinnacle Point caves, which served as a home to the ancient inhabitants of the coast. The second day's hike (12 km) follows the magnificent sandy beach to Boggomsbaai, with ample time for a quick dip. Highlights of the day include sightings of the rare African (black) oystercatcher, after which the trail was named, and a visit to an ancient Khoisan shell midden. On the third day (15 km), hikers make their way past Fransmanshoek where they can snorkel in the rock pools before continuing to Kanonpunt. The final day's hike (5 km) ends at the Gourits River mouth with a boat trip up the river, weather permitting. Hikers are transported to Boggomsbaai, where oysters and sparkling wine are served, and are then dropped off in Mossel Bay, or at George airport.

The only difference between the long trail and the shorter two-night, three-day option is that the shorter trail starts at Boggomsbaai.

9. ST BLAIZE TRAIL
Mossel Bay

Trail: 13.5 km; 5 hours; open-ended.
Permits: Not required.
Maps: Available from Mossel Bay Tourism or download from www. visitmosselbay.co.za/listing/stblaize/, email: info@visitmosselbay.co.za.

Facilities/Activities: None.
Pertinent information: As there are high cliffs, children must be accompanied by adults. Beware of high waves along the coast. It is inadvisable to walk the trail in strong winds. There is parking at both the start and end of the trail. Hikers must take their own water along.

The trail starts at the St Blaize Cave. The cavern has a height of 8 m, a depth of 13 m and a width of 28 m. Archaeological research has shown that the cave was inhabited as far back as the Middle Stone Age. Nearby is a historic lighthouse, which came into operation in 1864.

From the lighthouse the route leads westwards along the coastal cliffs, an ideal vantage point for whale and dolphin sightings and also a popular site for angling. The Cape gannet, lesser black-backed gull and African (black) oystercatcher are among the birds you might see along the way. You might also spot grysbok, common duiker and bushbuck. The trail ends at Dana Bay.

10. GOURIKWA PRIVATE NATURE RESERVE
Mossel Bay

Trails: 2 walks; 75 minutes to 2 hours; circular and out-and-return.
Permits: All hikers must register at reception. Fee for day visitors, but in-house guests free.
Maps: Available at reception.
Facilities/Activities: Fully equipped self-catering fishermen's houses, cottages and villa accommodation; snorkelling; rock angling; mountain biking. Visits to lighthouse by arrangement; tractor rides for groups.
Pertinent information: Horseflies can sometimes be very irritating. Keep an eye out for puff adders and Cape cobra. Carry water.

Situated in a region known to the early Khoikhoi as Gouriqua, the Gourikwa Private Nature Reserve is a mere 45-minute drive from Mossel Bay. It covers 2,500 ha of unspoilt coastal fynbos fronting on a 5-km stretch of coastline.

1. Cormorant Trail follows the coast with its intertidal pools, ancient stone fish traps built by the Khoikhoi and the most extensive boulder beach along the South African coastline. **5 km; 2 hours; out-and-return.**

2. Gorge Trail makes its way up a shady gorge with overhanging trees festooned with beautiful old man's beard to emerge in the fynbos after about 45 minutes. From here the trail loops back to the villas or you can continue to the coast. **75 minutes; circular.**

11. WOLWEDANS DAM WALK
Great Brak River

Trail: 6 km; 3 hours; out-and-return.
Permits: Not required.
Maps: Not available, but route is marked.
Facilities/Activities: Restaurants in Great Brak River.
Pertinent information: It is advisable to walk in groups. The walk should not be undertaken when the level of the river is high. Wear footwear suitable for walking in water.

The Wolwedans Dam Walk meanders from the leatherworks in Willow Street along the lower course of the Great Brak River. The route initially makes its way up a slope and then follows the old water furrow built to provide water to Great Brak River and Searle's Tannery way back in 1896.

Further along, the path crosses the river and then alternates between the riverbank and the riverbed where you have to take care stepping on loose stones. Continue upstream until you reach the stairs to the viewing platform overlooking the Wolwedans Dam, which was completed in 1986. The 70-m-high dam wall has a crest length of 270 m. Once you've enjoyed the views and taken a rest, you retrace your tracks down the river again.

12. GREAT BRAK RIVER WALKS
Great Brak River

Trails: 7 walks; 50 minutes to 1.5 hours; circular, out-and-return.
Permits: Not required.
Maps: None. For more information, contact Great Brak Tourism Office, tel: (044) 620 2550, email: greatbrak@visitmosselbay.co.za.
Facilities/Activities: Picnic sites with braai facilities; swimming pool; mini-golf at Pine Creek Caravan Park.

1. Pepper Tree Walk Starting at Hough's Herb Garden in Mossienes Street, the trail owes its name to the biggest pepper tree in South Africa. Several interesting buildings, original factory workers' cottages and a hydro-electrical pump house can be seen along the way. **4 km; 50 to 75 minutes; out-and-return.**

2. The Circle Walk combines a ramble through the town with walking along the beach, estuary and the Great Brak River. Attractions in the town include the biggest known pepper tree in South Africa, the Searle Memorial Church and Searle Family Graveyard, where the town's founders are buried, and the Watson Shoe Factory, to which the town owes its existence. **5 km; 1.5 hours; circular.**

13. GLENTANA BEACH WALK
Glentana

Trail: 6 km; 3 hours; out-and-return.
Permits: Not required.
Maps: None. For more information, contact Great Brak Tourism Office, tel: (044) 620 2550, email: greatbrak@ visitmosselbay.co.za.
Facilities/Activities: Braai places, toilets and parking area at Glentana Beach.
Pertinent information: The walk can only be done at low tide. The trail is not marked.

This easy walk from Glentana eastwards to Cape Windlass alternates between stretches of sandy beach and rocky outcrops. The trail passes the rusty remains of a floating dock, which ran aground here while being towed between England and Durban in 1902.

14. OUTENIQUA NATURE RESERVE
George

Trails: 4 walks; 3 to 8 hours; open-ended and out-and-return.
Permits: CapeNature Contact Centre, cell: 087 087 8250, email: reservation. alert@capenature.co.za.
Maps: Sketch maps.
Facilities/Activities: None.

1. Pass to Pass Trail links the Outeniqua and the historic Montagu passes. An optional 2.6 km out-and-return detour to the summit of Losberg (851 m) will be rewarded with extensive views over George and the coastal plains. East of Losberg the trail drops down to the Keur River, with its delightful patch of indigenous forest, before ascending steeply to the end. This trail can be hiked in either direction. **4.7 km; 3 hours; open-ended.**

2. Cradock Pass Trail From Witfontein the route follows the George and Cradock peaks trails for about 1 hour and then branches off to cross Tierkloof. After that the trail ascends along a spur, following the old Cradock Pass. Built in 1812, this pass was the only way across the mountains until the completion of the Montagu Pass in 1847. After crossing the railway line the trail climbs steeply up Cradock Kloof, and at one point the grooves cut by wagon wheels into the rock can still be seen. You gain nearly 800 m in altitude as you climb to the top of Cradock Pass, from where it is a 2-km downhill walk to the Montagu Pass. **12.4 km; 6 hours; open-ended.**

3. George Peak Trail From Witfontein the trail climbs steeply up the slopes, through fynbos, for about 2.5 hours to a nek where the George Peak and Cradock Peak paths split. From this intersection it is a 30-minute climb to the 1,337-m-high summit of George Peak from where there are expansive vistas of George and the coastline stretching between Mossel Bay and Knysna. The trail gains over 1,000 m in altitude and is rated as strenuous. **17 km; 7 hours; out-and-return.**

4. Cradock Peak Trail follows the same route as the George Peak Trail for the first 2.5 hours. The trail then climbs steeply for about 1 hour to the summit of Cradock Peak, at 1,579 m the highest point in the area. This is an extremely demanding trail, with an altitude gain of nearly 1,300 m, but the views are ample reward for the effort. **19 km; 8 hours; out-and-return.**

15. GROENEWEIDE NATURE WALKS
Groenkop Forest, Garden Route National Park

Trails: 3 walks; 3 to 5 hours; circular.
Permits: Self-issue permits at start. Entry fees payable when access points are staffed.
Maps: Available at start.
Facilities/Activities: Picnic sites.

The Groeneweide Nature Walks start at the parking area 1.5 km beyond the entrance gate, which is reached just before the Saasveld Forestry College. The indigenous evergreen forest here is largely representative of the moist forest type. The network of walks traverses the 1,450-ha Groenkop indigenous forest with its numerous streams. Following forestry tracks and footpaths, the network offers three different hike options: the **Red Route** (13 km; 4 to 5 hours), the **Blue Route** (11 km; 4 hours) and the **Green Route** (9km 3 to 4 hours).

An enchanting pool in the Silver River is a highlight on the Red Route, which leads past a number of enormous Outeniqua yellowwoods. Other forest trees found here include real yellowwood, white stinkwood, terblans, stinkwood and wild peach.

Animals to look out for include baboon, vervet monkey, blue duiker, bushpig, bushbuck and caracal, and leopard also live here. Among the many forest birds to keep an eye out for are the Knysna turaco, Narina trogon, olive thrush, sombre greenbul, chorister robin-chat, crowned eagle and black sparrowhawk.

16. WILDERNESS WALKS
Garden Route National Park

Trails: 4 walks; 1 to 4 hours; circular and out-and-return.
Permits: Self-issue, except Half-collared Kingfisher Trail and Giant Kingfisher Extension obtainable at Ebb and Flow reception or start of trail.
Maps: Pocket guide of hiking trails.
Facilities/Activities: Self-catering accommodation and camping at SANParks' Ebb and Flow North and South rest camps; picnic sites; bird hide; pedal boats and canoes for hire; angling (permits required).

The Wilderness Section of the Garden Route National Park provides protection to a string of four lakes, two estuaries and 28 km of coastline. The three western lakes (Island Lake, Langvlei and Rondevlei) are connected to the Touw River by the Serpentine, a narrow 5.5-km channel that passes through a marshy area.

The wetlands are an important waterbird habitat, and are sometimes home to as many as 24,000 birds at a time. Waterbirds constitute over a third of the 240 bird species recorded to date, and among them are five of the ten kingfisher species that occur in South Africa, as well as red-knobbed coot, yellow-billed duck, African darter, reed cormorant and little grebe. The lake system has one of the country's largest populations of African marsh harrier.

In the indigenous forests, trailists may chance upon such mammals as blue duiker, bushbuck, bushpig and vervet monkey. The coastal scrub supports grysbok and a variety of rodents, including the Cape dune molerat.

1. Half-collared Kingfisher Trail and Giant Kingfisher Extension The route initially follows the western bank of the Touw River and then crosses to the eastern bank to join the Giant Kingfisher Trail. For most of the way you will be walking on a boardwalk that was built when the ageing water pipeline between the Touw River and the water treatment plant was replaced. The pipeline was buried where possible or suspended under the boardwalk. The trail ascends through magnificent forests of yellowwoods, white stinkwood, climbers, flowering bulbs and ferns. Keep an eye out for half-collared and giant kingfishers, Knysna turaco, Narina trogon, blue-mantled crested flycatcher, tambourine dove and white-starred robin. The trail ends at a small waterfall and a series of rock pools surrounded by huge boulders. **7.2 km; 3 to 4 hours; out-and-return.**

2. Brown-hooded Kingfisher Trail passes through lush riverine bush along the Duiwe River, which is crossed several times (slippery rocks necessitate caution at river crossings). Just before the junction of the Duiwe and Klein Keurbooms rivers an optional short steep climb leads to a viewsite. A short way on, the trail branches off to follow the Klein Keurbooms River to a magnificent pool. The start is signposted on the Lakes Road, east of Ebb and Flow North Rest Camp. **5 km; 2 to 3 hours; out-and-return.**

3. Cape Dune Molerat Trail traverses the area between Rondevlei and Swartvlei and offers excellent birding opportunities. Two interlinked options are available.

Route A winds along the base of the dunes to the shores of Swartvlei. At the eastern end of the dune the trail climbs steeply to the dune crest, which provides excellent views over Swartvlei and the coastal plains. It then follows the dune crest before winding down to the start. **6 km; 2 hours; circular.**

Route B splits off Route A after 1 km and then makes a wide loop, which winds partly along the banks of the Wolwe River. Birding in the reed beds along the river can be very rewarding, so remember to take binoculars. After 4 km the trail joins up with Route A, continuing to the shores of Swartvlei before returning along the dune crest. **8 km; 2.5 hours; circular.**

4. Woodville Big Tree Walk Reaching 33.5 m into the sky and with a stem diameter of 2.9 m and a crown spread of nearly 30 m, the Woodville Big Tree

ranks among the 'Big Five' Outeniqua yellowwoods (*Afrocarpus falcatus*) in South Africa. From the picnic area it is a short walk to the forest monarch estimated to be 800 years old. Once you have admired this forest giant you can follow a trail that meanders through the Hoogekraal indigenous forest. The walk is ideal if you are keen on ticking off some of the forest birds. **2 km; 30–45 minutes; circular.**

17. OUTENIQUA HIKING TRAIL
Garden Route National Park

Trail: 108 km; 7 days, with shorter options; open-ended.
Permits: SANParks, P O Box 3542, Knysna 6570, tel: (044) 302 5606, fax: (044) 302 5627.
Maps: Colour map and information pamphlet.
Facilities/Activities: Huts with bunk beds, mattresses, firewood and water.
Pertinent information: Be prepared for rain and mist. After rain the forest paths can be very slippery, necessitating footwear with a good grip.

The indigenous forests of the Knysna region constitute the largest natural forest area in the whole of South Africa, covering some 28,600 ha of state forest and 16,000 ha of private land. The forests are populated with some 142 woody tree and shrub species, among them real and Outeniqua yellowwood, stinkwood, ironwood, red alder, Cape beech, tree fuchsia, Cape holly and assegai. Along the stream banks there are a number of impressive fern, tree fern and colourful moss species to be seen.

On account of the dense vegetation and the high canopies, birds are more often heard than seen. Among the 40 typical forest birds you may tick are the Knysna turaco, Narina trogon, the chorister and Cape robin-chats, white-starred robin, olive thrush, and terrestrial brownbul.

The forests are the habitat of bushbuck, bushpig, blue duiker, vervet monkey and leopard, as well as a variety of seldom seen small mammals that are either elusive or nocturnal. On the second day of the trail, make sure that you keep an eye out for grey rhebok, klipspringer and baboon in the fynbos and mountainous areas.

This trail goes through majestic indigenous forest, aromatic pine plantations and fynbos-covered mountain slopes. Opened in November 1976, the original Outeniqua Hiking Trail was designed as an eight-day, 149-km hike between Witfontein, outside George, and Diepwalle. However, by the time many hikers had reached Tierkop Hut, after a murderous 22 km on the first day, their enthusiasm had gone. As a result, sections of the trail were rerouted, and the four-day trail between Witfontein and Windmeulnek was eventually closed. Although the trail still has its fair share of ascents and descents, as well as fairly long distances on some days, it is a pleasant hike, with several shorter options.

From Beervlei, day one's hike (16 km; 5.5 hours) traverses easy terrain through the Beervlei indigenous forest and then descends through pine plantations to the Hoëkraal River. The next 8 km to Windmeulnek Hut is a steady ascent through the pines of the Karatara Plantation.

The Windmeulnek/Platbos leg on day two (17 km; 5.5 hours) is through fynbos, except for the last 3 km, which is through pine plantations. From Windmeulnek the trail makes its way down to the Karatara River and then steadily upwards along the slopes of Spitskop before reaching a pool in the Plaat River. After a gentle ascent up the slopes of the Kagiesberg, the trail makes its way down to Platbos.

On day three (15.5 km; 7 hours) the trail initially ascends through indigenous forest and pine plantations to the Homtini River, and from here it follows a gently undulating route through plantations and indigenous forest to Jubilee Creek. After you pass Jubilee Creek there is a steep climb that has to be negotiated before you reach Millwood Hut.

Just over half of the fourth day's hike (17 km; 5 hours) is either level or downhill, passing first through pine plantations and then magnificent indigenous forest. Continuing through the forest, the trail gains over 300 m in altitude as it climbs out of the kloof carved by the Knysna River. An easy downhill stretch rounds off the day's hike at Rondebossie Hut.

Day five's hike (13 km; 5 hours) moves back and forth through forest and pine plantation margins, to fynbos and the indigenous forest of Diepwalle. The day begins with a sustained climb to the beacon on Jonkersberg, followed by a long, gradual descent to the Gouna River. The final section is an easy 2.5-km climb to Diepwalle Hut.

The sixth day's hike (16 km; 5 hours) follows a trail with gentle descents and ascents at the four rivers you encounter along the way. Most of the hike to Fisantehoek is through indigenous forest interspersed with fynbos islands.

The final leg of the trail, on the seventh day (12 km; 4.5 hours), is a relatively easy hike through indigenous forest, with only one gentle incline close to the beginning of the trail. The remainder of the day's hike to Harkerville is either level or downhill.

18. GOUDVELD FOREST
Garden Route National Park, Knysna

Trails: 3 walks; 1.5 to 3 hours; out-and-return and circular.
Permits: Self-issue permits at start. Entry fees payable when access points are staffed.
Maps: Sketch map available.
Facilities/Activities: Picnic sites at Jubilee Creek, Millwood and Krisjan-se-Nek; mining museum; Bendigo mining village; tea room at Millwood.

Covering 5,150 ha, Goudveld is the largest tract of indigenous forest in the Knysna area and was once the scene of frantic gold mining. Prospectors and miners began flocking to the Knysna forests after the discovery of a gold nugget in the Karatara River in 1876.

Following the discovery of rich alluvial gold in 1885, and reef gold the following year, mining activity in the Knysna area reached fever pitch. By 1887 Millwood had a permanent population of 400 inhabitants (as well as about 600 diggers), six hotels, three newspapers and various shops. Most of the miners left for the Witwatersrand with the discovery of gold there in 1886, and by 1893 Millwood's population had decreased to 74. As the remaining inhabitants drifted off, the ramshackle tin and iron houses were reclaimed by the forest and all that remains from this era are the mine shafts, pieces of mining machinery and a cemetery. Matterolli House, one of only two surviving corrugated iron houses, serves as a tea room. The other house was dismantled and re-erected in Knysna, where it serves as a museum.

1. Jubilee Creek Walk From the Jubilee Creek picnic site, the route follows a section of the Outeniqua Hiking Trail through indigenous forest along a tranquil stream. Relics of the frantic search for gold in the 1880s include the remains of an old diggings pit and a water furrow. The trail ends at a pool and waterfall, where you swim. **4 km; 1.5 hours; out-and-return.**

2. Millwood Mining Walk passes through pine plantations and then ascends to Nols se Kop before swinging back to the old Bendigo Mine. The mine forms part of the Millwood Mines Restoration Project and displays include a portable steam engine and stamp battery. Along the way there are also a few old mining adits. The trail starts and ends at the Millwood picnic site. **5.6 km; 2 hours; circular.**

3. Dalene Matthee Trail Originally named the Woodcutter Trail, the walk starts at Krisjan-se-Nek picnic site. There is a memorial to the author who found much inspiration for her books, *Fiela's Child* and *Circles in the Forest*, in these forests. The trail passes through a magnificent indigenous forest on the way to Forest Creek, then makes a wide loop to Langrugpad, which it follows to Jubilee Creek. The final section is a gravel road. **9 km; 3 hours; circular.**

19. GOUKAMMA NATURE AND MARINE RESERVE
Knysna/Sedgefield

Trails: 6 walks; 1.5 to 5 hours; circular and open-ended.
Permits: CapeNature Contact Centre, cell: 087 087 8250, email: reservation. alert@capenature.co.za.
Maps: Reserve pamphlet with trails indicated.
Facilities/Activities: Mvubu and

Groenvlei bush camps on the shores of Groenvlei (call (044) 802 5310 to book); picnic sites, swimming, sailing and canoeing on Goukamma River; sea and freshwater angling (permits required).
Pertinent information: The Galjoen Trail is inaccessible during high spring tide and is best hiked at low tide. Because of rip currents along the coast, swimming is dangerous.
Special notice: Due to a fire in the greater Knysna–Plettenberg Bay area in June 2017, the hiking trails in the reserve have been closed intermittently for maintenance work. Contact CapeNature for an update (tel: (021) 483 0190 or (044) 802 5310, www.capenature.co.za).

The 2,500-ha Goukamma Nature and Marine Reserve protects a 14-km-long stretch of beach, the Goukamma River Estuary, vegetated dunes, coastal forest and Groenvlei Lake. Landlocked Groenvlei is the only freshwater lake in the string of lakes between Wilderness and Sedgefield, and as it is not fed by any rivers it is recharged only by rainwater seeping from the surrounding dunes. The marine section of the reserve extends 1.8 km seawards.

The vegetation is characterised by coastal dune fynbos and coastal dune forest, with extensive stands of milkwood trees. Among the more than 220 bird species recorded to date are the African marsh harrier, African fish eagle, several waterfowl species, the giant and half-collared kingfisher and the African finfoot. Also look out for African (black) oystercatchers along the coast. Animals occurring in the reserve include bushbuck, grysbok, bushpig, water and grey mongoose, Cape clawless otter, caracal and porcupine.

1. Bush Pig Trail The trail starts at the Goukamma trail head and follows the western bank of the Goukamma River for a short way before ascending to a fynbos-covered ridge, from where there are wonderful views of the coast, the Goukamma River and its estuary. The trail then winds down the ridge and passes through a magnificent milkwood forest. The final stretch of the trail follows a valley back to the trail head. **6.5 km; 2 to 3 hours; circular.**

2. Galjoen Trail follows the coastline between Rowwehoek and Platbank. Here trailists can explore the intertidal zone and look out for dolphins. Between August and December there is the possibility of seeing southern right whales. You must arrange transport at Platbank, or you can hike an out-and-return route half the distance. **14 km; 4 hours; open-ended.**

3. Blombos Trail owes its name to the blombos (*Metalasia muricata*), a fynbos shrub commonly seen along the trail. Starting at the Groenvlei trail head, hikers have a choice of three routes, each offering a different perspective of the reserve. The trails meander along fynbos-covered ridges, through patches of milkwood forest and along the shore of Groenvlei. The longest of the three routes also incorporates a stretch of the coastline. **Short route: 6.5 km, 2 to 3 hours; circular. Medium route: 13 km, 4 hours; circular. Long route: 15 km, 5 hours; circular.**

20. GOUNA FOREST
Garden Route National Park, Knysna

> **Trail:** 6.5 km; 2 hours; circular.
> **Permits:** Self-issue permits at start. Entry fees payable when access points are staffed.
> **Maps:** Available at start.
> **Facilities/Activities:** Picnic site at Grootdraai.

Terblans Walk owes its name to the Terblans beech, known in Afrikaans as the terblans. A member of the protea family, the terblans occurs in the southern Cape in the Gouna Forest only, and has a limited distribution elsewhere in South Africa.

Starting at Grootdraai picnic site, the route passes through a section of the 3,450-ha Gouna Forest, the second-largest tract of indigenous forest in the Knysna area. Along the course of the trail there are a number of large Outeniqua yellowwoods and magnificent groves of ferns. At Witplekbos, just beyond the halfway mark, there is a delightful swimming pool. Except at the Rooiels River

crossing, where the descent is followed by a steep climb, the terrain is relatively flat.

21. DIEPWALLE FOREST
Garden Route National Park, Knysna

> **Trails:** 7 to 9 km; 2 to 3 hours; network.
> **Permits:** Self-issue permits at start. Entry fees payable when access points are staffed.
> **Maps:** Available at start.
> **Facilities/Activities:** Picnic sites at Ysterhoutrug, Big Tree and Velbroekdraai; cycle route to Garden of Eden.

The Diepwalle indigenous forest covers 3,200 ha and was once the last refuge of the famed Knysna elephants. Numbering between 400 and 500 in the 1800s, they were relentlessly hunted for their ivory following the Millwood gold rush, and by the early 1900s their numbers had declined to a mere 50.

By 1920 the population had decreased even further and for the next 50 years remained unchanged at between 11 and 13 animals. Only three elephants were found when a census was conducted in 1979, and a plan to resettle three young elephants from the Kruger National Park in 1994 was unsuccessful. Only one elephant, an old cow, was found during a search for the remaining elephants during the same year. Then, quite unexpectedly, a young bull was seen in the Gouna Forest in September 2000.

Elephant Walk This walk makes its way through indigenous forest, crossing streams and rivers. The trail network passes through moist, medium moist, wet and very wet forest types. Trees in the moist forest type reach heights of 15 to 30 m and this type of forest is, therefore, also referred to as 'high forest'. Typical species include real and Outeniqua yellowwoods, stinkwood, white pear and ironwood. The wet forest type is confined to river valleys and ravines, and is characterised by red and white alder, tree fuchsia, stinkwood and Cape holly.

The trail network offers a choice of three different colour-coded routes: **Red** (7 km; 2 hours), **White** (8 km; 2.5 hours) and **Black** (9 km; 3 hours).

22. HARKERVILLE COAST HIKING TRAIL

Garden Route National Park,
Plettenberg Bay

See no. 23 (this page) for walks.

Trail: 27 km; 2 days; circular.
Permits: SANParks, P O Box 3542, Knysna 6570, tel: (044) 302 5606, fax: (044) 302 5627.
Maps: Colour map with information.
Facilities/Activities: Huts with bunks and mattresses, fireplaces, water and toilets.
Pertinent information: Chains have been anchored into rock faces to assist hikers at difficult places along the coast. Assistance might be necessary for those afraid of heights.

A section of the trail winds through the Sinclair Nature Reserve, with its indigenous forest, and along the rugged coastline. The first day's route (15 km; 7 hours) is an easy ramble through indigenous forest for about 11 km and then a steep descent to the spectacular coast, with its sheer cliffs, small coves strewn with loose round rocks, gullies and rocky headlands. Wooden ladders and a chain handhold assist hikers in difficult places. The 2.5-km coastal stretch is followed by a steep climb up to the coastal plateau and the Sinclair overnight hut.

The second day's hike (12 km; 6 hours) traverses the coastal plateau for about 2 km, then descends a forested kloof, and wends its way through fynbos to the coast. There are many difficult sections. Further on, the trail passes through a rock arch and, after following the coastline for about 2 km, climbs steeply to the plateau. The trail ascends gradually through indigenous forest before levelling off.

23. HARKERVILLE FOREST

Garden Route National Park,
Plettenberg Bay

See no. 22 (this page) for hiking trail.

Trails: 2 walks; 3 and 3.5 hours; circular.

Permits: Self-issue permits at start. Entry fees payable when access points are staffed.
Maps: Obtainable at start.
Facilities/Activities: Picnic sites at Kranshoek Waterfall and Viewpoint.

1. Kranshoek Coastal Walk From the waterfall at the Kranshoek picnic site the trail descends steeply through indigenous forest down the gorge carved by the Kranshoek River. The route then follows the rugged coastline for about 3.5 km to the mouth of the Crooks River. A steep climb up to the coastal plateau is followed by an easy walk along a gravel road back to the picnic site. **9.4 km; 3.5 hours; circular.**

2. Perdekop Nature Walk Starting at Harkerville Forest Station, the walk takes an easy route through cool, indigenous forest to Perdekop, with its lovely stand of hard pear trees. The pool below the waterfall in the Perdekop River is an ideal spot for a break or a swim. From here the route ascends steeply to Kleineiland Pad. The remainder of the walk is an easy ramble through indigenous forest. **9.5 km; 3 hours; circular.**

24. ROBBERG NATURE AND MARINE RESERVE

Plettenberg Bay

Trails: 9 km; 3 hours, with shorter options; circular.
Permits: CapeNature Contact Centre, cell: 087 087 8250, email: reservation. alert@capenature.co.za.
Maps: Sketch map of trail.
Facilities/Activities: Picnic sites; interpretation centre; braai on wooden deck with sea views; abseiling; diving. Overnight at the point of the reserve at The Point Shack, tel: (044) 802 530 for bookings.
Pertinent information: Parts of the trail to The Point traverse high cliffs and difficult, rocky terrain, which can

be dangerous for inexperienced hikers. Freak waves and strong currents make swimming inadvisable. Do not climb the sand dune above Witsand, as it is unstable. There is no shade, water or toilet facilities on the trails. Remember to bring a sunhat, sunscreen and lots of liquids. The boardwalks criss-crossing the reserve are there for the protection and rehabilitation of the vegetation and to protect breeding seabirds. Visitors must stay on the boardwalks and be aware that they can be slippery when wet.

The 175-ha Robberg Nature and Marine Reserve protects the Robberg Peninsula, which is a 4-km-long promontory ranging in width from 250 m at The Gap to about 1 km in the vicinity of The Island. The vegetation alternates between coastal scrub and thickets, and among the animals you may come across on your walk are common duiker and Cape grysbok.

Highlights of the trail, which follows mainly the cliff edges, include the magnificent rock pools at The Point and the beautiful white beach at Percy's Bank. From the high cliffs there are also expansive views of the long sweep of white beach to Plettenberg Bay and the coastline to the west. There are two shorter options: a 2.1-km walk via The Gap and a 5-km walk via Witsand Island.

25. STINKHOUTKLOOF NATURE WALK
Garden Route National Park, Tsitsikamma Section

Trail: 8 km; 3 hours; circular.
Permits: Self-issue permit at start. Entry fees payable when access points are staffed.
Maps: Available at start.
Facilities/Activities: Picnic site at start; drinking water.

The trail, in Bloukrans Forest, initially goes through pine plantations before winding for a few hundred metres through the indigenous forest in the upper reaches of Stinkhoutkloof. It then returns to plantations for just over 1 km, passing through a small patch of fynbos before entering the indigenous forest once more. Several streams are crossed, and the tall tree ferns growing along the banks are unlikely to escape attention. Near the 5-km mark there is a lovely natural swimming pool. Continuing through forest, you reach the old Main Road, just beyond the 6-km mark, and follow it back to the Bloukrans Forest Station, which is also the start of the trail.

26. TSITSIKAMMA HIKING TRAIL
Garden Route National Park, Nature's Valley

Trail: 60.8 km; 5 days; open-ended.
Bookings: MTO Ecotourism, cell: 087 158 2110, email: info@mtoecotourism. co.za or book online at https://www.mto. group/eco-tourism/tsitsikamma-trail.
Maps: Detailed fold-out trail map.
Facilities/Activities: Overnight huts with bunks, beds, wooden benches/tables, cooking shelters, cold showers, hot-water shower buckets and flush toilets.
Pertinent information: An optional equipment porterage service, enabling hikers to carry only daypacks, is available.

This trail traverses the slopes of the Tsitsikamma Mountains, crossing amber-coloured streams and passing through small patches of forest, where leafy fern glades and colourful fungi create fairytale scenes. Most of the trail is, however, through mountain fynbos, with mountain scenery.

The Tsitsikamma region supports a richer birdlife than the fynbos areas further west, and more than 217 species have been recorded in the area. This is mainly due to the more varied habitat created by the mix of fynbos and indigenous forest patches. Species to look out for include the Knysna and Victorin's warbler, Cape sugarbird, the malachite and orange-breasted sunbird, the Cape rock-thrush and greater honeyguide.

The first day's hike (3.6 km; 1.5 hours) meanders from Nature's Valley along the eastern banks of the Groot River Lagoon to Kalander Hut.

Day two's hike (13.5 km; 6 hours) passes mainly through the indigenous forests of Grootkloof and Platbos. Except for the climbs at Douwurmkop, soon after the beginning of the hike, and Staircase Falls, the terrain is easy. Staircase Falls, which is reached 4 hours from the start, is an ideal lunch stop. The remaining 5 km to Blaauwkrantz Hut is through a series of pine plantations.

Day three (13.4 km; 4 hours) begins with a steep climb and then, save for the drop to the Bloukrans River, follows a gradual incline for most of the day. Most of the hike is through open fynbos, with small relic patches of forest at Buffelsbos and Benebos. Keurbos Hut is situated on the edge of a small patch of indigenous forest.

The gentle descent to the Lottering River on the fourth day's hike (13.4 km; 4 hours) is followed by a steady climb up the Rushes Pass. The trail then winds down to the Lottering River, from where you follow a gently undulating route through mixed vegetation and indigenous forest to Heuningbos Hut.

Day five's hike (14.2 km; 7 hours) is mainly through fynbos, and involves two fairly steep climbs: up the Splendid Pass and to Nademaalsnek. The Splendid Pass owes its name to the rare silver mimetes (*Mimetes splendidus*) which occurs here. If you make an early start, take your time, and enjoy the magnificent scenery, the day's hike will not be nearly as daunting as it appears. From Nademaalsnek the trail descends Teebosrug, a ridge named after the abundance of wild bush tea (*Cyclopia subternata*), and then descends through indigenous forest to Sleepkloof Hut.

The final day's hike (3.2 km; 1 hour) is an easy walk through indigenous forest and rank fynbos to the Storms River Bridge, where the trail ends. As an alternative (5.5 km; 2 hours), hikers can end the trail at Storms River village.

27. DE VASSELOT

Garden Route National Park, Nature's Valley

See no. 28 (p. 109) for walks at Storms River Mouth and no. 29 (p. 110) for hiking trail.

Trails: 6 walks; 2.5 to 7 hours; circular, open-ended.
Permits: Conservation fee. No booking required for day walks.
Maps: Colour trail map.
Facilities/Activities: De Vasselot camp site: self-catering forest cabins and camp sites with ablutions; canoes for hire.

The De Vasselot area lies at the western end of the Tsitsikamma Section of the Garden Route National Park, and includes the coastal plateau (which rises approximately 300 m above sea level), forested slopes and a section of rugged coastline. Indigenous forests account for nearly two-thirds of the 2,560-ha section of the park, while fynbos covers the remainder.

The area is named after the Comte Médéric de Vasselot de Regné, who was appointed in 1880 as Superintendent of Woods and Forests of the Cape Colony. The area was declared a forestry nature reserve in 1974. It became part of the former Tsitsikamma National Park in 1987.

The network of interlinking trails runs through coastal scrub forest, high indigenous forest, and fynbos vegetation on the plateau.

1. Kalanderkloof Trail owes its name to the colloquial name for the Outeniqua yellowwood, which grows in great abundance here. Starting opposite the entrance to the De Vasselot camp site, the trail ascends steadily through indigenous forest before emerging into fynbos. From the viewpoint here, you can enjoy beautiful, expansive vistas, including the lagoon and the densely forested kloofs. The return leg is through indigenous forest, along the kloof. **4.8 km; 2.5 hours; circular.**

2. Groot River Trail follows the eastern banks of the Groot River to its mouth, and continues along the sandy beach, eastwards, to The Gully. From here the trail follows the last section of the Otter Trail in reverse, ascending The Point (the promontory above The Gully) from where there are magnificent views over the coastline. From the gate on the promontory retrace your tracks, cross the Groot River mouth, and follow the road back to your starting point at the De Vasselot camp site. **6 km; 2.5 hours; circular.**

3. Salt River Mouth From the shop at Nature's Valley the trail ascends through scrub forest to a viewpoint, and a short way further along joins a jeep track. You turn left here and follow the path to the Salt River. The return leg leads through scrub forest, and then along and above the rocks, past Pebble Beach, named after the pebbles of different hues and sizes washed up here. **9 km; 2.5 hours; circular.**

4. Salt River via Keurpad initially follows the outward leg of the Kalanderkloof Trail, but from the viewpoint the trail continues to the head of Kalanderkloof. After crossing the R102 the trail continues through fynbos, along the Keurpad Route, named after a grove of blossom trees, which are known in Afrikaans as keurbome. About 2 km after crossing the Salt River the trail links up with Rugpad, which leads through indigenous forest to the Salt River mouth, from where you can follow the coast back to Nature's Valley. **15.1 km; 6 hours; circular.**

5. Varinghoek via Keurpad starts at the picnic site on the Plettenberg Bay side of the Groot River Pass. The route is mainly through indigenous forest, except along Keurpad, which traverses the coastal fynbos, and across two patches of fynbos along the Brak River Route. Keurpad is named after a grove of keurboom seen on the outward leg of the route. From the Salt River it is a steady climb back to the starting point. **16 km; 6 hours; circular.**

6. The Crags via Brak River Starting from the De Vasselot camp site, this route leads to Nature's Valley, from where you follow the Salt River Route across the Salt River. Further on, you make your way along the Brak River Route on a jeep track and a firebreak before joining a gravel road, which leads to the SANParks ranger's house, where parking is available. **17.1 km; 7 hours; open-ended.**

28. TSITSIKAMMA WALKS
Garden Route National Park, Storms River Mouth

See no. 27 (p. 108) for walks in De Vasselot and no. 29 (p. 110) for hiking trail.

Trails: 3 walks; 2 to 3 hours.
Permits: Conservation fee. No booking required for day walks.
Maps: Sketch maps.
Facilities/Activities: Self-catering accommodation; restaurant; scuba trail; boat cruises up Storms River Gorge.

Stretching between Grootbank in the west and the Groot River near Humansdorp in the east, the 4,172-ha Tsitsikamma Section of the Garden Route National Park is a kaleidoscope of sheer cliffs, secluded bays and deeply eroded gorges, as well as indigenous forests.

When the park, initially known as the Tsitsikamma National Park, was proclaimed in 1964 its offshore boundary extended about 300 m seawards, making it the first marine national park in South Africa. The marine boundary was subsequently extended to 5.5 km out to sea. The inland boundary more or less follows the 200-m contour line.

The vegetation of the coastal belt is typical scrub-like, dry forest, lacking the luxuriant undergrowth of the high forests further inland. Species found here include white milkwood and wild camphor, while Outeniqua yellowwood, stinkwood, red alder, small-leaved saffron and Cape beech also occur. The flora of the coastal plateau is characterised by fynbos.

Some 40 of the 210 bird species recorded to date (such as the African (black) oystercatcher, ruddy turnstone, white-breasted cormorant, Caspian tern and kelp gull) are associated with the sea and shore. Among the forest species to look out for are the Knysna turaco, emerald-spotted wood dove, terrestrial brownbul, white-starred robin, blue-mantled crested flycatcher and olive bushshrike.

Mammals inhabiting the forest include the rare blue duiker, bushbuck, bushpig, vervet monkey, leopard and caracal, while the Cape clawless otter favours the area's perennial rivers and marshes.

1. Waterfall Trail follows the first 2.6 km of the Otter Trail to a magnificent waterfall that cascades over several steps into an inviting pool. **6 km; 3 hours; out-and-return.**

2. Mouth and Lookout Trail passes through indigenous forest and then makes its way to the Storms River Mouth. The mouth is bounded by sheer cliffs, and hikers cross the suspension bridge to the other side. A steep climb to the plateau is rewarded with fine views over the rugged Tsitsikamma coastline. A different return path is followed to the start. **4 km; 2.5 hours; circular.**

3. Blue Duiker Trail makes its way through scrub to the Agulhas Lookout and then enters the indigenous dry forest, where you may chance upon a blue duiker. The trail crosses a small stream, with an enchanting cascade, and offers ample opportunity for birding. **3.7 km; 2 hours; open-ended.**

29. OTTER HIKING TRAIL
Garden Route National Park,
Storms River Mouth

See no. 27 (p. 108) and no. 28 (p. 109) for walks.

Trail: 41 km; 5 days; open-ended.
Permits: Book well in advance. SANParks, P O Box 787, Pretoria 0001, tel: (012) 428 9111, fax: (012) 343 0905, email: reservations@sanparks.org.
Maps: Colour map and trail pamphlet.
Facilities/Activities: Huts with bunks and mattresses, fireplaces, firewood, water and toilets.
Pertinent information: Consult a tide table and plan to cross the Lottering River (day 3) and the Bloukrans River (day 4) at low tide. A survival bag is useful to float your pack across if you must swim. Although firewood is usually supplied, it is not always available, making it advisable to carry a backpacking stove. Use water at the huts sparingly, as it comes from rainwater tanks filled by runoff from the hut roofs.

Twilight coastal forests, huge waves crashing against the rugged coastline, secluded bays and a coastal plateau covered with ericas and proteas – this is the beautiful scenery of the Otter Hiking Trail. The first official hiking trail to be opened in South Africa, in 1968, the route goes from the Storms River Rest Camp to Nature's Valley, along what is undoubtedly one of the most spectacular stretches of coastline in South Africa.

The trail owes its name to the Cape clawless otter, which lives in the perennial rivers and marshes along the coast. Along the Tsitsikamma coast they also frequent the intertidal zone and the sea. Shy and noctural creatures, they are very seldom seen, but with some patience and luck you may see one in the late afternoon, usually where a river enters the sea.

The first day's hike (4.8 km; 2 hours) wends its way along the edge of the coastal forest and takes you over rocks to Waterfall River, with its beautiful waterfall that cascades into a huge natural pool. A short climb through indigenous forest, followed by a descent to a valley, brings you to the first overnight stop, which is at Ngubu's huts.

At the very beginning of day two (7.9 km; 4 hours) the trail ascends steeply to the plateau. Beyond Skilderkrans the trail descends to a stream, before climbing once again, and then after a level stretch drops down to the Kleinbos River, with its narrow gorge, pools and waterfalls. From the Kleinbos River the trail returns to the plateau, only to lose height once again and, after a final steep climb, makes its way down to Scott's huts on the banks of the Geelhout River.

Day three (7.7 km; 4 hours) follows quite an undulating course across forested slopes, stretches of the coast and the plateau. At low tide the Lottering River-crossing is easy, but during high tide, or if a gully has been washed open after rains, you might be in for a swim. From here it is a 20-minute walk to Oakhurst huts.

Although the fourth day (13.8 km; 6 hours) is the longest stretch of the trail, the gently rolling terrain is fairly undemanding. Alternating between the coastline and the indigenous forest, the trail leads you to the Bloukrans River after 10 km. Beyond the river the path climbs steeply to the coastal plateau, from where there are fine views over the coastline. The trail then descends steeply to Andre's huts, which nestle in indigenous forest alongside the Klip River.

Day five (6.8 km; 3 hours) begins with a steep climb to the plateau and, except for a gentle descent and ascent at Helpmekaarkloof, this day involves just an easy ramble along the clifftops to The Point. From here you look down onto the Groot River Estuary and the spectacular white sandy beach of Nature's Valley. After climbing down to the beach and crossing the estuary you have an easy walk to either Nature's Valley or the Groot River camp site.

30. STORMS RIVER WALKS
Garden Route National Park,
Storms River village and bridge

Trails: 2 walks; 1.5 to 2.5 hours, shorter options available; circular.
Permits: Self-issue permits at start. Entry fees payable when access points are staffed.
Maps: Available at start.
Facilities/Activities: Picnic sites at Ou Brug and Storms River Bridge.

1. Ratel Nature Walk has been laid out in the area surrounding the famous Tsitsikamma Big Tree and consists of three interlinked routes. The **Green Route** is a 1.2-km circular walk to the Big Tree. Towering an incredible 36.6 m above the forest floor, this enormous Outeniqua yellowwood has a circumference of 8.5 m at chest height and a crown spread of 32.5 m. From the Big Tree, the **Yellow Route** (2.6 km) makes a wide loop, passing yet another enormous Outeniqua yellowwood along the way. The **Red Route** consists of a 1.6-km loop that branches off from the **Yellow Route**. There are also a number of huge hard pear trees that trailists will see during the course of the walk. **4.2 km; 1.5 hours, with shorter options; circular.**

2. Plaatbos Nature Walk makes its way through indigenous forests to the south of the N2. The trail network offers four options. The **Green** (5.1 km), **Red** (7.8 km) and **Yellow** (8.1 km) routes start and end at the Forestry Office in Storms River village, while the **Blue Route** (830 m) starts and ends at the Storms River Bridge picnic site. **8 km; 2.5 hours; circular.**

31. DOLPHIN TRAIL
Garden Route National Park,
Storms River Mouth

Trail: 17 km; 2 days; open-ended.
Permits: Dolphin Trail, tel: (042) 280 3588, fax: (042) 280 3577, email to fax: (041) 394 5114, email: info@dolphintrail.co.za.
Maps: Available from www.dolphintrail.co.za.
Facilities/Activities: Luxury overnight accommodation, with gourmet dinners, breakfasts, picnic lunches and a forest tea.
Pertinent information: Guided trail. Luggage is transported to overnight huts. Hikers carry only a daypack.

Trained field guides accompany hikers, introducing them to the wonders of nature and the marine environment. Distances on this luxury, fully catered trail are short, leaving ample time to enjoy the spectacular views, to take a dip or to go snorkelling in the rock pools with their interesting marine life.

On the first day of the trail (7.5km) hikers are met by their guides at Storms River Rest Camp before setting off along a 2-km boardwalk through magnificent indigenous forest to the Storms River, which is crossed by way of a suspension bridge. The crossing is followed by a steep climb to Lookout Point. After a short level section through fynbos, the trail descends through indigenous forest to the coast. The trail then climbs steeply to Steilkop and meanders to the Misty Mountain Reserve. Accommodation is in luxury chalets with magnificent views over the ocean.

Day two's hike (9.5 km) winds down steeply to the rugged coastline with its cliffs and natural rock pools, which can be explored with snorkelling gear. Most of the day's walk is along the coast, but there is a steep climb back to the plateau where hikers can take a breather in a delightful patch of forest. The remaining 3 km of the trail leads through fynbos to Forest Ferns where hikers are accommodated in chalets built on the edge of the Sanddrift River. Guests can visit the fernery and nursery here, do some cycling, boating, birding, or simply relax in the jacuzzi or sauna.

Guests are transported back to Storms River Rest Camp after breakfast the following morning.

32. CADEAU ADVENTURE TRAILS
Storms River Mouth

Trails: 2 trails; 5 to 6 hours; guided; circular.
Bookings: Book at least 2–4 days in advance. Cell: 083 462 2457 (Andries), email: cadeau.za@gmail.com or online at www.gardenroutehikingtrail.co.za.
Maps: Trails are guided – non-negotiable.
Facilities: Dome tents with double or twin beds; fully equipped communal kitchen; indoor braai areas; boma; communal ablutions with hot showers and flush toilets; mountain-biking trails.
Pertinent information: Hiking boots that provide ankle support are essential. Don't forget sunscreen, a towel and swimming costume.

The Tsitsikamma coastline is renowned for its rugged but spectacular scenery – sheer wave-cut cliffs, secluded coves and rocky shoreline. The Cadeau Adventure Trails are not your usual hiking trail or easy walk, but challenging yet exhilarating adventure trails guided by a qualified guide with the necessary medical knowledge.

Both trails are very strenuous as they involve a steep climb down to the coast, scrambling over rocks, exposed cliffs and a steep climb back onto the plateau, and should not to be attempted by people with a fear of heights. The trails are conducted from Cadeau, a 10-ha private property along the eastern reaches of the Garden Route National Park.

1. Garden Route Elands River Coastal Adventure
Trail is regarded as one of the most scenic and dramatic trails in South Africa. Ladders and ropes are provided to assist hikers to cross two challenging rocky areas. Be prepared for rock scrambling over most of the route, using all parts of your body. There are spectacular pools along the way to swim in and explore. **6 km; 5 to 6 hours; circular.**

2. Garden Route Bloubaai Coastal Adventure Trail
winds through fynbos, coastal forest and along the rocky coastline, where wooden ladders and bridges have to be negotiated. Along the way, you can cool off in delightful swimming pools. **7.8 km; 5 to 6 hours; circular.**

33. ANTJIE SE PAD
Kareedouw

Trails: 37 km; 3 days or 56 km; 5 days; circular. A slackpacking option is also available.
Bookings: cell: 082 741 2733, email: antjiesepad@gmail.com, web: www.antjiesepad.co.za.
Maps: Available.
Facilities: House at old school building at Witteklip base camp; two overnight huts with beds and mattresses, hot-water showers, toilets, kettle, braai grid and wood.
Pertinent information: Groups are limited to a minimum of 4 and a maximum of 12 hikers.

Stretching from Willowmore eastwards for 120 km to Patensie, the Kouga Mountains form a barrier between the Baviaanskloof to the north and the Langkloof in the south. It is a landscape of deep valleys, cliff faces and wild mountain scenery.

Wildlife includes grey rhebok, mountain reedbuck, klipspringer, baboon and rock dassie. The diversity of habitats supports an equally diverse birdlife.

The vegetation of the Kouga Mountain is dominated by mountain fynbos with a rich diversity of members of the protea family, ericas and a variety of reeds and rushes. Unlikely to escape your attention are the bitter aloe (*Aloe ferox*), Baviaanskloof cycad (*Encephalartos longifolius*) and the near threatened Baviaanskloof cedar (*Widdringtonia schwartzii*), which is restricted to a few isolated kloofs in the Kouga and Baviaanskloof mountains. Another noteworthy plant is the honeybush (*Cyclopia* spp.), which is cultivated and harvested commercially for honeybush tea.

The trail traverses Witteklip farm, a working small-stock farm. Honeybush tea is cultivated and harvested commercially on the slopes. The trail was started to

Left: Hogsback is renowned for its splendid cascades.
Below: In addition to the world-renowned Otter Hiking Trail in the Tsitsikamma Section of the Garden Route National Park, visitors can also explore several short day hikes around Storm's River and Nature's Valley.

Top: Oakhurst huts, the third overnight stop on the Otter Hiking Trail, are perched above the Lottering River.
Above: The Otter Hiking Trail follows the spectacular Tsitsikamma coastline for 41 km.

Top: Overnight trails along the Wild Coast take in a multitude of natural splendours along this unspoilt stretch of coastline.
Above: This is one of the basic shelters at Helderfontein where you'll sleep after your first day on the Boosmansbos trail.
Right: The Wild Coast is a very isolated area, where people still live quite traditionally, and many young, urban men return here for their initiation into manhood.

Top: Walk in the uKhahlamba-Drakensberg from May to August and you're likely to see the high peaks of the area covered in snow and ice.
Above: Hikers can visit the area's many open-air rock art galleries, containing over 35,000 rock paintings.
Left: The Tunnel Walk is one of the most popular with visitors to the Royal Natal National Park.

Right: To take a detour around The Tunnel and get to the Tugela River, you need to climb up a chain ladder on the uKhahlamba-Drakensberg's Tugela Tunnel and Gorge hike.

Below: The Amphitheatre forms an impressive backdrop to the Royal Natal National Park, and you'll see it from a number of different vantage points on the various trails through this hikers' Mecca.

Above: In the Little Berg the rivers and streams have carved striking gorges through the soft sandstone of the Clarens Formation, such as this one in the Royal Natal National Park.

Below: The rare bearded vulture, or lammergeier, is easily identified in flight by its distinctive wedge-shaped tail. The vulture 'restaurant' in the Giant's Castle reserve offers opportunities to spot this bird.

Opposite top: Outdoor enthusiasts have a wide choice of numerous easy day walks in the foothills of the uKhahlamba-Drakensberg or more challenging routes to the Escarpment.

Opposite bottom: Ferncliffe Nature Reserve near Pietermaritzburg offers several short trails through pleasant natural forest.

You can explore this magnificent gorge, hollowed out of the Oribi Flats by the Mzimkhulwana River, on several beautiful walks through the Oribi Gorge Nature Reserve.

generate funds for the Living Water Ministries, which holds leadership camps for underprivileged children.

Sections of the trail follow the footsteps of Antjie Stuurman, who walked 10 km every morning from the stock post where she lived with her husband to Witteklip, where she worked in the 1930s. At the end of the day's work, Antjie walked back to her house behind the Blouberg in the evening.

The trails alternate between deeply carved valleys and table-top mountain ridges, and several steep ascents and descents must be negotiated. Hikers will, however, be rewarded with sweeping views of the Tsitsikamma and Baviaanskloof mountains and the 1,768-m-high Cockscomb in the Groot Winterhoek mountains.

34. LEOPARD TRAIL
Baviaanskloof World Heritage Site Nature Reserve

Trails: 63 km; 4 days; circular; slackpacking; 2-day walks; 5 to 6 hours; circular.
Bookings: Call Catherine, cell: 074 939 4395, email: reservations@gobaviaans.co.za, web: https:gobaviaans.co.za.
Maps: Available.
Facilities: Various accommodation options at base camp. Three overnight huts, each accommodating 4 people, with bunks, mattresses, central kitchen area with gas stove, cooking and eating utensils, braai area, braai grid, splash pool, hot-water showers and flush toilets.
Pertinent information: Carry at least 2 or more litres of water on the Leopard Trail. Pools and rivers could be dry during drought periods. Although the Leopard Trail is a slackpacking trail, hikers must be fit.

Covering over 210,000 ha, the Baviaanskloof Mega-Reserve is the third-largest wilderness area in South Africa. The 120-km-long valley is bounded to the north by the Baviaanskloof range, while the rugged Kouga Mountains form its southern boundary. It is the easternmost of the eight clusters that make up the Cape Floral Region Protected Areas, which were declared a UNESCO World Heritage Site in 2004.

The vegetation ranges from mountain fynbos and patches of indigenous forest to spekboomveld, Karoo shrubs, succulents and valley bushveld. Animals you might find here include kudu, grey rhebok, mountain reedbuck, bushbuck and baboon. Leopard also occurs, but this shy and mainly nocturnal cat is seldom encountered. The rich diversity of habitats and vegetation types support some 300 bird species.

The Leopard Trail (63 km; 4 days) in the western reaches of the Kouga Mountains is an excellent example of collaboration between the Another Way Trust, a community development organisation, and the Eastern Cape Parks and Tourism Agency. Starting at Cedar Falls Private Nature Reserve, the trail meanders through spectacular scenery with awe-inspiring views and delightful pools where hikers can cool off after rains. Above all, hikers can enjoy solitude. As long distances are covered on the second and third days, and as there are some steep ascents and descents, hikers should be physically fit.

Hikers can also set off on two less challenging day hikes from the Cedar Falls base camp.

1. Cedar Falls Day Hike This trail follows the course of a deep gorge bounded by red sandstone cliffs. Be prepared for lots of boulder-hopping, river crossings and two compulsory swims of 10 m and 15 m. The trail ends at a magnificent waterfall that cascades into a pool with crystal clear water. It can only be hiked by overnight visitors staying at the Cedar Falls base camp. **4 to 6 hours; out-and-return.**

2. Gabriel's Loop combines the first half of the first day's hike of the Leopard Trail and the second half of day two. It is named after the pool situated on the trail. **12.7 km; 5 hours; circular.**

35. CHOKKA TRAIL (Slackpacking)
Oyster Bay to St Francis Bay

Trails: 62 km; 4 days.
Bookings: Email: chokkatrail@gmail.com; cell: 073 825 0835 (Esti).

Maps: Maps and directions handed to hikers on arrival.
Facilities: Accommodation for 3 nights in 3- and 4-star graded establishments.
Activities: Calamari tasting; chokka cleaning demonstration; visit to Seal Point lighthouse and St Francis canal cruise.
Pertinent information: Fully catered trail, excluding drinks and personal extras. Minimum group size 4, maximum 16. Local guides are provided on days two, three and four.

This trail in the Greater St Francis area between Oyster Bay and Port St Francis is named after the Cape hope squid, which is commonly referred to as chokka and calamari. The route alternates between white beaches, sections of rocky coastline, wetlands and dune fields along a section of the coast known as the Coastal Cradle of Humankind. Shell middens, stone fishing kraals and Early Stone Age artefacts testify to the presence of people along the coast over an extended period.

The first day's hike (18 km; 6 hours) meanders along the coastline and through fynbos and coastal thicket from Oyster Bay to Thysbaai. Along the way, the stone fishing traps built by Khoikhoi some 2,000 years ago can be seen at low tide. Although the full trail is 18 km, you can turn back at any point.

The second day's hike (16 km; 6 hours) is the most demanding, as hikers have to negotiate the dune field between Oyster Bay and St Francis Bay. A local guide accompanies hikers to guide them through the coastal thicket on the dunes and shifting dunes.

The third day's hike (15 km; 6 hours) starts with a walk through a coastal forest before ascending the coastal dunes. Further along, the route winds towards Mostertshoek on the coast and then follows the coastline to the Seal Point lighthouse and Cape St Francis beach to the overnight stop. Highlights of the day's hike include the second-largest blowhole in southern Africa and the rusty remains of the Osprey shipwreck.

On day four (13 km; 5 hours) the trail meanders from Cape St Francis beach towards Shark Point and Port St Francis, the only privately owned harbour in South Africa and the centre of the chokka industry. After a calamari tasting and farewell lunch, the route continues through the Cape St Francis Nature Reserve and back to the beach and your vehicle.

36. GROENDAL WILDERNESS AREA
Uitenhage

Trails: 4 trails; 16 to 38 km; 5 or 6 hours to 2 or more days; out-and-return and circular.
Permits: Groendal office, cell: 087 086 2499, or Eastern Cape Parks Board and Tourism Agency, tel: (043) 429 0881, email:reservations@ecpta.co.za.
Maps: Basic map.
Facilities/Activities: Camp sites with communal hot-water showers and flush toilets; 3-bedroomed Rooikrans Lodge; picnic sites for day visitors. There are no overnight facilities in the wilderness area and hikers must carry tents or sleep in caves.
Pertinent information: Suitable footwear for wading through water and swimming is advisable for the Lower and Upper Blindekloof routes, as well as the Emerald Pool route. A dry bag is essential for Upper Blindekloof.

Covering 21,793 ha, the Groendal Wilderness Area lies at the eastern end of the Grootwinterhoek Mountains. Groendal Dam is at the centre of the wilderness area, and its surrounding landscape is characterised by a plateau bisected by deep ravines set against a backdrop of rugged mountains. Strydomsbergpiek, the highest point in the wilderness area, rises to 1,180 m above sea level.

Vegetation at the lower elevations is mainly valley bushveld, dominated by soetnoors (*Euphorbia coerulescens*), while porkbush, sneezewood, honey-thorn and cat-thorn also occur here. Fynbos and grasses are found at higher altitudes: typical species are tall yellowbush, blue and large-leaved sugarbushes and the common pincushion. Deep ravines support forests of Outeniqua and real yellowwood, red alder and the Cape star-chestnut.

Several mammal species might be spotted along the way. Bushbuck, blue duiker and vervet monkey inhabit the forested areas, while the open mountain areas are home to grey rhebok, mountain reedbuck and baboon. Leopard also occur here, but these secretive predators are seldom seen.

The birdlife is diverse, and species you might see in the fynbos are Cape and red-necked spurfowl, Cape grassbird, Cape sugarbird and Cape siskin. In the valley bushveld, be on the lookout for Knysna woodpecker, white-browed robin-chat, African dusky flycatcher and southern tchagra. A variety of waterbirds are attracted to the Groendal Dam and the rivers.

1. Lower Blindekloof Route From the start at the Groendal office, the trail initially ascends steeply along a jeep track for about 2 km to the monument that marks the official opening of the wilderness area on 14 February 1976. A nearby shady tree with a bench provides a welcome breather before you head down into the Blindekloof valley. From here you make your way up the river, which is crossed about a dozen times. To return to the start you have to retrace your tracks. A steep ascent awaits you out of the valley, but once you reach the jeep track it's an easy downhill walk. **16 km; 5 to 6 hours; out-and-return.**

2. Unmarked Routes The unmarked routes should only be attempted by experienced and fit hikers with orienteering and map reading skills. The Upper Blindekloof Route (32 km; 2 days; circular), which explores the upper reaches of Blindekloof with its tranquil pools and waterfalls, involves several compulsory swims. The Emerald Pool Route (32 km; 2 days; circular) follows a demanding and undulating route to Emerald Pool in Upper Chase's Kloof. The Dam Route (38 km; 2 days; circular) is the most strenuous of the unmarked trails in the Groendal Wilderness Area because of its undulating nature.

37. KLEINRIVIER MOUNTAIN ESCAPES
Uitenhage

Trails: 21 km; 2 days; circular; 9 day walks; 800 m to 10 km; circular and out-and-return.
Bookings: Cell: 083 991 7021, email: reservations@kleinrivier.co.za.
Maps: Download from www.kleinrivier.co.za.
Facilities: Accommodation at tented camp; self-catering cabins and farm cottage; camp site with lapa with wood stove and sink, fireplace, braai facilities, hot-water showers and flush toilet; mountain-bike trail.
Pertinent information: Slackpacking option available, at an additional cost, for overnight trail.

Kleinrivier Mountain Escapes is situated near the eastern end of the Groot Winterhoek Mountains and borders the Groendal Wilderness Area on two sides. Deep ravines and valleys bounded by sheer cliffs dominate the landscape. The trails pass through a variety of landscapes, including subtropical thicket, fynbos and indigenous forests. Klipspringer, kudu, mountain reedbuck, blue wildebeest and red hartebeest are among the game occurring in the area.

1. Two Gorges Trail is regarded as Kleinrivier's flagship trail. The first day's hike (10 km; 7 hours) meanders along the Kleinrivier Gorge and then continues along Drielingkloof. The trail ascends to a ridge overlooking Chase's Kloof in the Groendal Wilderness Area and there are spectacular views of Uitenhage, Gqeberha, the Zuurberg and the Kirkwood Valley before you descend to Stone Lodge. The second day's hike (11 km; 6 hours) initially follows an easy route along the Palmiet River Gorge for about 2.5 to 3 hours. After ascending steeply to the Western Plateau for about an hour, the trail meanders gradually down to the office.

2. Day Walks Each of the nine day walks has its distinctive character. Trails vary in length from an easy 800-m walk to 10 km, but can be integrated to suit hikers' fitness and interests.

38. VAN STADEN'S WILDFLOWER RESERVE
Gqeberha

Trails: 2 walks; 1 hour; circular.
Permits: Entry free. No booking required for day walks.
Maps: Download from www.vanstadens.co.za.
Facilities/Activities: Information centre; picnic sites; toilets.

This 400-ha reserve consists of a cultivated section, where indigenous plants are propagated, and large tracts of natural vegetation. The reserve straddles the N2 and is bounded, to the west, by the impressive Van Staden's Gorge. The part of the reserve north of the N2, on the coastal plateau, contains mainly fynbos.

South of the N2, the coastal plateau gives way to slopes of Alexandria Forest (a type of coastal forest), representing the southwestern extension of the more tropical eastern forests. It is more drought-hardy than the coastal forests further east and is best developed in the Alexandria area, northeast of Gqeberha.

1. River Walk traverses natural fynbos and mass plantings of proteas, ericas and other species in the north of the reserve. It follows the edge of the Van Staden's Gorge, then swings back to the start. Cape sugarbird and six sunbird species are among the more than 100 bird species recorded here. **2.5 km; 1 hour; circular.**

2. Forest Walk, south of the N2, provides the opportunity to explore a fine tract of Alexandria Forest. Among the trees to be seen are yellowwood, bastard saffron, cabbage tree, white elder and black ironwood. The walk also offers excellent opportunities for ticking forest birds, such as the tambourine dove, Knysna turaco and forest canary. **3 km; 1 hour; circular.**

39. MAITLAND NATURE RESERVE
Gqeberha

Trails: 3 walks; 1.5 to 3 hours; circular.
Permits: Entry free. No permits required.
Maps: Sketch map.
Facilities/Activities: Maitland Resort, with camp sites and ablutions, nearby.
Pertinent information: Water in the reserve's streams is not suitable for drinking; carry water.

Situated at the mouth of the river to which it owes its name, the 127-ha Maitland Nature Reserve provides protection to a fine stand of coastal forest and bush consisting of, among others, yellowwood, milkwood and boer bean trees.

Among the animals you may chance upon are the bushbuck, blue duiker and grey mongoose, and the forest is also home to the Knysna turaco, African paradise flycatcher and emerald-spotted wood dove.

Starting from the entrance gate, all three trails initially follow the old wagon road to the long-abandoned lead mine at the top of the hill, outside the reserve.

1. Sir Peregrine Maitland Trail This trail follows the old wagon road and then loops back down the slope through coastal forest to the De Stades River, with its dense canopy of overhanging trees. **3 km; 1.5 hours; circular.**

2. Igolomi Trail From the turnoff onto the Sir Peregrine Maitland Trail continue for a short way along the wagon road to where the Igolomi Trail splits off to the right. The return leg goes through low bush and small trees and along the way there are fine views across the coast. **4 km; 2 hours; circular.**

3. De Stades Trail branches off to the left, opposite the Igolomi Trail turnoff, and then runs along the ridge of a forested dune, from where there are expansive views of the Maitland River Valley and the high sand dune at the river mouth. **9 km; 3 hours; circular.**

40. THE ISLAND NATURE RESERVE
Gqeberha

Trails: Network of several walks; 30 minutes to 5 hours; circular.
Permits: The Officer-in-Charge, The Island Nature Reserve, P O Box 50634, Colin Glen 6018, tel: (041) 378 1634, fax: (041) 378 1607.
Maps: Trail pamphlet with sketch map.
Facilities/Activities: Picnic sites, covered braai and eating area.
Pertinent information: Precautions against ticks are advisable.

The Island Nature Reserve stretches over some 500 ha. It is interspersed with pine and eucalyptus plantations, and also provides protection to a patch of Alexandria Forest. It is typically very dense, with a height of about 10 m, and represents the southwestern extension of the more tropical coastal forests occurring further east. It is composed of more plants specially adapted for dry areas than the coastal forests further east, but also contains species typical of the temperate forests further west.

Bushbuck Walk In addition to the antelope after which the walk is named, you might also chance upon common duiker and vervet monkey, while a variety of small mammals also live in the reserve. Among the bird species to look out for are the olive bushshrike, Narina trogon, Knysna turaco, dark-backed weaver and olive woodpecker.

Trees along the network of trails have been marked and can be identified by referring to the list on the trail pamphlet. Along the Bushbuck Walk, some fine examples of hard pear, cheesewood, Outeniqua yellowwood, veld fig, Cape teak and Cape chestnut can be seen.

The Alexandria Forest is on an ancient vegetated dune, which forms part of a series of dunes in this area of the Island Nature Reserve, with a height of up to 282 m above sea level. On the full circuit there are two good vantage points on the dune. At the 8.5-km point trailists can climb up an iron ladder to the top of a beacon, and at the 10.4-km mark there is a fire lookout. From here there are extensive views over the forest and the ocean beyond, with Jeffrey's Bay and Cape St Francis clearly visible on a clear day. Bushbuck Walk consists of a number of interlinked loops: **1.5 km; 30 minutes. 3.4 km; 45 minutes. 7.6 km; 2 hours. 16 km; 5 hours. All circular.**

41. SARDINIA BAY NATURE RESERVE
Gqeberha

Trail: 8 km; 3 hours; circular.
Permits: No booking required for day walk.
Maps: Sketch map.
Facilities/Activities: Picnic facilities; toilets.
Pertinent information: For your own safety it is advisable to walk in a group.

Covering 320 ha, this reserve was established in 1980 to protect the coastal dune fynbos vegetation and its associated fauna. From near Schoenmakerskop, westwards, to Bushy Park, the Sardinia Bay Marine Reserve extends 1 km out to sea.

As a result of the strong coastal winds, the milkwoods are stunted and low, sometimes only knee-high. In spring, numerous dusky pink sand onions (*Veltheimia viridifolia*) can be seen flowering under the coastal bush, and the gazania and red-hot poker flowers add colour to the rocks along the coast.

Sacramento Trail is named after the Portuguese galleon that ran aground just off Schoenmakerskop on 30 June 1647. Only nine of the 72 survivors reached Delagoa Bay (today Maputo) after a six-month, 1,300-km walk. A bronze cannon, salvaged from the wreck in 1977 and mounted on the coast just west of Schoenmakerskop, is a reminder of the disaster.

From the western end of Schoenmakerskop the trail follows the coast past the Sacramento Monument, and at the far end of Cannon Bay the ruins of a mill used to crush sea shells can be seen. Beyond Cannon Rocks there are numerous gullies where trailists can explore the local marine life or cool off. The return leg from Sardinia Bay follows a ridge linked to the reserve's network of bridle paths.

42. CAPE RECIFE NATURE RESERVE
Gqeberha

Trail: 9 km; 3 hours; circular.
Permits: No fee if vehicles are left outside gate. No permit required for walks.
Maps: Sketch map and information sheet.
Facilities/Activities: Information centre; bird hide; toilets.

This reserve, at the westernmost point of Algoa Bay, encompasses 336 ha of coastal dune flora and rocky shores. Dominating the reserve is a 24-m-high octagonal lighthouse, which has warned ships of the dangers of Recife Point and Thunderbolt Reef since 1851.

A variety of waterbirds, such as the black-winged stilt, pied avocet, African swamphen and waterfowl, are attracted to the water reclamation works, and a large number of terns roost on Recife Point. A rocky promontory has been set aside as a sanctuary for the endangered African penguin, and it is hoped that rescued and injured birds released here after rehabilitation will form a mainland breeding colony.

Trail of the Roseate Tern was named after a tern species occurring along the coast. The trail leads from the reserve gate to the water reclamation works, where a bird hide provides good birding opportunities. The route then follows the coastline, past the lighthouse and the African penguin sanctuary, before swinging away from the coast to the remains of a World War II military barracks. A short climb brings you to an observation post, built in 1940 as part of the city's harbour defences, from where you look out over the reserve, Algoa Bay and the notorious Thunderbolt Reef.

43. SETTLERS PARK
Gqeberha

Trails: 2 to 7.5 km; 1 to 3.5 hours; network.
Permits: No permit required.
Maps: Sketch map and information sheet.
Facilities/Activities: Flower display house; toilets; water.
Pertinent information: Don't drink water from the Baakens River.

Situated in the heart of Gqeberha, Settlers Park is a 54-ha greenbelt in the steep-sided Baakens River Valley. Amid the natural, mixed woodland are manicured lawns, pathways, benches and water features.

Jan Smuts Walk From the main entrance gate off Howe Street, the trail leads down into the valley with its high cliffs, springs, groves of exotic trees, and collections of proteas and cycads. There are numerous footpaths to follow, and along the way good birding can be enjoyed. The 120 species to be seen include the olive woodpecker, red-necked spurfowl, yellow-breasted apalis, forest canary and tambourine dove. Keep an eye out for peregrine falcon in the vicinity of Lovers' Rock.

44. LOWER GUINEAFOWL TRAILS
Gqeberha

Trail: 7.5 km; 2.5 hours; open-ended.
Permits: Not required.
Maps: Sketch map with information sheet.
Facilities: Flower display house, toilets and water in Settlers Park.
Pertinent information: For your own safety it is advisable to walk in a group. The Baakens River water is not drinkable, so you will need to carry water on your hike.

The Lower Guineafowl Trail follows the lower course of the Baakens River, which owes its name to the beacon that was erected in 1795 to indicate the spring where sailors of the Dutch East India Company obtained fresh water. The river meanders for 23 km from its source near Hunter's Retreat through the city centre and enters the sea through the Gqeberha harbour. Although urban expansion has encroached on the valley, it remains a scenic green space away from the hustle and bustle of the city.

The vegetation ranges from indigenous forest and fynbos to valley bushveld and succulents, while the valley is the habitat of no fewer than 18 plant species of conservation concern. Over 130 bird species have been recorded to date, while a variety of small mammals and reptiles also inhabit the valley.

Starting at the Third Avenue Dip in Newton Park, the trail initially meanders along the river's floodplain, which is bounded to the north by cliffs that are up to 40 m high in places. At Dodd's Farm the river makes a wide loop and further along you pass underneath the Target Kloof bridge. Settlers Park is reached a short way on and at around the 6-km mark you have the option of climbing up to the car park at the lower end of Howe Street or continuing for another 1.5 km to Brickmakerskloof. **7.5 km; 2.5 hours; open-ended.**

45. ZWARTKOPS NATURE RESERVE
Gqeberha

Trail: 10 km; 3 hours; circular.
Permits: No permit required.
Maps: Sketch map with information sheet.
Facilities/Activities: None.
Pertinent information: For your own safety it is advisable to walk in a group.

The Zwartkops Nature Reserve was established to protect the valley bushveld, salt marshes, tidal flats and pans of the Zwartkops Estuary, 15 km north of Gqeberha. The vegetation is characterised by boer bean, cabbage, white milkwood and porkbush trees. The reserve also contains aloes, which are especially attractive in June and July when they are in flower.

The wetlands and valley bushveld attract a diversity of birds, and to date some 220 bird species have been recorded in the Zwartkops Estuary. At times up to 1,000 flamingo congregate on the pan, and in summer a variety of waders and terns can be ticked. In the valley bushveld, keep an eye out

for the Knysna woodpecker, grey-winged francolin, southern tchagra and white-throated robin-chat.

The valley bushveld vegetation here in the Zwartkops Nature Reserve is home to Cape grysbok, blue duiker and bushpig, while the Cape clawless otter favours rank vegetation along the river.

Flamingo Trail starts at the Motherwell stormwater channel in the Zwartkops Nature Reserve, a few kilometres north of the city centre. From here the trail climbs through valley bushveld vegetation to the Escarpment, from where there are fine views over the Zwartkops Estuary. It then descends along a kloof to the saltpan and follows a track along the base of the Escarpment for a while, before climbing to the top of the Escarpment once more. A final descent to the saltpan is followed by a walk along the river to Redhouse, before the trail runs close to the edge of the saltpan.

46. ALOE TRAIL
Bluewater Bay, Gqeberha

Trail: 7 km; 2.5 hours; circular.
Permits: No permit required.
Maps: Sketch map with information sheet.
Facilities/Activities: None.

Aloe Trail is named for the profusion of aloes at the start of the trail, the outward leg of which runs along the Escarpment above Zwartkops Estuary. Just before the 1-km mark the Yellow Trail (a 2-km circuit) branches off, while the longer Red Trail makes a detour inland a short way on. It then returns to the Escarpment from where there are great views over the estuary, Zwartkops Nature Reserve further upstream, and the distant Cockscomb Peak. The trail then swings away from the Escarpment and makes its way through valley bushveld vegetation on the plateau, where it winds through a series of old wallows. These depressions are the only evidence that elephants once roamed the area. The last 1 km follows the return leg of the Yellow Trail. The trail starts at the top end of Tippers Creek Road, between Amsterdamhoek and Bluewater Bay.

47. VAN DER KEMP'S KLOOF TRAIL
Bethelsdorp

Trail: 8 km; 3 hours; circular.
Permits: No permit required for walks.
Maps: Sketch map and information pamphlet.
Facilities/Activities: None.

This trail starts in the heart of the historic settlement of Bethelsdorp, which was established in 1803 by Dr Johannes van der Kemp of the London Mission Society. Among the places of historic interest in the town are the Almshouse (1822), Van der Kemp's Church (built in 1903 on the site of the first church, which was destroyed by a fire in 1890, Church Square) and the Mission Bell, erected in 1815. Another noteworthy building that you can see here is Livingstone Cottage where the missionary and explorer is said to have stayed.

From the village centre the trail makes its way along the Little Zwartkops River in Van der Kemp's Kloof for about 3 km. Shortly after leaving the village, the trail passes the Washing Tree, a fig tree where women once gathered to do their laundry. The remains of stonewalls that demarcated agricultural plots further on are reminders of the kloof's farming history. Van Der Kemp's Kloof has the largest population of *Strelitzia juncea* in the world, a crane flower species endemic to Gqeberha. The trail then climbs onto the plateau, covered in grassy fynbos. Along the way there are views over Gqeberha's western suburbs, the kloof, Zwartkops Valley and Algoa Bay. A steep descent into the kloof, followed by a short walk, concludes the trail.

48. ZUURBERG
Addo Elephant National Park

Trails: 2 walks; 1 or 5 hours; circular.
Permits: Conservation fee. No bookings required for day walks.
Maps: Sketch map.

Pertinent information: The trails start at the Zuurberg office, 17 km from the Addo Main Camp. Hikers must start the Doringnek trail before 12:00.

Addo Elephant National Park was set aside in 1931 to protect the last remaining elephants in the Eastern Cape, and since then the park's elephant population has increased from 11 to over 420. It is also a sanctuary for black rhino and, at one stage, was home to the only population of foot-and-mouth-disease-free buffalo in southern Africa. Red hartebeest, eland, kudu, bushbuck and grysbok are among the antelope found in the park. Also of interest is the scarce flightless dung beetle, which is endemic to the Eastern Cape.

The Zuurberg section of the Addo Elephant National Park covers 35,000 ha of rugged mountain peaks and wild river valleys in the Klein Winterhoek Mountains. It was proclaimed a national park in 1985 and subsequently became part of the Addo Elephant National Park when land in between the two reserves was acquired.

The Zuurberg section of the park is home to a variety of animals, including kudu, mountain reedbuck, grey rhebok, bushbuck, common and blue duiker and bushpig. Cape mountain zebra, black rhino and hippo have been reintroduced here.

The valley bushveld vegetation of the area is considered the most pristine in the whole of the Eastern Cape. Fynbos dominates the higher altitudes, while patches of indigenous forest occur in the more sheltered kloofs. Noteworthy among the plants are three cycad species, as well as the grass aloe (*Aloe micracantha*) and the succulent cushion bush (*Ruschia rigens*).

1. Zuurberg Cycad Trail is named after the long-leaved cycad. The trail offers magnificent views of the rugged Zuurberg Mountains and passes through a delightful patch of indigenous forest. **3 km; 1 hour; circular.**

2. Zuurberg Doringnek Trail meanders across fynbos-covered plateaus and then descends into the Doringnek Kloof, with its riverine vegetation and Otto's Pool. The trail then climbs back to an open fynbos ridge, which you follow back to the start. **15 km; 5 hours; circular.**

49. WOODY CAPE
Addo Elephant National Park

Trails: 1 walk; 2 to 3 hours. Hiking trail; 32 km; 2 days; circular.
Permits: Camp Matyholweni, Addo Elephant National Park, P O Box 146, Colchester 6175, tel: (041) 468 0916, fax: (041) 468 0949, email: mathyholweni@ sanparks.org (for Alexandria Hiking Trail). Tree Dassie Trail: Conservation fee. No advanced booking required.
Maps: Sketch map.
Facilities/Activities: Two overnight huts at start of the trail, and Woody Cape Hut, with bunks, mattresses, water and ablutions.
Pertinent information: Hikers should wear brightly coloured clothing to make themselves visible in case of an air search. At Woody Cape Hut, no fires are permitted and refuse must be brought back. The only water available here is rainwater collected from the roof, which must be used purely for drinking and washing cooking utensils.

The Woody Cape Section of the Addo Elephant National Park contains the largest tract of Alexandria Forest in the country and the largest coastal dunefield in southern Africa.

The Alexandria Forest consists of low to medium-height (10-m-high) trees and often looks more like a thicket than a forest. Taller trees grow in the valleys. Alexandria Forest has an interesting composition, as it contains a mixture of coastal, tropical species, typically occurring further east, temperate montane species and Cape forest species.

Covering some 110 km², the Alexandria dunefield has evolved over the last 6,000 years. It ranks among the best examples of a mobile dune system in the world, and the influx of sand into the system is estimated at 375,000 m³ a year.

The forest is home to bushpig, bushbuck and blue duiker, while the dune thickets are inhabited by grysbok, common duiker, tree dassie and vervet monkey. Leopard, caracal, black-backed jackal and a variety of smaller mammals also occur here.

The Alexandria dunefield is an important breeding habitat of the Damara tern and the African (black) oystercatcher. Bird Island, the largest of a group of offshore islands, is home to some 140,000 Cape gannets and some 5,000 African penguins. Species to look out for in the forest include crowned and trumpeter hornbills, Narina trogon, chorister robin-chat, terrestrial brownbul and dark-backed weaver.

1. Alexandria Hiking Trail The first day's hike (18.5 km; 6 hours) alternates between plantations and indigenous forest for 4 km to the Waterboom (the 'Water Tree'), so named because early travellers were said to have used rainwater that collects in the hollow in the base of the tree. From here, the trail goes through magnificent Alexandria Forest before traversing private property and crossing a buffer dune to reach the coast. You then follow the coastline, with its white beach and dune cliffs, for 6 km. At high tide you will have no option but to take the 'high route' on the cliffs, but at low tide you can continue along the coast to a wooden ladder, which provides access to the top of the cliffs. The last section of both routes runs along the top of the cliffs.

The second day's hike (13.5 km; 5.5 hours) leads through the dunes with tall posts to guide hikers through the shifting dunes. The small 'islands' of bush pockets in the dunes are particularly striking. Beyond the dunefield the trail enters private property, where it traverses a large grassy plateau. You will pass a chicory roasting stack, used in the 1920s. The last section of the trail is once again through indigenous forest.

2. Tree Dassie Trail Tree Dassie Trail meanders through magnificent indigenous forest from Camp Mathyholweni. This easy walk is an ideal way to familiarise yourself with the trees and to do some birding. **7 km; 2 to 3 hours; circular.**

50. MOUNTAIN ZEBRA NATIONAL PARK
Cradock

Trails: 1 to 10 km; 1 guided hike and guided morning walks; 30 minutes to 4 hours; circular.

The Mountain Zebra National Park was proclaimed in 1937 when it became clear that the Cape mountain zebra was doomed to extinction. None of the original herd of six animals was still alive in 1950 and the survival of the Cape mountain zebra looked bleak. A donation of five stallions and six mares to the park by Mr J H Lombard of the neigbouring farm Waterval brought about a turnaround in the survival of the species. The population increased to 25 in 1964 and surpassed the 200 mark in 1980. Surplus animals have been translocated to the Karoo National Park at Beaufort West, the Camdeboo National Park at Graaff-Reinet, the De Hoop Nature Reserve near Bredasdorp and the Tsolwana Game Reserve west of Queenstown.

While mountain and plains zebra are the main attractions, the park, which covers a total area of 28,386 ha, also protects one of the highest concentrations of mountain reedbuck in South Africa, as well as common duiker, klipspringer, eland, kudu, springbok, blesbok, steenbok, black wildebeest and red hartebeest. Small herds of black rhino and buffalo occur, mainly in dense riverine thicket. Carnivores include caracal, small spotted cat, bat-eared fox, black-backed jackal and yellow mongoose. Cheetah were introduced in 2007 and lions in 2013.

African rock pipit, ground woodpecker, Drakensberg rockjumper, pale-winged starling, Cape and sentinel rock-thrush and mountain wheatear are among the 276 bird species to look out for. Verreaux's eagle, jackal buzzard, rock kestrel and booted eagle count among the raptors.

Rest Camp Walks

Hikers can explore the environs of the rest camp in safety along two short but enjoyable rambles in the fenced area. Soetkop, a large sandstone outcrop, dominates the scenery behind the rest camp. The walks present an ideal opportunity to take a closer look at the Karoo shrubs and plants. Be on the lookout for the tracks of small mammals that occur in the area. Among them are steenbok, common duiker, ground squirrel, Cape hare and scrub hare. African rock pipit and mountain wheatear are some of the species that can be ticked here.

1. Imbali Walk is an easy walk over flat terrain. It owes its name to the isiXhosa name for the rock dassie, a small herbivorous species that favours rocky terrain. Research has shown that these mammals feed on at least 80 different plant species. The dassie's main predators are Verreaux's eagle and caracal. **1 km; 30 minutes; circular.**

2. Black Eagle Walk is named after the Verreaux's eagle, one of 18 raptor species recorded in the park. This route is more demanding than the Imbali Walk, as it makes its way up Soetkop. From its summit you can enjoy spectacular views of the park. Looking to the south, the scenery is dominated by Bankberg and a deep valley carved by the Wilgerboom River. From here you make your way back to the start. **2.5 km; 1 hour; circular.**

Guided Walks

Morning walks are conducted from the rest camp and their distance and duration will depend on the level of fitness of the group.

1. Guided Morning Walks are undertaken in remote areas of the park and could include the original Idwala Trail, which ascends along Grootkloof to the Big Rock, called *idwala* in isiXhosa. On these walks, trailists will learn more about the fascinating Karoo plants, enjoy magnificent views of the surrounding countryside and perhaps see some wildlife on foot. **10 km; 2 to 3 hours; circular.**

2. Salpeterkop Hike is a challenging climb to the 1,514-m-high summit of Salpeterkop in the northwestern corner of the park. Rising more than 300 m above the surrounding countryside, Salpeterkop is a typical mesa. These isolated flat-topped mountains are characteristic of the Karoo landscape. **10 km; 3 to 4 hours; circular.**

51. COMMANDO DRIFT NATURE RESERVE
Tarkastad

Trail: 6 km; 2 hours; out-and-return.
Permits: Entrance fee. No bookings required for day walk.
Maps: Sketch map.
Facilities/Activities: Fully equipped self-catering chalet; three stone cabins with basic facilities; camping sites; bird hide; mountain biking; picnicking; boating; freshwater angling (permit required). Accommodation bookings: Eastern Cape Parks Board, P O Box 11235, Southernwood, East London 5200, tel: (043) 705 4400, fax: 086 611 1123, email: reservations@ecparks.co.za.
Pertinent information: Summer temperatures can be very high.

The Commando Drift Dam is the focal point of this 5,983-ha nature reserve, which is characterised by low, undulating hills. The reserve was proclaimed in 1980 and one of the management objectives is to restore the Karoo veld to its original state.

Game that occurred in the area historically has been reintroduced, including Cape mountain zebra, black wildebeest, red hartebeest, blesbok and springbok. Kudu, steenbok, mountain reedbuck, caracal, baboon and vervet monkey also occur here. Over 200 bird species have been recorded here.

Bushman Trail leads from the rest camp along the shores of the dam and then follows a jeep track up Palingkloof (*paling* is Afrikaans for eel). The open water and the shore attract a variety of waterfowl and waders, making this trail ideal for birding enthusiasts.

52. TWO RIVER HIKING TRAIL
Makhanda (Grahamstown)

Trails: 20 km; 2 days; circular. 2 day walks; 8.5 and 15 km; 4 to 7 hours; circular.

Bookings: Contact Megan, cell: 076 412 4608, email: 2rivertrail@gmail.com.
Maps: Available.
Facilities/Activities: Two rustic hiking cottages with beds with mattresses, braai facilities, dining area, communal hot-water ablutions and washing-up facilities. Two self-catering farm cottages.
Activities: Birding.
Pertinent information: Maximum group size is 12.

The Two River Trail meanders between the Kariega and Assegaai rivers on Mossland, a dairy farm with a history going back to the arrival of the British Settlers in the Eastern Cape in 1820. The trail alternates between farmland pastures, pockets of indigenous forest and valley bushveld vegetation characterised by tall tree euphorbias, aloes and diverse succulents.

Mammals you might chance upon include the diminutive blue duiker, common duiker, grysbok and bushbuck. Also keep an eye out for bushpig and mountain reedbuck. With a bird checklist of over 190 species, the trails offer excellent birding opportunities.

The 20-km overnight trail starts at Reed Cabins, which overlooks a dam, and meanders for 10 km along the banks of the Assegaai River to Medbury Cottage, a renovated 1820 Settlers cottage, on the first day. The second day's hike (10 km) partly follows the historic Old Bay Road, built by Andrew Geddes Bain in 1844, and then takes hikers through the valley carved by the Kariega River, a Khoekhoen name said to mean 'river of many steenbok', back to the start. Hikers can also opt to do the full 20-km hike in one day. This option should only be attempted by fit hikers.

The two day hikes partly follow the same route as the overnight trail before looping back to the start at Alldays and Onion cottages. **8.5 km; 4 hours, and 15 km; 7 hours; circular.**

53. ASSEGAAI TRAILS
Makhanda (Grahamstown)

Trails: 4 trails; 5 to 7.5 km; linear and circular.

Bookings: Assegaai Trails, tel: (046) 622 8619, cell: 082 445 1042, email: assegaaitrails@imaginet.co.za, www.assegaaitrails.co.za.
Maps: Colour map.
Facilities/Activities: Two hikers' camps with bunk beds, mattresses, hot showers, flush toilets and braai places; self-catering cottages; accommodation for groups.
Pertinent information: Temperatures can be very high in summer. It is advisable to treat boots and socks with a tick repellent.

Permits: Contact George Euvrard, cell: 082 921 2690, email: g.euvrard@ru.ac.za, www.indlelayobuntu.com.
Maps: Daily trail maps given to participants.
Facilities/Activities: Dinner, bed and breakfast provided. Accommodation and meals vary depending on overnight stop.
Pertinent information: Pilgrimage walks take place on scheduled dates. Groups are limited to a maximum of 12 people (including leader and driver). Trailists must provide their own sleeping bag and backpack and must arrange their own transport from the end point of the trail.

The walks that make up the Assegaai Trails, a network of four trails, owe their collective name to the Assegaai River that meanders through what was once a thriving pineapple farm. Now a private nature reserve, the former farm has been stocked with a variety of game: Burchell's zebra, giraffe, bushbuck, grey rhebok, common duiker and grysbok are among the species you are likely to encounter.

The vegetation varies from lush riverine forest and open grassland to wooded kloofs and valley bushveld. The diverse habitats and the Assegaai River attract a rich variety of birds and to date more than 180 bird species have been recorded here.

Although the distances are short, the terrain is undulating and the trails are graded as moderate.

Hikers have a choice of four colour-coded routes: **Blue Trail** (5 km), **Yellow Trail** (6.5 km), **Red Trail** (7.5 km) and **Purple Trail** (7.5 km).

All the trails have been linked with pink-coded paths to allow hikers to extend or shorten their chosen routes. Picnic facilities have been provided along the four trails and there are several delightful swimming stops along the way in which to cool down in the heat of summer.

54. INDLELA YOBUNTU PILGRIMAGE ADVENTURE WALKS
Makhanda (Grahamstown) to Cape Town

Trails: Guided pilgrimage walks on various sections of the trail. Daily distances vary between 18 and 33km.

When George Euvrard of Rhodes University in Makhanda did the well-known Camino de Santiago pilgrimage trail in Spain in 2008, it inspired him to create an African pilgrimage trail. This trail will ultimately stretch for 1,200 km from Grahamstown to Cape Town, following back roads and little-used jeep tracks. Pilgrims sleep on farms and at churches along the way.

Two sections of the trail have already been opened. The 'Crossing Over' section (Makhanda to Patensie) covers 275 km and is walked in 13 days, while the 'Kom Nader' section (Patensie to Knysna) covers 325 km and takes 14 days. The remaining 600 km of the trail is under development.

55. KOWIE CANOE/HIKING TRAIL
Port Alfred

Trails: 42 km canoeing out-and-return; 2 walks; 6 km and 12 km; circular.
Bookings: Cell: 082 491 0590, email: kowietrails@imaginet.co.za.
Maps: Not available.
Facilities/Activities: Wooden 4-room chalet, bunks, mattresses, small gas cooker, pots, kettle, crockery, cutlery, firewood, braai grid, cold-water showers, flush toilet.

This unique combination of canoeing and hiking, the only adventure of its kind in South Africa, starts at the small boat harbour at Port Alfred. After about 4 to 5 hours of paddling up the Kowie River, you reach the overnight hut, situated below the cliffs on the eastern bank of the river at Horseshoe Bend.

Birdlife is prolific and the African fish eagle, pied and giant kingfishers, Egyptian goose and white-breasted cormorant are likely to be seen while you paddle up the river, while the Knysna turaco also occurs.

A two-night stay will enable you to enjoy the peace and tranquillity of the Waters Meeting Nature Reserve – which is named after the point where the fresh water of the meandering Kowie River meets the sea water when the high tide pushes some 25 km upstream – and to explore the reserve.

From the hut, hikers can set off on two circular trails (6 km; 2 hours ,and 12 km; 3.5 hours). Covering 4,247 ha, the reserve's vegetation is dominated by dense valley bushveld, and tall euphorbias, cycads, aloes, wild date palms, wild banana (*Strelitzia nicolai*) and yellowwoods are conspicuous. Mammals to be on the lookout for include kudu, bushbuck, bushpig, baboon, vervet monkey, otter and blue duiker.

56. GREAT FISH RIVER RESERVE
Peddie

Trails: Guided walk; approximately 1.5 hours.
Permits: Entrance fee. Guided walks are conducted from Mvubu Camp along the Great Fish River. Book in advance with reserve, cell: 060 978 5573. Accommodation must be booked with the Eastern Cape Parks Board, P O Box 11235, Southernwood, East London 5200, tel: (043) 705 4400,

fax: 086 611 1123, email: reservations@ecparks.co.za.
Maps: Sketch map of reserve.
Facilities/Activities: Self-catering lodges; self-guided game drives; picnic sites; freshwater angling.

The Great Fish River Reserve complex, which bisects the Great Fish River, protects one of the best examples of valley bushveld vegetation in South Africa. Covering 45,000 ha, the complex comprises the Double Drift Game Reserve, the adjoining Andries Vosloo Kudu Reserve and the Sam Knott Nature Reserve.

In the northern part of this reserve is a fenced-off game-viewing area. Three of the Big Five, namely elephant, black rhino and buffalo, have been reintroduced. Other species occurring here include giraffe, kudu, eland, blue mountain reedbuck, red hartebeest, waterbuck, Burchell's zebra and impala, as well as numerous small mammal species. Hippo have been released in the Great Fish River.

The area is rich in the legacies of the frontier wars fought here between the early white settlers, the San, the Khoikhoi, the Xhosa and the British during the eighteenth and nineteenth centuries. Reminders of this turbulent era, which spanned almost a hundred years, include the ruins of several forts that once formed part of the Cape Colony's defences. Fort Willshire dates back to 1819, while Fort Double Drift and Fort Montgomery and the Botha's Post Garrison were built later. Fort Double Drift, with its imposing towers and perimeter walls, stands in a valley in the reserve.

57. HOGSBACK WALKS
Hogsback

Trails: 3 to 20 km; 1 to 6 hours; network.
Permits: Obtain from Visitor Information Centre.
Maps: Obtain from Visitor Information Centre.
Facilities/Activities: Hotels; guesthouses; camping site.

Pertinent information: Snakes (boomslang, cobras and puff adders) are plentiful, so you must be alert, especially in spring and summer.

Maps: Not available, but trails are clearly marked.
Facilities/Activities: Picnic area with braai places, tables and benches, toilets, lapa and safe parking.

Situated below the three ridged peaks of Hogsback, to which the mountain village owes its name, Hogsback is renowned for its beautiful indigenous forest, mountain streams, cascades and numerous magnificent waterfalls. The village is also well known for its masses of azaleas, rhododendrons and crabapple trees, which burst into bloom in spring.

A network of trails traverses the indigenous Auckland Forest along footpaths signposted with pig emblems. The pigs were emblazoned in different colours along the various walks years ago by the Hogsback Inn and are described in what are known as Piggy Books, on sale in the village.

Among the many attractions along these walks are waterfalls, with alluring names, and Hogsback's famous Big Tree. Also known as the Eastern Monarch, this ancient Outeniqua yellowwood towers 34 m above the forest floor. Among the splendid waterfalls are the 39 Steps, Madonna and Child, Swallowtail, Bridal Veil and Kettlespout. The last is so named because, when the southeaster wind blows strongly, water falling down the natural spout of the cliffs is blown back, creating what looks like steam.

Other trails lead through pine plantations to Tor Doone (1,565 m high) and if you are prepared for a full day's hike it is a steady climb to the summit of the 1,963-m-high Gaika's Kop. Another option is to hike to the base of the three Hogsback peaks. There are various explanations of the origin of the name Hogsback. Among these is that the rocky krantzes of the three Hogsback peaks resembles the bristles on the back of a hog. The name was originally given to what's now known as Hogsback Mountain.

58. KOLOGHA FOREST TRAILS
Stutterheim

Trails: 3 trails; 1 to 8 hours; out-and-return and circular.
Permits: Not required.

Situated at the eastern end of the Amatola Mountains, the indigenous forests at Stutterheim are one of the largest remaining tracts of natural forests in South Africa. The mistbelt caused by the progressive warming of the moist ocean air as it ascends the Escarpment results in rainfall throughout the year on the mountain's southern slopes, giving rise to delightful waterfalls, cascades and streams.

Outeniqua yellowwood is the dominant tree species, while the real yellowwood is also common. Knobwood, easily identified by its distinctive bark studded with big conical knobs, tree fuchsia, Cape chestnut and lemonwood are among the other species flourishing in the forest. A variety of ferns, clivias, spurflowers (*Plectranthus*) and the mauve twin sisters (*Streptocarpus rexii*) adorn the forest floor.

Samango monkey and tree dassie inhabit the trees, while the forest floor is home to bushpig, porcupine and the diminutive blue duiker. Small predators also occur but are seldom seen.

Be on the lookout for the Cape parrot, which is critically endangered and is restricted to the Afromontane forests of the Eastern Cape, Magoebaskloof and the Xumeni Forest in KwaZulu-Natal. Other typical forest birds include the Knysna turaco, the elusive Narina trogon, African olive pigeon, cardinal woodpecker and chorister robin-chat.

The trails start at the picnic site in the Kologha Forest Reserve and are clearly marked with colour-coded footprints.

The **Blue Trail** is an easy, but enjoyable ramble suitable for families. The trail winds along a stream with three delightful waterfalls and although you will walk on a wooden boardwalk for much of the way, there are some steep ascents. You then retrace your tracks back to the start. **3 km; 1 hour; out-and-return.**

The outward leg of the **Yellow Trail** meanders through the forests higher up on the mountain slope, and along the way you will pass two delightful waterfalls. After a steep descent you join a forestry road which takes you back to the start. **7 km; 3 hours; circular.**

The **Red Trail** initially follows the Yellow Trail and then zigzags steeply out of the forest onto the plateau. Here your efforts will be rewarded with expansive views over Stutterheim, Mount Kubusie and the patchwork of pine plantations and indigenous forest far below. The route then descends steadily and joins the return leg of the Yellow Trail. **17 km; 8 hours; circular.**

59. AMATOLA HIKING TRAIL
King William's Town/Hogsback

Trails: 100 km; 6 days; open-ended; 38 km; 2 days; circular.
Bookings: Permits only available through Amatola Trails. Book online at www.amatolatrails.co.za.
Maps: Available.
Facilities: Overnight huts with bunk beds, mattresses, showers, toilets and braai facilities.
Pertinent information: Amatola Trails offers various packages that include the permit fee, pre- and post-hike accommodation (dormitories or camping) at Hogsback, shuttle from Hogsback to the start, safe parking and hikers' assistance. Except for the first day, the trail covers long distances with steep ascents and descents and should only be attempted by very fit hikers. The cooler winter months are the best time for hiking, but even in winter you could have rain and the occasional snowfall. Sections of the trail can become very slippery during rain, while mist is not uncommon at higher elevations, especially during the summer months.

1. Amatola Hiking Trail From Maden Dam the first day's hike (11.9 km; 6 hours) makes its way through the Pirie Forest, a magnificent patch of indigenous forest. Although it is the shortest day of the trail, it is a steady ascent and you will gain about 750 m in altitude before reaching Gwiligwili Hut.

On the second day (19.4 km; 9 hours), the trail ascends through the Abafazi Forest and grasslands and then continues steadily through the Mvulu Forest and the Dontsa Main Forest. The path then drops down, crossing several streams with delightful waterfalls and pools in the Galarta Forest before heading up the Ngobazana River Valley to the Dontsa Hut.

The third day (20.6 km; 10 hours) is the longest and most difficult, making a very early start essential. The trail starts with a steady ascent through indigenous forest until you emerge into open fynbos on Mount Thomas, and continues to ascend steadily over the next few kilometres. It then descends to the Eseka Valley, where there is a series of delightful pools. From here the trail continues to the Cata Forest Station and over the final 5 km gains some 500 m in altitude through the appropriately named Waterfall Forest, with its numerous cascading splendours, to Cata Hut.

The fourth day's hike (14.5 km; 7 hours) starts with a steep climb along a tributary of the Cata River. A short way beyond the 2-km mark you have the option of heading for the nek between the two Geju peaks or following a loop to the left. The latter winds close to the edge of the cliffs and should be avoided in misty or bad weather. Along the way you will enjoy sweeping views of Gaika's Kop, Elandsberg and the Keiskamma basin far below. From Geju Peak (1,850 m), the highest point of the trail, you descend steadily along a kloof clad in indigenous forest to Mnyameni Hut.

On day five (19.4 km; 9 hours) the trail ascends through indigenous forest and along the ridge behind the highest of the Hogsback peaks (1,937 m). The route then descends along the Wolf River, where numerous crystal clear pools are especially inviting on a hot day. After following the river for about 3 km, the trail climbs out of the valley, traversing fynbos and grasslands, and then descends through the Schwarzwald Forest to Zingcuka Hut.

After making your way through the Schwarzwald Forest at the start of day six (16.2 km; 8 hours), a steep climb up the slopes of the Hogsback peaks awaits you and you will gain some 800 m in altitude. The trail then descends into the Tyume River Valley and the end of the trail. You can either follow the easy Wolf River Ridge road for 4 km to Hogsback or make your way through the Auckland Forest past the Madonna and Child waterfall to the Big Tree and Hogsback. **100 km; 6 days; open-ended.**

2. Zingcuka Loop Trail starts 3 km from Hogsback on the Wolf Ridge Road, at the western end of the Amatola Hiking Trail. The first day's hike (22 km; 7 hours) climbs out of the Tyume River, ascending steadily to a nek between the Hogsback peaks. The route then winds down the Wolf River, where hikers can refresh themselves in the inviting mountain pools. Leaving the Mnyameni Valley, the trail ascends and then goes along the edge of Zingcuka Krantz before dropping down sharply to the overnight hut. On the return leg (16 km; 6 hours) the same route is followed as on day six of the Amatola Hiking Trail, namely a demanding climb to the rocky ridge of Hogsback Peak, followed by a descent to the Tyume River/Wolf Ridge Road. **38 km; 2 days; circular.**

60. PIRIE FOREST
King William's Town

> **Trails:** 2 walks; both 3 hours; circular and out-and-return.
> **Permits:** Not required, but the register at the information kiosk must be signed.
> **Maps:** Indicated on Amatola Hiking Trail map available from Department of Agriculture, Forestry and Fisheries, Private Bag X7485, King William's Town 5600, tel. and fax: (043) 642 2571, cell: 082 886 1061, e-mail: amatolhk@dwaf.gov.za.
> **Facilities/Activities:** Picnic sites at Maden Dam; information kiosk.

Situated in the transitional zone between the indigenous forests of the southern Cape and the more subtropical forests of the northern part of the Eastern Cape and KwaZulu-Natal, the Pirie Forest is an excellent example of typical Eastern Cape, indigenous high forest. The indigenous forests are dominated by Outeniqua and real yellowwoods, while stinkwood, Cape chestnut, red currant,

Cape beech, forest elder and lemonwood are also to be seen here. The forests reach up to 25 m in height and are an excellent example of the high forests typical of the Eastern Cape. These forests comprise some 250 woody species – double that of the southern Cape forests. Unlike the southern Cape forests with their luxuriant undergrowth, there is very little undergrowth because of the dense canopy. The mauve *Streptocarpus* and several ground and tree orchids are among the eye-catching flowering species of the forest to look out for. At higher elevations the forests are replaced by dense sour grassveld which has been invaded by fynbos and grassland vegetation. Typical fynbos species include the common sugarbush and the white sugarbush (*Protea lacticolor*).

Exploitation of the forest began in 1819 when trees were felled to build Fort Willshire on the Keiskamma River. In the late 1890s the sole right to extract wood from the forest was granted to Mr J E Howse, and reminders of this era can still be seen more than a century later (see under 'Pirie Walk', below).

The two walks start at the information kiosk above Maden Dam, reached 11 km off the King William's Town/Stutterheim road.

1. Pirie Walk follows the track of the 4-km-long narrow-gauge railway line that linked Howse's sawmill to Timber Square, where, between 1910 and 1917, the logs were loaded onto a 5-ton locomotive and transported to the mill. Still to be seen here are a section of the original track, hand-hewn lemonwood sleepers, and a trestle bridge across the Hutching's Stream. At Timber Square the trail splits off the Amatola Hiking Trail (see p. 135) and after crossing the Buffalo River meanders along the banks of the river, through indigenous forest, back to the start. **9 km; 3 hours; circular.**

2. Sandile's Walk honours the Paramount Chief of the amaRharhabe clan of the Xhosa nation, Sandile, who led his people in three Frontier Wars against the British military. During the 1877–8 Frontier War, Sandile used the Pirie Forest and a deep cave at the base of what became known as Sandile's Krantz as a refuge. He was shot dead in a skirmish with the volunteer forces of Captain Lonsdale in May 1877 and buried with full military honours at the foot of Mount Kemp on 9 June 1878.

Sandile's Walk leads along the western bank of Maden Dam and, after crossing the Buffalo River and Artillery Stream, steadily ascends through indigenous forest to Sandile's Cave. Carry water and take a torch to explore the cave. **9 km; 3 hours (or 4 hours if exploring the cave); out-and-return.**

61. WILD COAST AMBLE
Qolora River to Glen Garriff

Trail: 56 km; 4 days; open-ended (transfer provided).
Permits: Wild Coast Holiday Reservations, P O Box 8017, Nahoon 5210, tel: (043) 743 6181, fax: (043) 743 6188, email: meross@iafrica.com.
Maps: Trail brochure with map.
Facilities/Activities: A combination of hotels and cabanas for five nights. The last night at Glen Gariff can be substituted for a night at Inkwenkwezi Game Reserve.
Pertinent information: Fully inclusive package including transfers from and back to East London, hotel accommodation with all meals for five nights and the services of a guide. Porters can be hired to carry hikers' backpacks, which must be kept below 10 kg each.

Starting at either Trennery's or Seagulls Beach Hotel, the first day's hike of 12 km ends at Morgan Bay. The trail follows the same route as the Strandloper Hiking Trails (this page). Overnight accommodation is provided at Morgan Bay, Haga Haga, Cintsa East and Glen Garriff.

62. WILD COAST MEANDER
Kob Inn to Morgan Bay

Trail: 56 km; 5 days; open-ended (transfer provided).

Permits: Wild Coast Holiday Reservations, P O Box 8017, Nahoon 5210, tel: (043) 743 6181, fax: (043) 743 6188, email: meross@iafrica.com.
Maps: Trail brochure with map.
Facilities/Activities: Hotel accommodation for five nights.
Pertinent information: Fully inclusive package including transfers from and back to East London, hotel accommodation with all meals for five nights and the services of a guide. Porters can be hired to carry hikers' backpacks, which must be kept below 10 kg each.

The section of the coastline between the Qora River and Morgan Bay has proved a popular holidaying and angling destination for many years, and this packaged hike allows hikers to explore this part of the Wild Coast in real luxury.

The trail alternates between beach walking and hiking over grassy headlands with a number of river crossings. Daily distances are generally short – between 6 and 21 km – leaving ample opportunity for hikers to enjoy the superb scenery. The area is of historic interest, as it was at the enchanted pools in the Gxara River where Nongqawuse heard the voices that prompted the slaughter of livestock and resulted in the national suicide of the Xhosa people in 1856–7.

Hotel accommodation is provided at Kob Inn, Mazeppa Bay, Wavecrest, Trennery's or Seagulls Beach, and Morgan Bay Hotel.

63. STRANDLOPER HIKING TRAILS
Kei Mouth

Trails: 2 trails; 57 km; 3 nights/4 days; open-ended. 42 km; 4 nights/5 days; open-ended (transfer provided for Strandloper Sundowner Trail).
Permits: The Reservations Manager, Strandloper Hiking Trail, P O Box 86, Kei Mouth 5260, tel. and fax: (043) 841 1046, email: info@strandlopertrails.co.za.

Maps: Trail map and information brochure.

Facilities/Activities: Strandloper Hiking Trail: overnight huts with bunks, mattresses, fireplaces (except at Cape Henderson Hut) and water. Strandloper Sundowner Trail: fully inclusive package on DBB-basis, picnic lunch, shuttle and baggage transfers.

Pertinent information: Many rivers are crossed; carry a tide table and plan to cross at the turn of low tide or beginning of an incoming tide. Take precautions against sunburn. Fires are not allowed at Cape Henderson Hut and you will need to carry a backpacking stove.

On these trails you follow in the footsteps of the San and Khoikhoi who exploited the marine resources along the coast, and in those of the hapless mariners who were cast ashore after their ships ran aground. Among the shipwrecked vessels is thought to be the famed *Santo Alberto*, wrecked off Cintsa East in 1593. The route takes you along rocky shores and sandy beaches, and through grassland and coastal bush.

1. Strandloper Hiking Trail was first established in the 1980s and was revived more recently by the Strandloper Ecotourism Board.

The trail starts at the Strandloper Ecotourism Centre at Cape Morgan, where you will meet the Trail Manager. The first day's hike (15.75 km) incorporates an 8.75-km circuit of the town of Kei Mouth, the Kei River and coastal walking. The next 7 km (3 hours) is over uneven, rocky terrain and a long sandy beach to Morgan Bay. From here the trail heads through grassland above the Morgan Bay cliffs before returning to the coastline, which you follow to Double Mouth Hut.

Soon after setting off on day two (14 km; 7 hours) you cross the Quko River Estuary and the trail then passes Bead Beach. Beyond Haga Haga, the coastline is characterised by a wave-cut platform and there are numerous opportunities for snorkelling in the gullies.

From the Cape Henderson Hut, the first 10 km of the third day's hike (13 km; 5 hours) is along a wide sweep of sandy beach, with four estuaries to be crossed. You will reach Beacon Valley Hut a short way beyond Cintsa East and Cintsa West.

The final day's hike (14 km; 5 hours) makes its way to Gonubie, mainly along the rocky coastline. **57 km; 3 nights/4 days; open-ended.**

2. Strandloper Sundowner Trail Hikers on this trail have the luxury of carrying only a daypack. Hikers are transferred from Cintsa East to Trennery's Hotel on the first day of the hike. From here you can walk to the wreck of the *Jacaranda* or opt for another excursion. On the second day's hike you head for Kei Mouth/Morgan Bay. The sheer Morgan Bay cliffs are a highlight of the third day's hike to Haga Haga. All but the first 4 km of the final day's hike to Cintsa East is along a magnificent stretch of sandy beach. **42 km; 4 nights/5 days; open-ended (transfer included).**

64. PORT ST JOHNS TO COFFEE BAY HIKING TRAIL
Port St Johns to Coffee Bay

Trail: 81 km; 5 hike days; linear; guided.
Bookings: Active Escapes, tel: (033) 329 5259, email: tours@active-escapes.co.za.
Maps: *Wild Coast: The Touring Map* by Slingsby Maps. Online orders http://slingsby-maps.myshopify.com.
Facilities/Activities: Accommodation for 6 nights at homestays (village homes) and backpackers, dinners and breakfasts at village homes and dinners at backpackers. Optional upgrades to more upmarket accommodation on some nights.
Pertinent information: Price includes return shuttles to Mthata and Port St Johns. Hikers must be fit, as the trail traverses undulating terrain with steep ascents and descents and includes long stretches of beach walking. Hikers also negotiate exposed steep-sided hill slopes.

Starting at Second Beach, Port St Johns, the first day's hike (18 km; 6 to 7 hours) meanders through dune forest in the Silaka Nature Reserve, past Sugarloaf Rock and down to the Mngazi River. From here the beach is followed to the first overnight stop at the Mngazana River with its large estuary.

The second day's hike (14 km; 4 to 5 hours) is mainly on inland footpaths, with several ascents and descents, passing rural villages and forested valleys. Mpande Beach, just south of the Sinangwana River, is the second overnight stop.

From Mpande Beach the trail (18 km; 6 to 7 hours) again winds inland until you descend to the Mnenu River. The trail then continues along the coast to the Hluleka Nature Reserve and the homestay overnight stop just outside the reserve.

Day four (21 km; 8 hours), the longest leg, features undulating hills and pretty coves, such as those at Banana and Strachan's bays. After crossing the mangrove-lined Mtakatje River, the route continues to Presley Bay, Lwandile and the overnight stop at Mdumbi.

The final day is a mere 10 km and after crossing the Mthata River you head over the hills to reach Coffee Bay after a four-hour walk.

65. PONDO VOYAGER HIKING TRAIL
Mtamvuna River to Mbotyi

Trails: 73.5 to 77.5 km; 5 hike days; linear; guided except through Mkambati Nature Reserve.
Bookings: Active Escapes, tel: (033) 329 5259, email: tours@active-escapes.co.za.
Maps: *Wild Coast: The Touring Map* by Slingsby Maps. Online orders http://slingsby-maps.myshopify.com.
Facilities/Activities: Accommodation for 5 nights – 1 village homestay, 1 eco-backpackers, 2 tented camps and 1 night lodge with meals as specified. Canoes are available at the Mtentu and Msikaba overnight stops.
Pertinent information: Package includes return transfer to Port Edward/Wild Coast Casino Hotel.

The 125-km stretch of the Wild Coast between the Mtamvuna River at Port Edward and the Mzimvubu River at Port St Johns is without doubt one of the most beautiful stretches of coastline in the world. Dramatic cliffs, rolling hills, tranquil estuaries, unspoilt beaches and fascinating rock formations sculpted by the ocean characterise the coast. Set against the grassy slopes and ridges of the rolling hills dropping down to the sea are the rondavel homesteads of the amaPondo people.

This section of the Wild Coast falls within the Pondoland Centre of the Maputaland-Pondo Region of biological diversity and endemism – one of 34 floristic hotspots on earth. Over 200 of the more than 2,250 plant species occurring in the Pondoland Centre are endemic. The vegetation is dominated by grasslands, extending down to the sea at places, with patches of coastbelt dune forest and a few small mangrove communities. The northern banks of the Mtentu and Msikaba rivers are the only places in the world where the endemic Pondo palm occurs.

Among the more than 200 bird species recorded here are the African fish eagle, several kingfisher species, including the mangrove kingfisher, and a variety of seabirds. The sheer cliffs of the Mtentu and Msikaba gorges provide nesting and roosting places for Cape vultures.

The 5-day Pondo Voyager Hiking Trail stretches between the Wild Coast Casino and Mbotyi along one of the most spectacular coastlines in the world. It alternates between walking along the beach and footpaths close to the shore, but where the coastline becomes impassable, the trail heads inland. You will also pass by settlements and homesteads, providing a fascinating insight into the rural way of life of the amaPondo people.

About 2 km after setting off on the first day (14 km; 7 hours), the trail passes the Mzamba cretaceous deposits, the earliest Upper Cretaceous fossil deposit known, dating back to between 80 and 86 million years ago. Here, numerous tree trunks, marine shells, ammonites and sea urchins are exposed at low tide in the rocky reefs and in a 10 m-high cliff. From here, the route alternates between the sandy beach and footpaths close to the coast until you reach Mnyameni, the first overnight stop.

The second day's hike (12 to 14 km; 6 to 7 hours) follows the beach and footpaths until the Shikombe River is reached. Here, the coastline becomes too rocky and the route takes you over a hill before dropping down to the Mtentu River, the second overnight stop. The Mtentu forms the northern boundary of the Mkambati Nature Reserve.

After crossing the Mtentu River on day three (12 to 15 km; 6 to 7 hours), hikers can explore the Mkambati Nature Reserve. Attractions include the Mtentu Gorge, Horseshoe Falls and Four Waterfalls Viewpoint. The day's hike ends on the southern bank of the Msikaba River.

From Msikaba the trail on day four (16 km; 8 hours) follows the coastline past Kilroe Beach to Port Grosvenor, where a derelict tunnel is a reminder of the numerous attempts to recover the fabled riches of the *Grosvenor*, which ran aground on 2 August 1782. Flat rock shelves extending into the sea characterise the coast between the Mkweni River and Luphuthana, where the fourth overnight stop is made. During high tide the spray of the pounding breakers shoots up to 15 m in the air.

The final day's hike (18.5 km; 8 hours) is the longest, but also the most spectacular, so an early start is essential. The route continues along the coast past Top Hat, a flat rock resembling a top hat, and after about an hour you will reach Grotto Cave at the start of Waterfall Bluff. The Mlambomkulu Falls, one of only 19 waterfalls that drop directly into the sea, is reached a short way on. You will have to retrace your tracks for a short way as the trail veers inland onto Waterfall Bluff and crosses the river about 1 km inland, where there are some inviting pools – an ideal place for a rest and a swim.

Other highlights of Waterfall Bluff, which extends for about 5 km along the coast, include Cathedral Rock, a huge sea stack with the breakers pounding through its arches, the 80-m-high Mfihlelo Falls, which also plunge directly into the sea, and the Citadel. After ascending Mgcagcama Hill, Drew's Camp is passed and the final stretch of the hike is along the beach to Mbotyi with its beautiful lagoon.

66. WILD COAST PONDO WALK
Lusikisiki

Trail: 3 multi-directional day walks; 13 to 22 km per day; 6 to 9 hours per day; circular.

Permits: Wild Coast Holiday Reservations, P O Box 8017, Nahoon 5210, tel: (043) 743 6181, fax: (043) 743 6188, email: meross@iafrica.com.

Facilities/Activities: Accommodation at Mbotyi River Lodge, inclusive of meals, guides and transfers to and from certain sections; optional visit to a Xhosa village; horse-riding; canoeing; angling.

With Mbotyi River Lodge as a base, there are guided walks to some of the most dramatic sights along the Pondoland Coast.

On the first day (13 km; 6 hours) the walk follows the unspoilt coastline south to Ilityelentaka (Bird Rock) and alternates between sandy beaches and rocky headlands. The return route makes its way inland over grassy hills and past traditional Xhosa villages. Along the way hikers are rewarded with stunning views of the coast, valleys and patches of lush indigenous forest.

The second day's hike to Waterfall Bluff and back covers 22 km (9 hours) and this coastline is regarded as one of the most spectacular sections of the Wild Coast. The near-vertical sandstone cliffs of Waterfall Bluff tower some 100 m above the ocean for about 6 km along the coast and up to 5 km inland. Cathedral Rock, a huge rock formation with waves pounding through its arches, the Citadel rock formation and the Mfilelo Falls are among the many spectacular sights encountered along this route. The Mlambomkulu River has a series of pools and a waterfall that plunges directly into the sea.

On the third day (14 km; 6 hours) the trail meanders along a scenic valley dotted with patches of natural forest. The trail then ascends quite steeply before making its way down again into another valley with an 80-m-high waterfall and an inviting rock pool where weary hikers can cool off. The route is fairly demanding, but along the way hikers will be able to enjoy spectacular views and gain an insight into the daily lives of the amaPondo people.

67. LAMMERGEIER HIGHLANDS RESERVE
Lady Grey

Trails: 6 trails; 11 to 22 km; 5 hours to 2 days; out-and-return, open-ended and circular.
Bookings: Lammergeier Highlands Reserve, cell: 082 929 9729, email: info@adventuretrails.co.za, web: www.adventuretrails.co.za.
Maps: The trails are indicated on the 1:50,000 topographical map.
Facilities/Activities: Overnight huts with bunks, mattresses, hot showers, flush toilets and braai facilities; trout fishing; tubing; swimming; horse trails; greywing shooting.

The 7,500-ha Lammergeier Highlands Reserve lies in the Witteberg, the southwestern spur of the southern Drakensberg. The vegetation is typically grassland, and among the reserve's 282 bird species are the bearded vulture, or lammergeier (after which the reserve is named), Verreaux's eagle, Cape vulture and jackal buzzard. A 'vulture restaurant' (feeding station) offers good opportunities for viewing raptors. The trail network consists of several interlinked loops, offering a choice of hikes:

1. Black Eagle Trail leads into the Karringmelkspruit Valley, with its inviting pools, and further along offers great views of Olympus Gorge. From the Karringmelkspruit and Olympus Gorge junction the trail ascends to Olympus Hut. **11 km; 5 hours; out-and-return.**

2. Witteberg Sky Walk offers a strenuous walk to the summit of the Witteberg. Starting at Olympus Hut, the route ascends steeply up the mountain slopes, but the far-reaching views over the area north of the Kei River and Lesotho make this a worthwhile walk for fit hikers. **12 km; 6 hours; circular.**

3. Cheese Factory Trail is named after a cheese factory, which operated until 1929. From Olympus

Hut the trail follows the krantzes above the Karringmelkspruit and continues along the Five Oaks Valley past the Roman Baths (a lovely pool) to Upper Pelion Hut. **Distance and type not available; 5 to 6 hours.**

4. Pelion Valley Walk leads from Upper Pelion Hut along Pelion Valley, with its rich diversity of flora, pools and waterfalls. The Main Waterfall plunges 45 m into a pool, and a short detour leads to the nearby Hidden Waterfall. **11 km; 5 hours; out-and-return.**

5. Table Mountain Traverse From the Upper Pelion Hut the route descends into the Keiskamma Valley and then rises steeply to the summit of the flat-topped Table Mountain (not to be confused with Cape Town's famous World Heritage Site). After stopping to enjoy the views south towards Barkly East and Lesotho, you follow the trail down the mountain's western slopes to the starting point at Tempe. An alternative, as well as easier, option skirts the mountain. **Distance not available; 5 to 6 hours; open-ended.**

6. Snowdon Peak offers a challenging walk to the peak's 2,750-m-high summit. Cape and bearded vultures are often seen high up in the mountains. There are no facilities here and hikers must provide their own tents. **22 km; 2 days; out-and-return.**

68. TELLE FALLS HIKE
Rhodes

Trail: Approximately 13 km; 6 to 8 hours; out-and-return.
Permits: Not required. As Tiffindel Ski Resort is closed at the time of publication, it is advisable to make arrangements for a guide.
Maps: None.
Facilities/Activities: Various accommodation options are available in Rhodes.
Pertinent information: Check weather conditions the night before the planned hike. Beware of strong winds and

crumbling rock at the cliff edge near the waterfall.

Starting at Tiffindel Ski Resort on the slopes below Ben Macdhui, this difficult but rewarding trail leads to the 200-m-high Telle Falls, a spectacular waterfall seen by few people, owing to its remote location. From the resort the trail gains 280 m in altitude to the summit of the Drakensberg and then descends along the slopes above the Telle Valley. A pool below a small waterfall marks the halfway mark. The trail continues its descent along the western slopes of the valley to the waterfall. The return journey consists of a steep walk back to the Drakensberg summit. From here you retrace your tracks to the Tiffindel resort.

69. WOODCLIFFE CAVE TRAIL
Nqanqarhu (Maclear)

Trail: 54 km; 5 days; circular.
Bookings: Woodcliffe Country House, cell: 082 925 1030, email: info@woodcliffe. co.za, web: www.woodcliffe.co.za.
Maps: Photocopy of 1:50,000 map of area.
Facilities/Activities: Overnight huts and cave; water; firewood at Tok's Cave.

Situated in the Joelshoek Valley, this circular trail traverses a sheep and cattle farm, with scenery ranging from steep grassy hills and sandstone cliffs to mountain streams, with natural pools, and large patches of indigenous forest. Cave rock paintings are reminders of the original inhabitants, the San and the Khoikhoi.

Among the 170 bird species encountered here are the grey crowned crane, Cape and bearded vultures, Verreaux's eagle, mountain wheatear, mocking cliff-chat and African paradise flycatcher. Antelope species you may spot are the grey rhebok and mountain reedbuck. Porcupine, caracal and other species also occur, but are seldom seen.

The first day's hike (5 km; 1.5 hours) is an easy walk along a 4x4 track along the Little Pot River to Tok's Cave, an overhang with four huts built inside.

On the second day (13 km; 7 hours), you backtrack to Woodcliffe farmhouse and follow a circular route to Redcliffe Pool. From here the trail ascends to a saddle above a waterfall and then descends to Skinny Dip Pool before returning to Tok's Cave.

Day three (13 km; 7 hours) follows a jeep track to the base of the Drakensberg and climbs steeply along a ridge to Vlak Nek at the top of the High Berg. Then it is a gentle descent to the Reed Park overnight stop.

The fourth day's hike (13 km; 7.5 hours) begins with a steep climb to the Escarpment where hikers are rewarded with spectacular views of the landscape far below. The remainder of the day's hike follows Sephton's 4x4 Pass down to Wide Valley Hut.

Day five (10 km; 3 hours) follows a 4x4 track for 2 km and then climbs along a path to the top of a ridge before dropping down into Woodcliffe Valley. From the Pot River it's about an hour's walk to the end of the trail.

70. MEHLODING ADVENTURE TRAIL
Matatiele

Trail: 58 km; 4 days; open-ended.
Permits: Mehloding Community Trust, P O Box 406, Matatiele 4730, tel. and fax: (039) 737 3289, email: mehloding@ telkomsa.net
Facilities/Activities: Four overnight chalets with twin-bedded rooms or dormitories (linen and towels provided), hot showers, flush toilets, boma, communal lounge and kitchen; guided tours to a sangoma; horse-rides on Basotho ponies (suitable for beginners).
Pertinent information: The trail can be booked on a fully inclusive basis (dinner, bed and breakfast) or for self-catering. Transport back to the start can be arranged through the Trust.

This guided trail was launched in October 2003 by the Mehloding Community Trust, which aims to create work for residents of more than 25 villages in the northern Alfred Nzo region.

The trail passes through rural villages and follows stock paths through grassland, proteaveld and indigenous forest in the foothills of the southern Drakensberg. Attractions include rock painting sites, and along the way you will learn more about the medicinal uses of the plants and the culture and way of life of the people. The trail leads hikers along the foothills of the Eastern Cape Drakensberg and you will enjoy expansive views of the 'Berg'. Situated in the border region with Lesotho, it is not uncommon to meet Basotho, clad in their traditional blankets and travelling on horseback, along the trail. From Malekhalonyane Chalet, the first overnight hut near Motseng village, it is a 14-km (7-hour) hike to Makhulong Chalet below. The second day's hike (19.5 km; 8 hours) to Machekong Chalet is the longest. On the third day (12.5 km; 6 hours) the trail continues to Madlangala Chalet. Day four's hike (12 km; 6 hours) is a pleasant walk through a diversity of landscapes and vegetation types. The trail ends near Qachas Nek Border Post where hikers can be collected by prior arrangement with the Mehloding Community Trust.

UKHAHLAMBA-DRAKENSBERG & KWAZULU-NATAL

From the challenging mountain peaks of the uKhahlamba-Drakensberg and the rolling grasslands of the Midlands, to the pristine beaches of the Maputaland coast and the mosaic of wetlands that is St Lucia, KwaZulu-Natal offers an incredible diversity of landscapes and attractions. So it is perhaps not surprising that two of the first four World Heritage sites to be declared in South Africa, the iSimangaliso Wetland Park (formerly the Greater St Lucia Wetland Park) and the uKhahlamba-Drakensberg Park, are situated in the province.

The uKhahlamba-Drakensberg Park covers some 243,000 ha and stretches over a distance of 150 km, from Royal Natal in the north to the Mkhomazi Wilderness Area in the south. The park was created in 1986 when five former Natal Parks Board reserves were amalgamated with four wilderness areas and state-owned forestry land. The uKhahlamba-Drakensberg was proclaimed a World Heritage Site in 2000 and is one of only 23 'mixed' sites (one with cultural and natural significance) on the World Heritage List. Another exciting development involving the uKhahlamba-Drakensberg is the recent creation of the Maloti-Drakensberg Transfrontier Conservation Area (TFCA) with Lesotho. Of the TFCA's total 8,113 km^2, 5,170 km^2 (64 per cent) falls within Lesotho, while the remaining 2,943 km^2 (36 per cent) lies within South Africa. The TFCA aims to conserve the biodiversity and cultural resources of the Maloti-Drakensberg area and will be managed as an undivided ecosystem. It will also promote the economic development of the transfrontier area.

Part of the Southern African Escarpment, the uKhahlamba-Drakensberg is South Africa's highest and most spectacular mountain range. Several peaks rise over 3,000 m above sea level. Their isiZulu name, uKhahlamba, means 'barrier of spears'; in winter the highest peaks are covered in snow.

These mountains were once the stronghold of the San who left a rich legacy of rock art on the walls of caves and overhangs in the 'Berg', as the mountains are affectionately known to outdoor enthusiasts. With over 35,000 individual rock paintings, it has one of the largest concentrations of rock art in the world. Well-known sites include Battle Cave in Injisuthi, Main Caves in Giant's Castle, and Ndedema Gorge.

Those accustomed to the floral wealth of the Western Cape fynbos are often disappointed by the flora of the uKhahlamba-Drakensberg. However, to date more than 1,600 flowering plants and 72 fern species have been recorded here. Many species are obscured in the grasslands, or grow in protected places, and so are easily missed. Delightful patches of yellowwood forest occur in protected valleys and kloofs. Spring is full of surprises, as brown grass is brought to life, with numerous plants bursting into flower. In August the Natal bottlebrush with its magnificent red flowers is conspicuous among the Clarens sandstone cliffs.

The Berg's unique wetland system of marshes, lakes, vleis and networks of streams and rivers is of great natural significance. At least 36 plant species are unique to the 11 wetland plant communities occurring in the uKhahlamba-Drakensberg.

For bird-watching enthusiasts the uKhahlamba-Drakensberg offers several specials among the 246 species recorded to date. Heading the list is the rare bearded vulture, a species that has its last stronghold here. Its distinctive wedge-shaped tail and wingspan of between 2.5 m and 3 m make it easily identifiable in flight, as well as an unforgettable sight. It has extremely powerful wings, and gliding speeds of 105 km/h have been measured. The cliffs of the uKhahlamba-Drakensberg also serve as a refuge for the rare southern bald ibis and Cape vulture, while the wetlands provide a habitat for rare and endangered species such as the wattled crane and the striped flufftail. Other specials include the Drakensberg siskin and the Drakensberg rockjumper, as well as the yellow-breasted and mountain pipits.

The uKhahlamba-Drakensberg is the country's most popular walking and backpacking destination. Options range from numerous self-guided and interpretive walks in the Little Berg to overnight trails in remote wilderness areas. The Little Berg consists of the lower mountains and hills, below what is called the High Berg. Several passes link the Little Berg to the Escarpment, and there are dramatic hikes between the two.

Another unique area of KwaZulu-Natal is the iSimangaliso Wetland Park, awarded World Heritage status in 1999. It covers some 332,000 ha and has as its focal point Lake St Lucia, Africa's largest saltwater lake and home to the highest concentration of hippo and crocodile in South Africa.

The park consists of five distinct ecosystems: the marine ecosystem, with its sandy beaches and the southernmost coral reefs in the world; the forested dunes of the Eastern Shores; the 38,000-ha Lake St Lucia; the Western Shores with their sand forests and marine fossils; and the Mkhuze swamps.

With 521 bird species, the iSimangaliso Wetland Park offers exceptional birding. The lake supports large breeding colonies of pelicans, herons, storks, terns and a variety of waterfowl, while the patches of sand forest harbour species such as Neergaard's sunbird, eastern nicator and Rudd's apalis.

Four of the Big Five species (rhino, elephant, buffalo and leopard) occur in the park, and among the other mammals to be seen are reedbuck, blue wildebeest, waterbuck, nyala, impala, Burchell's zebra, and red duiker. Cheetah and a variety of smaller predators are also well represented.

Visitors can explore the park on foot, along many self-guided, interpretive walks laid out near the various rest camps, join a guided day walk or undertake a wilderness trail in the Tewate Wilderness Area along the Eastern Shores of the park.

In the northeastern corner of KwaZulu-Natal lies another unique tract of land, Maputaland. Bounded by the Ubombo and Lebombo mountains in the west, this fascinating region covers some 8,000 km² and encompasses the coastal plains from just south of the iMfolozi River, northwards, right up to the border with Mozambique.

Maputaland is a patchwork of forested dunes, swamp forest, marshes, lakes, grasslands and miles of pristine beaches. Among its many features is the Kosi Lake system with its raffia palms, palm-nut vultures and unique mangrove community. Other attractions include Lake Sibaya, the country's largest freshwater lake, the unique sand forests of Tembe Elephant Park and Ndumo Game Reserve. For those seeking an encounter with the Big Five, the Hluhluwe-iMfolozi Park offers a top-class wildlife experience. Hluhluwe and iMfolozi were proclaimed in 1897 as two separate parks. They, together with St Lucia Park, are the three oldest conservation areas in Africa. The first wilderness area in South Africa was set aside in iMfolozi in 1959, and it was here that the first guided wilderness trails were conducted. iMfolozi also played a crucial role in saving the white rhino from extinction, and the park has one of the largest populations of black rhino in the world. Opportunities to explore the park on foot range from guided game walks to overnight trails in the wilderness area.

Other scenic highlights of KwaZulu-Natal include the magnificent Mthamvuna and Oribi gorges in the south of the province. There are also several small, but worthwhile, nature reserves and green spaces within the densely populated urban areas of Pietermaritzburg and Durban.

KwaZulu-Natal enjoys a warm subtropical climate, but it is much cooler up in the mountains. Summers are hot and humid along the coast, while the winter months are pleasant. Further inland winter days are generally pleasant, but at night temperatures often drop to below 5 °C. Summer days in the interior are pleasant, as are the night-time temperatures.

In the uKhahlamba-Drakensberg foothills summer temperatures range between 13 and 32 °C. In winter they are generally between 5 and 16 °C, although they can drop to well below freezing.

KwaZulu-Natal has summer rain, which falls mainly between October and March in the heavy thunderstorms. The average annual rainfall over most of the uKhahlamba-Drakensberg is 1,250 mm, but as a general rule the rainfall increases from the valleys to the upper part of the Little Berg.

During summer the Little Berg and the summits are often blanketed by heavy cloud and mist, which can take up to two weeks to lift. Frost occurs about 150 nights a year, snow falls a few times a year. Although snow can be expected any time of year, it generally falls between April and September. In the southern Berg snowfalls are more frequent and heavier than in the northern Berg. Although usually restricted to the summit and near summit, snow occasionally reaches down to the 1,800-m level.

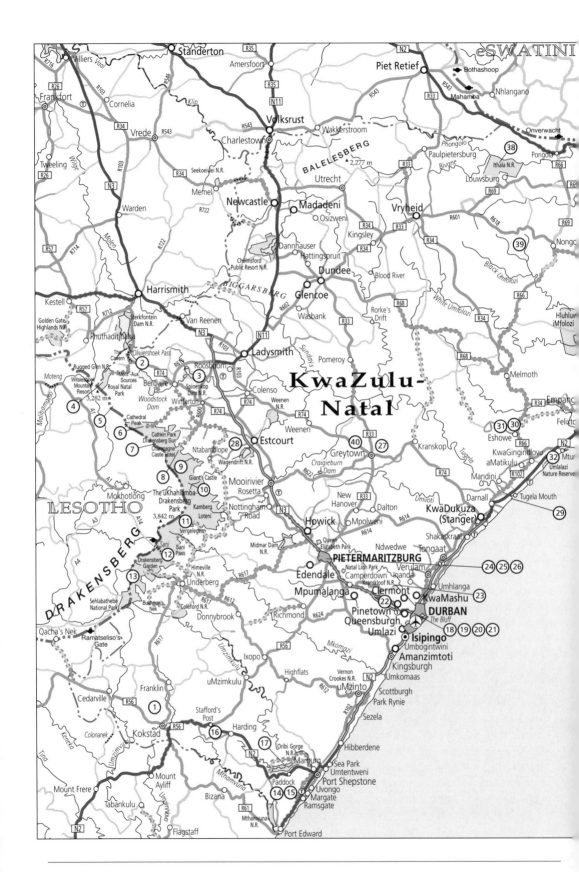

INDIAN
OCEAN

IMPORTANT INFORMATION

UKHAHLAMBA-DRAKENSBERG

Weather conditions here can change rapidly, and this range has probably claimed more lives than any other in South Africa. Always be prepared for adverse weather conditions and bear the following in mind when doing long walks or overnight hikes:

➤ Groups for overnight hikes are limited to a maximum of 12 persons.

➤ Do not venture into the High Berg if you are unfamiliar with the area.

➤ A good map is essential. The best maps are the six-part series of maps covering the entire uKhahlamba-Drakensberg from Mont-aux-Sources in the north to Sehlabathebe in the south. The maps are available from the Ezemvelo KZN Wildlife Reservation Office or Ezemvelo KZN Wildlife Drakensberg Centre.

➤ It is compulsory to complete the mountain register upon entering any of the mountain areas. Do this as accurately as possible as this information will speed up assistance or rescue operations, should these be necessary.

➤ On completion of your hike, note the time and date of your return in the register and inform the Officer-in-Charge.

➤ You can find yourself trapped in heavy mist, the visibility reduced to a few metres, with very little warning. Do not attempt to descend from the Escarpment. Rather pitch your tent and stay put until the mist lifts.

➤ Never pitch camp close to streams or rivers, as flash floods are not uncommon after heavy thunderstorms. These thunderstorms might break high in the catchment areas of rivers and you may not even be aware of them.

➤ In the event of snow, try to move to lower ground as soon as possible but, if the snow is too deep, try to get to the nearest cave or improvise an emergency shelter.

➤ Always carry at least two days' worth of high-energy spare rations in case you become trapped by mist or snow.

➤ There are certain caves that can be booked for the exclusive use of one group. Reservations should be made with the relevant Ezemvelo KZN Wildlife office.

➤ Even if you have booked a cave, you must always carry a tent, as bad weather or other factors may prevent you getting to it and force you to spend a night in the open.

➤ No open fires are permitted on trails in the Berg, so trailists must carry a lightweight backpacking stove and fuel.

➤ Other essentials for overnight hikes are a good down sleeping bag (rated at least -5 °C), a high-density ground pad, waterproof rain gear and cold-weather clothing.

➤ A valid passport is required for excursions beyond the Escarpment into Lesotho.

➤ Treat Basotho herdsmen that you might encounter on the Escarpment courteously.

SAFETY GUIDELINES

In view of sporadic attacks on hikers, especially on the Escarpment, the following safety measures are suggested:

➤ Contact the warden in charge of the area where you intend hiking to enquire about safety in the area.

➤ Groups should consist of at least four people, including an experienced leader who knows the Berg well.

➤ Avoid camping at the head of frequently used mountain passes or along major trails.

➤ Pitch tents in an inconspicuous place on high ground where you enjoy the advantage of visibility.

➤ Do not camp below rocky outcrops, as rocks can be hurled onto tents pitched below.

1. MOUNT CURRIE NATURE RESERVE
Kokstad

Trails: No demarcated trails, but hikers can follow old cattle tracks and paths.
Permits: Conservation fee. No permit required for hiking.
Maps: Not available.
Facilities/Activities: Camp sites (some with electrical plug points), communal dishwashing and hand laundry facility, communal ablutions with hot-water showers; angling, picnicking.
Pertinent information: Not necessary to book for camping, but overnight visitors must arrive before 18:00 when the reserve gate closes. It is advisable to hike in small groups in case of an accident or emergency.

The Mount Currie Nature Reserve is situated in the foothills of the southern KwaZulu-Natal Drakensberg. The area was used for grazing until it was declared a nature reserve in 1963 (the Phil Leary Nature Reserve). In 1981 it was declared a provincial nature reserve under the Natal Parks Board and renamed.

Covering 1,777 ha, the reserve is characterised by hills, ridges and deep river valleys. The landscape rises some 800 m from Crystal Dam at the lower end of the reserve to Mount Currie (2,224 m), which is capped by a 30-m-high band of sheer dolerite. Wetlands fed by springs occur between Crystal Spring and the Crystal Dam along the reserve's western boundary. The 28-ha Crystal Dam, the main source of water for Kokstad, is fed by water from the Crystal Spring and a tributary of the uMzimtlava River which flows into the dam.

The reserve is of great cultural and historical importance to the Griqua people who settled below the iconic Mount Currie. After leaving Philippolis in the southern Free State in 1862 with 2,000 people, 300 wagons and 20,000 head of livestock, under the leadership of Adam Kok III, they settled at Mount Currie in what was then known as Nomansland on 12 May 1863. The laager site where they lived until they relocated to Kokstad in 1872 and the foundations of Adam Kok's house were declared a national monument in 1949.

Mountain reedbuck and blesbok are common and there is a healthy population of oribi – an endangered species. Other antelope to be seen include grey rhebok, common duiker and bushbuck, while serval, Cape clawless and spotted-necked otters also occur.

The reserve has a bird list of some 230 species, including one of the highest densities of striped flufftail in the country. Grass owl, crowned crane and African marsh harrier are species to look out for in the wetlands and grasslands. Keep an eye out for Drakensberg rockjumper, sentinel rock thrush and Gurney's sugarbird in montane areas and on rocky slopes.

The vegetation is dominated by grasslands which are especially attractive in spring when a rich diversity of flowers burst into bloom. Common sugarbush (*Protea caffra*) and silver sugarbush (*Protea roupelliae*) are characteristic in open woodland areas, while stands of ouhout occur in the river valleys and along streams.

There are no demarcated trails, but hiking in the reserve will appeal to those who enjoy the freedom of blazing their own trails.

2. VERGEZIENT BERG TRAILS
Bergville

Trails: 2 day walks; both 13.5 km, with shorter options; network from base camp.
Bookings: Fagala Voet, cell: 082 776 5540 or 081 894 9802, email: bookings@fagalavoet.co.za or online at www.fagalavoet.co.za.
Maps: Trail map incorporated in trail pamphlet.
Facilities/Activities: Base camp with bunks/beds, mattresses; kitchen with fridge, microwave, three-plate cooker, pots, cooking utensils, crockery and cutlery; braai areas; showers and toilets.

The various trails at Vergezient Mountain Retreat are located on the edge of the uKhahlamba-Drakensberg Escarpment, and offer wonderful views of the Amphitheatre, Cathkin Peak and Champagne

Castle to the southeast, the Maluti Mountains to the southwest, and the town of Colenso to the east.

The trail network passes through open short grassland interspersed with proteas, kloofs with delightful patches of indigenous forest, tranquil streams, and two 40-m-high waterfalls. Hidden behind one of the waterfalls is an overhang decorated with rock paintings. Also of interest is a huge ancient landslide, which provides the setting for a rather unusual wetland.

Mountain reedbuck and blesbok count among the many animals you may see, while a rich diversity of birds is attracted by the varied habitats. For those interested in history, Retief Pass (along which the Voortrekkers first entered what is now KwaZulu-Natal in 1838) and the Retief Rock are situated nearby.

Trail possibilities include short strolls, three rambles ranging from one to three hours and two 13.5-km routes, which can be combined into an overnight trail from the base camp.

3. DISCOVERY TRAIL
Spioenkop Game Reserve, Bergville

Trails: 3 or 6 km; circular.
Permits: Conservation fee. No booking required for walk.
Maps: Trails are clearly marked.
Facilities/Activities: Fully equipped self-catering chalets; camp sites; Anglo-Boer War museum; watersports.

Spioenkop Game Reserve covers 5,400 ha of thornveld and grassland around Spioenkop Dam, which was completed in 1973. Numerous Late Iron Age stone structures testify to the presence of Late Iron Age people in the area.

The reserve owes its name to the highest hill in the vicinity, Spioenkop, meaning 'spy hill'. It was the setting for one of the bloodiest battles in KwaZulu-Natal during the South African War (1899–1902). While attempting to break through the Boer lines to relieve the siege of Ladysmith, the British suffered a crushing defeat against the Boers here on 24 January 1900.

White rhino, giraffe, Burchell's zebra and a variety of antelope have been reintroduced, among them eland, blesbok and waterbuck.

Some 290 bird species have been recorded to date, including Cape vulture, lammergeier, blue and crowned cranes, southern ground hornbill, grass owl and white-backed night heron.

The trail consists of two loops on the slopes overlooking the southern shores of the dam. The shorter option has a few short, steep climbs and descents, while the longer loop partly follows the shoreline of the dam.

4. ROYAL NATAL NATIONAL PARK
uKhahlamba-Drakensberg Park, Bergville

Trails: 24 walks; 45 minutes to 2 days; circular, out-and-return, open-ended.
Permits: Conservation fee. No permit required for walks.
Maps: Excellent guidebook with map.
Facilities/Activities: Self-catering accommodation; camp sites at Mahai and Rugged Glen; picnic sites; trout fishing; swimming; horse-riding.

Covering 8,094 ha in the northern uKhahlamba-Drakensberg, the Royal Natal National Park (the term 'royal' being added after a visit from the British royal family in 1947) is dominated by the awe-inspiring Amphitheatre, a sheer basalt wall that rises over 700 m above the Little Berg. This imposing natural wonder stretches from the Eastern Buttress, westwards, for 8 km to the Sentinel. The 500-m-high Tugela Falls, among the highest in the world, plunge over the edge of the Amphitheatre in five gigantic leaps. Other well-known attractions in the area include a sandstone formation, appropriately named the Policeman's Helmet, and the spectacular tunnel carved by the Tugela River.

The Amphitheatre wall forms an impressive backdrop to the Clarens sandstone formations of the Little Berg. At the lower elevations the vegetation is typically grasslands, with scattered stands of proteas, while indigenous forests of yellowwood, Cape beech, assegai and white stinkwood occur in sheltered valleys and kloofs. From the upper edge of the Little Berg to just below the summit, the vegetation is characterised by grasslands, with the alpine belt occurring above altitudes of 2,865 m. In this belt the grasslands are interspersed by *Erica* and *Helichrysum* species.

The park's bird list of over 130 species features several noteworthy birds, such as the bearded vulture, peregrine falcon, grey crowned crane, Drakensberg rockjumper, Cape grassbird and Gurney's sugarbird. Other species to keep an eye out for are the Cape vulture, Verreaux's eagle, Swainson's spurfowl, ground woodpecker, sentinel rock-thrush, white-starred robin and Cape longclaw.

Mammals are mainly small and nocturnal and thus easily overlooked. Among the more conspicuous species are grey rhebok, mountain reedbuck, klipspringer, common duiker, baboon and dassie. Carnivores include caracal and serval.

The park is traversed by a network of trails covering over 100 km, including six short walks, with a total duration of two hours or less.

Mahai Car Park

1. Cascades and McKinlay's Pool The trail follows the road past the trout hatchery and after about 15 minutes you will reach the Cascades, with its delightful setting against the backdrop of a patch of indigenous forest. The trail now continues along the left bank of the Mahai River to reach McKinlay's Pool at the junction of the Mahai and Gudu rivers, about 15 minutes beyond the Cascades. From here you can either retrace your tracks or continue with the path, which ascends steeply to Lookout Rock, where you join the Tiger Falls path. **8 km; 3 hours; circular.**

2. Fairy Glen and the Grotto Cross the Mahai River at the eastern end of the camping site and follow the Fairy Glen and Sunday Falls path. Just before the path crosses the Golide Stream, the Fairy Glen route turns off to the left, ascending gently to Fairy Glen, a popular picnic spot. From here the trail ascends steadily to below the Plowman's Kop cliffs, where you turn right. A short way on the path zigzags steeply and then levels off before reaching a split. The left-hand path leads to the head of the Grotto, where a waterfall plunges over the cliffs. Despite the name, the Grotto is not a cave, but two impressive gorges eroded through the sandstone. **10 km; 4 hours; out-and-return.**

3. Gudu Falls, the Crack and Mudslide Initially this trail follows the Tiger Falls path, which you join behind the hotel, and passes below the sandstone cliffs of Dooley. It then drops down to Gudu Bush where a path leads along the right-hand bank of the Gudu River to the falls at the head of the valley.

Continuing up the Mahai River Valley along the Basotho Gate path, you reach the turn-off to the Crack after about 1.2 km. Here a steep climb along a crack in the sandstone cliffs has to be negotiated, and at one difficult section there is a chain ladder. The trail now traverses the high ground and crosses the Gudu River about 50 m upstream of the falls; an excellent spot for a refreshing dip and a lunch stop.

After traversing Plowman's Kop, the route continues down the Mudslide where a short chain ladder assists trailists at the start. Owing to the steep gradient and loose surface, which becomes very slippery after rain, the Mudslide is not suitable for young children and those with a fear of heights. From the base of the cliffs follow the Gudu Bush path to the first turn-off on your left and make your way back to the car park. **11 km; 5 hours; circular.**

4. Sunday Falls, Surprise Ridge and Cannibal Cave This walk follows the route to the Fairy Glen turn-off, where you turn right instead, continuing to Sunday Falls, which you reach about an hour after setting off. The turn-off to the falls is signposted and, after crossing above the falls, keep an eye out for a track leading to the base of the falls.

Continuing along the main path, the trail crosses the Sunday Falls Stream and then the Sigubudu River. A short climb brings you to Surprise Ridge, with its unexpected views that extend as far as Cathedral Peak, Cathkin Peak and Champagne Castle in the south. Cannibal Cave lies outside the park boundaries, and is reached after a short walk westward along the ridge.

Instead of retracing your tracks, you can return via the Grotto and Fairy Glen trails, a full day's hike, but very rewarding. **22.5 km; 8 hours; circular.**

1. Tugela Tunnel and Gorge This is without doubt the most popular and scenic walk in the park. From the car park the path follows the right-hand bank of the Tugela River past a sandstone ridge dominated by the Policeman's Helmet. The sandstone ridge on which this well-known landmark is perched has the only population of one of South Africa's most endangered proteas, the cloud sugarbush (*Protea nubigena*). The Latin species name means 'born of the clouds' – a reference to its habitat which is often shrouded in clouds. The trail passes through several patches of forest and as you continue you become increasingly aware of being enclosed by the gorge. Over the last 1.5 km of the hike you cross the river three times and then reach the Tunnel a short distance beyond a chain ladder on the right-hand bank of the river.

Depending on the level of the river, you can either walk up the Tunnel for about 65 m or use the chain ladder to skirt it and boulder-hop up the Tugela River for about 800 m.

On the left-hand bank of the river, almost directly opposite the chain ladder, there is a steep path leading to Tunnel Cave, from where you overlook the Tunnel, with the Amphitheatre forming an impressive backdrop. **22.5 km; 7 hours; out-and-return.**

2. Devil's Hoek Valley From the car park follow the Gorge path to the signposted turn-off to the right. The trail now climbs out of the valley and after a short while there is a split, where you turn left to bypass Thendele Camp. From here the path continues along the right-hand bank of the valley, passing through two delightful patches of forest. The path ends at Second Bush. **9 km; 4 hours; out-and-return.**

3. Vemaan Valley This path follows the Devil's Hoek Valley route for about 1.6 km to a split where you turn left. After crossing the Devil's Hoek River the trail makes its way around to the Vemaan Valley, which you follow to a small patch of forest. From here the trail doubles back along the Policeman's Helmet Ridge, which can be ascended from further back. **9 km; 4 hours; out-and-return.**

5. SENTINEL PEAK TO CATHEDRAL PEAK TRAVERSE
uKhahlamba-Drakensberg Park, Bergville

Trail: 60 km; 5 days; open-ended.
Permits: Toll gate and hiking fees must be paid in cash at Witsieshoek Mountain Lodge, cell: 082 609 8988.
Maps: Covered by *uKhahlamba-Drakensberg Map* series by Slingsby Maps. Online orders http://slingsby-maps.myshopify.com.
Facilities: Various accommodation options at Witsieshoek Mountain Lodge near start. Camp site at Cathedral Peak; caves on traverse.

Starting at the Sentinel car park, this traverse features some of the most dramatic scenery found in the uKhahlamba-Drakensberg. The first day's hike (12 km; 6 hours) ascends along a chain ladder to the top of the Amphitheatre and then heads south to the Kubedu River. From here the trail ascends gently along a tributary of the Kubedu and, after skirting the Ifidi Pinnacles, you reach Ifidi Cave.

On the second day (11 km; 4 hours) the route heads inland to avoid the deep cutback between Ifidi and Icidi buttresses, before swinging to the Escarpment. Continuing along the Escarpment you will enjoy spectacular vistas of the Fangs and Madonna and her Worshippers. You can overnight in Fangs Cave, situated a short way down Fangs Pass.

The third day's walk (11 km; 4 hours) offers magnificent views of the Mweni Pinnacles and the Mweni area. The path detours inland around the Mweni Cutback and crosses the Senqu River. From the headland on the Escarpment edge there are imposing views of the Mweni Needles and the Rockeries Tower. Mponjwane Cave, a short distance north of the Rockeries Pass, is a popular overnight stop.

Day four's hike (15 km; 6 hours) takes you to the head of the Rockeries Pass, from where there are stunning views of the eight peaks of the Rockeries. At the top of the pass there is a path that leads

Above: The Hoopoe Falls are the highlight of the eponymous walk in the Oribi Gorge Nature Reserve.
Below: This is an easy river crossing for hikers on the Primitive Trail in Hluhluwe-iMfolozo Park.

Above: The Kosi Bay section of the iSimangaliso Wetland Park is a mosaic of lakes, high dunes, swamp forests, mangrove communities and unspoilt beaches. It is also a sanctuary to several rare plant and bird species.

Above: Loggerhead turtle hatchlings begin their perilous journey across the sand at Kosi Bay, towards the relative safety of the sea.
Below: Lake Makawulani (below), the first of the four interconnected lakes making up the Kosi system, contains several Thonga fishtraps.

Opposite and below: The Golden Gate Highlands National Park is a wonderful hiking destination with spectacular scenery dominated by rugged sandstone outcrops.

Above: The park has some amazing rock formations, such as the incredible stratified Mushroom Rocks.

Above: This wooden bridge helps trailists up a sheer rock face on the Holkrans Trail at Golden Gate Highlands National Park. **Below:** The park boasts many striking, natural features, such as the Sentinel, or Brandwag, as well as caves hikers can explore on the Holkrans Trail.

Above: The imposing roof of Cathedral Cave (above) is another of the impressive rock formations at Golden Gate Highlands National Park.

Above: The Forest Falls Walk, near Sabie in Mpumalanga, takes its name from these magnificent falls.

Below: You'll find numerous reminders of the gold rush era of the 19th century on the Prospector's Hiking Trail near Pilgrim's Rest.

This page: You can enjoy beautiful hikes in Mpumalanga: along a grassy ridge overlooking the Sabie Valley (above) on the Loerie Walk; past Lone Creek Waterfall (left) on one of the Fanie Botha hikes; and to the famous Bourke's Luck Potholes (below) – the highlight of the Blyderivierspoort Hiking Trail.

to a waterfall in the Senqu River, which is some 4 km away. You then follow the Kokoatsan River upstream from the waterfall. After a steep climb up a ridge the trail descends steeply to the head of the Ntonjelana Pass. From here the route follows the Escarpment above the Cathedral range to the Mlambonja Pass. Twins Cave, the overnight stop, is just a short way down the pass.

On the final day of the hike (11 km; 4 hours) the route descends along the Mlambonja Pass to the Cathedral Peak Hotel. The route is scrubby and you will lose some 1,500 m in altitude over the course of your descent to the hotel.

6. CATHEDRAL PEAK AND MLAMBONJA WILDERNESS AREA

uKhahlamba-Drakensberg Park, Winterton

Trails: 120-km network of footpaths; 1 to 18 km; 30 minutes to overnight hikes; circular, out-and-return and open-ended.
Permits: Conservation and overnight hiking fees. The Officer-in-Charge, Cathedral Peak, tel: (036) 488 8000.
Maps: Covered by *uKhahlamba-Drakensberg Map* series by Slingsby Maps. Online orders https://slingsby-maps.myshopify.com.
Facilities/Activities: Luxury chalets, restaurant, swimming pool and tennis court at Didima Camp. Camp site with ablution facilities at Cathedral Peak. Didima Rock Art Centre at Cathedral Peak. Certain caves can be reserved in advance for the exclusive use of a group.

Covering 31,500 ha, Cathedral Peak and the adjoining Mlambonja Wilderness Area are among the most favoured Berg destinations for outdoor enthusiasts. Bounded to the north and northwest by the Upper Tugela River and to the south by the Mdedelelo Wilderness, the area is dominated by the Cathedral range. The 4-km-long row of free-standing peaks, also known as the Ridge of

the Horns, includes some of the most spectacular peaks in South Africa, among them Cathedral Peak (3,004 m), Bell (2,930 m), Outer Horn (3,005 m), Inner Horn (3,005 m) and the Chessmen. In addition to these tall, free-standing peaks are those of the Escarpment here, which are all over 3,000 m.

There are numerous opportunities for short walks in the Little Berg and extended overnight hikes in the Mlambonja Wilderness Area.

1. Ndedema Gorge is accessible only by undertaking a guided walk. The gorge, about 8 km long, is internationally renowned for its rock art, and 3,909 rock paintings at 17 sites were painstakingly recorded by the late Harald Pager in the 1960s. Sebayeni Cave, the first shelter in the sandstone band on the southern side of the valley, is the largest of the decorated shelters in the gorge and contains over 1,100 paintings. Other well-known rock art sites in the gorge include Poacher's Cave and Leopard Cave. The gorge has one of the most extensive patches of indigenous forest to be found in the Drakensberg. **9.5 km; 3 hours, to start of the gorge; open-ended. Guided walks only.**

2. Tarn and Tryme Hills This pleasant walk, with its splendid views of the Little Berg, starts off at the Cathedral Peak Hotel and ascends relatively steeply to the Mushroom Rock. From here the trail climbs along a ridge to Tarn Hill, named after the small tarn on the plateau. After about 4 km you will join a jeep track, along which you ascend steadily for about 1 km before turning left. The trail then winds down the slopes, crosses a stream and then ascends the slopes of Tryme Hill before dropping down into the forested valley of the Mhlonhlo River, which you follow back to the start.

There are also worthwhile detours, which can be made to the Ribbon, Albert and Doreen falls. **10 km; 4 hours; circular.**

3. Organ Pipes Cathedral Peak is the only Berg area from which you can drive to the top of the Little Berg. Access is via the 10.5-km-long Mike's Pass, which gains some 500 m in altitude to Arendsig Gate, the starting point of the route to the Organ Pipes and the Escarpment. The start of the ascent is signposted, about 6.5 km from Arendsig. Over the next 7 km the path gains more than 900 m in altitude, passing an assembly of spires and buttresses known in isiZulu as *Qolo la Masoja*, or the Ridge of Soldiers. This is either due to apparent resemblance of the fluted columns to a regiment of soldiers standing to attention, or the name could be derived from a tradition associated with military action; the origins of the name are not certain. **13.5 km; 7 hours; open-ended.**

From the top of Organ Pipes Pass you can do a traverse along the Escarpment to Gray's Pass, ending at Monk's Cowl office. **50 km; 5 days; open-ended.**

4. Rainbow Gorge Starting at the Cathedral Peak Hotel, this delightful and relatively easy walk follows the deep gorge carved by the Ndumeni River, which has its source below the Organ Pipes. From the hotel the path skirts the base of Tryme Hill and after about 4 km descends into the Ndumeni Valley.

As you make your way up the forested valley you reach a beautiful pool into which two waterfalls cascade. The going now becomes more difficult as you have to cross the river several times before reaching the gorge, which can be explored by crawling underneath a boulder jammed in the gorge.

From the head of the gorge you can either retrace your tracks or clamber up the steep right-hand bank of Tryme Hill to join a footpath at the top of the hill. Turn right here and follow the path back to the hotel. **11 km; 5 hours; out-and-return or circular.**

5. Cathedral Peak with its spire-like outline reaches a height of 3,004 m and dominates the Cathedral Range – a line of free-standing peaks extending up to 4 km from the Escarpment. An ascent of Cathedral Peak involves an altitude gain of over 1,600 m. An entire day should be set aside for this strenuous 18-km round trip. The final ascent to the summit of Cathedral Peak involves a C-grade scramble and this hike is, therefore, not recommended for inexperienced hikers.

On a clear day the view from the summit is magnificent, with Cathkin Peak to the south and Eastern Buttress to the north clearly visible. To the southeast the scenery is dominated by the deep valley carved by the Mlambonja River. **18 km; 10 hours; out-and-return.**

7. CATHEDRAL PEAK TWO PASSES HIKE
uKhahlamba-Drakensberg Park, Winterton

Trail: 37.5 km; 3 days; open-ended.
Permits: Conservation and overnight hiking fees. The Officer-in-Charge, Cathedral Peak, tel: (036) 488 8000 or (036) 488 1346.
Maps: Covered by *uKhahlamba-Drakensberg Map* series by Slingsby Maps. Online orders https://slingsby-maps.myshopify.com.
Facilities/Activities: Luxury chalets, restaurant, swimming pool and tennis court at Didima Camp. Camp site with ablution facilities at Cathedral Peak. Didima Rock Art Centre at Cathedral Peak. Certain caves can be reserved in advance for the exclusive use of a group.

This is a demanding but rewarding hike that should only be attempted by fit and experienced hikers. From the Arendsig Gate at the end of Mike's Pass, the route continues for 3 km along a jeep track to the Contour Path, where you turn left, continuing for 3.5 km to the turn-off to Organ Pipes Pass. Over the next 7 km you will gain over 900 m in altitude as you go past the imposing Organ Pipes. The wide valley between Ndumeni Dome and Castle Buttress, reached after the day's strenuous 13.5-km hike, is a good place to overnight in a tent, or continue to the Ndumeni Caves, two small shelters high up on Ndumeni Dome.

On account of the undulating terrain an early start is recommended for the second day's hike (12.5 km). For the best views, follow the watershed over Castle Buttress and Cleft Peak (at 3,281 m, the highest point between Mont-aux-Sources and Cathedral Peak). Further along, the path traverses the watershed close to the edge of the Escarpment, revealing awe-inspiring views. Prominent landmarks include the Column, Pyramid, Cockade and Elephant, and beyond Xeni Pass you look down onto the Cathedral Range. The overnight stop, Twins Cave, is situated a short way from the head of the Mlambonja Pass.

Day three's hike (11.5 km) involves a steep descent along the Mlambonja Pass. Because of the steep gradient and loose scree in the rock bands near the head of the pass, and the slippery grass, great caution must be exercised; you would be well advised to take your time. The Inner and Outer Horn are outstanding features along the descent.

8. CATHKIN PEAK AND MDEDELELO WILDERNESS AREA
uKhahlamba-Drakensberg Park, Winterton

Trails: 185-km network of footpaths; 1 to 58 km; 30 minutes to overnight hikes; circular, out-and-return, open-ended.
Permits: Conservation and overnight hiking fees. The Officer-in-Charge, Monk's Cowl, tel: (036) 468 1103 or (036) 468 1150.
Maps: Covered by *uKhahlamba-Drakensberg Map* series by Slingsby Maps. Online orders https://slingsby-maps.myshopify.com.
Facilities/Activities: Camp site with ablution facilities at Monk's Cowl. Certain caves can be reserved in advance for the exclusive use of a group.

Monk's Cowl and the adjoining 29,000-ha Mdedelelo Wilderness Area are characterised by deep valleys, impressive peaks and caves with rock paintings. Familiar landmarks include Cathkin Peak, Gatberg and the Dragon's Back, an impressive range of free-standing block-shaped peaks. Backpacking is made easier by a contour path that links popular destinations and passes to the Escarpment. The area is bordered in the north by Cathedral Peak and in the south by the Injisuthi section of the Giant's Castle Game Reserve. The scenery in this area is spectacular.

1. Contour Path via the Sphinx One of the most popular routes onto the Little Berg from Monk's Cowl is via the Sphinx and Verkykerskop. This is the usual route onto the Contour Path and hence also to the higher peaks and passes. Some 450 m is gained in altitude before the gradient levels off at Breakfast Stream, beyond which the trail ascends gently to the Contour Path. Dominating the scenery ahead is Cathkin Peak (3,149 m). **5.5 km; 3 hours; open-ended.**

2. Gray's Pass is reached by following the path via the Sphinx to the Contour Path where you turn right, continuing for 2.5 km to Hlatikulu Nek. Remain on the Contour Path for another 1.5 km and turn left to reach Keith Bush Camp after a steady climb of about 4 km. It is a beautiful camp site, situated at the head of the Mhlawazini River and surrounded by cliffs on three sides. Although only 2.5 km long, Gray's Pass is not only eroded and exposed, but also steep, and you will gain some 700 m in altitude.

Shortly after starting the climb up the pass you will get your first uninterrupted view of Monk's Cowl (3,234 m). Nkosazana Cave, near the top of the pass, is a good place to spend the night on the Escarpment. From the top of the pass it is an easy walk of about 3 km to Champagne Castle (3,377 m). You can either backtrack down Gray's Pass, or descend along Ship's Prow Pass, immediately south of Champagne Castle. Do not attempt to descend along the northern fork of Ship's Prow Pass, which is extremely dangerous, but take the south fork. Loose scree makes this a difficult descent, so take care. **45 km; 3 days; circular.**

3. Monk's Cowl to Ndedema Gorge Monk's Cowl owes its name to the 3,234-m-high peak resembling a hooded figure. It is obscured by Cathkin Peak (Mdedelelo) and the first uninterrupted views can be enjoyed on the ascent of the Escarpment along Gray's Pass. Monk's Cowl is one of the most challenging peaks in the uKhahlamba-Drakensberg and was first successfully scaled only in 1942.

Another option when joining the Contour Path via the Sphinx and Breakfast Stream is to hike to Ndedema Gorge. This is a rather strenuous walk, which takes you through two river valleys with long descents followed by steep ascents.

Gatberg, a peak with a hole (estimated to be 9 m in diameter) through its base, is a prominent landmark along this route. The isiZulu word *intunja* is variously translated as 'the eye of the needle' and 'the hole in the mountain through which the shepherds can creep'. Further along the scenery is dominated by the Dragon's Back, an impressive range of block-shaped peaks. Some 400 m in altitude is lost over the last 4 km of the hike to Ndedema Gorge, which is reached about 28 km from the Monk's Cowl Office. From here it is about 9.5 km (3 hours) to Cathedral Peak.

9. INJISUTHI
uKhahlamba-Drakensberg Park, Estcourt

Trails: 5 walks; 6 to 15 km; 3 hours to overnight hikes; circular, out-and-return, open-ended. 6-hour guided walk to Battle Cave.
Permits: Conservation and overnight hiking fees. The Officer-in-Charge, Injisuthi Camp, tel: (036) 431 9000 or (036) 431 9001.
Maps: Covered by *uKhahlamba-Drakensberg Map* series by Slingsby Maps. Online orders https://slingsby-maps.myshopify.com.
Facilities/Activities: Self-catering cabins; camp site; guided walks to Battle Cave; trout fishing (permit required).

South Africa's two highest peaks, Mafadi (3,446 m) and Injisuthi Dome (3,379 m) form an impressive backdrop to the wild Injisuthi Valley in the north of the Giant's Castle Game Reserve. Other prominent peaks to be seen in this area include Old Woman Grinding Corn, The Injisuthi Triplets and The Molar. Dominating the skyline to the northwest of the Injisuthi Valley are three particularly impressive peaks – Champagne Castle, Monk's Cowl and Cathkin Peak.

1. Grindstone Caves owe their name to a grindstone that was placed there many years ago. The trail leads to a delightful yellowwood forest and then meanders up mountain slopes towards the sandstone cliffs before levelling off. **6 km; 3 hours; out-and-return.**

2. Van Heyningen's Pass is a favourite walk to the top of the Little Berg. After passing through a patch of forest the route ascends along Van Heyningen's Pass to a viewpoint, where trailists are rewarded with spectacular views of Monk's Cowl and Champagne Castle. Looking southwards along the line of jagged peaks, the view extends as far as the impressive wall of Giant's Castle. **8 km; 3 hours; out-and-return.**

3. Cataract Valley is reached by continuing from Grindstone Caves down to the Old Woman Stream, which you cross above a waterfall. The path then climbs to the top of a ridge and drops down into Cataract Valley, crossing Cataract Stream three times before reaching the Delmhlwazine River. From here the trail veers back to the camp. **13 km; 5 hours; circular.**

4. Battle Cave can only be visited if you join a guided walk from Injisuthi Camp. The cave owes its name to a scene depicting a battle between two feuding San clans. Also depicted are a small group of lion, animals superimposed on humans, eland, rhebok and masked figures. **15 km; 6 hours; out-and-return.**

5. Wonder Valley is reached by hiking to the top of Van Heyningen's Pass. From here, continue heading up the path towards a ridge, which is crossed further along. The route now descends gradually and there are some fine views of Wonder Valley. Continue to Wonder Valley Cave, from where it is best to retrace your tracks. **15 km; 5 hours; out-and-return.**

10. GIANT'S CASTLE
uKhahlamba-Drakensberg Park, Estcourt

Trails: 285-km network of footpaths; 3 to 30 km; 1 hour to overnight hikes; circular, out-and-return, open-ended.
Permits: Conservation and overnight hiking fees. The Officer-in-Charge, Giant's Castle, tel: (036) 353 3718 or (036) 353 3775.

Situated on a grassy plateau among deep valleys and below the dramatic, sheer cliffs of the Escarpment, the Giant's Castle area is a hiker's paradise. The Escarpment here is dominated by a number of well-known natural landmarks, such as Giant's Castle, the Long Wall, Carbineer Point, The Thumb and Bannerman Face.

Giant's Castle Game Reserve, proclaimed in 1903 to protect the declining population of eland, extends from Giant's Castle Ridge, northwards, for 25 km to the Injisuthi River. In addition to eland, the reserve is also home to blesbok, mountain and southern reedbuck, grey rhebok, grey duiker and baboon.

With an extensive bird checklist of about 160 species, Giant's Castle offers birding enthusiasts exciting opportunities. Topping the list of noteworthy species is the rare bearded vulture, which is often seen flying overhead. Not to be missed is a guided walk to the vulture hide at Bamboo Hollow, where carcasses are placed between May and September especially to supplement the diet of the bearded vultures. Other raptors you might see at the hide include Cape vulture, Verreaux's eagle, lanner falcon and jackal buzzard.

The southern bald ibis has been recorded in the area, and among the other species you may tick here are Cape longclaw, ground woodpecker, Drakensberg rockjumper, Drakensberg siskin and Gurney's sugarbird.

There are in excess of 25 walks in the reserve (excluding the Injisuthi area), ranging from a 1.9-km round trip from Giant's Castle Camp to Main Ridge, to a four-day hike.

Short Walks

1. River Walk The outward leg takes the Main Caves path to Rock 75 and then doubles back through grassveld and light bush along the eastern bank of the Bushman's River. **3 km; 1 hour; out-and-return.**

2. Bushman's River Trail, an interpretative walk starting at the hutted camp, is one of the most popular walks in the reserve. Points of interest along the way include Sandstone View and the historic Rock 75, where the camp cook of the 75th Regiment on Foot carved the figure 75 into a boulder during the Langalibalele rebellion in 1874. The Main Caves are the highlight of the trail. One of the best-known rock art sites in South Africa, the two large overhangs contain some 540 individual paintings. A recorded commentary on the San is given hourly, and the site museum provides an invaluable insight into the life of these early inhabitants of the Drakensberg. **3.2 km; 2 hours; out-and-return.**

3. Grysbok Bush Trail follows the path past Main Caves and then ascends steadily through grassland and oldwood. Further along, the valley closes in and becomes more densely wooded with oldwood and wild olive trees. About 4 km after setting off from the Main Camp you will reach the first pool and Grysbok Bush, a delightful patch of indigenous forest. **8 km; 4 hours; out-and-return.**

Longer Walks

1. Giant's Hut via Giant's Ridge Follow the path past the Main Caves turn-off for about 500 m. The trail climbs steeply out of the Bushman's River Valley and two short but steep ascents, with more gentle terrain in between them, have to be negotiated. The path then follows the spine of a ridge and traverses the slopes of another ridge before joining the Contour Path. Turn left here and follow the Contour Path as it winds below Giant's Castle to reach Giant's Castle Hut after 2 km. The return leg along Two Dassie Stream is reached a short way on and initially follows the stream's western bank. Lower down you will cross the stream a number of times, and there are several inviting pools. After 8 km the trail joins the path to the Main Caves and the remainder of the walk is an easy stroll back to Main Camp. **20.5 km; 9 hours; circular.**

2. Langalibalele Pass is reached by taking the Main Caves and Grysbok Bush paths (see 'Short Walks', this page). From the lower end of Grysbok Bush the trail ascends steadily along the spine of a ridge, gaining some 400 m in altitude over 2 km to the Contour Path. A 1-km walk along the Contour

Path takes you to the turn-off to Langalibalele Pass, which gains some 670 m in altitude over 3 km. At the top of the pass a short walk to the south leads to a stone cairn that marks the spot where three carbineers of Major Durnford's forces and two auxiliaries were killed in a skirmish with Chief Langalibalele's Hlubi (the Sesotho-speaking people of Zululand) on 4 November 1873. Five of the peaks to the south of the pass – Erskine, Bond, Potterill, Kambule and Katana – were named in honour of those killed. The same route is followed back. **21 km; 10 hours; out-and-return.**

3. Giant's Castle Pass and Giant's Castle From the Main Camp follow the path up Giant's Ridge to the Contour Path where you turn right, continuing for 2 km to the turn-off to Giant's Castle Pass. Over the next 2 km you will gain some 770 m in altitude to the top of Giant's Castle Pass. The last section is steep, so beware of landslides and avoid gullies branching off to the left as they are impassable. From the pass a path leads eastwards for about 2 km, and reaches the summit of Giant's Castle (3,314 m) after a gentle ascent of about 230 m. Return to Main Camp along the same route. **30 km; 2 days; out-and-return.**

Overnight Hiking

This route has no particular name, but offers a rewarding circular, four-day hike, incorporating two of the mountain huts. On the first day (10.5 km; 4 hours) you hike from Main Camp via Two Dassie Stream to the Contour Path and Giant's Hut.

Giant's Hut is the ideal base for an ascent of Giant's Castle (18 km; 9 hours) on day two. From the hut, follow the Contour Path for about 2 km beyond the Giant's Ridge path until you reach the foot of Giant's Castle Pass. A steep 2-km climb brings you to the top of the pass, where a path leads eastwards for about 2 km to the summit of Giant's Castle. Return along the same route to the hut. Day three's hike (17.5 km; 7 hours) to Bannerman Hut follows the Contour Path, at an altitude of about 2,300 m. Except for several mountain stream crossings, the walk is fairly easy. Dominating the Escarpment are some prominent landmarks: the Long Wall, Katana, Carbineer Point, Kambule, Mount Durnford, Potterill, Bond and Erskine. About 9.5 km after setting off you will reach the base of Langalibalele Pass. Further along, the path passes below the

Thumb and Bannerman Face, before reaching Bannerman Hut at the foot of Bannerman Pass.

On the fourth day, backtrack for 4 km to join the Secretary Bird Ridge path, or continue for another 500 m to join a more direct route back to the Main Camp. The total distances for this day are 12 km (4 hours) and 10.5 km (3.5 hours) respectively. **56.5 or 58 km; 4 days; circular.**

11. MKHOMAZI WILDERNESS AREA AND KAMBERG, LOTHENI AND VERGELEGEN NATURE RESERVES
uKhahlamba-Drakensberg Park, Nottingham Road

Trails: 465-km network of footpaths; 3 to 80 km; 1.5 hours to overnight hikes; circular, out-and-return, open-ended.
Permits: Conservation and overnight hiking fees.
The Officer-in-Charge, Mkhomazi, tel: (033) 266 6444.
The Officer-in-Charge, Highmoor, tel: (033) 267 7240.
The Officer-in-Charge, Lotheni, tel: (033) 702 0540 or (033) 702 9018.
The Officer-in-Charge, Vergelegen, tel: (033) 702 0712, cell 082 762 9884.
The Officer-in-Charge, Kamberg, tel: (033) 267 7251.
Maps: Covered by *uKhahlamba-Drakensberg Map* series by Slingsby Maps. Online orders https://slingsby-maps.myshopify.com.
Facilities/Activities: Highmoor: camp sites. Kamberg: self-catering accommodation and trout fishing. Lotheni: self-catering accommodation, camp site, trout fishing and Settlers' Museum. Vergelegen: self-catering accommodation.

Mkhomazi Wilderness Area

Proclaimed in May 1973, the Mkhomazi Wilderness Area of some 54,000 ha is not as well known as the areas further north. The spurs of the Little Berg extend further east from the Escarpment than they do towards the north, and the deeply incised valleys give the landscape a rugged appearance and a sense of isolation and tranquillity. Soaring buttresses and several unnamed peaks of over 3,000 m dominate the Escarpment.

The area is rich in history, and was the scene of many bitter clashes between the San and the early white settlers.

Highmoor

To the north and east of the wilderness is Highmoor. Kamberg, Lotheni and Vergelegen, which serve as convenient access points for the Mkhomazi Wilderness Area, adjoin the wilderness area to the south and east. Despite the rugged terrain there are numerous footpaths, but they are mainly restricted to the occasional spur and to river valleys, often making it necessary to boulder-hop up a valley to reach higher ground.

Kamberg

This reserve, on the northeastern boundary of the Mkhomazi Wilderness Area, covers 2,232 ha and is renowned for its scenery, as well as for its excellent trout fishing. Game to be seen includes mountain reedbuck, reedbuck, blesbok, eland, grey rhebok and oribi.

1. Mooi River Trail takes its name from the Mooi River, which has its source in the adjoining Mkhomazi Wilderness Area. This walk consists of a main trail with three 1-km loops and has been designed as a wheelchair trail. **7 km, with shorter options; 2 to 3.5 hours; circular.**

2. Game Pass Trail This guided walk starts at the Kamberg Rock Art Centre with a DVD presentation on the rock art of the uKhahlamba-Drakensberg. The cave has some of the best-preserved paintings in southern Africa, including fine polychrome eland and human figures. Trails depart from Kamberg Camp at 08:00, 11:00, 12:30 and 13:00 and are limited to 10 people at a time. **6 km; 2.5 to 3 hours; out-and-return.**

Lotheni

Lotheni covers 3,984 ha and has some of the most spectacular scenery in the Drakensberg, including a number of waterfalls. Among these are Jacob's

Ladder Falls, which cascade down the mountain slopes in several tiers. Prominent peaks, such as the Tent, Hawk and Redi peaks, are clearly visible on the Escarpment.

1. Gelib Tree Trail starts about 500 m from the Settlers' Museum and leads to the Gelib Tree. The acacia tree grew from seed collected by an officer of the 1st Royal Natal Carbineers, Captain Charles Eustace, in what was then Italian Somaliland during World War II. He planted the seed years later on his farm (which became part of the Lotheni Nature Reserve) in memory of 13 carbineers who were killed during the campaign to take the village of Gelib from the Italian military forces. **1.3 km; 30 minutes; circular.**

2. Yellowwood Cave From Simes's Cottage the trail follows the left-hand bank of the Lotheni River upstream past the eMpophomeni Falls. Further along it continues along Ka-Masihlenga Stream, flanked by indigenous forest, to a cave situated on the right-hand bank of the stream. **10.6 km; 4 hours; out-and-return.**

3. Emadundwini Trail starts at the Lotheni Camp huts, from where it ascends steadily to just below Sheba's Breasts, gaining some 770 m in altitude. A short way on you join the Contour Path to Giant's Hut and from here you continue in a northwesterly direction until you reach the Taylor's Path junction. Turn left and follow Taylor's Pass, which descends steadily and crosses a tributary of the Elandshoek River. The trail winds above the Elandshoek River, and a short walk along the Lotheni River returns you to the start. **11.5 km; 5 hours; circular.**

4. Eagle Trail leads from the Lotheni camp site past the 12 points of interest that are discussed in the trail brochure. Aspects covered include the geology of the region, the Drakensberg as a water catchment area, sandstone formations, grasslands and fire, as well as tree ferns. The terrain is moderate, but you will encounter one or two fairly steep gradients. **12.8 km; 6 hours; circular.**

5. Bhodla River Canyon From the Lotheni Camp huts the trail initially follows the Gelib Tree Trail and then continues towards the game guard huts below Ka-Zwelewle. However, before reaching the huts, the path splits off to the right, continuing to the magnificent canyon carved by the Bhodla River. **12.6 km; 6 hours; out-and-return.**

6. Hlathimbe Pass Ascending the Escarpment via the historic Hlathimbe Pass, you will gain 880 m in altitude over 9 km to the Contour Path linking the Hlathimbe and Ka-Masihlenga passes. You follow the Contour Path for about 3.5 km, and over the last 4 km the trail gains 440 m in altitude up the Hlathimbe Pass. **35 km; 2 days; out-and-return.**

Vergelegen

Cradled by the Mkhomazi and Mlahlangubo rivers, this Y-shaped reserve covers 1,159 ha of deep valleys and steep grassy hillsides. It is a sanctuary to eland, mountain reedbuck, reedbuck, grey rhebok and oribi.

Mohlesi Pass should only be attempted by trailists who are physically fit as it is a demanding hike with an altitude gain of about 1,600 m to the top of the pass. The 3,482-m-high Thabana Ntlenyana, the highest point in Africa south of Kilimanjaro, lies about 5 km away in Lesotho. **50 km; 2 days; out-and-return.**

12. MZIMKHULU WILDERNESS AREA AND MZIMKHULWANA NATURE RESERVE
uKhahlamba-Drakensberg Park, Himeville

Trails: 220-km network of footpaths; 3 to 35 km; 1.5 hours to overnight hikes; circular, out-and-return, open-ended.
Permits: Conservation and overnight hiking fees. The Officer-in-Charge, Cobham, tel: (033) 703 0831, cell: 086 240 1274. The Officer-in-Charge, Garden Castle, tel: (033) 701 1823, cell: 083 962 3934 or 086 505 8599.
Maps: Covered by *uKhahlamba-Drakensberg Map* series by Slingsby Maps. Online orders https://slingsby-maps.myshopify.com.

Facilities/Activities: Camp sites at Cobham and Garden Castle. Certain caves can be reserved in advance for exclusive use.

The southern uKhahlamba area has spectacular sandstone formations and numerous streams and rivers. Those seeking to escape from the more popular areas further north will find Mzimkhulu a haven of tranquillity. Although the area lacks a well-defined contour path, the northern section has an extensive network of trails, while in the southern section you can ascend the Escarpment along several passes.

The Mzimkhulu Wilderness Area extends from Sani Pass in the north to Griqualand East in the south, and is bounded to the east by the Mzimkhulwana Nature Reserve. The two areas cover a total of 57,000 ha. Despite the absence of prominent free-standing peaks, which are so characteristic of the central and northern Berg, several unusual buttresses and rock formations create some quite stunning scenery. Access to the greatest concentration of the area's footpaths is from the Cobham office.

1. Rhino Peak (3,051 m) juts out from the Escarpment for about 2 km and is one of the most conspicuous peaks in the southern Drakensberg. The isiZulu name *ntabangcobo* means 'rhino's horn peak'. The peak is reached by following a well-defined path from the Garden Castle office along the Mlambonja River. From Pillar Cave, reached 2 km from the start, the path climbs 500 m in altitude over 3.5 km, and then by another 400 m over the final 1.5 km along the Mashai Pass. Once you reach the Escarpment, the path swings eastwards, and after about 2 km you come to Rhino Peak, which is easily ascended. To the south lies Wilson's Peak (3,267 m), Mashai (3,313 m), Walker's Peak (3,306 m) and the Devil's Knuckles, also known as *Baroa-Ba-Bararo* or The Three Bushmen. **18 km; 12 hours; out-and-return.**

2. Sipongweni Shelter is reached, from the Cobham office, by following the course of the Pholela River upstream for about 7 km before turning left. You will come to the shelter about 1 km further on. It is regarded as one of the best rock art sites in the entire Drakensberg, taking into consideration the number of paintings found here, their state of preservation and the interesting themes depicted. It is best known for the scene showing men spearing fish from small canoes. **16 km; 4 hours; out-and-return.**

3. Hodgson's Peaks Captain Allen Gardiner noted the 'singularly indented outline' of the twin peaks just south of Sani Pass when he first saw them in 1835, and this prompted him to name them the Giant's Cup. The peaks were later renamed in memory of Thomas Hodgson, who was accidentally wounded during a punitive expedition organised in 1862 to take back cattle and horses from the San. He died of his wounds a day later and was buried at the top of the pass. A cairn was erected on the site a year later. The trail from the Cobham office follows the Pholela River upstream, and the final ascent is along the Masubasuba Pass. About 1,400 m is gained in altitude to the top of the pass. **36 km; 2 days; out-and-return.**

13. GIANT'S CUP HIKING TRAIL
uKhahlamba-Drakensberg Park, Himeville

Trail: 59.3 km; 5 days; open-ended.
Permits: The Reservations Officer, Ezemvelo KZN Wildlife, P O Box 13069, Cascades 3202, tel: (033) 845 1000, fax: (033) 845 1001, email: bookings@kznwildlife.com.
Maps: Colour trail map with information on the reverse.
Facilities/Activities: Five overnight huts with bunks, mattresses, cold water and toilets.
Pertinent information: There is no overnight hut at the start of the trail. Arrangements must be made for transport at the end of the trail, as it is open-ended.

This relatively easy trail traverses the foothills of the southern Berg and is an ideal introduction for those unfamiliar with the Berg. Stretching from the foot of the Sani Pass in the north to Bushman's Nek in the south, the trail winds past eroded sandstone formations, across grassy plains and through spectacular valleys with inviting pools. Herds of eland are sometimes encountered along the way, while raptors such as the bearded and Cape vultures are occasionally seen overhead.

The first day's hike (13.3 km; 6 hours) traverses easy terrain and you will reach Ngenwa Pool after 5 km. Although short of the halfway mark, the pool is an ideal lunch stop, especially on a hot day. From here the trail ascends gently and then levels off as it skirts the base of Ndlovini, before dropping down to the first overnight hut in the Pholela Valley.

Day two (9 km; 3.5 hours) begins with a gentle climb before plateauing at the Tortoise Rocks – round flattened rocks resembling prehistoric tortoises. Further along you will reach Bathplug Cave, named after the small waterfall that cascades through the cave's roof after rain and then disappears through a natural drain-hole, before reappearing a little further along. The walls of the cave are decorated with several hundred small paintings of stick-like human figures, horses and animals. From here the trail descends to the overnight hut in the Mzimkhulwana Valley.

The third day's hike (12.2 km; 5.5 hours) begins with an easy ascent towards the Little Bamboo Mountains, and after about 4 km reaches its highest point at Crane Tarn. A short way on, the trail passes an interesting site where the remains of petrified trees can be seen exposed in the Beaufort Group. The trail then follows Killiecranckie Stream, and halfway between the 5- and 6-km markers you come to a beautiful pool beneath a massive boulder. A gentle descent brings you to the Mzimkhulu Valley, and from here it is an easy 2-km walk to the overnight hut.

A short, but steep climb up the slopes of Garden Castle awaits hikers at the start of day four of the hike (12.8 km; 6 hours). The trail then levels off just above the 1,900-m contour, and further along you will find yourself looking down onto the Drakensberg Gardens Hotel. After about 8 km the trail descends steeply, and the remainder of the day's hike is over level terrain.

On the final day's hike (12 km; 5 hours) the trail takes you up an easy climb to Bucquay Nek and then descends to the Mzimude River, which you can cross by means of a suspension bridge. Over the next 2 km you will gain approximately 200 m in altitude as you make your way to Langalibalele Cave on the western slopes of Langalibalele Peak. The remainder of the trail to Bushman's Nek Hut is mostly downhill.

14. UMTAMVUNA NATURE RESERVE
Port Edward

Trails: 6 walks; 1 to 8 hours; circular and open-ended.
Permits: Conservation fee. No booking required for walks.
Maps: Comprehensive brochure with sketch maps of trails.
Facilities/Activities: Braai facilities; toilets at Beacon Hill entrance.
Pertinent information: Accommodation is available at Clearwater Cabins and Trails, cell: 083 549 6710 (Natalie), e-mail: info@clearwatertrails.co.za. Access to the reserve can be arranged for guests.

Situated on the northern bank of the Mthamvuna River, which forms the boundary between the Eastern Cape and KwaZulu-Natal provinces, the Umtamvuna Nature Reserve covers 3,257 ha of spectacular scenery. Highlights of the reserve include the deep gorge carved by the Mthamvuna River, its riverine forest, steep rocky cliffs, waterfalls and magnificent views.

The reserve is said to contain more species of rare trees than anywhere else in southern Africa and, despite its small size, a staggering 1,250 flowering plants, ferns, mosses and lichens have been recorded. The Pondoland coastal grassland that lies above the gorge is especially eye-catching in spring, when flowers in different hues come into bloom.

Umtamvuna's bird checklist stands at 259 and includes species such as crowned eagle, African green pigeon, secretarybird, Cape rock-thrush, Knysna woodpecker and Gurney's sugarbird. The cliffs are also home to a steadily increasing population of Cape vulture, and there are rewarding views from the vulture hide.

Antelope you may chance upon include blue and common duiker, bushbuck and reedbuck. Other mammals to keep an eye out for are samango and vervet monkeys, thick-tailed bushbaby, baboon, rock dassie and Natal red hare.

The trails have been laid out in the vicinity of the Pont and Beacon Hill entrances.

Pont Entrance

1. Lourie Trail, an easy walk, meanders above the Mthamvuna River before swinging away to partly ascend the slope on the eastern bank of the Mthamvuna River. The trail then works its way back through a forest, where there is a possibility of seeing blue duiker and bushbuck. **2 km; 1 hour; circular.**

2. Fish Eagle Trail follows the course of the Mthamvuna River upstream for some 3 km, before taking the Dog's Leg to ascend steeply to the grassland. It continues along the krans edge, and there are some spectacular views over the gorge and the landscape south of the Mthamvuna River further along. The path then descends back to the start. **8 km; 4 hours; circular.**

Beacon Hill Entrance

1. Ingungumbane Trail involves a steep climb down to the Bulolo River, which you cross twice before the trail ascends steeply through magnificent forests back to the grasslands. Despite its steep gradients the trail is regarded as one of the most delightful walks in the reserve. **4 km; 3 hours; circular.**

2. uNkonka Trail drops down to the Bulolo River, which is followed downstream to its junction with the Mthamvuna River. Although the terrain along the river is difficult in places, there are numerous good swimming spots in which to cool down. A steep climb (with an altitude gain of more than 300 m) along the Razorback takes you back to the grassland, from where there are excellent views over the gorge. **8 km; 6 hours; circular.**

3. iMpunzi Trail leads through grassland along the eastern boundary of the nature reserve and later links up with the Fish Eagle Trail to end at the Pont Entrance. Along the way there are sweeping views across the gorge. **8 km; 4 hours; open-ended.**

4. iMziki Trail This trail descends to the Bulolo River and then gains some 200 m in altitude on the ascent to the Western Heights, the largest grassland area in the reserve. Along the way you will be able to explore hidden kloofs, streams, forests and a pristine vlei, and enjoy spectacular views. **12 km; 8 hours; circular.**

15. MPENJATI NATURE RESERVE
Margate

Trails: 2 walks; 1.2 and 1.8 km; 1 to 1.5 hours.
Permits: Conservation fee. No booking required for walks.
Maps: Trails are clearly marked.
Facilities/Activities: Picnic places with braai facilities; children's playground.

This coastal nature reserve, situated 20 km south of Margate, is a mosaic of coastal lowland forest (which covers about one-third of the 60-ha reserve), grasslands, as well as the wetlands of the Mpenjati River and its lagoon.

The coastal red milkwood, coast silver oak, big num-num and Natal wild banana are typical species of the dune forest. Other species include lagoon hibiscus, wild date palm and pigeonwood. The reserve lies near the northern limit of the distribution of *Prionium serratum* – a palmiet that resembles a dwarf palm.

The mammals you might chance upon in the reserve include vervet monkey, bushbuck, duikers (blue, red and grey), and smaller species such as Cape clawless otter, spotted genet and large grey mongoose.

Despite the reserve's small size, birding can be rewarding and you could tick green twinspot, Narina trogon, Knysna and purple-crested turaco.

The 1.2-km-long **iPithi Trail** (the name means 'blue duiker' in isiZulu) meanders along the southern bank of the Mpenjati River.

The **Yengele Trail** (1.8 km; 1 hour) meanders through the Yengele Forest – one of the largest tracts of dune forest along the south coast of KwaZulu-Natal.

16. ANEW RESORT INGELI FOREST
Harding

Trails: 3 walks; 1.8 to 9 km; 30 minutes to 3 hours; circular.
Permits: Tel: (039) 553 0600, email: ingelires@anewhotels.co.za, web: www.anewhotels.com.
Maps: Sketch map.
Facilities/Activities: Log cabins, deluxe rooms, rooms with garden and forest views; swimming pool; tennis court; adventure golf course; birding; mountain biking (from 3 to 30 km); trail running tracks.

The Ngele area is a mosaic of pine plantations (the Weza Plantation here is the largest in South Africa), patches of indigenous forest and mountain grasslands. Typical species to be seen in the Ngele Forest include lemonwood, knobwood, Natal krantz ash, Outeniqua yellowwood, red stinkwood and sneezewood.

The grasslands are the habitat of myriad flowers belonging to the lily, orchid, iris and aster families. Among the many species occuring here are brunsvigias, nerinas, watsonias, wild dagga, red-hot pokers and a variety of herbaceous plants. The Christmas bell (*Sandersonia aurantiaca*) with its bright orange-yellow bell-shaped flower is frequently seen near vleis.

The forest patches and plantations are inhabited by one of the largest populations of bushbuck in South Africa, while common vervet and samango monkeys also occur here. The Ngele Forest is home to a large population of the rare serval, although they are seldom seen because of their shy nature. Mountain reedbuck, grey rhebok and baboon occur in the more mountainous areas.

Among the more than 220 bird species that have been recorded in the Weza/Ngele area are eastern bronze-naped and African green pigeons, Cape parrot, long-crested eagle, forest buzzard, Knysna turaco, Narina trogon, Knysna woodpecker and yellow-throated woodland warbler. Grassland species include secretarybird, grey crowned crane and orange-throated longclaw.

1. Blue Trail alternates between indigenous forest, plantation and grassland in the Mackton Plantation, close to the lodge. **3.1 km; 1 hour; circular.**

2. White Trail starts with a steep climb through the Ngele Forest, one of several patches of indigenous forest covering a total of 3,670 ha. You will gain over 300 m in altitude before you reach the grassland, so take your time and enjoy the magnificent forest scenery along the way. The route then follows the upper edge of the forest to a fire lookout point, from where you will be treated to expansive views over the patchwork of plantations, indigenous forests and grasslands. Dominating the scenery to the southwest is the 2,268-m-high Ngele Peak. The return leg is a steady descent through the Ngele Forest. **9 km; 3 hours; circular.**

17. ORIBI GORGE NATURE RESERVE
Port Shepstone

> **Trails:** 3 walks; 2.5 to 5 hours; out-and-return.
> **Permits:** Conservation fee. No booking required for walks.
> **Maps:** Sketch map.
> **Facilities/Activities:** Self-catering cottages and huts; picnic sites.
> **Pertinent information:** The river water is not fit for human consumption. On account of the danger of bilharzia it is inadvisable to swim in the river.

In its wanderings across the Oribi Flats, the Mzimkhulwana River has carved a 24-km-long gorge to create one of South Africa's least-known, but nonetheless spectacular natural wonders: Oribi Gorge.

Located 25 km from the Indian Ocean, the Oribi Gorge has a depth of up to 500 m and a width of up to 5 km. The vegetation includes scarp forest, valley bushveld and coastal sourveld, and the scenery ranges from indigenous forest to towering sandstone cliffs. The most scenic section lies in the 1,873-ha Oribi Gorge Nature Reserve.

The reserve has an excellent example of evergreen coastal scarp forest, with typical species such as forest bushwillow, Cape beech, red quince, rock ash and tarwood. The striking large-leaved dragon tree and the Drakensberg cycad are also found here.

Animals you may see on the walks in the reserve include blue and common duiker, common reedbuck, bushbuck, baboon and samango monkey. More elusive are leopard, which do occur here but are seldom encountered. A small number of other carnivores, including several species of mongoose, also inhabit the reserve.

With a bird checklist of over 220 species, birding can be especially rewarding in this reserve. Species to look out for include Narina trogon, trumpeter hornbill, eastern bronze-naped and African green pigeons, lemon dove, Knysna turaco and green twinspot. The variety of habitats also attracts several raptor species, among them booted, martial and crowned eagles, African marsh harrier and lanner falcon.

1. Nkonka Walk Starting at the Gorge picnic site, this route passes through the forested slopes above the Mzimkhulwana River. It then continues along the base of the drier west- and north-facing slopes, with their valley bushveld vegetation. **5 km; 2.5 hours; out-and-return.**

2. Hoopoe Falls Walk follows an easy route from the Gorge picnic site along the northern banks of the Mzimkhulwana River for about 1.5 hours. Flanked by majestic sandstone cliffs and forested slopes, the trail then follows the Mbabala Stream to where the Hoopoe Falls plunge into a deep pool. **7 km; 4 hours; out-and-return.**

3. Mziki Walk owes its name to the isiZulu word for the reedbuck (*mziki*). Starting at the Gorge picnic site, the route ascends along a narrow gully to the top of the cliffs. From here it makes its way through grassland, with wonderful views over the gorge. It can also be started at the rest camp. **9 km; 5 hours; out-and-return.**

18. BURMAN BUSH NATURE RESERVE
Durban

> **Trails:** 3 walks; 500 m to 5 km; 30 minutes to 2 hours; circular.
> **Permits:** Entrance fee. No booking required for day walks.
> **Maps:** Enquire at the reserve.

Burman Bush Nature Reserve lies 8 km north of the bustling metropolis of Durban, near the Moses Mabhida Stadium. It provides protection to approximately 50 ha of coastal dune bush, regarded as one of the best preserved relic patches of coastal bush in the greater Durban area. Typical tree species to be seen include flat-crown, forest feverberry, Natal mahogany, pigeonwood and white stinkwood.

Among the many interesting birds to look out for are the lanner falcon, green wood-hoopoe, fork-tailed and square-tailed drongo, red-capped robin-chat, yellow-breasted apalis and African paradise flycatcher. Also to be seen are the orange-breasted bushshrike, dark-backed weaver, green twinspot and pin-tailed whydah.

Animals found here include the blue duiker, known in isiZulu as *pithi*, common duiker and vervet monkey. Banded and slender mongoose and porcupine also occur here.

The trail network consists of three circular trails: the **Pithi Trail** (500 m; 30 minutes), the **Hadeda Trail** (1 km; 1 hour) and the **Forest Olive Trail** (5 km; 2 hours). A definite highlight is a viewing platform at canopy level from where there are sweeping vistas of the Umgeni River – from the Connaught Bridge downstream to the river mouth at the Blue Lagoon.

19. PARADISE VALLEY NATURE RESERVE
Durban

Trails: 4 walks; 10 minutes to 1 hour; network.
Permits: Entrance fee.
Maps: Available at reception.
Facilities/Activities: Picnic areas, braai facilities, toilets; birding.

Despite its relatively small size, the 100-ha Paradise Valley Nature Reserve is an important link in the green corridor along the Umbilo River between Pinetown and Durban. The reserve was proclaimed as a provincial nature reserve by the Natal Parks Board in 1965 to protect the coastal, riverine and scarp forest, as well as remnant patches of grassland in the valley, but was deproclaimed in 1980 and falls under the eThekwini Municipality.

Of historical interest are the remains of the old Umbilo Waterworks, Durban's first water supply scheme, which was completed in 1887. Although it was destroyed by floods when 450 mm of rain fell in the river's catchment area in a 24-hour period in 1905, what little remained was proclaimed a national monument in 1994.

Visitors can explore the reserve along four short walks which can be combined into a much longer walk. Walks have been colour-coded in accordance with their gradient.

1. Waterfall Trail is an easy walk along the Umbilo River and leads past the remains of the Umbilo Dam wall and the filter beds to the viewing platform overlooking the Umbilo Falls. **705 m; 10 minutes.**

2. Duiker Trail meanders through coastal forest and grassland, passing an avenue of mango trees that leads to the demolished caretaker's residence and the spillway abutment. **642 m; 10 minutes.**

3. Bushbuck Trail leads through coastal forest and along the way passes the exposed roots of Natal wild fig trees. **861 m; 15 minutes.**

4. Dormouse Trail, the most demanding trail, winds through grasslands and coastal forest to above the Umbilo Falls. **1.3 km; 20 minutes.**

20. PALMIET NATURE RESERVE
Durban

Trails: 10 km network; 15 minutes to 3 hours.
Permits: Entrance free, but donations can be made to the reserve.
Maps: Trail booklet.
Facilities/Activities: Braai and picnic sites. Guided trails 1st Sunday of each month.

This 90-ha nature reserve, in the heart of Westville and a mere 10 km northwest of Durban, provides protection to the rugged Palmiet River Valley, which is home to blue duiker, bushbuck and vervet monkey. The trail network (15 km in total) alternates between coastal and riverine forests, the Nkawu cliffs, grassland and the course of the Palmiet River. Although the routes are not difficult there are some steep ascents.

Among the interesting birds to keep an eye out for are Narina trogon and lanner falcon, while the red-capped robin-chat is common. In the forested parts of the reserve you may catch a glimpse of the blue duiker.

21. KENNETH STAINBANK NATURE RESERVE
Durban

Trails: Mkumbi Trail: 6 km; 2 hours; circular. Several short rambles also available.
Permits: Conservation fee. No booking required for walks.
Maps: Sketch map.
Facilities/Activities: Camp site; picnic site with braai facilities; toilets; cycling trails.

Situated in the southwestern suburbs of greater Durban, this nature reserve provides protection to 211 ha of coastal forest and grassveld.

Along the trails you may come upon common reedbuck, bushbuck, red and blue duiker, impala, nyala and vervet monkey. There is also a rich diversity of smaller mammals, among them the Cape clawless otter and banded mongoose.

Birding here can be rewarding – among the noteworthy species to be seen are the white-eared barbet, green malkoha and spotted ground thrush. Other species you may tick include the long-crested eagle, golden-tailed woodpecker, various species of kingfisher and the green-backed heron.

Mkumbi Trail This route initially winds through grassland past a dam, where antelope are often seen

drinking. Further along, the grassveld gives way to indigenous coastal forest. The trail then follows the Little Umhlatuzana River, which you cross twice before the trail loops all the way back to the start. **6 km; 2 hours; circular.**

22. NEW GERMANY NATURE RESERVE
Pinetown

Trail: 2.5 hours; circular
Permits: Entrance fee. No booking required for walk.
Maps: Sketch map of trail.
Facilities/Activities: Picnic and braai facilities; interpretative centre; walk-in aviary.

The vegetation of this small reserve in the hills of New Germany is dominated by coastal grassland interspersed by clumps of coastal bush and protea communities. The grassveld is attractive in spring when masses of spring flowers are in bloom, while the purple *Watsonia densiflora* is especially eye-catching in late summer.

Trees include the forest toad tree, thorny elm, forest bushwillow, flat-crown, mitzeeri, forest feverberry, wild date palm and thorny rope. Wildlife includes impala, bushbuck, blue duiker, vervet monkey, three mongoose species (slender, water and banded mongoose) and cane rat.

Red-capped robin-chat, Narina trogon, purple-crested turaco, green coucal, violet-backed starling and gymnogene can be ticked, while raptors include lanner falcon, black sparrowhawk and long-crested eagle.

The first white settlers arrived in the area from Bremen, Germany, in 1848 to grow cotton. The reserve was set aside as a commonage for the grazing of livestock and firewood collecting and, although the felling of trees for firewood collecting was prohibited in 1924, grazing was still permitted. As a result of overgrazing the grassland is dominated by *Aristida junctiformis*, a secondary grassland type.

The **Imbali Trail** traverses the northern section of the reserve, which lies between the freeway and the Palmiet River. The route alternates between grassland and clumps of bush.

23. KRANTZKLOOF NATURE RESERVE
Kloof

Trails: 12 trails; 0.8 km to 11.8 km; 45 minutes to 7 hours; out-and-return, circular, open-ended.
Permits: Conservation fee. No booking required for walks.
Maps: Reserve information brochure with map.
Facilities/Activities: Picnic sites; small interpretative centre.

The Krantzkloof Nature Reserve, which nestles against the coastal Escarpment, was proclaimed in 1950 to protect the spectacular forested gorges created by the Molweni and Nkutu rivers. The reserve is renowned for its breathtaking views over the Molweni River Valley, orange-red sandstone cliffs, the Ipithi and Nkutu waterfalls and the 90-m-high Kloof Falls on the Molweni River.

Despite its small size (668 ha), the nature reserve boasts a great diversity of flora, including several rare species. Among these is one of South Africa's rarest trees, the Natal quince, which occurs only in a few scattered localities. Other interesting species include the Pondo rose-apple, tarwood, rock ash and the Natal flame bush.

The reserve is home to thick-tailed bushbaby, bushbuck, blue and red duiker and tree dassie. Noteworthy species that birders may tick include crowned eagle, Wahlberg's eagle (the reserve is home to the southernmost known breeding sites of this species) and African broadbill. Also recorded are Knysna and purple-crested turacos, Narina trogon, brown scrub robin and trumpeter hornbill.

Three trails in the reserve are described below.

1. Nkutu Falls Trail starts at the Nkutu picnic site and meanders mainly through grasslands along the cliffs above the Nkutu River. A detour, reached about 1 km after setting off, leads to the base of the first waterfall. After retracing your tracks to the main trail, the route continues along the cliff edge, and further along you reach another detour to the second waterfall. Still further on there are spectacular views into the lower gorge. **1.5 hours, or 3 hours if visiting both falls; out-and-return.**

2. Molweni Trail has three starting points: Kloof Falls Road picnic site, Uve Road car park and Nkutu picnic site. All three trail options begin with a descent of some 350 m into the gorge and an equally strenuous climb out. This is the only trail that provides access to the bottom of the Kloof Falls. Trailists are advised not to walk downstream of Splash Rock, owing to the troublesome behaviour of residents outside the reserve. **5 hours; open-ended.**

3. Beacon Trail Starting at the Kloof Falls picnic site, this route initially follows the Molweni Trail, and then passes through grassland to a trigonometric beacon. The trail winds down into the gorge to Splash Pool. From here you follow the Molweni Trail back to the start. **6 hours; circular.**

24. FERNCLIFFE NATURE RESERVE
Pietermaritzburg

Trails: 7 walks; 10 km (in total); 10 minutes to 1 hour; circular, out-and-return.
Permits: Entrance fee. No booking required for walks.
Maps: Enquire at reserve.
Facilities/Activities: Picnic sites; parking.

Ferncliffe lies just below the Escarpment, about 12 km northwest of Pietermaritzburg, and covers some 250 ha of exotic plantations and indigenous forest, with species such as lemonwood, forest fig and clivia. The reserve's network of short trails takes in scenic attractions such as Breakfast Rock, with its fine views over Pietermaritzburg, a cave that houses four species of bat, Boulder Dam, tranquil streams and the Maidenhair Falls. A variety of birds are attracted to the plantations and forests, and you may come across bushbuck, provided you move about quietly.

25. KWAZULU-NATAL NATIONAL BOTANICAL GARDEN
Pietermaritzburg

> **Trails:** Network of footpaths; each no longer than 1 hour.
> **Permits:** Entrance fee. No booking required.
> **Maps:** Map of botanical garden available.
> **Facilities/Activities:** Restaurant; public toilets; nursery.

One of ten National Botanical Institute gardens, the KwaZulu-Natal National Botanical Garden dates back to 1874. A focal point of the garden is the magnificent plane tree avenue planted in 1908, while stately camphor, magnolia, tulip and swamp cypress trees testify to the early Victorian influence. Also of interest is a traditional Zulu hut, surrounded by an indigenous medicinal garden that forms part of a *muthi* (medicine) plant display.

The garden specialises in plants from the eastern grasslands of South Africa, and the grassland project contains fine collections of red-hot pokers (*Kniphofia*), watsonias and *Dieramas*. The northeastern section of the garden is characterised by indigenous scrub forest with a mixture of thicket, thornveld and mist-belt species and consequently attracts a wide variety of birds. A section of the forest forms part of the garden's clivia conservation project where four species of clivia are cultivated under irrigation.

To date more than 130 bird species have been recorded in the garden. Among the ones to be seen are crowned eagle, black crake, lemon dove, black-headed oriole, pied and giant kingfisher, chorister robin-chat and dark-backed weaver. Careful and persistent searching may yield elusive species such as buff-spotted flufftail, tambourine dove and green twinspot.

1. Turraea Trail makes its way along the shores of Kingfisher Lake and through indigenous forest, thickets and tangled scrub. The trail is especially rewarding for birding enthusiasts and includes a section planted with indigenous plants that attract birds and butterflies.

2. Forest Footpath offers wonderful views over the garden, and provides good chances to tick typical forest species such as the crowned eagle, African goshawk and dark-backed weaver.

26. BISLEY VALLEY NATURE RESERVE
Pietermaritzburg

> **Trails:** 2 walks; both 1 hour; circular.
> **Permits:** Not required.
> **Maps:** Enquire with Pietermaritzburg Conservation and Environment Department, tel: (033) 392 3241/2.
> **Facilities/Activities:** Picnic areas.

This small reserve on the southern outskirts of Pietermaritzburg provides protection to 350 ha of thornveld, grassland and tree-lined watercourses. A small wetland is one of the reserve's star attractions and offers good birding opportunities. There are two bird hides in the reserve, and more than 160 bird species have been recorded to date.

27. BLINKWATER HIKING TRAILS
Greytown

> **Trails:** 100 km (in total); 2 to 6 days; network of trails.
> **Bookings:** Rebecca van der Linde, cell: 082 776 0435, email: gohike@ blinkwatertrails.co.za or book online: www.blinkwatertrails.co.za.
> **Maps:** Trail pamphlet with map.
> **Facilities/Activities:** Two overnight huts with bunks, mattresses, showers, toilets, fireplaces and firewood; mountain-bike trails.
> **Pertinent information:** Success and iPhasiwe huts are no longer available.

Situated in the KwaZulu-Natal Midlands, this magnificent trail is a joint venture between the Umvoti Branch of the Wildlife and Environment

Society of South Africa, two timber companies (Sappi and Mondi) and Ezemvelo KZN Wildlife.

The area is dominated by commercial plantations, but patches of indigenous forest occur in the river valleys and on the southern slopes, while grasslands are found at higher elevations. Typical forest species occurring here include real, Outeniqua and Henkel's yellowwoods, knobwood, Cape chestnut, sneezewood, pompom tree and tree fuchsia. Ferns, begonias and *Streptocarpus* plants provide a touch of colour to the forest floor, while clivias grow in the forks of trees. The common tree fern is conspicuous along stream banks in the grasslands.

Among the animals you may see in the grasslands are the endangered oribi and mountain reedbuck. Most noteworthy among the birds are the endangered blue swallow, which breeds in the area, and the wattled crane, an endangered species that breeds in the vicinity of Island Dam. Raptors are represented by some 21 species, including martial and crowned eagles, Cape vulture, forest buzzard and African marsh harrier. Among many other species you may tick are buff-spotted flufftail, lemon dove, Cape parrot, African grass owl, trumpeter hornbill, red-capped robin chat, white-starred robin, Cape grassbird and Cape longclaw.

The trail network consists of two sections: the Southern Section, which is accessed through Mondi's Seele Estate, and the Northern Section, which starts at Mountain Falls in Sappi forests. All the trails are circular and interlinked, providing hikers with several options. The trails follow forestry roads, boundary firebreaks and footpaths, passing through plantations, indigenous forests and grasslands. Adding to the diversity of landscapes are tranquil streams, waterfalls and dams. There are also lovely views of the Albert Falls Dam.

As much as possible of the area's fascinating local history has been incorporated into the trail network. Reminders of the early settlers include an old grave site of the Wesleyans, who came to KwaZulu-Natal from Yorkshire to practise their religion without fear of persecution. Also to be seen is an old railway line, constructed at the start of the twentieth century to extract timber from the indigenous forests and sawpits.

Mountain Falls Hut, which owes its name to the nearby series of attractive waterfalls, is accessible by car. From the workshop at the Mondi Seele Estate in the Southern Section it is a 10-km walk to the Douglas Smit Cottage. From here, hikers have a choice of an 8.6-km walk to the Mountain Falls Hut or a longer 11.4-km walk through the Blinkwater Forest.

28. MOOR PARK NATURE RESERVE
Estcourt

Trail: 6 km; 3 hours; out-and-return.
Permits: Conservation fee. No booking required for walk.
Maps: Trail booklet.
Facilities/Activities: Picnic site; education centre; camp site at adjacent Wagendrift Dam Resort.

This small nature reserve, which covers 264 ha and lies at the head of the Wagendrift Dam, is dominated by Makabeni Hill. The landscapes range from exposed cliffs and deep gullies to a high plateau and the Bushman's River, which forms the reserve's southern boundary. The vegetation of the lower areas is dominated by acacia thornveld, while sourveld is characteristic of the higher elevations.

The vegetation is bushveld, thornveld, tall grassland and Highveld sourveld, and among the game reintroduced are Burchell's zebra, blesbok, mountain reedbuck, black wildebeest and impala.

Archaeological excavations on Makabeni Hill have provided evidence that Iron Age people lived here some 1,000 years ago. Of more recent historical interest is Veglaer, where the Voortrekkers fought a three-day battle against a large Zulu force from 13 to 15 August 1838.

Birding can be rewarding as the reserve has a checklist of some 200 bird species despite its small size. Birds attracted to the Wagendrift Dam include South African shelduck, southern pochard and whiskered tern. Raptors are represented by Verreaux's and martial eagles, Cape vulture and lanner falcon. Blue crane, western osprey, Cape longclaw and arrow-marked babbler count among the other species you might tick.

Old Furrow Trail is a self-guided, interpretative trail that leads along a historic irrigation furrow built by the Moor family between 1900 and 1903 to divert water from the Bushman's River to land that became submerged after the completion of the Wagendrift Dam in 1964. Marked points of interest along the trail include the area's history, vegetation types, trees and the ecology of the Bushman's River, and are described in the trail booklet.

29. HAROLD JOHNSON NATURE RESERVE
Darnall

Trails: 2 walks; 1 to 3 hours; circular.
Permits: Conservation fee. No booking required for walks.
Maps: Information booklet on Muthi Trail and map of Bushbuck Trail available from reserve office.
Facilities/Activities: Camp sites with ablution facilities; picnic sites; education centre.

Situated on the southern bank of the Tugela River, the Harold Johnson Nature Reserve covers 104 ha of grassland, bush and well-preserved tracts of coastal bush. The reserve is noted for its rich variety of epiphytic orchids. Among the trees commonly found here are the wild date palm, brackthorn, small knobwood, white milkwood, Kei-apple and black monkey orange.

The reserve is home to Burchells's zebra, impala and smaller mammal species such as the common, red and blue duiker, bushbuck and bushpig. Among the typical coastal birds you may tick are the dark-backed weaver, Narina trogon, red-capped robin-chat, purple-crested turaco and white-eared barbet.

The area is also rich in history. Of historic significance are the ruins of Fort Pearson, which served as a launching point when British troops invaded Zululand in 1879, and the Ultimatum Tree, where the British ultimatum to Cetshwayo was read out to his chiefs on 11 December 1878.

1. Muthi Trail is a self-guided, interpretative trail focusing on the Zulu people and the way they use some of the trees and plants in the area for medicinal

and other uses. Sixteen trees along the trail have been marked and are described in the trail booklet. **1.8 km; 1 hour; circular.**

2. Bushbuck Trail wanders down the steep slopes above the Tugela River to a stream bed and then ascends to a ridge overlooking the Tugela River Valley. **5 km; 3 hours; circular.**

30. DLINZA FOREST
Eshowe

Trail: 2 km; 1 hour; circular.
Permits: Conservation fee. No booking required for walk.
Maps: Trail is clearly marked.
Facilities/Activities: Forest canopy walkway; picnic and braai facilities.

The 250-ha Dlinza Forest on the outskirts of Eshowe features a delightful patch of coastal scarp forest – a transitional forest type with a mixture of typical coastal trees and mist-belt species. The giant umzimbeet and forest mangosteen are among the rare and unusual trees occurring here.

Dlinza is an important breeding site of the spotted ground thrush, while yellow-streaked greenbul, eastern bronze-naped pigeon and grey cuckooshrike can also be ticked. Other species to keep an eye out for are green twinspot, crowned eagle, trumpeter hornbill and green coucal.

Bushbuck, blue and red duiker, bushpig and vervet monkey inhabit the forest.

The trail offers a short option and a longer route of about 2 km. Visitors can also walk along the tracks that have been cut through the forest, sections of which were cut by British soldiers stationed here after the Anglo-Zulu War in 1879.

31. ENTUMENI FOREST
Eshowe

Trails: 2 trails; 2 and 4 hours; circular.

Situated about 15 km south of Eshowe, this 750-ha reserve was proclaimed in 1970 and provides protection to a stand of coastal scarp forest which contains several rare tree species.

The forest offers excellent birding, and yellow-streaked greenbul, African broadbill and eastern bronze-naped pigeon count among the many sought-after species.

Bushbuck, bushpig and blue and red duiker are some of the forest mammals you are likely to chance upon. Other, less conspicuous, species to look out for are water, slender and white-tailed mongoose, as well as Cape clawless otter.

Visitors can explore the forest along two trails, the **iPithi Trail**, named after the blue duiker, and the **iKhozi Trail**. The trails start at the car park and, after following a ridge for a while, there is a choice between the iPithi Trail for about 2 hours, or the iKhozi Trail, which takes about 4 hours to complete. Both routes drop steeply into the valley before climbing back to the start.

32. UMLALAZI NATURE RESERVE
Mtunzini

Bounded by the Mlalazi River in the north and the Amatikulu Nature Reserve in the south, this wonderful nature reserve has several very special attractions. The raffia palm reaches the southern limit of its natural distribution at Kosi Bay. However, the palms at Mtunzini grew from seeds that were planted by a former magistrate, C C Foxon, in 1915. The grove of palms was proclaimed a heritage site in 1943 and the reserve was established five years later.

The forest of black and white mangroves that fringes the Mlalazi River ranks as one of the finest mangrove communities in South Africa. A swamp forest, which is dominated by the powder-puff tree, occurs along the Siyayi Lagoon. The dune forest is one of the finest examples of its sort in South Africa. Coastal red milkwood, Natal guarri and dune false currant are among the typical species that can be seen here.

The reserve is home to a small population of palm-nut vultures – the southernmost limit of this species. Birdlife is as diverse as the habitats. White-eared barbet, yellow-bellied bulbul, purple-crested turaco, eastern bronze-naped pigeon, African finfoot and grey sunbird can be ticked. Be on the lookout for spotted ground thrush between April and September.

Sightings of blue and red duiker, bushpig and reedbuck are possible, while crocodile occur in the Mlalazi River.

A short 2-km walk provides a fascinating insight into the mangroves and the animals associated with these communities, such as mud-skipper, fiddler crab and mangrove snails. The second walk leads through the dune forest and, after crossing the Siyayi River, meanders down to the beach.

The longest walk (8 km) meanders through dune forest and mangroves along the southern bank of the Mlalazi River.

33. ENSELENI NATURE RESERVE
Empangeni

The Enseleni Nature Reserve is a beautiful mosaic of coastal grassland and forest, including riverine and swamp forest, along the Enseleni River, and is a sanctuary for several animal species, such as waterbuck, reedbuck, nyala, blue wildebeest and Burchell's zebra. Bushbuck, bushpig, red, blue and common duiker also occur, while the aquatic habitats are home to hippo, crocodile and monitor lizards.

Birding is excellent and the Enseleni River is a good place to seek out African finfoot, while white-backed night heron and Pel's fishing owl can be sought out in the adjoining forest. Other species to keep an eye out for include purple-crested turaco, white-eared barbet, black-throated wattle-eye and green malkoha.

The **Nkonkoni Trail** (4.8 km) alternates between Umdoni parkland, scattered ilala palms, mangroves, wild fig trees and grasslands. The **Mvubu Trail** (5.2 km) follows a route through swamp and riverine forest and across grassland.

34. ISIMANGALISO WETLAND PARK
St Lucia village, Sodwana Bay, Mkhuze village

Trails: Self-guided trail; 1.5 km; 30 minutes (St Lucia village). Guided forest walk 3 km; 1 hour (Mkhuze Game Reserve). Guided morning and afternoon walks; 4 km; 3 hours (Mkhuze Game Reserve). Unguided beach walks at Sodwana Bay.
Permits: No park permit fee for St Lucia Estuary. Park permit fee for Mkhuze Game Reserve. Guided walks must be booked and paid in advance at Mantuma Camp office.
Maps: Colour tourist map of the park.
Facilities/Activities: Various accommodation options, from self-catering accommodation and tented camps to private bush camps and camp sites, at St Lucia village, Sodwana Bay and in the Mkhuze Game Reserve.
Pertinent information: Precautions should be taken against malaria, especially during the rainy season. Swimming and wading in all the lakes are forbidden, because of hippo and crocodile.

The 332,000-ha iSimangaliso Wetland Park is a mosaic of unspoilt coastline, pristine lakes, swamp forests, magnificent dune forest, savannah woodland and grassland. The park's shores are the breeding grounds of leatherback and loggerhead turtles, while the offshore coral reefs are the southernmost on the African continent.

The park's historic core, the St Lucia Reserve, was proclaimed in 1895. Together with Hluhluwe-iMfolozi Park, which was established in the same year, it is the oldest conservation area in Africa. Several areas of state-owned forest land, game reserves and parks were subsequently amalgamated and the reserve was renamed the Greater St Lucia Wetland Park. The park was inscribed as South Africa's first UNESCO World Heritage Site in 1999, after which it was given its current name, iSimangaliso Wetland Park. *iSimangaliso* means 'miracle and wonder' in isiZulu.

Lake St Lucia, the largest estuarine system in Africa, is one of the important habitats of hippo and crocodile in South Africa. The main lake, which is about 40 km long and between 3 and 8 km wide, is connected to the sea by way of the Narrows, a 21-km-long winding channel. The lake is also an important breeding area for waterbirds in South Africa and at least 48 species are known to reproduce here. More than 70 species of fish are found in the lake. The St Lucia system was designated a Ramsar site in 1986.

Reaching heights of close to 200 m, the dune forests of the Eastern Shores are among the highest in the world. They were formed by wind-blown sand which accumulated on the underlying rock bed 12,000 to 20,000 years ago.

Other outstanding features of the park include Lake Sibaya, the largest natural freshwater lake in South Africa, and the Kosi lake system (both are Ramsar sites). Situated in the northeastern corner of the park, the system consists of four interconnected lakes which are linked to the sea by an estuary.

Just over a hundred mammals have been recorded in the park and the rich variety of game, which includes the Big Five, is one of the park's main attractions. White and black rhino, elephant, lion, buffalo, African wild dog and cheetah are among the 20 different species of game that have been reintroduced into the park since 2001. As a result of the reintroduction of animals such as buffalo, rhino, elephant and lion, most of the self-guided walks and longer trails that were once accessible have been closed down. There are, however, still a number of short walks and guided walks along which visitors can explore the park.

With a checklist of 526 species, birding is another major attraction of iSimangaliso. Heading the list of birding destinations is the Mkhuze Game Reserve, with some 450 species recorded to date.

St Lucia Village

Lake St Lucia and its estuary are some of the key attractions of the southern region of iSimangaliso. The lake is located north of the holiday village of St Lucia, close to the southern entrance to the park.

The vegetation here ranges from dune forest, grassland and Umdoni parkland to deep marshes, reed swamps and impenetrable mangroves along the estuary. Among the large game species to be seen are blue wildebeest, reedbuck, Burchell's zebra, waterbuck, impala and bushbuck. Smaller species to look out for include red and common duiker, vervet monkey and side-striped jackal. Hippo and crocodile can often be seen from the banks of the estuary or on a cruise offered by a licensed operator.

Not to be missed is a visit to the Crocodile Centre, which aims to educate visitors about the importance of these reptiles in nature. Interesting displays provide a fascinating insight into their biology and the way of life of these misunderstood reptiles.

Igwalagwala Walk at St Lucia village derives its name from the isiZulu word for the purple-crested turaco and Livingstone's turaco. This almost-level, easy, circular walk begins near the Eden Park camp site in the village. Originally laid out by honorary game rangers of Ezemvelo KZN Wildlife, the trail meanders through a patch of coastal dune forest along the shores of the St Lucia Estuary.

The forest is an excellent place for birding, and Narina trogon, white-eared barbet, golden-tailed woodpecker, blue-mantled crested flycatcher, trumpeter hornbill and Rudd's and yellow-breasted apalis are among the species recorded to date. Keep an eye out for green malkoha, Woodward's batis and broad-billed roller, a noteworthy species present during the summer months. A short detour takes you to the estuary shore where you chance ticking a variety of waterbirds, including lesser jacana and various kingfisher species.

A variety of mammals, such as vervet monkey, red duiker, tree squirrel and bands of banded mongoose, inhabit the forest. You might even chance upon a bushbuck or a warthog on your walk. Hippo are also present and as they usually leave the water before sunset to graze, it is inadvisable to do the trail in the late afternoon.

Trees you will encounter during the walk include Cape ash, pigeonwood, jackalberry, milkpear, flat-crown, common cabbage and white stinkwood. **1.5 km; 30 minutes; circular.**

Mkhuze Game Reserve

The 40,000-ha Mkhuze section was established as a game reserve in 1912, before being deproclaimed in 1939. Some 38,000 head of game occuring in the area were killed in an effort to eradicate *nagana* – a cattle disease borne by the tsetse fly – between 1944 and 1949. The reserve was reproclaimed in 1954 and opened to the public four years later.

The reserve was linked to the Greater St Lucia Wetland Park in 1992 when the Mkhuze Swamps were incorporated into the park. Bounded by the Ubombo Mountains in the west, its spectacular landscapes include bushveld, riverine forests dominated by sycamore figs, fever forests and the Nsumo Pan.

Wildlife is abundant and black and white rhino, elephant, buffalo, leopard, lion, hippo, giraffe, warthog and Burchell's zebra are just some of the mammals that can be seen here. Antelope are represented by red and common duiker, kudu, nyala, reedbuck and impala. The rare suni occur in the sand forest east of the rest camp.

With a checklist exceeding 450 species, Mkhuze is an excellent birding destination. Here you may find African broadbill, crested guineafowl, pink-throated twinspot and Neergaard's sunbird. The hides along Nsumo Pan offer good opportunities for spotting waterbirds, especially when the water level is low.

1. Fig Forest Walk is a guided walk in the southeastern section of the reserve, east of Nsumo Pan. From the parking area the route heads through stands of fever and umbrella thorn trees and ilala palm. After crossing two inlets of the Mkhuze River by way of a suspension bridge, the route enters the Fig Forest. This type of forest is extremely rare in South Africa – of the 1,800 ha in KwaZulu-Natal, 1,400 ha are located in Mkhuze. The circular route through the forest meanders along a boardwalk and a canopy walk with several interlinked viewing platforms.

The forest supports a rich variety of birdlife, and crowned and trumpeter hornbills, square-tailed drongo, golden-tailed woodpecker, red-billed wood-hoopoe, Narina trogon and crowned eagle are among the many species to be seen. Also be on the lookout for white-eared barbet, purple-crested turaco, green malkoha and broad-billed roller. The elusive Pel's fishing owl is another possibility in the forest. **3 km; 1 hour; circular.**

2. Guided Game-viewing Walks are conducted at 06:30 and 14:00 from Mantuma Hutted Camp. The excursion includes the drive to the area where the walk is conducted and back. While getting close on foot to game is often the highlight of such a walk, you will also learn more about the animals and their behaviour. It is advisable to book your walk on arrival or two days in advance by calling (035) 573 9004. **4 to 5 km; 3 hours; circular.**

35. KOSI SLACKPACKING TRAIL
iSimangaliso Wetland Park, KwaNgwanase

Trail: 39 km; 3 days; guided.
Bookings: Active Escapes, tel: (033) 329 5259, email: tours@active-escapes.co.za.
Maps: Google Earth route map sent after booking, but trail is fully guided.
Facilities/Activities: Accommodation at beach camp and tented camp with en-suite facilities, hot-water showers and communal dining. Snorkelling; birding.
Pertinent information: Fully catered including all meals, local guide, luggage transfers and boat trips.

Extending over a distance of about 18 km, the Kosi system consists of a string of four interconnected lakes and an estuary, which links the system to the sea. Surrounding the lakes is a mosaic of swamps, marshes and pans, while a strip of high dunes separates the lakes from the sea.

Nhlange, or Third Lake, is the largest of the four lakes, covering an area of between 3,000 and 3,700 ha; with a maximum depth of 31 m, it is also the deepest of the four. Mpungwini, or Second Lake, has less than 10 per cent of the surface area of Nhlange, and attains a maximum depth of 18 m. Makawulani (First Lake) is the smallest of the lakes and is approximately 8 m deep. Amanzimnyama, or Fourth Lake, the southernmost lake in the system, is in many respects unique. In addition to its swamp forests it has the most extensive occurrence of the rare raffia palm in South Africa. This species is confined to KwaZulu-Natal, and there are scattered groups near Manguzi (a small settlement outside the reserve). The palms at Mtunzini (south of Richards Bay) were established from seed. Also of interest here is Kosi Mouth, which is the only place in South Africa where five mangrove species occur together.

Among the more than 250 bird species recorded in the area is South Africa's rarest breeding bird, the palm-nut vulture – a fantastic tick for any birder. The breeding and feeding habits of the palm-nut vulture are closely associated with oil palms. Another noteworthy species, Pel's fishing owl, occurs in the swamp forest of Lake Amanzimnyama. Other species found here include the African fish eagle, white-faced whistling duck, African pygmy goose, green malkoha, broad-billed roller, African broadbill and Stierling's wren-warbler.

The coast of Maputaland is the most important breeding ground of the leatherback turtle in the southern Indian Ocean. Between October and February the females come ashore at night to lay their eggs on the beach.

Of cultural interest here is the complex system of fish traps at Lake Makawulani. These traps, which consist of wooden and reed fences designed to trap the fish in funnel-shaped baskets, have been used by the local Thonga people for over 500 years.

The first day's hike (13 km; 6 hours) from Beach Camp alternates between mangrove swamps, a fern forest and the Zilonde dunes close to the Mozambican border. The trail then makes its way to Kosi Mouth, where trailists can snorkel in the estuary with its amazing variety of fish before heading back to Beach Camp.

On the second day (7 km; 5 hours, including a boat trip), trailists set off to the Kosi estuary and then hike south to First Lake for a boat cruise on the lake, with its complex system of Tonga fishing traps, Second Lake and Third Lake, the largest lake. After disembarking along the western shore of Third Lake, trailists make their way to Kosi Bay Lodge.

On the third and final hike day (17 to 19 km; 7 hours), a trail is followed to the western shores of Fourth Lake, where the narrow channel between Third and Fourth lakes is crossed with a raffia pontoon. At Fourth Lake you will see the rare raffia palm and, if you are very lucky, the equally rare palm-nut vulture. From there the hike continues to Bhanga Nek where the dune barrier that separates Third Lake from the Indian Ocean is a mere 250 m wide. Trailists then head back to Third Lake for a boat crossing to the western shore and a hike up to Kosi Bay Lodge.

36. HLUHLUWE-IMFOLOZI PARK
Mtubatuba and Hluhluwe villages

Trails: Guided day walks; 4 to 5 km; 2 to 3 hours; circular. Five guided wilderness trails; distances vary from 7 to 14 km per day; 2 to 4 nights; walks from base camp or sites selected by trails officer on Primitive and Explorer trails.
Permits: Ezemvelo KZN Wildlife, P O Box 13069, Cascades 3202, tel: (033) 845 1067, fax: (033) 845 1001, email: trails@kznwildlife.com.
Maps: Colour tourist map of park.
Facilities/Activities: Self-catering and catered accommodation, restaurant and swimming pool at Hilltop Resort in Hluhluwe section; self-contained cottages, chalets and safari tents at Mpila Resort in iMfolozi section; lodges and bush lodges; self-drive game-viewing; morning and afternoon guided walks; guided morning and night drives, picnic sites, game-viewing hides.
Pertinent information: Groups must consist of a minimum of 4 and a maximum of 8 people, except on the Explorer Trail where the minimum group

size is 6. Children under the age of 16 are not allowed on any of the wilderness trails. All trails depart from Mpila Resort and are fully catered. Trailists are advised to take precautions against malaria and ticks. Trails are conducted between early/mid-February and late November/mid-December depending on the trail selected.

The Hluhluwe-iMfolozi Park is without doubt one of South Africa's most celebrated wilderness areas. Hluhluwe and iMfolozi were proclaimed in 1897 as two separate game reserves, making them among the oldest in Africa.

iMfolozi is the birthplace of the wilderness concept in South Africa, pioneered by visionary conservationist Ian Player. (This concept is to take an intrinsically wild area and conserve it in its natural state, with minimal human interference.) The first wilderness area was set aside in the southern part of the reserve in 1959 and it was here that South Africa's first wilderness trails were conducted. iMfolozi has also played an important role in the conservation of South Africa's white rhino population.

Originally separated by a strip of land known as the Corridor, the two reserves were amalgamated in 1985 and now form a 96,000-ha game park.

Home to the Big Five, the park is renowned for its large population of white rhino, as well as black rhino. Leopard, cheetah, spotted hyaena and African wild dog occur, while the large antelope are represented by eland, kudu, nyala, impala, common and mountain reedbuck, waterbuck and blue wildebeest. Burchell's zebra, giraffe, warthog and hippo are among the many other species that can be seen.

With a checklist exceeding 330 species, Hluhluwe-iMfolozi is a popular birding destination. Specials include African finfoot, Narina trogon, southern ground hornbill, white-backed night heron and southern bald ibis (winter only). White-backed and white-headed vultures and bateleur are among the 36 raptor species recorded to date.

The first wilderness trails in iMfolozi were conducted in the 25,000-ha wilderness area in 1959. Trails are conducted by a trails officer and a field guide assistant, both of whom are armed to ensure your safety. Although seeing game on foot is obviously a highlight of these trails, it is not the main objective.

The trails officers have an intimate knowledge of the wilderness area and will interpret the signs of the wilds and explain the intricacies of nature on the trails. In addition, trailists will learn more about the philosophy and principles of the wilderness concept.

Pack clothing that blends in well with the environment, as well as a pair of comfortable shoes that can be used for river crossings. Decisions about the daily routine, routes and distances are at the discretion of the trails officers and will depend on the time of the year that the trail is being conducted and the overall fitness of the group. Although the trails are not too demanding, trailists must be physically fit, especially those doing the Primitive Trail and the Explorer Trail, as backpacks have to be carried.

1. Base Camp Trails are conducted from the comfortable Mndindini Trails Camp on the banks of the White iMfolozi River. The facilities at Mndindini include four two-bed tents, communal ablution with a hot-water shower and a flush toilet, and an open-plan communal lounge area with a fridge and a kitchen. Trailists must check in at Mpila Resort by 13:00 and will then be directed to the Mndindini Trails Camp, where they will be briefed. Generally, trailists set off after breakfast and need to carry only a daypack containing lunch, water and personal effects. The final day ends after a morning walk and a snack at Mndindini. Trailists leave by 11:00. **Distances range from 7 to 14 km per day; 3 nights/4 days; walks from trails camp.**

2. Primitive Trails combine the features of a wilderness trail and a backpacking trail and will appeal to outdoor enthusiasts who like to be completely self-sufficient for the duration of a trail. Trailists must carry all their equipment, clothing, food and bedding and, although the daily distances are not excessive, they must be physically fit. On the first day of the trail, trailists must report by 09:00 at Mpila Resort where they will be advised on how to pack their backpacks. After a late breakfast and trail briefing the group sets off into the wilderness. The route is selected by the trails officer and sleeping is in the open under the stars at suitable sites selected by the officer. Lightweight rain shelters are provided in case of bad weather. Trailists take turns on the night watch, with only a fire to keep them company. Camp is generally made close to the White iMfolozi River,

usually the only source of drinking water. There are no showers or toilets, but the river can be used to freshen up after the day's walk. Trails end at 10:00 at Mpila Resort on the last day. **Distances range from 7 to 14 km per day; 4 nights/4 days.**

3. Short Wilderness Trails are ideal for people with limited time. Trails depart on Tuesdays and Fridays from Mpila Resort, where trailists must report by 11:00. After a briefing, participants set off on a 7-km walk to the Mndindini Trails Camp, carrying their personal equipment. Hikers who overnight at Mpila Resort can drop most of their gear off at the resort before 16:00 on the day before the trail starts, from where it will be transported to the wilderness camp by donkeys. Food, too, is transported to the camp by means of donkeys. Accommodation at the camp is in dome tents, which are equipped with mattresses. Shower facilities are limited to a hot-water bucket shower, while conventional toilet facilities are limited to a spade, toilet paper and matches. Up to 15 km is covered on the second day. On the final day, trailists walk back to Mndindini Trails Camp, where the trail ends at 13:00. **Distances range from 7 to 14 km per day; 2 nights/3 days; walks from base camp.**

4. Extended Short Wilderness Trails are essentially the same as the Short Wilderness Trails (see above), but offer trailists the opportunity to spend an additional day and a night in the wilderness. Trails depart from Mpila Resort on Tuesdays. **Distances range from 7 to 14 km per day; 3 nights/4 days; walks from base camp.**

5. Explorer Trails combine the relative comfort of the Base Camp Trails – the first and last nights are spent at the Mndindini Trails Camp – with the rough-and-ready amenities of the Primitive Trails. From Mndindini, trailists set off into the wilderness with backpacks. Sleeping is under the stars at a site selected by the trails officer, and lightweight rain shelters are provided in case of bad weather. At the discretion of the trails officer, equipment can be left at the overnight stop from where day walks are undertaken. **Distances range from 7 to 14 km per day; 2 nights/3 days; walks from base camp.**

6. Guided Morning and Afternoon Walks depart from Hilltop and Mpila resorts and are conducted by armed game guards. These informative walks, which include the possibility of encountering game on foot, are a wonderful way of experiencing the park at its best. Groups are limited to a maximum of eight people and children must be older than 12 years. **Distances range from 3 to 4 km; 2 to 3 hours; circular.**

7. Umbombe Walk is a short, 10-minute ramble which owes its name to the isiZulu word for the common wild fig. Starting at the swimming pool at Hilltop Resort, the trail meanders through a delightful patch of forest which attracts a rich diversity of forest birds such as lemon and tambourine doves, crowned and trumpeter hornbills, African goshawk, chorister robin-chat, yellow-bellied greenbul and bar-throated and yellow-breasted apalis. Trees marked along the way include stinkwood, thorny rope, forest feverberry, common cabbage and marula. **10 minutes; open-ended.**

37. NDUMO GAME RESERVE
Ndumo

> **Trails:** 5 guided day walks; 4 to 6 km; 2 to 3 hours; circular.
> **Permits:** Conservation fee and fee for guided walks, which must be booked at reception.
> **Maps:** Sketch map.
> **Facilities/Activities:** Self-catering accommodation; luxury tented camp; picnic sites; community camp site just outside reserve; guided drives to the pans; self-drive game-viewing.

Bounded by the Usutu River in the north and the Lebombo Mountains to the west, the Ndumo Game Reserve is known for its great birding. The reserve covers 12,420 ha and contains a variety of vegetation and scenery, including sand forest, floodplains, wetlands, riverine forest, woodlands and the dense Mahemane bush. A prominent feature of the reserve is the system of seasonal and permanent pans, fringed by the distinctive fever tree, and vleis. Well-known pans include Nyamithi and Banzi in the east of the reserve and Shokwe Pan in the west.

Established in 1924 as a sanctuary for the declining number of hippo, the park now has a healthy hippo population, as well as large numbers of crocodile. The nyala is the most common antelope in the park – Ndumo has one of the highest concentrations of nyala in South Africa. Also well represented are black and white rhino, giraffe, kudu, reedbuck, bushbuck, blue wildebeest, Burchell's zebra, red duiker, bushpig and spotted hyaena. Of special interest in the sand forest are the diminutive suni and the Tonga red squirrel. Buffalo occur, but as they favour the rank grass of the floodplains they are seen only occasionally.

Ndumo is a birding hotspot. With over 420 bird species it is, considering its size, undeniably South Africa's top birding destination. At least 17 of the 21 species that reach the southern limit of their distribution in Maputaland have been recorded here. Exciting species you may tick include eastern nicator, white-eared barbet, Stierling's wren-warbler, Woodward's batis, purple-banded sunbird and pink-throated twinspot. Of special interest is the system of wetlands, with a rich diversity of waterfowl and waders. Among these are African pygmy goose, lesser moorhen, Baillon's crake, great white and pink-backed pelicans, and the African finfoot. Raptors are also well represented.

Guided Walks Five guided walks are conducted through different landscapes and vegetation types in the reserve, ensuring that each trail offers a totally distinct experience, including the chance to see game.

The **Manzimbomvu Walk** explores the southwestern corner of the park, and the **Shokwe Pan Walk** is conducted in the vicinity of the seasonal pan of that name. Two walks focus on the Pongolo River with its interesting riverine vegetation: **North Pongolo Walk** and **South Pongolo Walk**. The **Nyamithi Pan Walk** leads to a bird hide overlooking a small reed-fringed pan that lies on the northeastern corner of Nyamithi Pan. **4 to 6 km; 2 to 3 hours; circular.**

38. ITHALA GAME RESERVE
Louwsburg

> **Trails:** Self-guided walks; 1 to 4 hours;

network from rest camp. Guided walks; 2 to 3 hours; circular.

Permits: Conservation fee. No booking required for self-guided walks. Fee for guided walks, which must be booked at Ntshondwe Camp reception office.

Maps: Sketch map of self-guided walks in Ntshondwe Camp; colour map of park.

Facilities/Activities: Ntshondwe Camp: fully equipped self-catering chalets, restaurant, pool, bird hide and jungle gym. Ntshondwe Lodge: self-catering lodge with en-suite bathrooms, own pool, jacuzzi and braai facility on deck. Rustic camp sites. Three bush camp lodgings for 4, 8 and 10 people, inclusive of one game walk per day. Self-drive game-viewing, morning and sunset game drives.

Bounded by the Pongolo River in the north, the Ithala Game Reserve covers 29,653 ha of rugged countryside, ranging from Drakensberg highlands to typical Lowveld. The reserve is renowned for its excellent game-viewing and the superb facilities offered by Ntshondwe Camp.

To date over 900 plant species have been recorded in the reserve, including approximately 320 tree species, one of the greatest diversities of trees in KwaZulu-Natal. The vegetation over much of the reserve is dominated by sweet and scented thorn woodlands, ranging from open savannah to dense thickets. The woodlands are interspersed with patches of tall grassland, consisting mainly of thatch grasses, while the plateau areas are characterised by short grassveld.

The many different habitats support a variety of animals and birds. Ithala is a sanctuary to rhino (both black and white), elephant, buffalo, leopard, giraffe, kudu, eland, waterbuck, nyala, impala, red hartebeest, blue wildebeest, mountain reedbuck, bushbuck and klipspringer. It is also home to the rare roan antelope and to the only population of tsessebe in KwaZulu-Natal.

With a checklist of over 314 bird species, Ithala offers good birding and counts among its noteworthy species the southern bald ibis. Raptors are represented by 29 species, including the white-backed vulture, Verreaux's, martial, and crowned eagles, African

fish eagle, bateleur, and African harrier-hawk. Also recorded are the brown-headed parrot, purple-crested turaco, several kingfisher species, blue swallow, violet-backed starling and red-billed oxpecker.

1. Self-guided Walks have been laid out below the cliffs in the Ntshondwe Camp. The **Plum-coloured Starling Walk** and **Porcupine Walk** both take about an hour to hike, while the **Klipspringer Walk** takes 90 minutes.

About four hours must be set aside for the longest route, the **Bushpig Walk**. Hikers are cautioned to keep a sharp lookout for dangerous animals such as leopard, black rhino and snakes.

2. Guided Walks are conducted twice daily; in the early morning and in the mid-afternoon. Trailists are accompanied by a game guard. **4 to 5 km; 2 to 3 hours; circular.**

39. NTENDEKA WILDERNESS AREA
Ngome State Forest, Vryheid

Trails: Network of several trails; 57 km (in total); 3 hours to full day; circular and open-ended.

Permits: State Forester, Ngome State Forest, Private Bag X9425, Vryheid, tel. and fax: (034) 967 9100.

Maps: Wilderness area brochure with map.

Facilities/Activities: Camp site with fireplaces, firewood and ablutions.

Pertinent information: Camping is not permitted in the wilderness area.

Ntendeka, an isiZulu name meaning 'place of precipitous heights', is a wonder-world of spectacular cliffs, tropical indigenous forest and grassland. The wilderness area is rich in the history of the Zulu nation and was used as a refuge by Mzilikazi when he was pursued by Shaka. In 1879 the Zulu king Cetshwayo took refuge in a cave at the base of one of the cliffs, following the defeat of the Zulu by the British.

Just under half of the 5,230-ha wilderness area consists of grasslands, while indigenous forest covers the remaining 2,635 ha. The Ngome Forest is considered one of the most beautiful in KwaZulu-Natal and is the habitat of more than 60 fern species, including *Didymochlaena truncatula*, a fern with 2.5-m-long dark green fronds, and forest tree ferns growing up to 8 m tall. The forest is also home to 19 epiphytic orchid species and the giant-leaved *Streptocarpus*, which has leaves up to 1 m long. Typical forest species include the real yellowwood, lemonwood, thorny rope, red alder, forest elder and some large specimens of forest waterwood. Of particular interest is the forest fig, also known as the strangler fig.

Among the 200-odd bird species recorded in this wilderness area are several noteworthy ones, including the southern bald ibis, eastern bronze-naped pigeon, wattled crane, green twinspot and blue swallow. Other species to look out for include the crowned and martial eagles, trumpeter hornbill and Narina trogon.

The wilderness area is traversed by a network of interlinking footpaths, which can be explored as day walks from the camp site. The shortest circuit is 8 km, and the detour to Cetshwayo's Refuge will add another 5 km to the trail distance. A full-day circular route of 19 km meanders below and over the Ntendeka cliffs. **57 km (in total); 3 hours to a full day; circular and open-ended.**

40. MHLOPENI NATURE RESERVE
Greytown

Trails: Numerous trails ranging from orientation, leisure, educational and archaeological trails to four-day trails suitable for beginners as well as serious hikers
Bookings: Contact Andy, Sat phone 087 095 1042, email: andy@mhlopeni.co.za.
Maps: Available. Guided trails can be arranged.
Facilities/Activities: Umphafa self-catering bush camp for maximum 10 people. Fully contained kitchen, communal hot-shower ablutions and braai place. There is also space for tents.

Pertinent information: The access road to Mhlopeni Nature Reserve is not suitable for low-slung sedan vehicles. Use the R74 from Greytown to Muden and after 27 km turn onto the L3230, which is followed for 7 km to the Warden's office.

In 1977 a group of conservation-minded business people bought an 808-ha piece of land in the Tugela River Basin northwest of Greytown. The vegetation was severely overgrazed and the landscape scarred by erosion. They set about rehabilitating the land to allow nature to reclaim its former glory. As pioneer of the conservancy movement, Mhlopeni was declared a nature reserve in 1977 and on 25 October 1994 it was declared a natural heritage site No. 223. An additional 517 ha were purchased in 1993, bringing the total area under custodianship to 1,325 ha. It is a member of the Conservancies Association of KZN.

Situated in the rain shadow of the greater Tugela River Basin, the vegetation is classified as dry valley bushveld, the smallest and least protected biome. Mhlopeni acts as the last genetic reserve for many hardwood species endemic to dry valley bushveld. Early Stone Age and Iron Age sites in the reserve testify to a long history of occupation of the area.

Mhlopeni, an isiZulu name meaning, 'Place of White Stones', has a healthy bushbuck population and fine specimens of kudu. Impala and plains zebra, as well as a large number of small mammals, also occur.

The reserve is situated at the intersection of the northern, southern, coastal and inland limits of distribution of birds. The bird list therefore exceeds 320 species and birding is rewarding. Cape vulture, African fish eagle and Verreaux's eagle are among the 24 raptor species recorded to date. Also to be seen are sought-after species such as bald ibis, blue crane, buff-spotted flufftail, southern ground hornbill, Narina trogon and African green pigeon.

Mhlopeni offers something for everyone, irrespective of whether visitors simply want to enjoy nature or are pursuing a special interest. The scenic, archaeological and botanical trails are customised to the needs of visitors, and newcomers are guided at no charge. Once visitors are familiar and confident they can explore the reserve on their own.

The Tugela Gorge Walk is one of the most popular walks in the Royal Natal National Park.

FREE STATE

Bounded by the Orange River in the south and the Vaal River in the north, the Free State lies on the great southern African central plateau, or Highveld. This province's landscape is predominantly flat, although sometimes gently undulating, and it is characterised by maize farms and extensive grasslands, where cattle are reared. In the east and northeast of the Free State, however, the rolling grasslands give way to dramatic sandstone rock formations, rugged mountains, challenging peaks and deep valleys, all of which create numerous opportunities for hikes, walks and other outdoor activities.

Situated at an altitude of between 1,000 and 1,800 m, the Highveld has a severe climate, with temperatures ranging from below freezing point during winter to 30 °C in summer. Under these extreme conditions only the hardiest plant and tree species can survive, so the vegetation found here is mainly grasslands, with few trees and shrubs, although proteaveld sometimes occurs on the slopes below sandstone cliffs.

Among the many prominent landmarks in the northeastern Free State are formations shaped like a camel and the profile of Queen Victoria, and Lesoba, a Sesotho name referring to a hole eroded through the mountain. Well-known formations in the Golden Gate Highlands National Park include Brandwag Buttress, also known as the Sentinel, the spectacular Mushroom Rocks and Gladstone's Nose, a formation resembling the profile of a former British Prime Minister.

The rock paintings on the walls of many of the *holkranse* (overhangs) in the northeastern Free State bear testimony to the San who once lived here. Also of interest is Salpeterkrans, which lies near Fouriesburg, where many women bring offerings to the spirits in the belief that it will increase their fertility.

After the harsh winter months the grasslands are brown and uninviting, but in spring a variety of flowering plants provides a touch of colour. Among these plants are *Gladiolus*, *Agapanthus*, *Hypoxis*, *Watsonia* and *Brunsvigia* species, as well as pineapple flowers (*Eucomis*), red-hot pokers (*Kniphofia*) and berg lilies (*Galtonia*).

In the more mountainous eastern and northeastern parts of the province, oldwood trees are conspicuous along the river courses. Wild sage trees, wild peach, Cape myrtle, small-leaved guarri and bladder nut, as well as nana berry, can all be found in sheltered valleys and ravines. Cabbage trees can be seen in rocky outcrops.

Typical game species of the Highveld include Burchell's zebra, black wildebeest, blesbok, eland and smaller antelope such as common duiker and steenbok. Also found here are springbok and oribi, while the grey rhebok and mountain reedbuck favour the mountainous areas. Smaller mammals found here include baboon, black-backed jackal, caracal, African wild cat and Cape hare.

For birding enthusiasts the eastern parts of the province and the northeastern highlands offer the opportunity to tick several noteworthy species. Among these are bearded and Cape vultures, southern bald ibis and yellow-breasted pipit. Typical grassland species that you should be on the lookout for include the sentinel rock-thrush, buff-streaked chat, blue korhaan and grey crowned crane. Ground woodpecker and Drakensberg rockjumper favour the rocky, higher elevations, while Gurney's sugarbird can be spotted in proteaveld. Rudd's and Botha's larks are two threatened species to look out for in the high-altitude grasslands of the northeastern corner of the Free State.

The landscape of the northeastern highlands is dominated by imposing cliffs, buttresses and outcrops of the Clarens Sandstone Formation, which forms the upper part of the Karoo Supergroup. The sandstone cliffs were formed by fine windblown sand that was deposited in a huge basin, when climatic conditions became increasingly dry during the Karoo times.

The many striking sandstone formations were shaped by a combination of several processes. The spectacular Mushroom Rocks in the Golden

Gate Highlands National Park, for example, were created as a result of the calcification of the sandstone at different levels, which in turn resulted in differences in resistance to weathering. Another process, salt weathering, was also at work here. This takes place when salt solutions seep out near the base of a cliff and crystallise, gradually eroding the cliff surface. In addition, groundwater is forced to seep out near the base of the sandstone when it reaches the impermeable mudstone, undermining the base of the sandstone cliff.

The Drakensberg Formation is another arresting natural feature in this area, and reaches a thickness of 600 m at Ribbokkop in the Golden Gate Highlands National Park. It was formed some 190 million years ago, when vast flows of lava covered large parts of southern Africa. The lava subsequently solidified to form thick layers of basalt, which are today the high mountains of the park.

A number of fossils have been discovered in the Golden Gate Highlands National Park and in the surrounding area of Clarens. The most exciting discovery to date has been that of a clutch of six dinosaur eggs (the first record of fossil eggs of the Upper Triassic period), which date back to between 185 and 195 million years ago.

Over much of the Free State summer days are warm, and evening temperatures are pleasant. In the northeastern highlands, however, temperatures are typically a few degrees lower and evenings can be cool. Winter days are generally mild, but can be bitingly cold when the southerly winds blow from the uKhahlamba-Drakensberg and the Malutis. At night temperatures frequently drop below freezing point and heavy frost is not uncommon. Mid-winter snow occasionally falls on the high mountains in the northeast.

Rainfall ranges from 600 mm in the northwestern Free State to 900 mm in the northeastern highlands. Most rain is recorded between November and March, with January and February being the wettest months, and June, July and August being the driest. The rains are typically accompanied by dramatic thunderstorms and displays of lightning, usually in mid-afternoon.

Opportunities for walks and hikes in the Free State range from easy rambles among the dolerite hills in the Free State National Botanical Garden to easy day walks and hiking trails. In the eastern and northeastern Free State there is an extensive network of hikes and walks on private farms and in conservancies. Hikers can also explore the high mountains of the Golden Gate Highlands National Park, or undertake a fairly demanding hike to the top of the Amphitheatre and the summit of Mont-aux-Sources.

IMPORTANT INFORMATION

➤ When planning a winter hike, bear in mind it can become extremely cold, so ensure that you pack enough warm clothing. A good-quality sleeping bag, rated below zero degrees, is essential.

➤ Lightning poses a threat in summer. Start walking early in the morning and aim to get to the overnight stop before the thunderstorm breaks. If caught in a storm, try to avoid exposed high ground, boulders and trees.

➤ Thunderstorms also pose the risk of flash floods on trails where rivers have to be crossed. Do not try to cross a river that is flowing strongly, but wait until it has subsided to a safe level.

➤ Firewood is not provided on some hikes, so check with the relevant trail authority when making reservations. Woody vegetation is in short supply and you should never collect firewood unless this has been authorised.

➤ Make fires only where permitted. Smokers must take great care – matches and cigarette ends may not be discarded on the trail. The risk of fire is very high during the winter months when the dry grass is extremely flammable.

➤ Many streams are dry in winter, so it is essential to set off with a full water bottle (of at least 2 litres) and use water sparingly until you can fill up again.

➤ Most Free State trails traverse private farmland and you must always use stiles where provided. Gates found closed must be shut behind you, and open gates left open. Visit a farmhouse only by invitation from the owner, or in cases of extreme emergency.

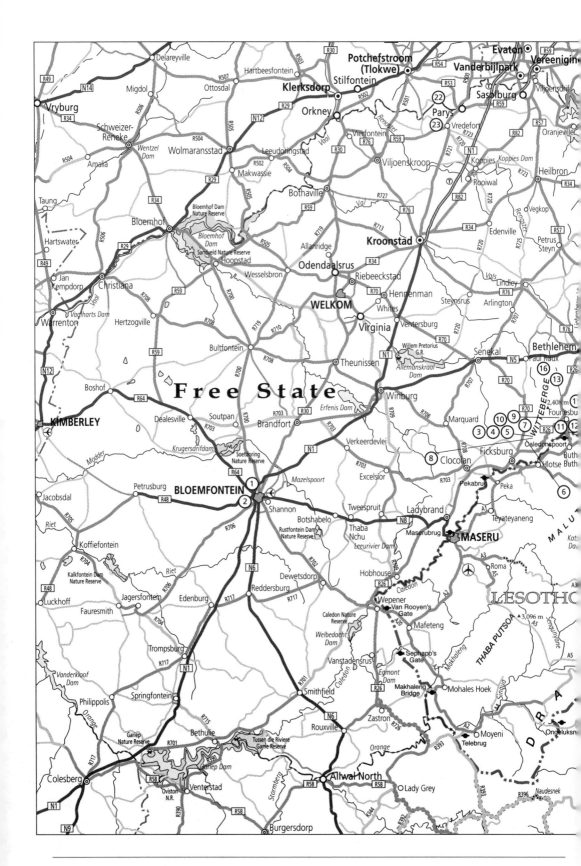

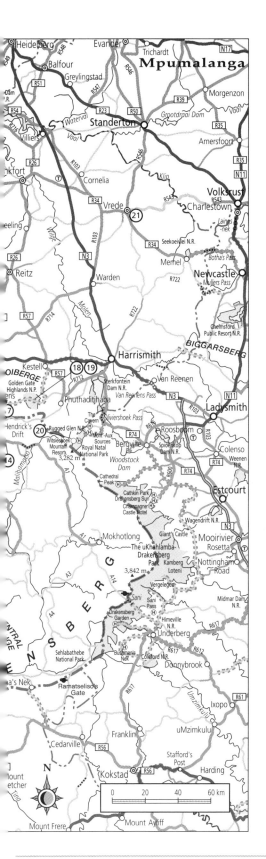

HIKING TRAILS

1. FRANKLIN NATURE RESERVE
Bloemfontein

> **Trail:** 9 km; 3 hours; circular.
> **Permits:** Entrance free.
> **Maps:** Not available.
> **Facilities/Activities:** Toilets;
> planetarium; restaurant.

Covering 250 ha, the Franklin Nature Reserve was established on Naval Hill in Bloemfontein in 1928. It is named after a former mayor of the city, Sir John Stuart Franklin. The reserve is home to a variety of game, including small numbers of giraffe, red hartebeest, Burchell's zebra, blesbok, eland and springbok, which can often be seen at close range. Several bird species can also be observed here.

Historical attractions in the reserve include the site where, during the South African War (1899–1902), two naval guns were positioned to fortify the remount camp established at the base of Naval Hill after Lord Roberts captured Bloemfontein from the Boers on 15 March 1900. Another reminder of this era is the White Horse, laid out in rocks painted white on the eastern slopes of Naval Hill. The stone figure – 20 m long and 12 m high – served as a direction marker for British troops taking horses to the remount camp.

Also of interest is the former Lamont-Hussey Observatory, which was established by the University of Michigan. It opened in 1928 and remained in operation until 1971, after which it was transformed into a theatre by the then Performing Arts Council of the Orange Free State. The site was later converted into a digital planetarium. The facility, the first of its kind in southern Africa, opened its doors to the public in November 2013.

Another attraction is the 6.5-m-high bronze statue of former President Nelson Mandela in the south of the reserve. The larger-than-life statue, which was unveiled in December 2012, faces towards the Wesleyan Church in Waaihoek where the African National Congress (ANC) was founded a century earlier.

The **Madiba Trail**, a marked walk in the south of the reserve, can be extended by following the network of tar and gravel roads as well as footpaths marked with a yellow horse. There are several viewpoints along the way, some providing panoramic views of the City of Roses – as Bloemfontein is also known. The reserve is especially busy on Saturday mornings when the Naval Hill park run takes place.

2. FREE STATE NATIONAL BOTANICAL GARDEN
Bloemfontein

> **Trails:** 4 km; 1.5 hours; network.
> **Permits:** Entrance fee. No permit
> for walks.
> **Maps:** Available at entrance.
> **Facilities/Activities:** Picnic areas;
> restaurant; Visitors' Centre, environmental
> education centre; plant sales.

The Free State National Botanical Garden straddles a valley located between three dolerite koppies that are situated on the outskirts of Bloemfontein. The garden was established on the farm Winter Valley, which was bought by the City of Bloemfontein in 1965 for the preservation and cultivation of the province's flora.

Ranging from tall grassland to gentle woodland, and characterised by species such as buffalo-thorn, karee, white stinkwood and wild currant, as well as succulent Karoo-like vegetation, the natural flora was largely pristine; only seven of the garden's 70 ha have been developed.

There are more than 400 plant species, and the plant collections include grass and bulb gardens. The pleasant area is especially attractive between November and March when a rich variety of trees is in full leaf.

Of special interest is a traditional Basotho homestead with a stone wall, a patrol path on one of the koppies, and the main dam, left by British troops, reminders of the South African War (1899–1902). There are two demonstration gardens: a medicinal plant and a 'water-wise' garden.

The garden is traversed by a network of footpaths that wind around the dolerite koppies and to rocky outcrops, from where there are stunning views over the valley, with its three dams, and the cultivated section of the garden.

3. WATERKLOOF HIKING TRAIL
Ficksburg

See no. 4 (this page) for hiking trail and no. 5 (p. 196) for walks.

Trails: 21 km; 2 days, or 26.7 km; 3 days; circular.
Bookings: Fagala Voet, cell: 082 776 5540 or 081 894 9802, email: bookings@fagalavoet.co.za or book online at www.fagalavoet.co.za.
Maps: Trail pamphlet with map available.
Facilities/Activities: Langesnek Base Camp: beds with mattresses, two-plate gas stove, pots, pans, kettle, braai facilities and hot-water ablutions. Barolong Overnight Camp: three wattle-and-daub rooms, or sleep in cave (bring own ground sheets or pads), braai facilities, cast-iron pots, water and pit toilets. Sphinx Mountain Hut: 22 beds, mattresses, braai facilities, pots, cast-iron potjie, cold-water showers and pit toilets.

This trail lies in the Moolmanshoek Private Game Reserve near Ficksburg in the eastern Free State. The vegetation ranges from typical grassland to wooded kloofs, and some of the nearly 90 tree and shrub species occurring in the area have been marked along the trail.

Game you might encounter includes Burchell's zebra, black wildebeest, blesbok, springbok and red hartebeest. In the more mountainous areas you might chance upon grey rhebok and mountain reedbuck, as well as numerous small mammals. The trail environs are home to an estimated 200 bird species.

Overlooked by the 2,410-m-high Visierskerf, the first day's route (10.5 km; 5 hours) ascends along a well-watered kloof with magnificent pools and then follows a contour at the base of the sandstone cliffs, passing several large overhangs. An optional detour takes hikers to the summit of the 2,312-m-high Sekonyela Peak, a climb involving a 240-m gain in altitude. From here the trail continues to the second kloof, where there is an inviting rock pool, perfect for a lunch stop. The path then wanders down to the Bamboeskloof, situated close to the overnight stop.

The second day's hike (10.5 km; 5 hours) initially rambles along the sandstone cliffs to a junction, where there is an option of ascending the Visierskerf. This 4-km out-and-return detour leads to the highest point in the Free State outside of the Malutis. From here the trail continues to a kloof with a delightful series of seven pools, where the route splits. The two-day route passes the pools and then descends through grasslands back to the start, while the three-day route continues along a contour on the slopes of Jacobsberg to the Sphinx overnight hut.

The third day's hike (5.7 km; 2 hours) winds below the Second and First Pyramids and then passes through ancient oak trees and along a willow tree lane to a large swimming pool. The remainder of the hike is mainly through cultivated lands.

4. SPHINX HIKING TRAIL
Ficksburg

See no. 3 (this page) for hiking trail and no. 5 (p. 196) for walks.

Trail: 15.5 km; 2 days; circular.
Bookings: Fagala Voet, cell: 082 776 5540 or 081 894 9802, email: bookings@fagalavoet.co.za or book online at www.fagalavoet.co.za.
Maps: Trail brochure with map.
Facilities/Activities: Langesnek Base Camp: trail hut with bunk beds, mattresses, two-plate gas stove, pots, pans, kettle, hot-water ablutions, lapa, braai facilities and swimming pool. Sphinx Mountain Hut: 22 beds, mattresses, braai facilities (firewood), pots, cast-iron potjie, cold-water showers and pit toilets.

This trail takes in a number of well-known rock formations, such as the Sphinx and the Pyramids in Moolmanshoek Private Game Reserve.

From the Moolmanshoek Valley the first day's trail (10.5 km; 4 hours) gradually ascends the slopes of the Witteberg through grassveld and then follows a contour to Spiraalgat. The 4.5-m-deep pool, shaped like an upside down ice-cream cone, is an ideal place for a tea stop. A short way on, the trail passes another inviting swimming hole, Witgatbad, and, still further on, the detour to the summit of the 2,410-m-high Visierskerf is reached. From here the route continues behind the Sphinx and then follows the contours on the slopes of Jacobsberg. A ladder leads down into a ravine and for the next 1 km the route is through dense indigenous forest. The Sphinx overnight hut overlooks a natural swimming pool, and a nearby dam provides good birding possibilities.

The second day's hike (5 km; 2 hours) traverses the contours below the two Pyramid mountains. A large overhang, which according to local lore served as an arsenal during the South African War (1899–1902), is passed further along the trail. The path then descends to a swimming pool and a dam, with a reed bird-watching hide, before reaching the base camp.

5. MOOLMANSHOEK DAY WALKS
Ficksburg

Trails: Several walks ranging from 1.7 km; 1 hour to full day from Moolmanshoek Lodge.
Bookings: Moolmanshoek Private Game Reserve, cell: 082 788 6623, email: info@moolmanshoek.co.za, www. moolmanshoek.co.za.
Map: Available.
Facilities/Activities: Various options for accommodation at Moolmanshoek Lodge and at Langesnek; horse-riding; fishing; mountain biking; game drives; 4x4 trails.

The Moolmanshoek Private Game Reserve nestles in a valley surrounded by several high peaks of the Witteberg in the eastern Free State. The 3,300-ha reserve was declared a South African Natural Heritage Site in 1994.

The vegetation ranges from grasslands to wooded kloofs where the mountain bamboo (*Thamnocalamus tessellata*) can be seen. It is endemic to mountains from the eastern Cape to the Drakensberg, Free State, Lesotho and Swaziland, growing at altitudes between 1,500 m and 2,000 m. Other noteworthy species include the red hairy heath (*Erica cerinthiodes*) and the parasitic white ink flower (*Harveya capensis*).

Game to be seen includes plains (Burchell's) zebra, black wildebeest, blesbok, springbok, red hartebeest, gemsbok and eland. Grey rhebok and mountain reedbuck inhabit the more mountainous areas. Several small mammal species also occur. The area supports a rich diversity of birds, including Verreaux's eagle, bald ibis, jackal buzzard and the ground woodpecker. A variety of birds is also attracted to the dams and wetlands.

In addition to two overnight trails, the Waterkloof Hiking Trail (See no. 3) and the Sphinx Hiking Trail (See no. 4), outdoor enthusiasts have a choice of several day walks. The **Five Dams Walk** (2.5 km; 1 hour) is an easy stroll through poplar groves past five dams. The walk to **Aunt Mitchell's High Tea Overhang** (4.5 km; 2 hours) ascends to the spot where Mrs Mitchell regularly enjoyed traditional English high tea. Other options include **Eco Cave** (6 km; 3 hours) and the **Seven Pools Hike** (1.7 km; 1 hour).

Energetic and fit hikers can ascend three high peaks. **Visierskerf** (2,407 m), **Sekonyela's Hat** (2,312 m), named after the leader of the Batlokwa Chief who settled with his people near the Caledon River in 1824, and the **Pyramid** (2,167 m).

6. KUTUTSA HIKING TRAIL
Ficksburg

Trail: 22 km; 2 days; circular.
Bookings: Earthrise Mountain Lodge, tel: 087 808 2709, email: earthrisemountainlodge@gmail.com
Maps: Sketch maps.
Facilities/Activities: Various accommodation options, including basic accommodation with self-catering kitchen; mountain biking; horse-riding; fishing; yoga and meditation.

The Kututsa Hiking Trail traverses the western aspects of the Witteberg Mountain and crosses several farms in the Witteberg Conservancy. It features magnificent sandstone overhangs, a rich diversity of flora and expansive views of the Maluti Mountains in Lesotho.

The first day's hike (12 km; 4 to 5 hours) starts with a pleasant walk along the Franshoekspruit and after about 5 km you start climbing to the Angel's Wing. Further along, the trail contours along the mountain slopes above the cliff line to the cave which the Sotho inhabitants named Kututsa. From here you can walk to a nearby cave which has a waterfall during the rainy season. The second day's hike (10 km; 4 hours) winds below the cliff line back to the start.

7. MOSAMANE HIKING TRAIL
Ficksburg

Trail: 10 km; 4 hours; circular.
Bookings: Fagala Voet, cell: 082 776 5540, 081 894 9802, email: bookings@fagalavoet.co.za, web: fagalavoet.co.za.
Maps: Sketch maps.
Facilities/Activities: Barn with beds, mattresses, hot-water showers, toilets, kitchen with fridge, gas cooker, two pots, cast-iron pot, kettle, limited cooking utensils and braai facilities.

The Mosamane Trail (*mosamane* is the Sesotho name for ground squirrel) meanders through grasslands, along valleys and past sandstone cliffs that have been weathered and sculpted by the elements into fascinating shapes. You will be able to see the Owl's Eyes, Cathedral, Pulpit and numerous other features, with little imagination. Several natural 'showers', formed by streams cascading down the mountain slopes, are another highlight, as is the Fairy Garden. On the second day you can do geocaching – an exciting treasure hunt.

8. THABA THABO NATURE RESERVE
Ficksburg

Trail: 4 trails; 2 hours to 8 hours; circular.
Bookings: Cell: 082 344 9100 WhatsApp only, email: info@thabathabo.co.za, web: www.thabathabo.co.za.

Maps: Available.
Facilities/Activities: Self-catering rondavel-style sandstone chalets and dormitory-style accommodation (not included in hike fee). No camping facilities but camping allowed anywhere in the reserve. Cycling, off-roading, fishing, swimming, rowing, horse-riding, abseiling.
Pertinent information: Access road only accessible with suitable off-road or high-clearance vehicles. Hiking trails are guided. Minimum of 2 hikers required.

The trails on Thaba Thabo (the name means 'Mountain of Happiness' in Sesotho) traverse a 1,500-ha nature reserve in the Witteberge (White Mountains) in the eastern Free State.

The reserve's vegetation is representative of the Drakensberg and Free State Highveld, and game to be seen includes black wildebeest, red hartebeest, blesbok, mountain reedbuck and southern reedbuck. Birdlife is prolific, with typical high-mountain species such as grey-winged francolin, ground woodpecker, Drakensberg rockjumper, rock kestrel, southern bald ibis and Verreaux's eagle.

The **Orange Trail** is an easy late afternoon or early morning walk. From the highest peak you will enjoy expansive views of Thaba Thabo, and along the trail you are likely to see a variety of game. **5 km; 2 hours; circular.**

The **Yellow Trail**, rated average to moderately difficult in places, ascends along a basalt ridge to Mount Gilboa, from where you can see up to 100 km on a clear day. After a steep descent, the trail follows an easy route to the start. **8 km; 4 to 5 hours; circular.**

The **Blue Trail** initially follows a contour along the sandstone outcrops before continuing below high sandstone krantzes. It then ascends steadily to the watershed and a promontory before joining a mountain track back to the camp. **12 km; 5 to 6 hours; circular.**

The **White Trail** is strenuous. Highlights along the trail include corbelled huts dating back some 300 years, as well as a cave with rock paintings. **15 km; 8 hours; circular.**

9. DE LUSTHOF WALKS
Fouriesburg

Trails: 2 walks; 2 and 5 hours; out-and-back, circular.
Bookings: Mr & Mrs N Roos, P O Box 88, Fouriesburg 9725, tel. and fax: (058) 223 0465, cell: 072 455 6895, email: delusthofplaas@gmail.com.
Maps: Map available from guesthouse.
Facilities/Activities: Fully equipped, self-catering guesthouse; trout angling.

These walks on the farm De Lusthof, a few kilometres northeast of Fouriesburg, allow visitors to enjoy the breathtaking beauty of the eastern Free State at leisure. De Lusthof, a working dairy farm, is situated in an area of great historical and cultural interest and also offers good bird-watching opportunities.

White Clarens sandstone outcrops and rock formations dominate the valleys, which have been carved by the numerous tributaries of the Little Caledon River. The high peaks, such as Ventersberg (2,270 m) and Snymanshoekberg (2,488 m), are composed of Drakensberg lava. The valleys are intensively cultivated.

Sour grassveld dominates the natural vegetation. The river valleys and valley slopes are covered with scrub forest. Everlastings (*Helichrysum*), red heath (*Erica cerinthoides*), red-hot pokers (*Kniphofia*), gazanias and a variety of other flowering plants add splashes of colour to the grasslands, especially in spring. Weeping willows are common along the banks of the Little Caledon River.

Birdlife is typical of the highland grassveld of the eastern Free State. Species to look out for include ground woodpecker, Cape and sentinel rock-thrush, Drakensberg rockjumper, Cape longclaw and African rock pipit.

The monument at nearby Surrender Hill is a reminder of one of the most crushing defeats suffered by the Boers during the South African War (1899–1902). Following the advance of the British forces from Lindley, President Marthinus Steyn and the Orange Free State forces retreated to the Brandwater Valley, a horseshoe-shaped basin encircled by the Witteberg in the west, the Rooiberg in the north and the Malutis in the east. The valleys, sandstone passages and caves provided ideal cover for the Boer forces. Fouriesburg served as provisional capital of the Free State for a short while. But with only a few passes into the basin, the Boers were at risk of being trapped by the advancing British troops.

President Marthinus Steyn and a column of 2,600 men commanded by General Christiaan de Wet escaped over Slabbert's Nek in the northwest of the basin on 15 July. The remaining Boer commandos were, however, encircled by the British forces on 24 July. General Marthinus Prinsloo and a force of close to 3,000 men surrendered on 31 July 1900 at what has become known as Surrender Hill. A further 1,544 Boers were captured at Golden Gate and by 9 August a total of 4,314 Boers had surrendered.

The **Salpeterkrans Walk** (4 km; 2 hours) meanders along the Little Caledon River to what is believed to be the largest overhang in the southern hemisphere. This enormous sandstone overhang is a place of worship for pilgrims who come from all over southern Africa to communicate with their ancestors. Women bring offerings to the ancestral spirits in the belief that this will increase their fertility. It is also used as a 'school' by sangomas who bring their pupils to the cave to instruct them and to get visions on how to heal their people. There are numerous small stone enclosures where regular visitors have staked out their claims and many names have been painted on the walls of the overhang.

Another option, a circular walk of about 10 km (5 hours), meanders along a valley and then ascends to the summit of the sandstone cliffs. This ascent used to be the emergency route, when the Little Caledon River was impassable, of the five-day Brandwater Hiking Trail. (The Brandwater trail is now unfortunately closed.) From the cliffs you can enjoy stunning views of Snymanshoekberg, the highest point in the area, and the Malutis in Lesotho. The path follows the watershed for about 30 minutes before descending to the Little Caledon River. After crossing the river, a short uphill walk brings you to the Salpeterkrans. The remaining 2 km of the walk follows the course of the Little Caledon River back to the farm.

10. WELGELEGEN CHERRY ESTATE HIKES
Fouriesburg

Trails: 4 unmarked routes on farm; 3 to 6 hours; 3-day (unmarked) hike to Visierskerf.
Bookings: Cell: 074 131 3617, fax: 086 618 2106, email: info@cherryestate.co.za.
Maps: Not available.
Facilities/Activities: Self-catering houses and chalets; bass angling; canoeing; mountain biking.
Pertinent information: There are no fixed routes and only experienced and fit hikers should attempt these hikes. Permission must be obtained from neighbouring farmers for the hike to Visierskerf.

Welgelegen Cherry Farm lies 16 km west of Fouriesburg in the eastern foothills of the Witteberg. The cool winter temperatures of the eastern Free State are ideal for the cultivation of cherries, which need a dormant period of about 850 hours from May to July. The first trees were planted on a farm in the Clocolan district by Henry Pickstone in 1904. Virtually the entire South African cherry crop is produced in the eastern Free State. A visit to the region is especially rewarding during the first three weeks of September when the white blossoms are spectacular. The fruit ripens from the end of September to the end of November. Harvesting is labour intensive as each cherry has to be picked ripe.

Some 10,000 cherry trees and thousands of apple trees thrive under ideal conditions at Welgelegen Cherry Farm. Nine varieties of red cherries are grown for fresh consumption, while the seven varieties of yellow cherries are mainly used for glazing as well as in the baking industry.

This is not your usual hiking trail or walk, but rather a relaxing way of exploring this scenic region. Visitors can amble through the orchards (and pick cherries during the season), inspect the caves on the farm, or explore the Witteberg, which reaches a height of 2,410 m at Visierskerf further south. The three-day hike to Visierskerf should only be attempted by experienced hikers, since the route is unmarked.

Highland sourveld, with attractive flowering plants, dominates the vegetation of the Witteberg, while thickets of oldwood, sagewood and karee occur in the valleys. The grasslands are home to mountain reedbuck, grey rhebok and a variety of smaller mammals.

Welgelegen has a breeding colony of southern bald ibis, while raptors include Verreaux's eagle and jackal buzzard. Sentinel rock-thrush, ground woodpecker, buff-streaked chat, Cape grassbird and blue and grey crowned cranes are among the other species you might tick.

11. CAMELROC HIKING TRAIL
Fouriesburg

Trails: 2 day walks; 9 and 3 km; 4 to 6 and 1.5 hours; circular.
Bookings: Camelroc Guest Farm, tel: (058) 223 0368, fax: (058) 223 0012.
Maps: Sketch map of trails with information.
Facilities/Activities: Fully furnished self-catering chalets; three-bedroom guesthouse; swimming pool; 4x4 trail; two mountain-bike trails.

Named after a sandstone formation resembling a camel's head, Camelroc Guest Farm lies between two rivers – the Caledon River and the Little Caledon River. Attractions include far-reaching views of Lesotho and the Maluti Mountains, dramatic rock formations and sandstone overhangs.

The 9-km route is short, but should not be underestimated, as there are several steep climbs along the way. Depending on the fitness levels of the trailists in your group, it can take between 4 and 6 hours to complete the hike.

From the camping area the path climbs steeply to God's Window, a sandstone overhang with splendid views of the landscape below. Adventurous hikers can approach the overhang via The Ledge, a sandstone ridge with steep slopes, while the Chicken Run offers a safer alternative for the less adventurous. A steep ascent leads to the plateau, where a wooden bridge spans the gorge between the mountain and the free-standing Camel Head rock formation. The trail then continues across the plateau towards Caesar's View, with its magnificent views of the Rooiberg and the Malutis, and then descends into a shady gorge.

Highlights of the 3-km walk include expansive views over the Free State and the Grot Woning (translated as 'cave dwelling'). The overhang with its rock paintings is reached by means of a bridge across the Little Caledon River. The final stretch of the trail meanders through poplar groves along the course of the river. There are numerous opportunities to cool off in the river pools.

12. SHUMBA VALLEY GUEST FARM
Fouriesburg

Trails: 3 walks; 30 minutes to 3 hours; self-guided.
Bookings: Shumba Valley Guest Farm, tel: (058) 223 0277, cell: 072 227 6752, email: barmour@worldonline.co.za.
Maps: Not available.
Facilities/Activities: Fully equipped self-catering cottages; en-suite rooms; camping sites with hot-water showers; mountain biking; quad biking; horse-riding.

Shumba Valley Farm lies about 12 km southeast of Fouriesburg. It is just a few kilometres from the Caledon River, which forms the border between South Africa and Lesotho. The landscape here is characterised by Clarens sandstone cliffs and deep valleys set against the backdrop of the mighty Maluti Mountains to the east and the Witteberg to the west.

The area is rich in history. It was at Butha Buthe, about 15 km east as the crow flies, where the Basotho leader, Moshoeshoe I, began uniting scattered tribal groups into a single nation in 1824. The lowlands west of the Caledon River,

the Conquered Territory, saw several battles between the Free State Boers, British troops and the Basotho from 1851 to the Gun War of 1880–81. During the South African War (1899–1902), the nearby Brandwater Basin became the last refuge of 8,000 Boer fighters following the occupation of Bloemfontein by the British forces in March 1900.

Three walks are available at Shumba. The shortest walk is an easy 30-minute ramble to the Caledon River. A second trail, also relatively short, takes you up the mountain. The third, and longest, walk is a more demanding three-hour route to Destiny Castle. This imposing structure was built on the edge of a sandstone cliff in the 1970s. However, the owner ran out of money and the building remained unfinished for more than three decades before its new owner completed it and turned it into luxury guest accommodation.

13. SPOREKRANS HIKING TRAIL
Fouriesburg

Trail: 18 km; 2 days; circular.
Bookings: Fagala Voet, cell: 082 776 5540, 081 894 9802, email: bookings@fagalavoet.co.za, web: fagalavoet.co.za.
Maps: Rough trail map.
Facilities/Activities: Base camp: huts with bunks, mattresses, kitchen with fridge, hotplate, pots, pan and electric kettle, lapa with braai facilities, hot showers and toilet. Overnight cave: log beds with mattresses, water, kettle, iron pot, braai facilities and toilet. Horse-riding; abseiling (minimum of 10 people); sunset game drives.

Laid out on Bergdeel Private Nature Reserve, this trail wanders through forested kloofs, across mountain streams and through grassland, in the heart of the Witteberg. The reserve is home to a variety of game species, among them eland, blue and black wildebeest, kudu, red hartebeest, blesbok and Burchell's zebra. Noteworthy among the birds is the rare southern bald ibis, which breeds in the sandstone cliffs of Bergdeel.

On the first day's hike (12 km; 5 hours) you walk along Stinkhoutkloof, with its white stinkwood trees, and then ascend a ladder to Angel's Corner and God's View, where you are rewarded with wonderful vistas. About 1 km on, you reach the scenic Bushman Baths and, further along, the trail follows Kudupoort before reaching two of the trail's main attractions: the scenic Bamboeskloof and Mermaid Pool, where you can take a refreshing swim. From here it is a 4-km walk to the overnight stop, Bushmen's Cave.

The second day of this route (6 km; 2 hours) retraces the last section of the previous day's hike to Sporekrans, after which the trail is named, and then takes trailists in an anti-clockwise direction, back to the start.

14. LESOBA HIKING TRAIL
Fouriesburg

Trails: 3 day walks; 6 to 14 km; 2 to 6 hours; network from base camp.
Bookings: Fagala Voet, cell: 082 776 5540, 081 894 9802, email: bookings@fagalavoet.co.za, web: fagalavoet.co.za.
Maps: Sketch map.
Facilities/Activities: Huts with beds, kitchen with two-plate stove, fridge, kettle, hot showers, toilets and braai facilities.

The Lesoba Hiking Trail traverses the mountains between Clarens and Fouriesburg, on the border between South Africa and Lesotho. It takes its name from the Sesotho term for the prominent hole that has been eroded through a mountain dominating the area.

The vegetation is mainly grassland, interspersed with proteas and mountain cabbage trees. Old-wood is also found here, occurring along the stream banks. The grasslands are especially eye-catching in spring when watsonias and a variety of other indigenous bulbous plants and orchids can be seen in full bloom. The stands of Lombardy poplar found here look beautiful in autumn.

From the base camp, the first day's hike (14 km; 6 hours) ascends to the summit of a mountain,

where trailists are rewarded with far-reaching views over the Caledon River and the distant Maluti Mountains in neighbouring Lesotho. Lesoba is also visible from here. The trail then strikes westwards across the plateau and descends to the Church Door, an overhang with several red and black San rock paintings.

On the return leg the trail passes a site where a fossilised dinosaur femur bone and shoulder blade can be seen. It then winds its way past Queen Victoria, a rock formation, named after the former British monarch.

In the northeastern Free State fossils have been unearthed at several sites in the region. They are reminders of the Karoo era when large tracts of South Africa were covered by shallow lakes and when dinosaurs reigned supreme. Some dinosaurs died naturally, while others were trapped in the mud – a perfect medium to preserve their bones as the climate became drier.

The second day's hike (12 km; 5 hours) makes its way past Lesoba and then climbs steeply to the top of a mountain, where hikers can once again enjoy stunning views of the surrounding landscape. On the descent, the trail passes another hole in the mountain and then skirts a grassy basin, where blesbok can usually be seen.

A shady day hike (6 km; 2 hours) is also available for those seeking more exercise or who would like to extend their stay.

15. MEIRINGSKLOOF NATURE PARK
Fouriesburg

Trail: Various short walks in Meiringskloof Nature Park; 20 minutes to 1 hour; longer walks in Didibeng Nature Park.
Bookings: Tel: 058 223 0067, email: admin@meiringskloofpark.co.za, web: www.meiringskloof.co.za.
Maps: Available.
Facilities/Activities: Fully equipped self-catering chalets; shady camp sites with power points, communal hot-water ablutions, braai facilities, swimming pool

Set against the backdrop of Ventersberg, the Meiringskloof Nature Park and adjoining Didibeng Mountain Park are dominated by white sandstone outcrops, overhangs and rugged mountain kloofs. The resort lies at the head of a narrow kloof bounded by sandstone cliffs in the area where the municipal waterworks were located from 1940 to 1973.

The vegetation is dominated by sour grassveld with patches of scrub forest in the river valleys and on the valley slopes. With the arrival of spring, the grassveld is transformed when spring flowers come into bloom. The birdlife is typical of the eastern Free State highlands.

1. Water Tunnels Trail Several interconnected short walks are available from the rest camp. Soon after setting off, you cross to the right-hand side of the Meiringskloofspruit. A short way on, you get to Holkrans, an enormous sandstone overhang which is about 100 m long and 30 m deep.

Continuing further, you reach one of the highlights of the walk as you enter a long, narrow, tunnel-shaped chasm with ferns and mosses clinging to the damp cliffs. Where the gorge comes to an end, a chain ladder takes you onto the sandstone cliffs, or you can opt to climb out of the tunnel at Jacob's Ladder.

From the chain ladder the route takes you along the right-hand side of the dam, which was built in 1973 to meet Fouriesburg's increasing water needs. Further along you reach the Water Tunnels, which were carved into the sandstone by the Meiringskloofspruit. From here you retrace your tracks. **2 to 3 hours; out-and return.**

2. Didibeng Mountain Park From the Water Tunnels you can continue to Ouhout Camp, named after the oldwood trees growing in the river valley. Take time to look back at the cultivated farmlands below and the Malutis in Lesotho in the distance. If you still have enough energy, you can continue to the top of Ventersberg via Maluti View, but bear in mind you still have to retrace your tracks. **8 to 9 hours; out-and-return.**

16. HOLHOEK HIKING TRAIL
Paul Roux

Trails: 2 day walks; 13 and 7 km; network from base camp.
Bookings: Fagala Voet, cell: 082 776 5540, 081 894 9802, email: bookings@fagalavoet.co.za, web: fagalavoet.co.za.
Maps: Sketch map of trail available.
Facilities/Activities: Two thatch-roofed stone huts with hot-water showers, flush toilets, lapa with kitchen, gas fridge, hotplate, two pots, pan, kettle and braai facilities.

On this trail hikers experience a combination of spectacular scenery and several historical and archaeological sites. The figure-eight layout has the advantage that hikers only need to carry a daypack as both nights are spent in the base camp.

The first day's hike (13 km; 6 to 7 hours) leads past a waterfall and ascends to the top of a sandstone ridge where the route meanders to several interesting rock overhangs, including one with San rock paintings of eland and therianthropes (animal-headed figures). Also of interest are two stone-and-mud shelters built against the rear wall of the second overhang. The shelters were most likely built by Sotho people some 200 years ago. Another overhang is close to a waterfall which plunges into a pool.

The second day's hike (7 km; 3 hours) starts with a climb and highlights include the Fairytale Wonderland overhang, a 500-m-long overhang clad with masses of ferns and mosses, and a cave where Boer women and children took refuge during the South African War (1899–1902).

Hikers have to negotiate numerous ladders and bridges – which might be daunting for those with a fear of heights – on both days.

17. MOUNT PERAZIM HIKING TRAIL
(previously Cannibal Hiking Trail)
Clarens

Trail: 16 km; 2 days; circular.
Bookings: Fagala Voet, cell: 082 776 5540, 081 894 9802, email: bookings@fagalavoet.co.za, web: fagalavoet.co.za.
Maps: Available.
Facilities/Activities: Two dormitories (The Cottage and The Melkstal) with bunks and mattresses, electricity, kitchen with stove, fridge, pots and kettle, communal hot showers and toilets at start. Cave with mattresses, fireplace, firewood, flush toilet and cold running water.

This easy to moderately difficult trail takes trailists past imposing sandstone outcrops, along densely wooded ravines and across grassveld in the Rooi and Witteberg Mountains, about 5 km south of Clarens. According to legend, the trail owes its previous name to a former Sotho Chief, Lesoeana, who took refuge in the overhangs with his followers during the turbulent days of the *Difaqane* in the nineteenth century. They allegedly turned to cannibalism in order to survive. Dominating the surrounding landscape is a 1,824-m-high peak, The Fort.

The first day's hike (9 km; 4 hours) follows a route along the base of the sandstone cliffs, past five overhangs. These shelters, once the home of San hunter-gatherers who left a legacy of rock paintings on the cave walls, were later inhabited by Sotho herders. The route also incorporates four ravines, and there are numerous wooden bridges and ladders to assist hikers. A swimming hole at the halfway mark makes an ideal place to stop for a rest. The overnight stop is in a large cave equipped with mattresses.

The second day's hike (7 km; 3 hours) affords hikers splendid views of the high peaks of the area, including George's Pimple, Wodehouse, Generaalskop and Visierskerf. The 125-step Step Ladder brings you down to a wooden bridge over the Little Caledon River. The trail follows the course of the river, with an optional ascent to the rock formation, Mushroom Rocks, before crossing the river for a second time.

18. RIBBOK HIKING TRAIL
Golden Gate Highlands National Park, Clarens

See no. 18 (p. 204) for walks.

Trail: 29 km; 2 days; circular.
Permits: SANParks, P O Box 787, Pretoria 0001, tel: (012) 428 9111, fax: (012) 343 0905, email: reservations@sanparks.org.
Maps: Trail pamphlet with sketch map.
Facilities/Activities: On the trail: overnight hut with bunk beds and mattresses, fireplace, firewood, hot shower and toilet. Glen Reenen Rest Camp: semi-equipped stone rondavels with shower; camp sites with hot-water ablutions, scullery and braai places; shop. Brandwag Rest Camp: single and double rooms with en-suite facilities, telephone and television; chalets with bedroom, living room, semi-equipped kitchen, braai places and bathroom. Short self-drive game drives; guided night drives; guided walks to Cathedral Cave; vulture hide.

Laid out in the foothills of the Malutis, the Ribbok Hiking Trail traverses the Golden Gate Highlands National Park. The trail winds through open grassland, passing impressive sandstone formations, which are especially attractive in the late afternoon when they are transformed from pink and yellow to a glowing golden colour.

Since it was proclaimed in 1962, the Golden Gate Highlands National Park has increased in size from its original 4,792 ha. Currently 32,608 ha in extent, the park is renowned for its spectacular sandstone formations, among them the Golden Gate (after which the park is named), the Sentinel or Brandwag Buttress, the imposing Mushroom Rocks and Cathedral Cave. There are also numerous *holkranse* ('hollow crags') and overhangs along the base of the Clarens Sandstone Formation.

The park has one of the largest herds of black wildebeest in the country. Other game species typical of the highlands include eland, blesbok, Burchell's zebra, mountain reedbuck and grey rhebok, while oribi and springbok also occur here.

To date some 160 bird species have been identified, among them the Verreaux's eagle and the southern bald ibis, which breeds in the park, while the rare bearded vulture is sometimes seen soaring overhead. Other species you may tick include Cape longclaw, grey-winged francolin, sentinel rock-thrush and Drakensberg rockjumper.

When you are walking through flat or gently sloping grasslands, keep an eye out for the tunnels of the giant girdled lizard, also known as the sungazer because of its habit of staring into the sun for hours.

The park has a surprising diversity of butterflies, and among the 78 species recorded are several endemic and rare species.

The grasslands are a key feature of this sanctuary, with Golden Gate being the only national park in the country that protects the grasses of the Highveld. The vegetation is characterised by dense montane sour grasslands, with species such as red grass, common thatch grass, iron grass and weeping lovegrass occuring in the park's highlands. To date some 65 grass and over 200 flowering plant species have been identified.

Trees and shrubs are scarce in the grasslands and are dominated by oldwood, wild peach and sagewood, while woody vegetation is restricted to the Little Caledon River Valley, sheltered ravines and sandstone crevices. Fynbos species include silver sugarbush and common sugarbush.

Starting at the Glen Reenen Rest Camp, the first day (16 km; 7 hours) is a steep hike up the well-known Brandwag Buttress, overlooking the Little Caledon River Valley. It then climbs steadily up the slopes of Wodehouse Peak before winding to Boskloof (not to be confused with Boskloof in the cliffs above Glen Reenen). From Tweelingskop the trail drops down to Wilgenhof, and then follows an easy route to the overnight hut situated next to a stream in Oudehoutskloof.

On day two's hike (13 km; 6 hours) the trail ascends along the Ribbokspruit, continuing past interesting rock crevices and an impressive waterfall. You gain about 700 m in altitude to the 2,732-m-high summit of Generaalskop, the park's highest point, from where there are magnificent views over Lesotho. The trail then descends along a spur, which offers dramatic views over the Little Caledon River Valley and the Mushroom Rocks. The slopes attract several game species, such as black wildebeest, blesbok and Burchell's zebra. From Langtoon Dam it is a short walk past a natural rockslide and pool to the Glen Reenen Rest Camp.

19. GOLDEN GATE HIGHLANDS NATIONAL PARK
Clarens

See no. 18 (p. 203) for hiking trail.

Trails: 4 walks; 1 to 4 hours; circular, out-and-return.
Permits: Conservation fee payable at Glen Reenen Rest Camp for walks. Reservations for guided walks to Cathedral Cave can be made at the reception office of the Glen Reenen Rest Camp.
Maps: Sketch map.
Facilities/Activities: Glen Reenen Rest Camp: semi-equipped stone rondavels with shower; camp sites with hot-water ablutions, scullery and braai places; shop. Brandwag Rest Camp: single and double rooms with en-suite facilities, telephone and television; chalets with bedroom, living room, semi-equipped kitchen, braai places and bathroom. Short self-drive game drives; guided night drives; guided walks to Cathedral Cave; vulture hide.

Glen Reenen Rest Camp

1. Wodehouse Kop is reached by following the path to the top of Brandwag. From here you follow the Ribbok Hiking Trail across a plateau before it climbs steeply up a grassy slope. Just beyond a band of dolerite the route splits off to the right, following a faint footpath to the 2,438-m-high Wodehouse Kop. **4 km; 4 hours; out-and-return.**

2. Golden Gate Highlights From Glen Reenen Rest Camp you can undertake several short walks under an hour to well-known features such as Echo Ravine, Boskloof, the Brandwag (Sentinel) and Mushroom Rocks, or do a longer hike combining all of these.

From the rest camp take the footbridge over the Little Caledon River and then climb to the base of the sandstone cliffs and Echo Ravine, a deep gorge, which can be explored if you wish.

Backtrack to the base of the split to Echo Ravine, turn right and continue to a right-hand fork, which leads deep into the wooded Boskloof. Once again you need to backtrack to the split (as the trail to Boskloof eventually peters out) where you turn right, continuing through boulders to the base of Brandwag. A chain ladder has been provided to help you negotiate the last 20 m of the cliffs. From the top of Brandwag there are fine views over the Little Caledon River and the park surroundings. You now have to backtrack to the first split to Echo Ravine, from where the trail hugs the base of the sandstone cliffs beneath the Mushroom Rocks until it eventually joins the park road. From here you can either backtrack, or follow the road back to the rest camp. **5 km; 2.5 hours; circular or out-and-return.**

3. Cathedral Cave is a guided walk that should not be missed, but is only conducted outside the August to end-November breeding season of the southern bald ibis. The cave is one of the most spectacular examples of sandstone weathering in South Africa. From a narrow opening in the roof at the end of the cave a stream plunges some 30 m to the floor, and below the lip of the waterfall the ceiling has been weathered into a magnificent dome, hence the name. Walks are conducted as part of the park's holiday programme but can also be arranged on request. Reservations can be made at the reception office of the Glen Reenen Rest Camp. **Approximately 7 km; 4 hours; out-and-return.**

Brandwag Rest Camp

Brandwag, the park's main rest camp, nestles below a sandstone outcrop that provides the setting for one of the most interesting walks in the park.

Holkrans From the rest camp the trail ascends steeply to the base of the sandstone cliffs behind the rest camp. The trail now hugs the base of the cliffs, leading to some spectacular caves eroded into the sandstone over countless aeons. Wooden steps provide access to the caves, which are a delight to photographers, as the rounded entrances provide perfect frames for the vistas across the valley. Where the trail eventually breaks away from the cliffs, a long wooden ladder provides access to a valley, which you follow back to the rest camp. **2 km; 1 hour; circular.**

20. SENTINEL TRAIL AND MONT-AUX-SOURCES
Phuthaditjhaba

Trail: 14 km; 7 to 8 hours; out-and-return, or 2 days with overnight on Escarpment.

Permits: Toll gate and hiking fees must be paid in cash at the Witsieshoek Mountain Lodge, cell: 082 609 8988.

Maps: The area is covered by *Map 1 (Royal Natal)* in the *uKhahlamba-Drakensberg* series by by Slingsby Maps. Online orders http://slingsby-maps.myshopify.com.

Facilities/Activities: Witsieshoek Mountain Resort, 7 km from the Sentinel Car Park, offers a variety of accommodation options. No facilities are available on the summit.

Pertinent information: Weather conditions on the Escarpment can change rapidly. Keep an eye out for possible weather changes, especially mist, which can set in with little warning. In winter, you must pack warm clothing, as a snowfall is always a possibility. Carry a tent if you plan to spend a night on the summit.

Safety: Sporadic attacks on hikers occur from time to time on the summit, making a group size of four people advisable.

Starting at the car park at the end of the Mountain Road, the path zigzags uphill and you pass the Witches, from where there are magnificent views of Eastern Buttress (3,047 m) and the Devil's Tooth (3,019 m). You will reach the Contour Path at the foot of the Sentinel after gaining some 300 m in altitude, and you then follow the path below Western Buttress (3,121 m).

At Kloof Gully there is a steep, rocky route that leads to Beacon Buttress (2,899 m) on the Escarpment, providing an alternative route for those wishing to avoid the chain ladders about 1 km further along the path. However, in winter, Kloof Gully is often blocked by snow and ice. In the early days this gully was the usual way to the summit and climbers often slept in Sentinel Cave, a short way beyond the gully.

Two sets of chain ladders, the first set installed by the then Natal Section of the Mountain Club of South Africa in 1930 and the second set in the 1980s, provide access to the Escarpment. The first ladder scales a near-vertical cliff for about 17 m, while the second ladder is about 13 m long.

From the top of the ladders it is approximately 1.5 km to the Escarpment edge, crossing the Tugela River en route. From the precipitous edge there are awesome views over the Royal Natal National Park, Eastern Buttress, the Devil's Tooth, the Devil's Toothpick and the Tugela Falls. With a total height of 948 m, the river plunges over the Escarpment's edge in five clear leaps – the longest single drop being 411 m. The World Waterfall Database recognised the Tugela Falls as the highest in the world in 2021, after it was found that the height of the Angel Falls in Venezuela had been calculated incorrectly.

If you are planning to overnight on the Escarpment to explore the area and Mont-aux-Sources, the Crow's Nest Cave can accommodate up to six people, but as it could be occupied, it is advisable to carry a tent. It is situated less than 1 km southwest of the old Natal Mountain Club hut.

Mont-aux-Sources (3,282 m), the highest point of the uKhahlamba-Drakensberg Amphitheatre, is situated approximately 5 km southwest of the ruin. It is reached by following the Tugela River upstream to its source and then to the beacon that marks the boundary between Lesotho and the South African provinces of Free State and KwaZulu-Natal.

The summit was first ascended by two French missionaries, Thomas Arbousset and François Dumas, while they were exploring the highlands of Lesotho in 1830. Realising the importance of the peak as the source of five major rivers, they named it the 'Mountain of Sources'. The Bilanjil and the Tugela rivers flow eastwards into KwaZulu-Natal, while the Western and Eastern Khebedu form the upper source of the Orange River. The Elands River, which flows into the Free State, can be seen tumbling over a precipice near the chain ladders.

21. LANGBERG TRAILS
Vrede

Trails: 2 day walks; 8 and 14 km; 3 and 6 hours; network from base camp.
Bookings: Fagala Voet, cell: 082 776 5540, 081 894 9802, email: bookings@fagalavoet.co.za, web: fagalavoet.co.za.
Maps: Sketch map.
Facilities/Activities: Base camp: double-storey building with bunks, mattresses, lounge, dining area, electricity, fridge, cooking utensils, fireplace and ablutions. Mountain biking; rock climbing; abseiling; caving.

This trail on Koefontein Farm traverses the slopes of the Langberg Mountains and the easy terrain makes it an ideal introduction for novice hikers. The first day's trail (14 km; 6 hours) alternates between winding above and below the sandstone cliffs. Highlights of the first day include the Waenhuis (Coach House), an enormous cave where women and children hid during the South African War (1899–1902), and a second cave with numerous passages.

The second day's hike (8 km; 3 hours) makes its way along an easy route across the lower slopes of the mountain. The trail partly follows the course of the Spruitsonderdrif, with its delightful natural pool, where you can enjoy a swim to cool off. There are also good birding opportunities.

22. KOEDOESLAAGTE TRAIL PARK & VENUE
Parys

Trails: 30.5 km; 1 hour to 5 hours; network.
Bookings: cell: 071 233 2777, email: reception@cycling-sa.co.za, web: www.koedoeslaagte.com.
Maps: Available.
Facilities/Activities: Picnic sites; cycling, trail running, swimming, canoeing.
Pertinent information: Open weekends and certain public holidays. Pre-booking required. Groups limited to 10, unless permission granted.

Situated in the Vredefort Dome, a UNESCO World Heritage site, the trails on Koedoeslaagte meander over hillsides and along the Vaal River. Due to the diversity of habitats in the area, birding can be rewarding, and to date over 120 species have been identified.

Trails range from a 3.5-km network on Ou Plaas, where the remains of Anglo-Boer War trenches can be seen, to an integrated network which allows hikers to plan their hike according to their fitness. Starting from the easy **Likkewaan Trail** (5 km; 1.5 to 2 hours), hikers can expand their hike by following several loops. The **Koedoe/Witkop route** (11 km; 3 to 5 hours) is the longest and most demanding, but can be shortened by taking the **Witkop/Witklip** (7 km; 2 to 3.5 hours).

23. VREDEFORT METEORITE HIKING TRAIL
Vredefort Dome

Trails: 60-km network; overnight trails (2 to 4 days); day trails (3 to 15 km).

Bookings: Fagala Voet, cell: 082 776 5540, 081 894 9802, email: bookings@ fagalavoet.co.za, web: fagalavoet.co.za.
Maps: Colour map available.
Facilities/Activities: Three well-equipped overnight camps ranging from thatched chalets at Deelfontein to an old farmhouse at Baskop and permanent tents at Thwane.

Vredefort Dome, a semi-circular range of hills with a diameter of 380 km, is not only the largest meteorite impact structure in the world, but also the oldest. Researchers have attributed the dome to a gigantic meteorite, with an estimated diameter of 10 km, which struck the earth's surface about 2 billion years ago. The immense force of the impact forced granite upwards and turned the edges of the adjacent strata outward. Erosion over countless millennia has left only a semi-circle of hills in the northwest of the original crater, while the southwestern part of the dome was subsequently covered by Karoo sediments. Vredefort Dome, also known as the Vredefort Impact Structure, was inscribed as a UNESCO World Heritage Site in 2005.

The area is also noteworthy for its large concentration and variety of stone-walled Iron Age settlements. Some of the early sites may have been inhabited as long as 1,500 years ago, while occupation of other settlements dates back to between the 1500s and the dispersal of the Tswana people, after the arrival of the Zulu chief Mzilikazi on the Highveld in the 1820s.

The vegetation is dominated by common hook thorn. Wild olive, white stinkwood, sweet thorn, mountain karee, blue guarri, velvet bushwillow and small knobwood are also common. The largest stand of proteas in the Free State can be seen at Dwarsberg – the highest point of the Dome. Lush riverine forest fringes the Vaal River where hikers can take a refreshing dip.

The Vredefort Meteorite Hiking Trail meanders over several properties in the southwestern part of the Dome. The trail has been designed as a figure-eight network with the Deelfontein Hikers Camp in the middle, Baskop in the west and Thwane northeast of Deelfontein.

The network of overnight trails has options from two to four days. Distances range between 8 km and 15 km over terrain varying from easy to moderately difficult. Each of the three base camps has its own network of day trails, ranging from 3 km to 15 km.

This leaves hikers with ample time for birding, taking in the fascinating geology and enjoying the scenery and magnificent views over the Vredefort Dome.

Depending on the route, hikers can view Iron Age stone enclosures as well as historical artefacts,

The uKhahlamba-Drakensberg is renowned for its spectacular scenery.

including relics from the South African War (1899–1902) and evidence of early gold-mining activity in the area.

Baskop Camp is situated on the Vaal River, and part of the route winds through lush riverine forest, with opportunities to cool off in the river. The northern loop of the Deelfontein to Thwane route winds along Dwarsberg, the highest point in the southern part of the Dome, and offers the best views of the impact structure.

MPUMALANGA & LIMPOPO

Situated in the northeastern and northern part of South Africa, Mpumalanga and Limpopo are renowned for their diverse landscapes, magnificent scenery and numerous other natural attractions. Mpumalanga shares a border with Eswatini to the southeast, while the Lebombo Mountains form a natural boundary with Mozambique to the east. Limpopo also borders on two countries; the Limpopo River forms the northern border with Zimbabwe, and to the west the province borders on Botswana.

There are numerous opportunities for outdoor enthusiasts to explore the plentiful natural attractions of these two provinces. These range from short, easy interpretative walks and overnight hiking trails to guided walks in the Kruger National Park and the Wolkberg Wilderness where backpackers can blaze their own trails.

Most of Mpumalanga lies on the Highveld, an upland region ranging in altitude from 900 m in the west to 2,277 m at the top of Mount Anderson in the Mpumalanga Drakensberg. The vegetation of the Highveld is characterised by grassland, ranging from almost pure grassveld with few trees and shrubs to grassveld interspersed with patches of woodland in the valleys and against hill slopes. Large areas that were formerly grassland are now planted with maize, wheat, sorghum and sunflowers, and additional vast stretches have been planted under pine and eucalyptus plantations. In addition, little remains of the large herds of game that once roamed the Highveld plains.

The Mpumalanga Drakensberg Escarpment is an area of scenic grandeur, featuring many waterfalls and well-known attractions such as the Blyde River Canyon, Bourke's Luck Potholes and God's Window. In the 1880s fortune seekers flocked to the area in search of gold, and the historic gold-mining towns of Pilgrim's Rest and Kaapschehoop serve as reminders of this era.

The vegetation of the Escarpment is characterised by mountain grassland, punctuated by rocky outcrops, weathered into fascinating shapes. In spring a variety of flowering plants provides a touch of colour to the grasslands.

Except for the indigenous forests of Mount Sheba only small patches of montane forests are found, in sheltered kloofs and ravines, on the Mpumalanga Escarpment. Typical species include Outeniqua and real yellowwood, lemonwood, Cape beech, white stinkwood and forest bushwillow.

Large mammals are neither abundant nor spectacular on the Escarpment. Antelope occurring naturally include grey rhebok, mountain reedbuck, klipspringer, common duiker, oribi and bushbuck. Also to be found are all five South African primates (baboon, vervet monkey, samango monkey, thick-tailed bushbaby and lesser bushbaby), bushpig, as well as a variety of small carnivores and rodents.

The montane grasslands near Graskop and Kaapschehoop are an important habitat of the endangered blue swallow, and southeastern Mpumalanga is home to several grassland specials, such as Botha's and Rudd's larks, yellow-breasted pipit and grey crowned crane, as well as the largest southern bald ibis breeding colonies in the world. Other grassland species found here include Cape rock-thrush, Swainson's spurfowl, Gurney's sugarbird, striped flufftail and buff-streaked chat. Among the forest species are crowned eagle, Knysna turaco, African paradise flycatcher, chorister robin-chat, sombre greenbul and olive woodpecker.

Minimum temperatures of below freezing point are not uncommon in winter, while days are cool. Frost can occur from May to September, and summer temperatures are moderate. Most of the Highveld's rainfall is recorded between November and March and is usually accompanied by violent mid-afternoon thunderstorms and lightning. Annual rainfall varies from less than 400 mm in the west to over 2,600 mm at God's Window, where the moisture-laden easterly winds are forced into an updraught, causing the formation of heavy mist and rain. Mist is especially common between December and March.

The Escarpment falls away to the Lowveld, a landscape of low-lying plains with altitudes ranging from 150 to 600 m above sea level. These dry woodlands contain a wealth of trees, with over 300 species recorded in the Kruger National Park alone. Typical species include mopane, bushwillow, leadwood, umbrella and knob thorns, apple-leaf, marula, Lowveld and silver cluster-leaf, baobab and fever trees.

Often regarded as 'the essential Africa', the Lowveld is synonymous with large herds of game and the Big Five (elephant, rhino, buffalo, lion and leopard). Stretching southwards from the Limpopo River for 350 km to the Crocodile River is the world-renowned Kruger National Park. This wildlife sanctuary of nearly 2 million ha is home to some 147 mammal species, 114 different reptile species and over 500 bird species.

The Lowveld has a subtropical climate. Winter days are mild, but in mid-winter minimum temperatures can drop to about 5 °C. During mid-summer maximum temperatures can reach up to 35 °C in January. Rainfall varies between 350 and 600 mm per year (November to February being the wettest months). Thunderstorms and lightning are common during this period.

Limpopo is a region of plains and hills, punctuated by the Soutpansberg in the north, the Waterberg in the west and the northern Drakensberg Escarpment in the east. The vegetation of the Escarpment is typically montane grasslands with small patches of indigenous forest in sheltered kloofs. Grootbosch near Magoebaskloof and the Wonderwoud in the Wolkberg Wilderness Area are the only two places where extensive patches of indigenous forests have survived.

Except for the Escarpment and the Lowveld, the vegetation over the rest of Limpopo consists of bushveld – a landscape of mixed trees and shrubs lower than 10 m, generally with their canopies touching. It is composed of, among others, a variety of bushwillow and euphorbia tree species, marula, red syringa, buffalo-thorn and vast stands of mopane.

On many farms in Limpopo cattle farming has been phased out in favour of game ranching, and the once prolific herds of game have begun to re-establish themselves. The Waterberg is a stronghold of the rare roan, while sable, kudu, reedbuck and impala are among the antelope species found here.

Birdlife is prolific and ranges from woodland species, such as white-throated robin-chat, Kalahari scrub robin, southern yellow-billed hornbill, barred wren-warbler and Burchell's starling to the rich diversity of birds attracted to the Nylsvley Wetlands. One of South Africa's top birding hotspots, Nylsvley has a bird checklist of 426 species, including breeding populations of several rare and threatened species. On occasion the wetlands can attract up to 80,000 birds at a time. The cliffs of the Waterberg are home to the largest breeding colony of the Cape vulture in the world.

Winter temperatures in the bushveld can be quite mild, but in mid-summer they often exceed 40 °C. Mpumalanga and Limpopo lie within the summer-rainfall region.

IMPORTANT INFORMATION

➤ Minimum temperatures can be extremely low on the Highveld and at high altitudes on the Escarpment, especially in winter, so hikers must pack sufficient warm clothing and a good sleeping bag.

➤ Mist is common along the Escarpment between September and April. If it is very thick you should wait until it has lifted (usually around mid-morning) or you could easily miss trail markers and get lost.

➤ Heavy thunderstorms occur in both Mpumalanga and Limpopo during summer, and are often accompanied by lightning. Plan to reach the overnight stop by mid-afternoon to avoid being caught in a thunderstorm or trapped by a river in flood.

➤ Always be aware of the risk of fire when walking through grassland. Smokers should be very cautious and fires must be made only where permitted.

➤ Ticks can be a problem in summer. It is advisable to take precautions, such as treating your socks with a tick repellent.

➤ Malaria is endemic in the Lowveld, while most of the rest of Mpumalanga and Limpopo fall within an epidemic malaria area. Consult a doctor about anti-malaria medication before you set off for the area.

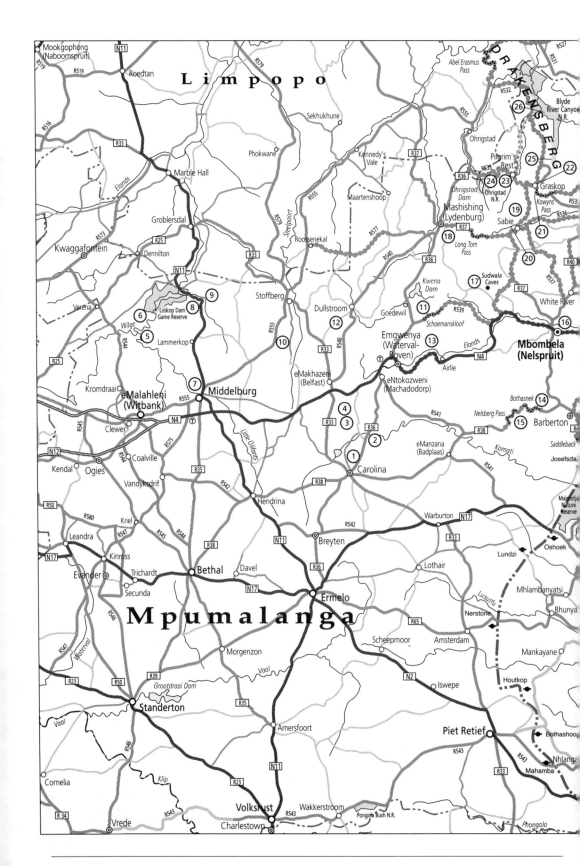

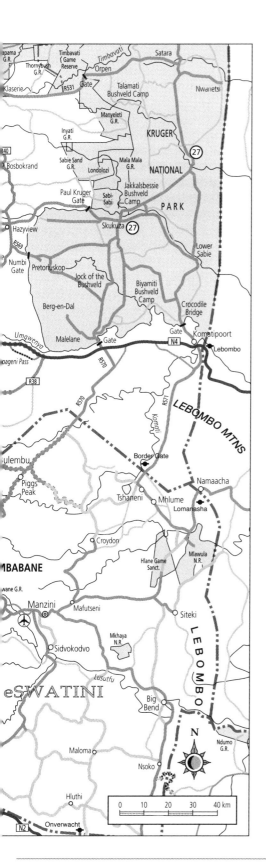

Continued on pp. 214–215

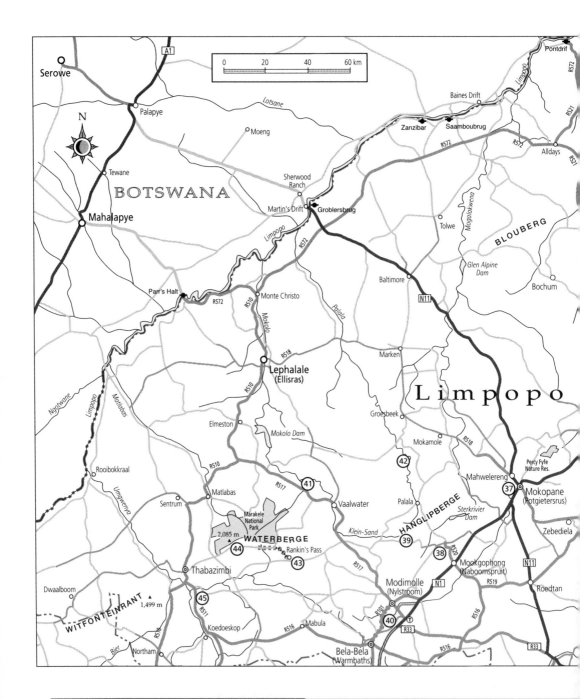

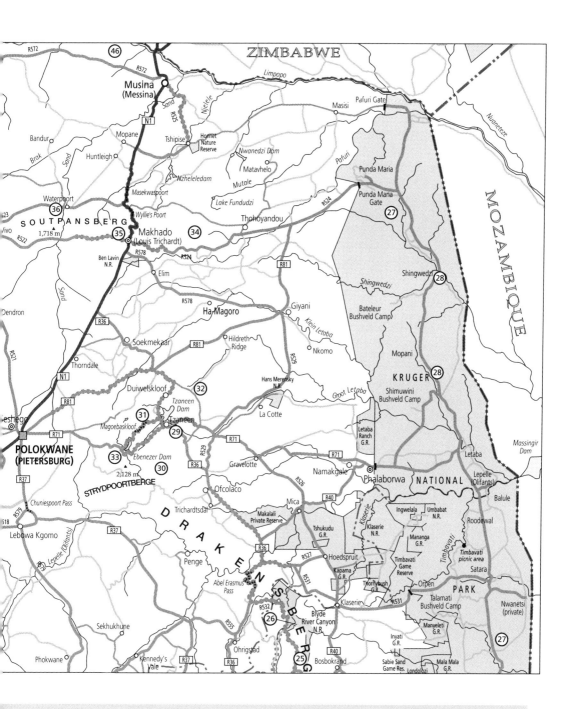

1. SUIKERBOSCHFONTEIN HIKING TRAIL
Carolina

Trail: 19.5 km; 2 days; circular.
Bookings: Fagala Voet, cell: 082 776 5540, 081 894 9802, email: bookings@ fagalavoet.co.za, web: fagalavoet.co.za.
Maps: Trail pamphlet with map.
Facilities/Activities: Rooikrans Camp: huts with beds and mattresses, kitchen with kettle, pots, pans; braai facilities; toilets and hot showers. Oom Japie's House: house with beds, mattresses, kitchen with kettle, pots, pans; braai facilities; toilets and hot showers.

Situated on the Escarpment, 20 km northeast of Carolina, the Suikerboschfontein Hiking Trail traverses grassland interspersed with patches of common sugarbush, also known as Highveld sugarbush. Tracts of indigenous forest with yellowwoods occur in sheltered kloofs, while common tree ferns are conspicuous along stream banks. Of historical interest are the ruins of shrines, temples and several other structures built by Dravidian (Indian) gold-seekers who prospected and traded gold with the Khoikhoi, and later the Nguni people, during the first and early second millennia.

From Oom Japie's House the first day's hike (9.3 km; 4 hours) descends steadily to the Yellow-wood Cliffs. The trail then traverses the plateau before descending to a swimming hole and a waterfall, which is reached further on. The final section of the day's hike meanders alongside a stream.

The second day's hike (10.2 km; 4 hours) from Rooikrans Camp passes through narrow gorges and you will reach Grootkloof and the 23-m-high Mooifontein Waterfall just over 2 km from the start. From here the trail follows a contour to S-bend Kloof and then leads along a stream, with beautiful waterfalls and pools. The trail makes its way through Gladdekloof, which is a good lunch stop. After negotiating Gladdekloof (a rope assists hikers up the wet cliffs) you follow the trail across Suikerbosrand, with its profusion of common sugarbushes, and then head for the Rooirant. The descent into Oom Japie's Gorge, with its magnificent tree ferns, is followed by a steady climb to Oom Japie's House.

2. KRANSKLOOF HIKING TRAIL
Carolina

Trails: 1 hiking trail: 18.5 km; 2 days; circular. 3 day walks: 3.5 to 5 km; 2 to 3 hours; circular and out-and-return.
Bookings: Fagala Voet, cell: 082 776 5540, 081 894 9802, email: bookings@ fagalavoet.co.za, web: fagalavoet.co.za.
Maps: Trail pamphlet with map.
Facilities/Activities: Kranskloof: stone huts with bunks and mattresses, kitchen with two-plate gas stove, pots, pans; braai facilities; toilets and hot showers. Inkungu: timber huts with the same amenities as Kranskloof.

1. Kranskloof Hiking Trail The first day (10 km; 4 hours) of this trail, also known as the Grey Rhebok Route, steadily ascends along the edge of a kloof, passing through a stand of milkplum trees. On reaching a waterfall, which plunges over a cliff edge, the trail climbs through interesting rock formations and grassveld before gently descending to the overnight stop, Inkungu.

Day two's hike (8.5 km; 3 hours), the Oribi Route, climbs out of Kleinklofie, with its huge tree ferns, to the plateau and then ascends gently to the waterfall, where the outward route of the first day's hike is reached. From here you retrace your tracks back to the start. **18.5 km; 2 days; circular.**

2. Ruins Day Walk can also be done here. **3.5 km; 2 hours; circular.**

3. Cliff Route follows the outward route of the overnight trail to the waterfall, from where you can retrace your steps. **4.5 km; 2 hours; out-and-return.**

4. Gully Route can be combined with the Cliff Route by descending into the valley from the waterfall. The descent is steep, and you lose some 100 m in altitude on your way down to the river, with its waterchute and lovely pools. **5 km; 3 hours; circular.**

3. BERMANZI HIKING TRAIL
eNtokozweni (Machadodorp)

Trails: 2 day walks: 8 and 12 km; 4 and 6 hours; network from base camp.
Bookings: Anvie Ventures,
tel: (044) 696 6585, fax: 086 652 3288,
email: anvie@iburst.co.za.
Maps: Sketch map.
Facilities/Activities: Luxury thatched stone house: three bedrooms, bathroom, kitchen with gas stove and fridge, solar lighting, electricity, lounge with fireplace, and braai area. Hikers' huts: bunk beds, mattresses, pots, pan, kettle, small charcoal stove, braai facilities, toilets and hot showers.

The mountains between eNtokozweni (Machado-dorp), Emgwenya (Waterval Boven) and eManzana (Badplaas) provide the setting for this trail, southeast of eNtokozweni.

1. Route 1, the Main Trail, begins by following an old wagon road made by a family who found safety in these valleys during the South African War (1899–1902). After passing through a natural rock crevice, Houtkapperskeur, the route descends to the base of the cliffs overlooking the Komati Valley. It then joins the old wagon road. It descends steeply through indigenous bush to the Bushbuck Trail and the Bankspruit. The trail now ascends sharply to the summit of Rooikrans and then drops down to a delightful pool and rapids. Further along you reach the Uitkoms Waterfall, said to be the second highest waterfall in Mpumalanga, and then you climb steadily back to a plateau. The return leg follows the edge of the plateau back to the base camp. **12 km; 6 hours; circular.**

2. Route 2 is made up of a combination of several relatively short, scenic secondary trails, such as the **Boerperd**, **Rooikat**, **Tarentaal**, **Tierboskat**, **Bosvark** and **Duiker** routes. **8 km; 4 hours; circular.**

4. HIGH FIVE TRAILS
eNtokozweni (Machadodorp)

Trails: 100-km integrated network; 2 to 7 days.
Bookings: Escarp Adventures, cell: 082 950 2417, email: hiker@escarp.co.za, web: escarp.co.za.
Maps: Available.
Facilities/Activities: 4 base camps with communal kitchens, braai places and communal hot showers.
Pertinent information: The minimum group size is 4 people.

The spectacular Skurweberg ('rough mountains') in the north of the Mpumalanga Drakensberg Escarpment provides the setting for the High Five Trails, which was previously known as the Num-Num Hiking Trail.

Grasslands punctuated by proteas dominate the vegetation, while pockets of indigenous forests occur in the kloofs. Some 110 tree species have been recorded to date, among them yellowwood, cabbage tree and wild pear.

Herds of plains zebra, blesbok, red hartebeest and black wildebeest roam the plains. Also to be seen are mountain reedbuck, kudu, bushbuck, baboon and vervet monkey.

With habitats ranging from forests, grasslands, wetlands and cliffs, a rich diversity of birds can be seen, among them Knysna and purple-crested turaco, southern bald ibis, Cape vulture, African fish eagle and crested eagle, while a variety of waterbirds are attracted to the dams, rivers and streams.

Starting at the Pongola Express, the first day's hike (7 km; 4 hours) leads to Aloe Kaya Camp. On the second day (8 km; 4 hours), hikers make their way to Mount Komati Camp and continue to Candlewood Camp on day three (9 km; 4.5 hours).

On day four (8 km; 4 hours) the trail leads back to the Pongola Express, which serves as the base for a circular route of 8 km.

Highlights of the trail include the 60-m-high twin-stream Uitkomst Waterfall, the second highest waterfall in the Lowveld, spectacular sandstone labyrinths, weathered sandstone formations and natural aloe rock gardens. From the Escarpment, hikers are rewarded with spectacular views of the Komati River Valley.

The integrated trail network has been designed to enable hikers to plan their own trails lasting anything from two to seven days. Although daily distances between the overnight huts are short, hikers should be fit as there are steep ascents and descents that have to be negotiated. Wooden ladders and bridges are provided at sections that are difficult to negotiate.

5. OLIFANTS GORGE TRAILS
eMalahleni (Witbank)

Trails: 3 trails: 23 to 24 km; 2 or 3 days; networks from base camp and circular.
Permits: Anvie Ventures, tel: (044) 696 6585, fax: 086 652 3288, email: anvie@iburst.co.za
Maps: Sketch map.
Facilities/Activities: Kingdom Base Camp: stone huts with bunks, mattresses, shower and toilet; thatched area with kitchen and braai facilities, pots, pan, kettles and lanterns. Slagthoek: farmhouse with bunks, mattresses, braai and kitchen facilities, pots, pan and kettle. Grootdraai: hut with bunks, mattresses, braai facilities, pot, pan and kettle, shower and toilet.

This trail network traverses an area of 15,000 ha at the confluence of the Lepelle (Olifants) and Wilge rivers in the Loskop Dam area. The trail network consists of a two-day overnight hiking trail and two trails each composed of two circular routes that can be hiked individually, as day walks, or combined into overnight trails.

1. Slagthoek Hiking Trail traverses the section to the east of the Lepelle (Olifants) River. From the Slagthoek Base Camp, the God's Window Loop (12 km; 6 hours) climbs gradually amid rocks to a viewpoint overlooking the Hundred Hills. It winds down into a valley with striking rock formations to a viewpoint, where hikers can enjoy stunning vistas of the Lepelle River. From here the trail climbs gently to Gifkoppie, with its panoramic views over the rapids and cascades, and then drops down to the river. After crossing the river, the route follows a densely wooded kloof back to the base camp. The Cycad Loop (11 km; 5 hours) follows a track to Boschkloof plateau and then descends along a valley with a natural cycad garden. Further along it ascends gently to a viewpoint overlooking the river, after which it heads back down to the base camp. **23 km; 2 days; network from base camp.**

2. Kingdom Hiking Trail Starting at the Kingdom Base Camp, Route 1 (8 km; 4 hours) ascends a kloof with a seasonal waterfall to a plateau, where hikers are rewarded with magnificent views of the Wilge River from the Razor's Edge. After following a contour, the trail descends into the densely wooded Donkerkloof, with its springs and ancient white stinkwood trees. Further along, the path makes its way along the Nyala River to Black Rock Cascade and Kingdom Base Camp.

Route 2 (16 km; 7 hours) leads past Black Rock Cascade and then ascends a kloof to a plateau, with a viewpoint that overlooks the Olifants Gorge and Die Hel at the confluence of the Lepelle (Olifants) and Wilge rivers. The trail then descends a kloof to the Lepelle River, passing a magnificent old fig tree. On the river you will find the Hippo Pool swimming spot, good for a swim or just to rest for a while. The trail continues along the river below towering cliffs, crossing the river twice by means of a cable handhold. However, when the river is high, you will have to follow an alternative route, which bypasses the loop where the Lepelle River is crossed. After the second crossing, the path ascends gently to Snaaksekrans Viewpoint and 1 km on veers sharply to the right to pass through Sheba's Breasts. The final section descends along the valley of the Nyala River back to the base camp. An early start is recommended for this day's hike. **24 km; 2 days; network from base camp.**

3. Olifants Gorge Hiking Trail is a two-day hike, which can be extended to three or four days by adding any of the circular routes detailed below. Day one (12 km; 5 hours) follows Route 2 of the Kingdom Hiking Trail to the first crossing of the Lepelle (Olifants) River. Here the trail splits off to the left to follow a kloof back to Slagthoek. On day two (12 km; 6 hours) the trail heads through Bamboeskloof and then follows the river and several swimming spots. At Grootdraai Hut it joins the Paradors Loop and then follows the Nyala River back to the Kingdom Base Camp. **24 km; 2 days; circular.**

6. ROOIKRANS HIKING TRAIL
Loskop Dam area, Middelburg

Trails: 3 walks; 3 to 4 hours; network from base camp.
Bookings: Rooikrans Hiking Trail, tel: (061) 071 7251, cell: 082 443 8942, email: info@rooikranshikingtrail.co.za, web: www.rooikranshikingtrail.co.za.
Maps: Download colour map from website.
Facilities/Activities: Hikers' dormitory with bunk beds, communal ablutions (hot-water donkey), flush toilets and communal kitchen with basic equipment, braai areas. Two-bedroom rondavel with four single beds, hot-water shower, flush toilet, fully equipped kitchen, braai area. Mountain biking.

This network of trails has been laid out on a game and cattle farm bordering the Loskop Dam Game Reserve. The trails are well marked and chain handholds, steps and wooden bridges assist hikers at difficult places. Highlights include inviting rock pools, cascades and a ribbon-like waterfall after the summer rains.

The area lies in a transitional zone between the Highveld and Lowveld, and the flora and fauna are representative of both regions. The vegetation ranges from shady wooded kloofs and grassveld to bushveld with typical species such as Transvaal milkplum (moepel in Afrikaans), Transvaal bottlebrush and mountain seringa. A variety of flowers come into bloom at spring.

1. Job se Kloof Trail follows the same route as the Witpenskloof Trail for about 1 km before splitting off. After ascending gently initially, a steep climb awaits you up Job se Kloof and you will gain close to 200 m in altitude from the start. Once you've reached the Escarpment, the trail levels off and you can enjoy stunning views of the valley below. A stone fortification is a reminder of the South African War (1899–1902), and a viewpoint with far-reaching views of the Loskop Dam and its surroundings is reached a short way on. The trail then descends to the red cliffs to which Rooikrans owes its name and the onward route of the Witpenskloof Trail. **11.1 km; 4 hours; circular.**

2. Witpenskloof Trail initially follows an easy route before ascending past a waterfall and swimming hole, where you can cool off after it has rained, and up Witpenskloof to the Escarpment. The path then levels off on the Escarpment before winding down to the overnight camp. **7.6km; 3 hours; circular.**

3. Draadkloof Trail, the most demanding route, ascends up Draadkloof and levels off once the Escarpment is reached. It then descends steeply along Job se Kloof before levelling off as you make your way back to the overnight camp. **11.4 km; 4 hours; circular.**

Hikers can combine Job se Kloof and Witpenskloof, but this is only recommended for fit hikers. **15.8 km; 6 hours; circular.**

7. BOTSHABELO HIKING TRAILS
Middelburg

Trails: 3 day walks: 6 to 12 km; 3 to 6 hours; circular.
Permits: Entrance fee. No booking required for walks.
Maps: Sketch map.
Facilities/Activities: Restaurant; kiosk; curio shop; Botshabelo Site Museum; Ndebele Open-air Museum.

This trail network combines the natural beauty of the area, its history, and the culture of the

Ndebele people. Botshabelo, a name meaning 'place of shelter', was established by the Berlin Mission Society in 1865. To protect his followers against attacks from the Pedi leader, Sekhukhune, missionary Alexander Merensky built a stone fort. The mission station expanded rapidly and by 1873 there were 1,315 inhabitants. The fort, two churches, Merensky House Museum and numerous other buildings from this era form part of the Botshabelo Site Museum.

Botshabelo lies within a 2,306-ha nature reserve, and among the game species to be seen are eland, blesbok, red hartbeest, black wildebeest, springbok and Burchell's zebra. Smaller species include steenbok, common duiker, oribi, klipspringer, baboon and vervet monkey.

1. Botshabelo Trail focuses on the history of the mission station. Winding past Fort Merensky, it offers excellent views of the settlement. After passing through two kloofs, the trail descends to the Little Olifants River and then makes its way back to Botshabelo, leaving enough time to explore the settlement. **6 km; 3 hours; circular.**

2. Aasvoëlkrans Trail passes through stands of the endemic Olifants River cycad and offers fine views over the Little Olifants River. The outward leg of this trail initially climbs gently and then follows a route above the Little Olifants River Gorge to Aasvoëlkrans. After crossing the river, the trail remains parallel to the Little Olifants River all the way back to the start. **12 km; 6 hours; circular.**

3. Bobbejaanstert Trail offers a shorter option on the Aasvoëlkrans Trail. It follows the outward leg of the Aasvoëlkrans Trail and then descends into the gorge, continuing above the river, before linking up with the outward leg of the hike. **10 km; 5 hours; circular.**

8. ZIP X TRAILS
Middelburg

Trails: 2 trails; 2 to 8 hours or overnight; circular and out-and-return.

Bookings: Loskop Adventures, cell: 082 923 1982 (Thys), email: bookings@ loskopadventures.co.za.
Maps: Hels River Trail follows a gorge that is unmarked.
Facilities/Activities: Camp site with two dome tents, canvas canopy, chairs, table, kettle, braai facilities and pit toilet on Hel's River Trail; ziplining; abseiling.
Pertinent information: Keep a close watch on the weather, as the level of the Hels River rises rapidly after rain. Lightweight boots or sandals with a good grip are essential. It is advisable to make use of a guide for safety reasons or if you are not experienced at kloofing.

Loskop Adventures is situated on an escarpment that is bisected by narrow kloofs, the Lepelle (Olifants) River and the deep gorge carved by the Hels River.

The vegetation is typical bushveld with characteristic species such as bushwillows (*Combretum* spp.) and boekenhout (*Faurea saligna*) and proteaveld. Of special interest are the two cycad species of the Lepelle River catchment area: the Middelburg cycad (*Encephalartos middelburgensis*) and the woolly cycad (*Encephalartos lanatus*).

Among the animals you might chance upon are kudu, bushpig, mountain reedbuck, klipspringer and vervet monkey. There is also a rich diversity of birds to be seen.

1. Hel's River Trail is a challenging kloofing route, which involves scrambling over and around boulders, rock hopping, wading through pools and swimming. From the Zip X reception centre a road is followed for about 1 km and the trail then descends steeply to the Hels River, which is followed for about 4 km until its confluence with the Lepelle River. A two-seater canoe and life jackets are provided at the final pool of the day, which is too deep to wade through, to get hikers and their equipment to the overnight camp. From the overnight camp you have to retrace your tracks upstream. This involves a steep climb out of the river and gaining some 350 m in altitude back to the start. **10 km; 6 to 8 hours; out-and-return.**

2. Kranskloof Trail From the Zip X reception centre the trail winds up and along a ridge to the top of the cliffs overlooking the Hels River. It then descends down cliffs, where ropes have been provided, into the Hels River. After following the river for about 500 m, the route ascends steeply up a rocky kloof passing an abandoned mine halfway up the kloof. Although short, the trail is difficult, as the difference between the highest and lowest points is 276 m. **4.6 km; 2 to 3 hours; circular.**

9. BUFFALO GORGE HIKING TRAIL
Middelburg

Trails: 4 trails: 1 to 7 hours, circular.
Bookings: Ryk Diepraam, cell: 083 528 9586, email: info@buffalogorge.co.za.
Maps: Sketch map
Facilities/Activities: Tents with beds and mattresses; wood-fired hot water; toilets and shower; bush kitchen with pots, pans, three-plate gas cooker, fridge and freezer, braai place. Abseiling; rock climbing; horse-riding.

The base camp trails on the farm Buffelskloof offer a combination of spectacular scenery, and, with a checklist of 80 species, excellent birding opportunities. Kudu, klipspringer, common duiker, baboon and warthog are among the mammals you may chance upon. Some 80 tree species have been marked and can be identified along the day walks, which serve as an excellent introduction to the trees of the area. Historical sites on the farm include an old school building dating back to 1922 and Iron Age stone enclosures.

Hikers can combine their walks with adventure activities such as abseiling, horse-riding and mountain biking.

1. The White Trail alternates between dense indigenous forest, grassveld and proteaveld with fascinating rock formations. Highlights of the day's hike include spectacular views of the Avontuur Gorge and the Selons River some 240 m below. For adrenaline junkies there is a 50-m-high abseil down a cliff face.

The trail follows the edge of the Escarpment and passes the nesting site of a white-fronted bee-eater colony. Further along, hikers have the choice of extending the day's hike by doing a 3-km loop which leads to a viewpoint (the Big King's Chair) over the valley, or continuing to the base camp. Water bottles can be topped up at a fountain on the return leg, which traverses level terrain before descending to the base camp. **12 or 15 km; 6 or 7 hours.**

2. The Blue Trail is ideal for beginners and will appeal to those interested in learning more about the trees of the area. The trail ascends steeply along a stream in a forested kloof with two small waterfalls, passing boulders and stunted trees reminiscent of bonsais, and then joins the White Trail. **1 hour.**

3. The Yellow Trail offers a choice of three routes. The trail follows the Blue Trail to the waterfall, where it branches off, passing an abseiling spot. It then ascends to the top of the plateau where it follows the contours before descending steeply into the valley. **1, 2 or 3 hours.**

4. The Orange Trail meanders through indigenous forest. Trees have been marked to show the way. **1.5 hours.**

10. RIBBOKKLOOF HIKING TRAIL
Middelburg/Stoffberg

Trail: 6.7 to 9.5 km; 2 days; circular or network from base camp.
Bookings: Fagala Voet, cell: 082 776 5540, 081 894 9802, email: bookings@fagalavoet.co.za, web: fagalavoet.co.za.
Maps: Colour map.
Facilities/Activities: Stinkhout Chalet: 12-bed chalet, beds with mattresses, kitchen with gas stove, fridge, hot shower and flush toilet; braai facilities; no electricity. River Bed Camp: overnight lapa covered with a thatch roof and shade cloth; camp mattresses; showers (no hot water); toilets; braai facilities. Bushpig Shelter: no facilities; take everything you need.

The Ribbokkloof Hiking Trail, given Green Flag status by the Hiking Organisation of South Africa (HOSA), provides breathtaking views over the Uitkyk area. The trail can be hiked as an overnight route or as a network of trails.

The trails, rated as easy and moderate, meander across rolling grasslands and past waterfalls and inviting pools. The distances are short, which allows hikers ample time to enjoy the magnificent scenery. The varied flora includes the large blue scilla and wild sweet pea. Trailists might also encounter bushpig and mountain reedbuck along the way.

From Stinkhout Chalet the first day's hike (9.5 km; 4 hours) ascends to Gideon se Waterval. From there the trail winds down into a valley and then climbs again to a waterfall. It continues across a plateau to a large white stinkwood tree. After descending, the trail makes its way to a 10-ha bass dam from where it is a short walk to the River Bed Camp.

The second day's hike from River Bed Camp (6.7 km; 3 hours) traverses easy terrain on the southern side of the valley. It is a short distance to Daan se Koelte. From Daan se Koelte the trail follows the contours of the valley to Bushpig Shelter. From there the trail descends to Stinkhout Chalet and then follows the same route back along the valley to River Bed Camp.

11. INDABUSHE TRAIL
Schoemanskloof

> **Trails:** 2 walks, 4.5 and 7 km; 1.5 and 3 hours; circular.
> **Bookings:** Indabushe Eco Lodge, cell: 083 443 0827, email: info@indabushe.com.
> **Maps:** Available.
> **Facilities/Activities:** Various accommodation options, including a lodge, tents and grassed camping sites. Mountain biking; quad trails; fishing; archery.

The Indabushe Trail (7 km; 3 hours) is situated on a private farm in the scenic Schoemanskloof Valley, which links the Highveld and the Lowveld. The trail starts at the guesthouse at the foot of the mountain and initially ascends steeply to the plateau, passing through bushveld vegetation. Along the way hikers pass the ruins of a stone settlement, a reminder of much earlier human habitation in the area. Near the summit, the fig trees growing against the cliffs are conspicuous.

Grassland covers the plateau, and the effort to make it to the top is rewarded with spectacular views of the 50-km-long Schoemanskloof Valley. Looking to the northwest, the scenery is dominated by a patchwork of irrigated lands and the Kwena Dam, which was built in the Crocodile River (*kwena* is the Setswana name for 'crocodile'). The dam was constructed primarily for irrigation. A spring on the plateau is an ideal place to enjoy lunch or simply relax before starting the downward climb and making your way back to the start of the trail.

A shorter trail (4.5 km; 1.5 hours), ideal for the inexperienced, is also available on the farm.

As a result of the diverse habitats, from riverine bush to grassland, birding can be rewarding. Purple-crested turaco, African paradise flycatcher, Cape rock-thrush, mocking cliff chat and jackal buzzard are among the species that have been recorded, while the Buffelskloofspruit and its riverine vegetation attract a variety of kingfishers and other waterbirds.

Red and common duiker, steenbok, bushbuck, vervet monkeys and baboon are among the mammals you might chance upon.

12. AMA POOT POOT HIKING TRAIL
Dullstroom

> **Trails:** 2 walks, 6 and 13 km; 3 and 6 hours; circular, network from base camp.
> **Bookings:** Cell: 083 629 9412 (Vera) or 083 625 6806 (Kobus), email: vera@uitvlugt.co.za or kobus@uitvlugt.co.za, web: www.uitvlugt.co.za.
> **Maps:** Sketch map.
> **Facilities/Activities:** Base camp with bunks, mattresses, kitchen with cooking utensils and gas appliances, lounge with fireplace, braai facilities, hot showers and toilets. Trout angling; mountain biking.

The Ama Poot Poot Hiking Trail has been laid out on a private game farm between the towns of Dullstroom and Belfast. The two routes of the trail meander through grassland, where hikers may spot a variety of game. Hiking can also be combined with trout angling in the dams.

1. Trout Route This trail starts off by following a tranquil stream with two waterfalls. It then meanders past some trout dams before reaching the Witpoort River Gorge. Provided you take rope along and you are relatively agile and adventurous, or if a member of your party has some climbing experience, the gorge can be explored at your leisure. You can wade up to the falls which you may have passed while on the Mountain Reedbuck Route. From here the trail continues to a viewpoint that overlooks the river and then doubles back to the start. **6 km; 3 hours; circular.**

2. Mountain Reedbuck Route wanders along rocky ridges and above krantzes, where hikers are rewarded with stunning views of the surrounding landscape. After crossing the Witpoort River the trail ascends steeply up the mountain slopes before looping back along a kloof with an abundance of common tree ferns. One of the highlights of the trail is a 10-m-high waterfall with an enormous pool, making this spot an ideal location for a lunch stop. After crossing the Witpoort River again, the trail climbs out of the gorge and returns to the start. **13 km; 6 hours; circular.**

13. ELANGENI HIKING TRAIL
Emgwenya (Waterval Boven)

Trail: 25 km; 2 days; circular.
Bookings: Fagala Voet, cell: 082 776 5540, 081 894 9802, email: bookings@ fagalavoet.co.za, web: fagalavoet.co.za.
Maps: Colour sketch map.
Facilities/Activities: Base camp: eight cabins (sleeping four each) with single beds, mattresses, electricity, kitchen with stove, kettle, communal lapa, braai facilities, hot showers and flush toilets. Mountain cabin: four bedrooms (sleeping eight each) with hot showers, kitchen with stove, kettle, gas lamps and fireplace with limited firewood.
Pertinent information: Trailists must ensure they carry enough drinking water, as limited water is available, especially on the first day. Ticks occur here, and trailists should take preventative measures.

The trail starts at the Elangeni Holiday Resort, some 18 km east of the historic town of Emgwenya (Waterval Boven).

An early start to day one (14 km; 5 to 6 hours) is advisable, as a steep walk up the mountain lies ahead. The trail starts off by following the course of the Elands River for approximately 1 km. It then ascends for another 3 km, gaining some 600 m in altitude as it winds its way up to the Escarpment. This section of the trail is likely to take about 2 hours, depending on the fitness levels of the individual members in your group. The stunning views of the Elands River Valley far below are, however, more than ample reward for the demanding climb.

The trail now winds along the edge of the Escarpment, passing through land that belongs to the paper manufacturer, Sappi, and special care should be taken to avoid starting a fire. Approximately 3 km along the Escarpment there is a lookout point. This is a good spot for a lunch stop. After following the edge of the Escarpment for another 3 km, the trail drops into a shaded valley and descends further to a small waterfall. From here the path continues its descent through a patch of indigenous forest, eventually leading to inviting rock pools. The overnight hut is a short way further (about 500 m) and is reached by following a path through dense bush before emerging at a clearing.

Starting at the overnight hut, the second day's trail (11 km; 3 hours) ascends steadily for about 2 km, gaining some 160 m in altitude, before reaching the 65-m-high Elangeni Waterfall. After passing through a tract of indigenous forest, trailists will reach another waterfall, which is about 35 m high. Allow some time here to take a refreshing dip in the pools before continuing along the trail. From here, the path descends steadily down the valley.

The final stretch of the trail follows a gravel road which will take you back to the start of the trail at the Elangeni Holiday Resort.

14. KAAPSCHEHOOP HIKING TRAIL
Kaapschehoop

Trails: 3 trails: 23.8 to 38.9 km; 2 to 3 days; circular.
Permits: Komatiland Eco-Tourism, cell: 083 641 3089, email: ecotour@safcol.co.za, web: www.safcol.co.za.
Maps: A4 colour sketch map of trail.
Facilities/Activities: Kaapschehoop: hut with bunk beds, mattresses, pots, pans, kettles, braai area, firewood, toilets and hot showers. Barretts Coaches: railway coaches with electricity, pots, pans, braai area, firewood, hot showers and toilets. Wattles: hut with bunk beds, mattresses, pots, pans, kettle, braai area, firewood, toilets and hot showers. Coetzeestroom: hut with bunk beds, mattresses, showers and toilet; braai area, firewood.
Pertinent information: Hikes can be started from the Kaapschehoop Hut or Barretts Coaches.

Owned by Komatiland Forests, the Berlin Plantation on the Drakensberg Escarpment provides a spectacular setting for the Kaapschehoop Hiking Trail. The landscape here is characterised by undulating hills, deeply eroded valleys, vegetated gorges, patches of indigenous forest, sheer cliffs and clear streams.

Kaapschehoop was the focal point of a minor gold rush following the discovery of alluvial gold in the early 1880s on a nearby farm called Berlyn (the Afrikaans name for Berlin). Many artefacts of the early gold-mining days, such as the Gold Commissioner's house, the old post office and the jail in Kaapschehoop, as well as the original gold mine diggings, can still be seen here today. By 1886, a year after the De Kaap Goldfields were proclaimed a public goldfield, the area already had a few thousand inhabitants and several permanent buildings. However, following the discovery of gold on the Witwatersrand, combined with disappointing returns at Kaapschehoop, many diggers abandoned the area and the settlement became a ghost town.

Plantations have replaced much of the natural vegetation, but a few patches of grassveld and indigenous forest have been left untouched. At Coetzeestroom the vegetation changes dramatically to Lowveld bushveld savannah. A noteworthy plant species occurring in the area is the endemic Kaapsehoop cycad, which enjoys protection in the Starvation Creek Nature Reserve.

Mammals to be found here include baboon, vervet monkey, rock dassie, oribi, common and blue duiker, klipspringer, bushbuck and bushpig. Also of interest are the wild horses of Kaapschehoop, variously said to be descendants of pit ponies and/or Boer horses that ran wild during the South African War (1899–1902).

More than 200 bird species have been recorded, among them 8 to 12 breeding pairs of the endangered blue swallow. They breed on Blouswawelvlakte, southeast of Kaapschehoop. The area, which has been set aside as the Blue Swallow Natural Heritage Site, holds the third largest breeding population of this species in South Africa. Other species to look out for include chorister robin-chats and white-starred robins, Knysna turaco, forest buzzard and olive bushshrike.

This trail network offers trailists several options, ranging from four two-day trails to tailor-made three-and four-day trails. One of the three-day trails, incorporating most of the different options, is described here in detail.

Two Creeks Three-day Trail Starting at Barretts Coaches (or Kaapschehoop), this trail is a unique combination of the natural, historical and cultural highlights of the Battery Creek and Starvation Creek trails. The first day's hike (15.3 km; 6 hours) meanders above the cliffs of the Escarpment, alternating between patches of indigenous forest and pine plantations. The trail then descends steadily to the Starvation Creek Nature Reserve, set aside to protect the Kaapsehoop cycad. It then continues to a waterfall in the creek – an ideal lunch stop. From here the trail ascends steeply up the creek to the Starvation Creek Falls and then eases off as it continues to the Wattles Hut.

A ladder helps hikers up difficult sections of the
Magoebaskloof Trail, near Tzaneen.

Previous page: God's Window provides sweeping views of Blyde River Canyon, near the start of the Blyderivierspoort Hiking Trail.

Above: The Three Rondavels, overlooking the canyon, make a striking landmark.

This page: Kruger National Park is the ideal place to hike if you want to see a wonderful variety of animals. You're most likely to spot vervet monkey (above) in wooded country near water. Waterholes are a good place to find many animals, such as giraffe (left), which are particularly vulnerable to attack when drinking. You may even see the elusive cheetah (below) on one of the park's many wilderness trails.

Next page: The breathtaking Valley of Desolation is the focal point of the Camdeboo National Park at Graaff-Reinet. It was declared a national monument in 1939.

Top: Toorberg is one of three peaks ascended on the Karoo 3 Peaks Challenge near Graaff-Reinet.

Above: The Klipspringer Hiking Trail in the Augrabies Falls National Park meanders through a variety of landscapes.

On day two (13.8 km; 6 hours) the trail makes its way through eroded sandstone formations before snaking up Spitskop. Bannisters Gold Workings, reached further along, is a reminder of the old gold-digging days. The remainder of the day's hike follows an undulating course along the Escarpment edge to Kaapschehoop, where some beautiful examples of Victorian architecture can be enjoyed, before continuing to the Kaapschehoop Hut.

Day three's hike (9.8 km; 5 hours) descends steadily into Battery Creek and then winds up to the cliff edge, which is followed until you pass through a small patch of indigenous forest. A short, steep ascent follows before the trail levels off. **38.9 km; 3 days; circular.**

Other options include the **Battery Creek Trail** (23.8 km; 2 days; circular) and the **Starvation Creek Trail** (24.7 km; 2 days; circular).

15. QUEEN ROSE HIKING TRAIL
Barberton

Trail: 20.9 km; 2 days; circular.
Bookings: Cell: 076 825 5794 (Pieter) or 072 604 9600 (Jackie), email: pieter@queensriver.co.za or jackie@queensriver.co.za, web: https://queensriver.co.za.
Maps: Sketch map.
Facilities/Activities: Queen's View Hut at start with toilets and hot showers. Two overnight huts with bunks, mattresses, braai facilities, stove and fridge.
Pertinent information: The trail involves numerous river crossings, during which caution must be exercised.

Laid out in the mountains west of Barberton, near Nelshoogte, this trail passes through spectacular scenery as it follows the Montrose and Queen's rivers.

Starting from Queen's View Hut, the first day's hike (13 km; 6 hours) ascends steadily through pine plantations to the highest point of the trail, from where there are stunning views. The trail descends sharply to the wooded Montrose River Valley, where the Alvin Falls and a deep pool make an ideal rest stop. You cross the river several times to reach Marie's Picnic Place in time for lunch. The trail follows an easy contour path past interesting rock formations to Angel's View. A steep descent leads to Makesh Hut.

Day two (7.9 km; 4 hours) initially follows the Queen's River upstream and climbs steadily for about an hour before reaching a picnic area. There is a detour to a pool with a cable slide, a short way downstream of the picnic area, which is well worth the effort. The trail ascends again and rewards hikers with great views of the Queen's River, its wild kloofs and Kupid Falls. Depending on the level of the river, the top of the falls can be reached along Heaven's Staircase. After the final uphill section at Fountain Forest, it is an easy walk back to the start.

Names such as Angels' View Corner and Heaven's Staircase poetically describe the scenic beauty of this trail. On both days there is ample opportunity to stop for a refreshing swim and to absorb the atmosphere of the trail surroundings.

16. LOWVELD NATIONAL BOTANICAL GARDEN
Mbombela (Nelspruit)

Trails: Network of paths.
Permits: Entrance fee. No permit required.
Maps: Information brochure with map.
Facilities/Activities: Guided tours by arrangement; restaurant; parking; toilets; plant sales.

The Lowveld National Botanical Garden became a reality in 1969, 14 years after the Mbombela (then Nelspruit) municipality first mooted the idea. It was established on two tracts of land donated by the municipality and HL Hall and Sons.

Two highlights of the 159-ha Lowveld National Botanical Garden are the deep gorge, carved by the Crocodile River, and the Nels River that converges with the Crocodile after tumbling over a waterfall. About 600 plant species grow naturally in the garden, and a further 2,000 have been planted here. With over 650 of South Africa's approximately 1,000 tree and shrub species represented, the garden is a delight to tree-lovers. Tree families collected in the garden include those of the corkwood and cabbage tree, wild fig, baobab, bushwillow and legume.

Of specific interest here is the cycad collection, considered to be the best collection of African cycads in South Africa, and the tropical African rain forest collection, which represents the magnificent tropical rain forests of Central and West Africa.

The vegetation is the most attractive in autumn and spring when a variety of trees and plants burst into full bloom. During these seasons the temperatures and humidity are also more bearable. Birding can be rewarding in the Lowveld National Botanical Garden. Look out for purple-crested turaco and African green pigeon in the fig trees along the Crocodile River.

In addition to the paved footpaths that meander through the garden there is a 1-km-long walk, the **Riverside Trail**, along the Crocodile River. Visitors explore the forests along a 4-m-high boardwalk, built to enable the hippos wandering about the garden at night to have 'unrestricted access'.

17. UITSOEK HIKING TRAIL
Mbombela (Nelspruit)

Trails: Overnight trail: 29.5 km; 2 days; circular. 2 day walks: 11 km; 5 hours; circular.
Permits: Komatiland Eco-Tourism, cell: 083 641 3089, email: ecotour@safcol. co.za, web: www.safcol.co.za.
Maps: A4 colour sketch map of trail.
Facilities/Activities: Uitsoek Hut: bunks, mattresses, pots and pans, braai facilities, firewood, hot-water showers and electricity. Lisabon Hut: bunks, mattresses, toilets and cold water from river.
Pertinent information: There is neither electricity nor firewood at Lisabon Hut. A backpacking stove is therefore essential, as are cooking utensils. Mist is common throughout the year, so make sure you take warm clothes and rain gear, and waterproof your pack.

This trail in the southeast of Mpumalanga, between Mbombela and Sabie, takes the hiker through spectacular Lowveld scenery, from the foothills of the Drakensberg to the Escarpment and back. The route traverses deep valleys and high mountains, which offer some magnificent views. It passes through montane grassland, pine plantations and beautiful indigenous forests, which were a source of timber for the first Voortrekkers who began settling in the area in 1848.

The vegetation of the low-lying areas in the south of the Uitsoek Plantation is characterised by patches of semi-deciduous forest and Lowveld sour bush-veld. Above 1,200 m this vegetation is replaced by northeastern mountain sourveld, much of which has been cleared for pine plantations. Typical tree species include Transvaal and broad-leafed beeches, wild teak and oldwood. Among the grassland flowers found here are the dwarf red-hot poker (*Kniphofia triangularis*), pineapple flower (*Eucomis humilis*) and no fewer than eight disa species. Extensive patches of montane forest have survived in the Houtbosloop and Beestekraalspruit valleys. About 120 tree species have been recorded in the area.

The only large predator occurring in the area is the leopard. Antelope to be seen here include red and common duiker, oribi, grey rhebok, mountain reedbuck, bushbuck and klipspringer. Among the other mammals you may see are bushpig, baboon and vervet monkey.

To date more than 100 bird species have been recorded in the area. Among these are long-crested eagle, Cape rock-thrush, white stork, Narina trogon and buff-streaked chat. Grassland bird species you may be able to tick off include Kurrichane, buttonquail, Zitting cisticola and Cape longclaw.

1. Uitsoek Hiking Trail The first day's hike (15 km; 7 hours) begins with a steady 8-km uphill slog, during which you gain 700 m in altitude. The trail now more or less follows the 1,800-m contour on the southern slopes of Makobolwane for about 2 km, and then skirts the upper reaches of the Kwagga River. The steep drop into Clivia Gorge, with its profusion of forest lilies (*Clivia caulescens*), is followed by an exhausting climb to the Escarpment, during which you gain some 180 m in altitude in less than 1 km. The final section of the day's hike follows an easy route across a rocky hill to Lisabon Hut.

Except for two short uphill stretches, day two (14.5 km; 7 hours) is downhill. Near the 3-km mark the trail drops somewhat steeply into Grootkloof. In just over 3 km you will lose 500 m in altitude until you reach the Houtbosloop Valley. On the way you will be passing through beautiful indigenous forest. The trail then follows the course of the Houtbosloop, which is criss-crossed numerous times. Near the 9-km mark there is a detour to the Bakkrans Waterfall, where a large pool makes a perfect lunch spot. From here the trail continues along the course of the Houtbosloop, with the final section climbing gradually through proteaveld. **29.5 km; 2 days; circular.**

2. Beestekraalspruit Trail This route ascends steadily through pine plantations, indigenous scrub forest and grassland to the cliff edge of Beestekraalspruit. It then descends gradually into Beestekraalspruit-kloof, with its indigenous forest. For the next 4 km the trail follows the course of the river, which you cross 20 times by means of wooden bridges. On leaving the stream, the trail climbs gradually to the starting point. **11 km; 5 hours; circular.**

3. Bakkrans Trail This trail leads to the Bakkrans Waterfall, alternating between pine plantations above the Houtbosloop and indigenous scrub forest in the kloofs. From here the last 4.5 km of the Uitsoek Hiking Trail is followed back to the start. **11 km; 5 hours; circular.**

18. GUSTAV KLINGBIEL NATURE RESERVE
Mashishing

Trails: 3 day walks: 5 to 12 km; 2 to 6 hours; circular.
Permit: Entrance fee. No booking required for walks.
Map: Sketch map.
Facilities/Activities: Museum; toilets.

Situated just outside Mashishing, the Gustav Klingbiel Nature Reserve covers 2,200 ha of typical escarpment flora and fauna. The reserve has been stocked with eland, blue wildebeest, blesbok, kudu, grey rhebok, mountain reedbuck, common duiker, steenbok and oribi. Over 200 bird species have been recorded and a 'vulture restaurant' (feeding station) has been established in the reserve.

1. Pedi Route is named after the Pedi people, who lived here for centuries. The focal point of the trail is an early Pedi settlement, and along the way you will pass terraces, stone-walled paths and the ruins of homesteads. The settlement was abandoned in the 1820s after its inhabitants were attacked by the Zulu leader Mzilikazi. After fleeing from the Zulu king Shaka, Mzilikazi and his followers migrated to the Highveld, where he attacked and conquered the Sotho, Tswana and Pedi inhabitants. **5 km; 2 hours; circular.**

2. Crane Route leads to a dam, which offers excellent birding opportunities, and then winds around Aarbeikop to the vulture restaurant (where you might see the Cape vulture) on the slopes of Vyekop before looping back to the start. Pedi ruins are also seen along this route. **9 km; 4 hours; circular.**

3. Protea Route follows Crane Route to Aarbeikop and then gently ascends to a vantage point where the Boers deployed two of their Long Tom artillery guns to delay the British advance of General Buller's troops during the closing stages of the South African War (1899–1902). The return leg of the trail descends along a kloof. **12 km; 6 hours; circular.**

19. FANIE BOTHA HIKING TRAIL
Sabie

Trails: 5 trails; 17.7 to 75 km; 2 to 5 days; circular and open-ended.
Permits: Komatiland Eco-Tourism, cell: 083 641 3089, email: ecotour@safcol. co.za, web: www.safcol.co.za.
Maps: Colour sketch map of trail.
Facilities/Activities: Six overnight huts with bunks, mattresses, covered braai area, firewood, showers (in all except Mac-Mac Hut) and toilets.

Opened in 1973, the Fanie Botha Hiking Trail will always be remembered as one of the pioneer hiking trails of South Africa. Located on the Drakensberg Escarpment, the trail takes in pine plantations, grassland and patches of indigenous forest, offering many splendid views over a mosaic of plantations and the Lowveld below.

Antelope you might encounter en route include klipspringer, grey rhebok, mountain reedbuck, bushbuck and oribi. Other mammal species to keep an eye out for are bushpig, baboon and rock dassie.

Among the birds recorded on Hartbeestvlakte are blue swallow and broad-tailed warbler. Elsewhere along the trail you may tick off jackal buzzard, Swainson's spurfowl, Cape rock-thrush, Knysna turaco and Gurney's sugarbird. The indigenous forests are the habitat of the Knysna turaco, red-chested cuckoo, sombre greenbul and sunbirds.

The full course of the trail extends from the Komatiland Ceylon Plantation to Graskop and then doubles back to Mac-Mac.

1. Maritzbos Trail Starting at the Ceylon Hut, the first day's hike (8.7 km; 4 hours) makes its way steadily uphill through pine plantations for 3 km and then descends, passing the 68-m-high Lone Creek Falls. From here the trail gently ascends to the overnight hut on the edge of Maritzbos.

Day two's hike (9 km; 4 hours) initially follows the Lone Creek downstream along its northern bank, before joining the outward leg of the first day's hike, from where you backtrack to Ceylon Hut. **17.7 km; 2 days; circular.**

2. Bonnet and Mac-Mac Pools Trail This trail can be started either at Graskop Hut or the President Burger Hut at Mac-Mac Plantation. From the President Burger Hut the first day's trail (19.6 km; 7 hours) climbs gently through pine plantations and indigenous forest patches for about 7 km. Further along, it follows an old coach road on the eastern slopes of Stanley Bush Hill to The Bonnet, from where it descends through grassveld to Graskop Hut.

On day two (23 km; 9.5 hours) the trail passes through pine plantations and grassland before descending through indigenous forest to the Mac-Mac River, which you cross by means of a suspension bridge. From here the trail climbs steeply to Mac-Mac Bluff and then descends past Mac-Mac Pools and Mac-Mac Falls.

The final section ascends gradually through pine plantations to President Burger Hut. **42.6 km (the distance is the same from both starting points); 2 days; circular.**

3. Hartbeestvlakte Trail leads from the Ceylon Plantation to Maritzbos, a relic patch of indigenous forest, on the first day (13.3 km; 4 hours). On the second day (12 km; 8 hours) the trail ascends along the Lone Creek through Maritzbos. After you leave the forest, the trail climbs steadily up the slopes of Mount Anderson to Hartbeestvlakte. Further along, you follow a mountain stream with pools and waterfalls before the final section of the trail takes you down through a pine plantation to the Stables Overnight Hut.

The third day's hike (8.5 km; 3 hours) is an easy downhill walk through fresh pine plantations and patches of lovely indigenous forest. **30.5 km; 3 days; circular.**

4. Mount Moodie Trail gets under way at the Ceylon Plantation and follows the first two days of the Hartbeestvlakte Trail. From the Stables Overnight Hut the third day's hike (16.3 km; 8 hours) skirts the edge of pine plantations as it climbs steeply to the summit of Mount Moodie (2,078 m), where hikers are greeted with views of the Sabie Valley. From here the trail descends sharply down the slopes of Baker's Bliss to Mac-Mac Hut. Day four's hike (13.6 km; 6 hours) meanders to The Bonnet and then heads to Graskop. **51.9 km, 4 days; open-ended.**

5. Fanie Botha Five-day Trail follows the four days of the Mount Moodie Trail. On day five (23.1 km; 10 hours) hikers follow the trail from Graskop to the Mac-Mac River. The trail ascends steeply to Mac-Mac Bluff and passes Mac-Mac Pools and the Mac-Mac Falls before reaching the President Burger Hut at Mac-Mac Plantation. **75 km; 5 days; open-ended.**

20. LOERIE WALK
Sabie

Trails: 13.5 km; 6 hours; circular.
Shorter, 10.5-km option available.
Permits: Sabie Forestry Museum,
tel: (013) 764 1058.
Maps: Sketch map.
Facilities/Activities: None.

The Loerie Walk follows a route through the valleys of the Sabie River and passes mainly through pine and eucalyptus plantations. It can be started either at Castle Rock Caravan Park or the Ceylon Plantation office.

From the Ceylon Plantation office the trail passes through pine plantations and patches of grassveld to reach the Bridal Veil Falls. From here the trail climbs steeply through and along the edge of indigenous forests past the Glynis and Elna falls to a ridge, from where there are stunning views over the Sabie Valley. After following a gum belt (eucalyptus trees planted between plantation sections as a windbreak) the trail joins a forestry track and then descends to Castle Rock. The remaining part of the trail is an easy walk along the course of the Sabie River.

A shorter trail option branches off from the main route about 7 km before you reach the Ceylon Plantation and then winds down to reach the starting point after 3 km.

21. FOREST FALLS WALK
Sabie/Graskop

Trail: 3 km; 1 hour; circular.
Permits: Sabie Forestry Museum, tel:
(013) 764 1058 or Mac-Mac Forest
Retreat, tel: (013) 764 2376.
Maps: Sketch map.
Facilities/Activities: Picnic sites at start.

From the Green Heritage picnic site at Mac-Mac, the trail passes through pine plantations and along the edge of indigenous forest fringing a tributary of the Mac-Mac River, to reach the beautiful Forest Falls after 1.6 km. The return leg follows the eastern bank of the river past several old mines before reaching the starting point.

22. JOCK OF THE BUSHVELD TRAIL
Graskop

Trail: 8 km; 3 hours; circular.
Permits: Not required.
Maps: Sketch map.
Facilities/Activities: Graskop Holiday
Resort at start.

On this route hikers can follow in the tracks of the famous Staffordshire terrier, Jock of the Bushveld, a frequent visitor to the area with his master Sir Percy Fitzpatrick during the years 1885 to 1887. From the Graskop Holiday Resort the path makes its way to Paradise Camp, where Fitzpatrick used to camp. From here the trail continues to the Bathing Pools (mentioned in the book *Jock of the Bushveld*) in the Tumbling Waters Spruit, which cascades over numerous rapids further downstream. At its southern end the trail wanders past the Sandstone Sentinels, quartz rock formations resembling a sea horse, wolf, camel, sitting hen and vulture. Further along, you cross the Fairyland Spruit and the trail then passes the Window Rock on the way back to the start.

23. PROSPECTOR'S HIKING TRAIL
Pilgrim's Rest

Trails: 31.5 km; 3 days; circular.
Permits: Komatiland Eco-Tourism,
cell: 083 641 3089, email: ecotour@
safcol.co.za, web: www.safcol.co.za.
Maps: Colour sketch map of trail.
Facilities/Activities: Overnight huts at
Morgenzon, Black Hill and Excelsior with
bunks, mattresses, braai facilities, toilets
and hot showers.

Pertinent information: The trail can be extended by starting or ending at the Morgenzon Hut, about 2 km from the Morgenzon Forest Station.

This trail takes you along the Mpumalanga Drakensberg through an area that once attracted hordes of miners, prospectors, fortune-seekers, confidence tricksters and stagecoach robbers following the discovery of gold at present-day Pilgrim's Rest in 1873. More than 1,500 miners rushed to the valley where Alec 'Wheelbarrow' Patterson discovered gold, and Pilgrim's Rest became the gold-mining hub when the Gold Commissioner moved his office from Mac-Mac to the new settlement in 1874. By the end of 1875 the town consisted of 21 shops, 18 bars, three bakeries, several stores and a variety of other buildings. Mining operations ceased in 1971, but have again resumed at several places, resulting in the closure of the two-day Peach Tree Creek Trail.

Although much of the Prospector's Hiking Trail is along gravel roads through pine plantations, you also walk through montane grasslands and indigenous forest. Outeniqua and real yellowwoods, white stinkwood, assegai and Cape beech count among the forest trees. Krantz aloes create natural rock gardens and are especially eye-catching in winter when they are in full bloom and attract malachite and scarlet-chested sunbirds.

The animal life is similar to that found elsewhere in the Mpumalanga Drakensberg. Grey rhebok, mountain reedbuck and oribi favour open grassland. The oribi, one of the most graceful species of smaller antelope, can be distinguished by its white rump, striking black-tipped tail and golden body colour. Only the males carry horns, which are straight and slender with pointed tips. Klipspringer, baboon and dassie can be seen in rocky areas, while common duiker and bushbuck are encountered in the forests.

Birding can be rewarding, and Verreaux's eagle, rock kestrel, Swainson's spurfowl, Knysna turaco and stonechat are among the species you will tick.

The first day's hike (10.2 km; 6 hours) starts at the Morgenzon Forest Station office, where secure parking is available. Despite the short distance, this is the most demanding section of the trail and

an early start is advisable. From the forest station the trail descends steeply to the upper reaches of the Clever Valley. Brace yourself for the relentless ascent, as the trail gains over 800 m in altitude to Black Hill Hut. From Clever Valley the trail ascends steeply, first passing through a patch of indigenous forest and then along an old wagon path before linking up with a forestry road. The road then drops into a tree-clad valley, before climbing steeply through indigenous forest and past waterfalls. You then emerge in mountain fynbos vegetation before reaching Black Hill Hut. The hut, with its commanding view, served as a fire lookout for many years until it was put to use as a hikers' hut in 1992.

The second day's hike (10.5 km; 4 hours) initially meanders through fynbos to a viewpoint at the 2,079-m-high summit of Black Hill, the highest point on the trail. Far below your feet lies Pilgrim's Rest, with Graskop in the distance. The trail now winds through lichen-clad, weathered quartzite formations above the cliffs of Black Hill. The day's hike is relatively easy, passing through pine plantations before descending to Excelsior Hut. Situated at the edge of a pine plantation, the double-storey Swiss chalet was used as a holiday retreat by its former owner before the property was incorporated into the forestry plantation. Looking northwards, you will see a wide open expanse, aptly named The Prairie. Keep an eye out here for mountain reedbuck, grey rhebok and oribi.

The renowned wild horses of Morgenzon are often seen grazing on the grasslands around Excelsior Hut. This is one of only a few wild horse populations in South Africa, the others being at Kaapschehoop and the Bot River Lagoon near Hermanus.

The third day's hike (10.5 km; 4 hours) takes you across the southern edge of The Prairie where the rambling protea (*Protea parvula*) is conspicuous between December and March, when the delicate pink flowers are in full bloom. This species occurs along the Escarpment from Mariepskop and the Blyde River Canyon to the Mashishing (Lydenburg) and Dullstroom areas. The trail descends to a viewpoint overlooking the Ohrighstad Valley and then passes through rocky outcrops before reaching Vyehoekloop, where there are several small waterfalls and delightful rocky pools. The trail now disappears into pine plantations before emerging into grassland as it skirts two private properties, Themeda Hill and Crystal Springs. It then continues through pine plantations to Clivia Bush, a lovely tract of forest named after the forest lilies, also known as clivias, that grow here. The remainder of the day's hike to Morgenzon Forest Station is mainly through pine plantations. If you wish, you can spend the night at the Morgenzon Hut.

24. MOUNT SHEBA NATURE RESERVE
Pilgrim's Rest

> **Trails:** 2 day walks: 3 and 5 km; 1.5 and 2.5 hours; circular and out-and-return. Network of 12 other shorter options available.
> **Permits:** Not required by lodge guests.
> **Maps:** Brochure and map available.
> **Facilities/Activities:** Country lodge.

Situated on the slopes of Mount Sheba above Pilgrim's Rest, the 11,400-ha Mount Sheba Nature Reserve provides protection to one of the last remaining patches of unspoilt indigenous forest in the Mpumalanga Drakensberg. Dominant among the 110 tree species recorded in the forest are some exceptionally large yellowwood, red pear and Cape chestnut trees, and the forest floor has a rich diversity of ferns and mosses.

Baboon, samango monkey, thick-tailed bushbaby, blesbok, grey rhebok, klipspringer, red and common duiker, oribi, bushpig and rock dassie are all found here. The Afromontane forests offer some of the best birding opportunities in Mpumalanga.

The reserve is criss-crossed by a network of 14 trails, ranging from easy rambles to demanding routes.

1. Old Digging Walk This walk criss-crosses Kearney's Creek numerous times as it makes its way to old digging sites, dating back to the area's early gold- \rush days. Along the way you pass several fine yellowwood specimens and lovely pools. **3 km; 1.5 hours; out-and-return (from bridge over Kearney's Creek).**

2. Marco's Mantle Walk has justifiably been described as sensational. The first portion of the trail passes through indigenous forest to Marco's Mantle Falls, in the upper reaches of Kearney's Creek. Here the trail passes behind the falls and then leads down to the pool below the falls. **5 km; 2.5 hours; circular.**

Among the other walks that can be done here are the **Waterfall Trail**, which leads to two beautiful waterfalls in the Sheba Spruit, and a walk to the Lost City Viewpoint on Mount Sheba.

25. BLYDERIVIERSPOORT HIKING TRAIL
Blyde River Canyon Nature Reserve

See no. 26 (p. 240) for walks.

> **Trail:** 30.1 km; 3 days; open-ended.
> **Permits:** Mpumalanga Parks and Tourism Agency, tel: 013 759 5373, email: reservations@mtpa.co.za, web: www.mpumalanga.com.
> **Maps:** Sketch map of trail.
> **Facilities/Activities:** Two overnight huts with bunks, mattresses, pots, kettles, braai facilities, firewood and toilets.
> **Pertinent information:** Parking is available at Paradise Camp at owners' risk. The trail from Bourke's Luck to Swadini is closed and hiking is not permitted on this section.

The Blyderivierspoort ('Blyde River Canyon' in English) Hiking Trail traverses the southern half of the 30,000-ha Blyde River Canyon Nature Reserve, which contains well-known attractions such as The Pinnacle rock formation, God's Window and Bourke's Luck Potholes. Along the trail hikers will also enjoy expansive views of the Three Rondavels.

The vegetation in the high-lying southern parts of the reserve is dominated by montane sourveld, which consists of open grassveld with small patches of indigenous forest. The grassveld is devoid of tall trees, except for the occasional stunted Transvaal beech, and you can often see common tree fern lining the small streams in the area.

Among the mammals found in the reserve are baboon, vervet monkey, bushbuck, kudu, red and common duiker, grey rhebok, klipspringer and bushpig. Some 227 bird species have been recorded in the reserve. These include 25 raptor species, such as Verreaux's, martial and crowned eagles, black-chested snake eagle, jackal buzzard, rock kestrel, and peregrine and lanner falcons. Keep an eye out for Shelley's francolin, Denham's bustard, buff-streaked chat and Gurney's sugarbird, as well as southern bald ibis, a species that breeds in the cliffs near Bourke's Luck.

Starting at Paradise Camp, on the God's Window Loop Road outside Graskop, the first day's hike (3 km; 1 hour) meanders through weathered quartzite rocks and across grassland to the Watervalspruit Valley. From Paradise Pool the trail rises gently and then descends to Watervalspruit Hut, which is built against a slope.

Shortly after the start of the second day's hike (13.5 km; 5 hours), the trail makes its way past quartzite outcrops that have been eroded into interesting shapes, and eye-catching patches of mottled yellow, white and red-brown lichens growing on the rocks. The path then descends to the Clearstream Hut, which is situated just upstream of a magnificent rock pool, where you can spend the afternoon swimming and relaxing.

On day three (13.6 km; 5 hours) the trail closely follows the Sefogane (Treur) River, before passing the site from where the Voortrekker leader Hendrik Potgieter is thought to have set off to look for a route to the sea in 1840. The trail continues along the course of the Treur River past the New Chumm Falls and the Belvedere Hydro-Electric Station. It then skirts the Crocodile Valley Estates Plantation, descending gradually to Bourke's Luck Potholes and the Old Mine Hut.

26. BOURKE'S LUCK POTHOLES TRAILS
Blyde River Canyon Nature Reserve

See no. 25 (p. 239) for hiking trail.

Trails: 2 day walks; 180 m and 8 km; 30 minutes and 5 hours; circular.

Permits: Available from Bourke's Luck Potholes Information Office.
Maps: Available from Bourke's Luck Potholes Information Office.
Facilities/Activities: Visitors' Centre; kiosk; picnic and braai facilities.

The famous Bourke's Luck Potholes are one of the main attractions of the Blyde River Canyon Nature Reserve (also known as the Motlatse Canyon Nature Reserve). Here the Motlatse River (formerly called the Blyde River) has cut a deep gorge into the rock. At the Motlatse's confluence with the Sefogane River (previously known as the Treur River), the swirling waters of the two watercourses and water-borne pebbles have eroded spectacular cylindrical potholes into the rock.

The old Afrikaans names of the two rivers – *Blyde* and *Treur* – hark back to a more volatile period in the history of South Africa. The river Blyde, meaning 'joy', was named by Voortrekker women when their husbands returned from an expedition to find a route to Delogoa Bay (now Maputo Bay) in 1840. The Treur (meaning 'mourning') was given its name when, earlier, the women had thought that their husbands had died during the excursion.

The potholes were named after a certain Tom Bourke, who in the 1880s predicted that gold would be found in the vicinity. Ironically, Bourke's own claim turned out to be unproductive. Good views of the gorge and the potholes can be obtained from the three metal bridges spanning the gorge and from several lookout points.

Downstream of Bourke's Luck, the Motlatse River has carved a spectacular canyon that is up to 700 m deep and 32 km long. Overlooking the Blyde River Canyon, the centrepiece of the Blyde River Canyon Nature Reserve, are the well-known hut-shaped promontories, the Three Rondavels.

1. Lichen Trail is an interpretative walk with information points about lichens on boards along the trail. Information is also provided in large print, as well as in Braille, and there is a tapping rail for blind visitors. This walk is also suitable for those in wheelchairs. Although under an hour, this trail is still included here as it is one of the few walks available for the blind and physically disabled. **180 m; 30 minutes; circular.**

2. Belvedere Day Walk leads to the Belvedere Hydro-Electric Power Station at the confluence of the Motlatse and Belvedere rivers. The power station was built in 1911 to supply electricity to the 'gold crushers' (machines used for the crushing of ore) at Pilgrim's Rest. It was the largest plant of its kind in the whole of the southern hemisphere at the time. From the Bourke's Luck Visitors' Centre the trail descends steeply into the Blyde River Canyon, losing some 400 m in altitude. The return leg follows a different route back to the start. It is a strenuous trail, which should only be attempted by fit hikers. **8 km; 5 hours; circular.**

27. KRUGER NATIONAL PARK
Mpumalanga and Limpopo

See no. 28 (p. 243) and no. 29 (p. 244) for backpacking trails.

Trails: 7 overnight wilderness trails: variable distances, up to 20 km a day from base camp; 4 days each. Guided day walks: 4 to 10 km; 2 to 4 hours; usually circular.
Permits: SANParks, P O Box 787, Pretoria 0001, tel: (012) 428 9111, fax: (012) 343 0905, email: reservations@sanparks.org
Maps: General park map.
Facilities/Activities: Wilderness trails: rustic huts with beds, bedding, covered lapa that serves as a dining area, reed-walled showers and toilets. Day walks from rest camps and before and after trails:12 rest camps with self-catering accommodation; five bushveld camps; five satellite camps; camp sites in the park; luxury private camps; restaurants; shops. Wilderness trails are catered but trailists must provide their own drinks and snacks. Guided 4x4 group trail; guided visit to Thulamela archaeological site.

Pertinent information: Wilderness Trails: groups are limited to 8 persons, all of whom must be between the ages of 12 and 65 years. Trails are conducted from Sunday to Wednesday and from Wednesday to Saturday. A reasonable level of fitness is essential, as up to 20 km may be walked in a day. Anti-malaria precautions are essential.

Proclaimed in 1926, the Kruger National Park is one of Africa's great national parks and is renowned worldwide for its superb wildlife. The park was named after Paul Kruger, the president of the South African Republic, later the Transvaal, who proclaimed the first sanctuary in the region in June 1894. A second reserve, the Sabi Game Reserve, was established in March 1898, covering 460,000 ha between the Crocodile River in the south and the Sabie River in the north. Shortly after the end of the South African War (1899–1902) a third parcel of Lowveld land, between the Letaba and Luvuvhu rivers, was set aside for conservation when the 900,000-ha Singitswi Game Reserve was proclaimed. All three of these protected areas, as well as more than 80 privately owned farms in the area and a pocket of land between the Lepelle (Olifants) and Letaba rivers, were consolidated to form the Kruger National Park.

Today the park covers nearly 2 million ha of unspoilt wilderness and is the oldest and biggest park in South Africa. It stretches for approximately 350 km from the south to the north along the border with Mozambique and spans the Mpmulanga and Limpopo provinces. From east to west, it is 60 km wide.

Early human habitation in the area is evident at the many Earlier, Middle and Later Stone Age sites in the park, with stone tools, some dating as far back as 1.5 million years ago, having been found. The park also contains several San rock art sites, associated with the Later Stone Age, and it is estimated that the San occupied the area between 20,000 and 150 years ago. Iron Age settlements also occurred throughout most of the Kruger, and more than 350 sites have been recorded to date. Those open to the public include Thulamela, a fifteenth-century site in the far north of the park, and Masorini in the western section of the park on the road to Letaba Rest Camp.

However, for many visitors, Kruger's chief attraction is its wildlife, and the park is home to 147 mammal species. The main drawcard is the Big Five (elephant, rhino, buffalo, lion and leopard), but there is also a wide variety of antelope such as sable, nyala, kudu, waterbuck, tsessebe and impala (the most abundant of the antelope). Also to be seen are African wild dog, cheetah, herds of blue wildebeest, Burchell's zebra, giraffe and hippo.

Kruger National Park offers exceptional birding, with a bird checklist of 508 species. Especially rewarding is the northern corner, along the Luvuvhu River, where several uncommon species can be ticked off. More than 50 raptor species have been recorded in the park to date.

In July 1978 Kruger National Park's first hike, Wolhuter Wilderness Trail, was opened in the south of the park. Since then the number of wilderness trails has increased to seven, and they are spread throughout the park.

Trails are conducted by a fully trained and experienced armed trails ranger who works in tandem with a back-up armed trails ranger. And, although game-viewing on foot is an integral part of the experience, time is also spent learning more about the environment. The trails ranger will interpret the tell-tale signs of nature. In addition, tree identification, bird-watching and appreciating the beauty of nature all form part of the experience.

The trail camps are rustic, but comfortable, and serve as a base from where walks are undertaken. Simple, but wholesome, meals are provided.

1. Bushman Trail is conducted in the southwestern corner of the park in an area boasting over 90 rock art sites, as well as numerous Stone and Iron Age sites. The generally hilly terrain is punctuated by granite outcrops, which afford trailists magnificent views of the area. Among the animals trailists might find are white rhino, elephant, buffalo, mountain reedbuck, kudu, klipspringer, Burchell's zebra and giraffe. The Malelane Gate is the nearest entry point to the Berg-en-Dal Rest Camp, from where trailists are transported to the base camp.

2. Mathikithi Trail owes its name to a prominent sandstone hill that dominates the undulating terrain about 6 km southwest of Satara Rest Camp. The hill provides an ideal lookout point from which to watch game and is a good spot for enjoying sundowners in the late afternoon. Trailists leave for the wilderness camp from Satara, with the most convenient entrance gate for this trail being Orpen. The tented wilderness camp, which lies about 500 m west of the sandstone hill, is situated alongside the N'wanetsi River in an area criss-crossed by a network of game trails. Mammals to be seen in the vicinity include large concentrations of elephant and buffalo, Burchell's zebra, impala and blue wildebeest, as well as several predator species.

3. Napi Trail traverses the rolling landscape and granite hills midway between Skukuza and Pretoriuskop. The base camp is situated at the confluence of the Mbayamiti and Napi rivers in an area with a high white rhino population. Trailists may also chance upon black rhino, elephant, buffalo, sable, kudu and reedbuck. Predators such as lion, leopard and African wild dog occur in the area, which also supports prolific birdlife. Trailists meet at Pretoriuskop. Numbi is the entrance gate nearest to this camp.

4. Nyalaland Trail The Punda Maria area in the far northern region of the Kruger National Park is one of southern Africa's most outstanding wilderness areas. The landscape is characterised by mopane trees, extensive baobab 'forests' and stands of fever trees. Although not rich in game it is one of South Africa's birding hotspots, with several Red Data species such as mottled and Böhm's spinetails and the silvery-cheeked hornbill. Punda Maria Rest Camp, from where trailists are transported to the base camp on the banks of the Madzaringwe Stream, is best accessed through Punda Maria Gate.

5. Olifants Trail is found in the central part of the park, with a base camp on the southern bank of the Lepelle (Olifants River). The route follows the northern bank of the Lepelle River downstream across countryside encompassing rocky ground, gullies and hilly terrain. The trail offers excellent opportunities for observing a large variety of game, especially during the dry season when the animals tend to congregate along the watercourse. Hippo as well as crocodile can be seen in the river, while elephant, waterbuck, impala, Burchell's zebra and buffalo are some of the game species you are likely to encounter along the way. There is also a rich diversity of birds, including martial eagle, African fish eagle and pied kingfisher.

The vegetation along the river is characterised by riverine bush with typical species such as Lowveld cluster-leaf, red spikethorn, small lavender feverberry, matumi, apple-leaf, weeping boer bean and sycamore fig growing here.

The trail starts at Olifants Rest Camp where hikers are given an early morning briefing before departing in an open vehicle for a 3.5-hour drive to the start of the trail. The drop-off point is close to the park's western boundary where the Lepelle (Olifants) River enters the sanctuary. Camp is made after a relatively short walk of 4 to 7 km.

The same routine is followed on days two and three. An early morning start is made before stopping for breakfast, after which the trail continues along the watercourse. An extended lunch break is taken during the heat of the day, followed by a siesta. The walk after lunch to the overnight stop is usually only a few kilometres long.

On day four trailists have a relatively short walk (7 km) to the end of the trail, from where they are collected by park authorities and taken back to Olifants Rest Camp. Travel time back to the start is at least 45 minutes, giving hikers a final opportunity to spot more game animals.

28. LONELY BULL AND MPHONGOLO BACKPACKING TRAILS
Kruger National Park

Trails: 4 days; 3 nights; guided; distances variable.
Permits: SANParks, P O Box 787, Pretoria 0001, tel: (012) 428 9111, fax: (012) 343 0905, email: reservations@sanparks.org
Maps: General park map.
Facilities/Activities: None.
Pertinent information: Groups are limited to a minimum of 4 and a maximum of 8 people, all of whom must be between the ages of 12 and 65 years. Trails are conducted between 1 February and 30 November, departing on Sundays and Wednesdays. Trailists can leave their cars at Mopani Rest Camp (Lonely Bull trail) or at Shingwedzi Rest Camp (Mphongolo trail), in a specially demarcated area. Trailists must be self-sufficient and carry a lightweight tent, a sleeping bag, a small gas stove and their own food. The trail is self-catering and hikers must prepare their own food. A reasonable level of fitness is essential, as trailists have to carry their own equipment. Trailists must also take water purification tablets, as some of the rivers in Kruger are polluted by upstream use. Anti-malaria precautions are essential.

One of the attractions of these backpacking trails lies in the fact that hikers must be self-sufficient for the duration of their chosen trail. Although a variety of game animals is likely to be encountered during both hikes, game-viewing is not the major drawcard on these outings. Instead, it is the experience of true wilderness, completely devoid of anything human-made, that makes the Lonely Bull and Mphongolo trails so appealing.

1. Lonely Bull Backpacking Trail This trail traverses the area between the low-water bridge over the Letaba River and the Mingerhout Dam in the northern sector of the park. Although sections of the trail follow the Letaba River, the trail does not follow a specific route, as different parts of the wilderness area are utilised on a rotational basis. No trail is therefore the same, with the route being determined by the rangers leading the hike. Trailists depart from Mopani Rest Camp.

2. Mphongolo Backpacking Trail is a flexible trail with no set route, and it is up to the group and the trail leader to decide which route to follow and when and where to camp each night. The trail is conducted in the wilderness area between the Mphongolo and Shingwedzi rivers in the northern section of the park. Trails depart from Shingwedzi Rest Camp.

29. ROOIKAT NATURE WALK

Tzaneen

> **Trail:** 11 km; 5 hours; circular.
> **Permits:** The Forester, New Agatha Plantation, Private Bag X4009, Tzaneen 0850, tel: (015) 307 4310, fax: (015) 307 5926. Permits can be obtained at the start of the trail during office hours.
> **Maps:** Trail pamphlet with sketch map.
> **Facilities/Activities:** Picnic site and toilets at the halfway mark.
> **Pertinent information:** Arrangements to visit the area must be made well in advance. After heavy rains it is advisable to check whether the trail is open, as the Bobs River, which is crossed several times during the course of the hike, could be in flood.

This trail meanders through the New Agatha Plantation, 18 km east of Tzaneen, and is set against the backdrop of Krugerkop and Tandberg, two well-known landmarks of the Wolkberg.

Although pine and eucalyptus plantations have replaced much of the natural vegetation here, the banks of the Bobs River are still lined with magnificent indigenous forest. Some of the trees along the route have been marked with their national tree number and among the species common to this area are Natal mahogany, white stinkwood, mitzeeri, pigeonwood and forest cabbage tree.

In addition to the caracal, a small cat to which the trail owes its Afrikaans name, this area is also home to bushbuck, common duiker, bushpig and baboon, as well as vervet and samango monkeys. Birds you may tick off include the rare bat hawk (which breeds here), jackal buzzard, purple-crested turaco, black-headed oriole and southern brown-throated weaver.

You start off walking through pine plantations and then you follow the course of the Bobs River. The trail crosses the watercourse a number of times. There are several cascades, rapids and pools where you can cool off or simply nurse your weary feet. After about 7 km you reach Die Akker picnic site. Set among pin oaks, it is a great place to regroup and have a last snack before tackling the final 4 km of the trail through eucalyptus and pine plantations.

30. WOLKBERG WILDERNESS AREA

Tzaneen

> **Trails:** No set trails.
> **Permits:** Obtainable only at Serala Forest Station.
> **Maps:** 1:50,000 topographical map sections 2330CC and 2430AA are indispensable as the map available from the Serala office is inadequate.
> **Facilities/Activities:** No overnight facilities are available in the wilderness area, making it essential to carry a tent.
> **Pertinent information:** The maximum group size for overnight visitors is 10. Fires are strictly forbidden in the wilderness area. There is only one route down the northern face of the Devil's Knuckles to the Shobwe River valley. The descent should, under no circumstances, be attempted by inexperienced hikers or by those with a fear of heights, as there are exposed sections requiring rock climbing. Contact Grant Christie at grant@grantchristie.co.za for guided hikes in the Wolkberg.

Situated about 80 km southwest of Tzaneen, the Wolkberg forms an arc where the northern extension of the Drakensberg joins the eastern extremity of the Strydpoort Mountain. The wilderness area covers 19,145 ha of high mountain peaks, deep ravines, patches of indigenous forest and grasslands. Dominated by the 2,050-m-high Krugerkop, also known as Serala, the Wolkberg (meaning 'cloud mountain') frequently lives up to its name, especially in summer when the high peaks are often covered in a fine mist.

Most of the vegetation is dominated by montane sourveld interspersed with proteaveld, but the vegetation along the Mohlapitse Valley consists of sour grassveld and bushveld trees. Patches of indigenous forest occur in deep ravines and on the southern and eastern slopes of higher-lying areas.

Noteworthy trees include the Transvaal mountain sugarbush and the Modjadji cycad. Also keep a lookout for the Wolkberg cliff aloe.

The area does not support a rich diversity of large mammals. Species you might see include bushbuck, grey rhebok, reedbuck, klipspringer, common duiker, baboon, samango and vervet monkeys, and lesser bushbaby.

Among the more than 157 bird species recorded here to date are black-fronted bushshrike, crested guineafowl, western yellow wagtail, bat hawk and martial eagle. Also keep an eye out for secretarybird, Burchell's coucal, southern boubou, lilac-breasted roller and Marico sunbird.

Except for management tracks and footpaths, there are no set trails in the wilderness area. The rugged terrain is unrelenting on the body and the Wolkberg should only be explored by experienced and fit hikers, or you should be accompanied by an experienced leader who is familiar with the area. The Devil's Knuckles, an 8-km ridge of sheer quartzite cliffs, is a formidable barrier between the southern and northern sections of the Wolkberg. It is, therefore, advisable to plan your visit with this in mind.

Highlights in the northern part of the wilderness area include the three-tier Klipdraai Waterfall, the pristine Wonderwoud in the Shobwe River valley, Kruger's Nose and the Cleopatra Pools and waterfall. There are also several delightful waterfalls in the Mawedzi River in its tributaries north of Serala peak.

Attractions in the southern section of the Wolkberg include the tufa formations and waterfall in the Ashmole Dales River, the rugged Mampaskloof, the spectacular Thabina Waterfall and the magnificent views from the Devil's Knuckles across the Shobwe River Valley

31. MAGOEBASKLOOF HIKING TRAIL
Tzaneen

Trails: 63 km; 5 days; circular. 4 shorter options: 20.1 to 42.9 km; 2 to 3 days; circular.
Permits: Komatiland Eco-Tourism, cell: 083 641 3089, email: ecotour@safcol. co.za, web: www.safcol.co.za.

Maps: Sketch map of trail.
Facilities/Activities: Six overnight huts with bunk beds, mattresses, braai facilities, showers and toilets. Hot water is available at De Hoek and Broederstroom, with only cold water water available at Dokolewa Pools, Waterfall, Woodbush and Seepsteen Mule Stables.
Pertinent information: Starting points for the trail are at the De Hoek, Woodbush and Broederstroom huts. Dokolewa Pools Hut is a 1.5-km walk from De Hoek, and the distance from Woodbush Hut to Seepsteen Mule Stables Hut is also 1.5 km. Since the trail has some steep ascents and descents – with altitude differences of at least 500 m in places – trailists must ensure that they are fit before attempting this hike. Ticks are prevalent, and trailists should take preventative measures.

The indigenous forests of Magoebaskloof are undoubtedly among the most beautiful in South Africa, resembling a fairytale wonderland. Streams cascade down the mountain slopes over moss-covered rocks, while dense clumps of ferns line their banks. Overhead, large masses of clivias (*Clivia* spp.) nestle in the forks of tree branches, and the colourful Knysna turaco can be seen gliding from tree to tree. Some sections of the trail traverse commercial pine plantations.

The forest is home to red duiker, bushbuck and the elusive leopard, as well as vervet and samango monkeys. The latter can be identified by their call, which consists of a loud repeated 'nyah', often followed by a series of chuckles. Although bushpigs are mainly nocturnal, they are often seen in the Grootbosch forest during the daytime.

Grootbosch is the largest indigenous forest north of the Vaal River, covering some 4,600 ha. Among the dominant species here are Outeniqua and real yellowwoods, white stinkwood, lemonwood and ironwood. The area is also home to several epiphytic orchids, while forest montbretia (*Crocosmia aurea*), with its yellow-orange flowers, showy *Streptocarpus parviflorus* and impatients (*Impatiens* spp.) are among the flowering species on the forest floor.

Birdlife is prolific, with some 309 species being recorded in the De Hoek and Grootbosch areas. Species to keep an eye out for include crowned and long-crested eagles, black-fronted bushshrike, dark-capped bulbul, chorister robin-chat, white-starred robin and yellow-throated woodland warbler.

Of historic interest are the Seepsteen Mule Stables, the Woodbush Arboretum (established in 1907) and the oak trees planted along the Broederstroom by Lady Florence Phillips, who bred horses at the Broederstroom Stud Farm in the 1920s.

The trail network consists of several sections, which can be combined to form longer, more challenging trails.

1. Debengeni Trail starts at Woodbush Hut and descends steadily to De Hoek (11.7 km; 6 hours). Shortly before you reach De Hoek, a path leads to a viewpoint overlooking the spectacular Debengeni Falls. The return route (8.4 km; 3 hours) is an uphill haul, involving an altitude gain of some 500 m to Woodbush. Highlights include the Dokolewa Pools, exceptionally tall tree ferns and the walk along the Dokolewa Stream, with its pools and magificent indigenous forest. The trail can also be hiked in the opposite direction, starting at De Hoek. **20.1 km; 2 days; circular.**

2. Dokolewa Pools Trail This option starts at Dokolewa Pools Hut and day one's hike (8.4 km; 4 hours) ascends along the return leg of the Debengeni Trail before branching off to the Seepsteen Stables Hut near the end of the trail. Day two's hike (11.7 km; 5 hours) is a steady descent, which leads past Debengeni Falls and then to the Dokolewa Pools Hut. **20.1 km; 2 days; circular.**

3. Dokolewa Waterfalls Trail (from Woodbush Hut) From Woodbush Hut the first day's hike (13.7 km; 7 hours) leaves the arboretum and winds through pine plantations interspersed with several patches of indigenous forest. The trail passes what is reputedly the tallest planted tree in the southern hemisphere – a saligna gum tree with a height of 84.4 m. The trail climbs through indigenous forest and pine plantations, and then wends its way downwards. Further along, it passes through an avenue of oak trees planted in the early 1900s and ascends to a viewpoint overlooking the Dap Naude Dam. After skirting the dam you reach the turn-off to the Broederstroom Hut and Waterfall Camp.

The second day's hike (18 km; 7 hours) follows an easy route along a ridge, from where there are spectacular views of the forested valley below. Further along, the trail descends steeply to the top of a series of high waterfalls. Another waterfall is reached a short way on, and the trail then meanders past tall tree ferns lining the Dokolewa Stream, which you follow past several inviting pools to the Dokolewa Pools. The last 1 km ascends through pine plantations to the Dokolewa Pools Hut. The final day's hike (9 km; 5 hours) is a steady uphill climb back to the parking area at Woodbush Hut. **40.7 km; 3 days; circular.**

4. Dokolewa Waterfalls Trail (from De Hoek Hut) heads for the Dokolewa Pools Hut, and the first day's hike (9.9 km; 4 hours) climbs to the Seepsteen Stables Hut. Day two's hike (15 km; 6 hours) makes its way to Waterfall Camp, while the third day's hike (18 km; 7 hours) descends to Dokolewa Pools Hut and then continues to De Hoek Hut. Highlights include magnificent tree ferns, the walk along the Dokolewa Stream, with its inviting pools surrounded by indigenous forest, the arboretum at Woodbush, the waterfalls in Grootbosch forest and the Dokolewa waterfalls and pools. **42.9 km; 3 days; circular.**

5. Magoebaskloof Five-night Trail This trail combines all the highlights of the Magoebaskloof area. The first three days of the hike follow the same route as the Dokolewa Waterfalls Trail option, which starts at De Hoek parking area. From Dokolewa Pools Hut the fourth day of the Magoebaskloof Five-night Trail (8.4 km; 4 hours) ascends to Woodbush Hut, and the final day's hike (11.7 km; 5 hours) makes its way mainly downhill to De Hoek. **63 km; 5 days; circular.**

32. MODJADJI NATURE RESERVE (MODJADJI CYCAD RESERVE)
Tzaneen

Trail: 7 km; 3 to 4 hours; circular.
Permits: Entrance fee. No permit required for walk.

Maps: Sketch map.
Facilities/Activities: Information Centre; museum; picnic sites.

Covering 530 ha, the Modjadji Nature Reserve (also known as the Modjadji Cycad Reserve) provides protection to a unique and spectacular forest of Modjadji cycads on the slopes above the Modjadji Valley, about 35 km northeast of Tzaneen. This reserve is said to contain the highest concentration of a single cycad species in the world. The Modjadji cycad is the tallest-growing of all the 29 different cycad species indigenous to southern Africa, with at least 22 species taking on a tree-like form. Although the average height of the Modjadji cycad ranges between 5 and 8 m, large specimens can grow up to 13 m tall, and their golden-brown fruit can weigh a staggering 34 kg. Cycads are the living descendants of an ancient group of gymnosperms (cone-bearing plants) that grew abundantly on earth about 145 million years ago.

The cycad forest has enjoyed the protection of successive generations of Modjadji (Rain Queens), the hereditary female rulers of the Bolobedu people, who have lived in the area for over three centuries. The lineage of the Rain Queen can be traced back to the sixteenth century when her ancestors migrated from the Karanga kingdom in southeastern Zimbabwe to the Tzaneen area. Revered for her rain-making powers, she officiates at the annual ceremony at her royal enclosure in November. A museum dedicated to the Rain Queen gives a fascinating insight into the Bolobedu people and their mystical rulers.

The trail winds through the cycad forest down to the bushveld below, where trailists may see waterbuck, bushbuck, blue wildebeest, nyala and impala. More than 170 bird species have been recorded in the area, among them Verreaux's eagle, purple-crested turaco and bushshrike.

33. LOUIS CHANGUION HIKING TRAIL
Haenertsburg

Trails: 5 km or 10 km.
Permits: Entry free, but donations may be be made via the SnapScan QR code or electronic transfer (bank details on www.frohg.org) or may be placed in boxes at Tin Roof and Foodzone in Haenertsburg.
Maps: Download from www.frohg.org.
Facilities/Activities: Hiking.
Pertinent information: No smoking or lighting of fires. No littering (no toilets along the trail). Groups are limited to a maximum of 15 people.

The trail honours local resident, veteran hiker and historian, Professor Louis Changuion, who laid the trail out in 1993. It is maintained by the Friends of Haenertsburg Grasslands (FroHG), a non-profit organisation, and a wonderful example of local community engagement in conserving the environment.

The route meanders through the 126-ha Haenertsburg Nature Reserve, which was proclaimed in 2016 to protect the largest fragment of Woodbush Granite Grassland (WGG) in South Africa. The WGG is one of the most threatened vegetation types in South Africa and contains many endemic and threatened plant and animal species. Historically, the WGG covered 430 km² but has been drastically reduced to a severely fragmented 6 km².

The trail alternates between grasslands and delightful patches of indigenous forest. The walk is especially attractive in spring and throughout summer, when the grassland flowers come into bloom.

34. ENTABENI HIKING TRAIL
Makhado (Louis Trichardt)

Trail: 32 km; 2 days; circular.
Permits: Komatiland Eco-Tourism, cell: 083 641 3089, email: ecotour@safcol.co.za, web: www.safcol.co.za.
Maps: Sketch map of trail.
Facilities/Activities: Overnight hut with bunks, mattresses, braai facilities, firewood, toilets and hot showers.
Pertinent information: To reach Entabeni Hut, trailists will need a 4x4 vehicle or a vehicle with a high ground

clearance. Hikers must bring their own drinking water during the dry season. Do not drink water from the streams.

Entabeni Hut is the starting and end point for this hiking trail that follows a figure of eight, enabling you to carry only a daypack. The route alternates between patches of indigenous forest, pine plantations and grasslands. There are also shorter options of 8 or 12 km to choose from.

Highlights on the southern loop (16 km; 6 to 7 hours) include a magnificent tract of indigenous forest where you may spot samango monkeys and gigantic Californian redwood trees that were planted some 60 years ago. Along the trail you will enjoy expansive views of Hanglip to the west and the patchwork of fruit orchards and plantations of Levubu. On the return leg, the trail passes Vera's Tears Waterfall – a welcome oasis on hot days – and the Ebbe Dam.

On the northern loop (16 km; 6 to 7 hours) you will be rewarded with views of the Thathe Vondo area and the sacred Lwamondo Peak.

Hikers can choose shorter options on both loops.

35. SOUTPANSBERG HIKING TRAIL
Makhado (Louis Trichardt)

Trail: 18.7 km; 2 days; circular.
Permits: Komatiland Eco-Tourism, cell: 083 641 3089, email: ecotour@safcol.co.za, web: www.safcol.co.za.
Maps: Colour sketch map of trail.
Facilities/Activities: Two overnight huts with bunks, mattresses, braai facilities, firewood, hot (Zoutpansberg Hut) and cold (Hanglip Hut) showers and toilets.
Pertinent information: Zoutpansberg Hut is at the office, 2 km from the entrance gate. Hikers must arrive at the office before 18:00 on the day of arrival.

Laid out on the slopes of the Soutpansberg, South Africa's northernmost mountain, this trail follows the first day's route of the original Soutpansberg

Hiking Trail. Although most of the trail is through pine and eucalyptus plantations, sections wind through beautiful indigenous forest.

The vegetation of the area has been classified into three broad types: northern mistbelt forest, Soutpansberg mountain bushveld and Soutpansberg summit sourveld, and includes scrub forest, high indigenous forest and mopane bushveld.

Among the dominant tree species are yellowwood, lemonwood, forest bushwillow, forest waterwood and Cape beech. Other species found here include knobwood, Cape chestnut, Transvaal plane, assegai and forest elder.

Three primate species occur in the Soutpansberg (vervet and samango monkeys, and baboon), and antelope are represented by bushbuck, klipspringer, oribi and common duiker. Also inhabiting the range is the shy and secretive leopard.

Birdlife is prolific and includes the black sparrow-hawk, long-crested and crowned eagles, red-eyed dove, Narina trogon and Knysna turaco. You will also be able to tick off chorister robin-chat, white-starred robin, black-headed oriole, olive bushshrike and crested guineafowl.

From Zoutpansberg Hut the first day's hike (12.3 km; 6 hours) ascends steeply through pine plantations, gaining some 300 m in altitude. The trail passes through a patch of beautiful indigenous forest along Bobbejaanskraal and then ascends gradually along the lower slopes of Hanglip to the overnight hut.

Day two's hike (6.4 km; 2 hours) climbs gently to a small hill, from where there are expansive views of Makhado, the surrounding farms and Albasini Dam. The trail then descends through bushveld before entering pine plantations.

36. LESHIBA MOUNTAIN RETREATS
Makhado (Louis Trichardt)

Trails: 12 day walks, self-guided or guided; 1.5 to 7 hours; circular and out-and-return.
Permits: Tel: (011) 483 1841, cell: 082 881 1237, email: info@leshiba.co.za.

Situated on the summit of the western Soutpansberg, the unspoilt Leshiba forms part of the Western Soutpansberg Conservancy and has been declared a natural heritage site.

With a checklist of over 340 tree species, Leshiba offers excellent opportunities for amateur botanists. The vegetation ranges from bushveld to magnificent patches of montane forest, and several endemic succulents also occur in Leshiba. Among the trees recorded are Outeniqua and real yellowwoods, 12 acacia and nine fig species, common wild pear, marula, Transvaal milkplum, silver oak, forest bushwillow and common star chestnut. There are also several species of fern and moss.

Leshiba is a sanctuary for white rhino, giraffe, Burchell's zebra, bushpig and warthog, while large antelope are represented by, among others, sable, kudu, eland, red hartebeest, waterbuck, mountain reedbuck and impala. Common and red duiker, Sharpe's grysbok and klipspringer count among the small antelope species. Also occurring here are leopard and brown hyaena.

Birdlife is prolific and includes Verreaux's and martial eagles, tambourine dove, crested guinea-fowl, and Knysna and purple-crested turacos. Eastern nicator, white-browed robin-chat, lilac-breasted roller and Cape rock-thrush have also been recorded here. Hikers are also likely to spot Cape vulture and jackal and forest buzzards.

Visitors can opt to do Leshiba's 12 well-marked trails. These can be done either as self-guided routes or with the help of a knowledgeable guide. Although the guided walks usually follow the various marked routes, specific tree, bird and rock art trails that do not necessarily follow the marked routes are also offered at Leshiba.

The longest walk is about 6 km, and takes between 5 and 7 hours. Special features of the trails include baobab trees (in some areas), rock pools where you can enjoy a refreshing swim after the summer rains, deep gorges framed by high cliffs, and rock paintings. On some of the trails hikers are rewarded with incredible vistas from vantage points on the edge of sheer cliffs.

37. THABAPHASWA TRAIL
Mokopane (Potgietersrus)

Overlooked by Thabaphaswa (which means the 'black and white mountain'), Groenkop Farm lies in a lush basin just 16 km from the town of Mokopane. This network of three trails offers a number of different options, including a hike up the mountains behind the Kanniedood Camp, along the valley running through the farm, and across the flats in the western part of the farm. The various trail options are connected by links, which makes it possible to plan a route to suit trailists' particular level of fitness.

38. SERENDIPITY HIKING TRAIL
Mookgophong (Naboomspruit)

Bookings: Anvie Ventures,
tel: (044) 696 6585, fax: 086 652 3288,
email: anvie@iburst.co.za or contact
Serendipity Eco Trails, cell: 082 553 3266,
email: info@serendipitytrails.co.za.
Maps: Sketch map.
Facilities/Activities: Three camps: Berg,
Tierkloof and Bush Baby, with beds,
mattresses, braai facilities, showers and
toilets. Mountain biking; 4x4 trails.

These delightful trails traverse the 1,200-ha
bushveld farm Tierkloof, northwest of Mookgophong. Hikers have the choice of base camp day
hikes or an overnight hike. The route passes through
deeply incised gorges, with crystal clear pools, and
mountain streams, valleys and bushveld. From
viewpoints on the route you will be rewarded with
panoramic views of the Waterberg to the west. Trees
along the trail have been marked with their national
tree numbers, and among the species growing in
the patches of indigenous forests are yellowwood,
bladdernut, cheesewood and tree fuchsia.

Antelope occurring in this area include mountain
reedbuck, common reedbuck, kudu and klipspringer.
Among the more than 200 bird species recorded in
the area to date which you may be able to tick during
the course of the hike are Verreaux's and martial
eagles, terrestrial brownbul and Cape batis.

Starting at the Bush Baby Camp, the first day's
hike (12 km; 6 hours) makes its way through several
delightful kloofs to Berg Camp. The second day's
hike (10 km; 5 hours) leads past a waterfall and an
inviting swimming spot before heading back to
Bush Baby Camp.

Hikers can also opt to do two day trails from
Tierkloof: one is 12 km (6 hours) long and the other
is 6 km (3 hours).

39. SKEURKRANS HIKING TRAIL
Mookgophong (Naboomspruit)

Trails: 2 walks; 2 and 3 hours; circular
from base camp.
Bookings: Fagala Voet, cell: 082 776
5540, 081 894 9802, email: bookings@
fagalavoet.co.za, web: fagalavoet.co.za.
Maps: Basic sketch map.
Facilities/Activities: Three A-framed
huts with communal kitchen with fridge,
gas braai, pots, pans, kettle, iron pots;
flush toilets; mountain biking.

The Waterberg stretches in an arc from just above
the town of Thabazimbi for 150 km to northeast
of Mookgophong. It is renowned for its buttresses,
sheer sandstone cliffs, rocky crags, deep ravines,
mountain stream and delightful rock pools.

The vegetation is characterised by broad-leaved
woodland. Typical bushveld trees include wild pear,
Transvaal red milkwood (moepel), African beech,
white seringa, paperbark albizia and bushwillows.
The Transvaal milkplum (stamvrug) are conspicuous
in rocky areas.

Among the mammals you may see are bushbuck,
kudu, common duiker and klipspringer. Mountain
reedbuck and grey rhebok occur at higher altitudes.
Also keep an eye out for rock dassie, baboon and
vervet monkey.

Birdlife is prolific and the cliffs and rocky areas
provide roosting and nesting sites for Verreaux's
eagle. Other species to be on the lookout for include
the grey go-away-bird, crimson-breasted and
white-crowned shrikes, red-crested korhaan and
pied babbler.

The Skeurkrans Hiking Trail near the southeastern
edge of the Waterberg mountain range owes its
name to the horizontal fissures in the sandstone
cliffs that give the impression that the rocks have
been torn apart. Hikers have a choice of two trails:

1. The Leopard Trail meanders through dense
bushveld in the foothills of the Waterberg and
then ascends steeply for about 500 m as you make
your way up to the plateau – an ideal resting
spot to enjoy the view. The path then winds in
the direction of Hanglip, a sandstone buttress
resembling a face with a hanging lip. Another
short but steep climb takes you to a saddle, and
about 1 km on, the trail climbs to the top of the
Escarpment. Once again, slow down, take a well-
deserved break and enjoy the views around you.
The path remains on top of the mountain until you

reach a kloof where you descend along a stream that has beautiful rock pools to cool off in. From the kloof the trail is flat for about 1 km before another steep climb takes you to a plateau before descending to the camp. **9 km; 3 hours; circular.**

2. The Bobbejaan Trail starts off with a leisurely walk through indigenous forests. A steep climb then takes you to the top of the mountain where you can enjoy the views while enjoying breakfast. From here, the trail descends back to the camp. **6 km; 2 hours; circular.**

40. STAMVRUG HIKING TRAIL
Modimolle (Nylstroom)

Trails: Overnight trail; 20 km; 2 days; circular. 2 day walks; 8 and 13 km; 3 and 5 hours; circular.
Bookings: Fagala Voet, cell: 082 776 5540, 081 894 9802, email: bookings@fagalavoet.co.za, web: fagalavoet.co.za.
Maps: Trail pamphlet with map.
Facilities/Activities: Kloof Base Camp: farmhouse with beds, mattresses, kitchen with two-plate gas stove, pots, pans, braai facilities, firewood, hot showers and toilets. Stamvrug Camp: same facilities as at Kloof Base Camp.

Situated in the foothills of the Waterberg, the Bateleur Nature Reserve covers 2,000 ha of bushveld, rocky hills and kloofs with delightful streams.

Among the wide variety of bushveld trees to be seen is the Transvaal milkplum (stamvrug in Afrikaans), the species to which the trail owes its name. One of the largest concentrations of this species in the area can be seen in this reserve. Other typical bushveld species found here include velvet and large-fruited bushwillows, Transvaal beech, Waterberg medlar and the Transvaal cabbage tree.

Antelope you may encounter include kudu, blesbok, bushbuck, reedbuck, klipspringer, steenbok and common duiker. Leopard, aardwolf, brown hyaena, warthog, baboon and vervet monkey also occur here.

Birdlife is prolific, and species to be seen include raptors such as Cape vulture, African harrier-hawk, Wahlberg's eagle and black-chested snake eagle, as well as African wattled lapwing, black crake and greater double-collared sunbird. Blue crane breed in the reserve too.

1. Stamvrug Hiking Trail The first day's hike, the Kloof Route (13 km; 5 hours), begins with a steady climb to a koppie, from where there are extensive views of the Waterberg to the north, Kranskop to the east and the Nyl zijn Oog to the west. From here the trail descends gradually and then follows a ridge, which offers wonderful views of the Waterberg.

The remainder of the Stamvrug trail follows a gently undulating course to a patch of indigenous forest and a magnificent natural rock garden before descending to a farm dam, where you can cool off and rest before hiking the final 1 km to the Stamvrug Hut.

The second day's hike, the Stamvrug Route (7 km; 3 hours), gently ascends along a ridge to a koppie and traverses a grassy plateau, before reaching another koppie. The trail then descends to a patch of indigenous forest and, further along, a detour leads to the Krans Dam. An easy climb is followed by a descent into a delightful kloof, which you follow until the final climb back to the Kloof Base Camp. **20 km; 2 days; circular.**

2. Day Walks Visitors can also explore the reserve by way of a network of day walks, including the Leopard Trail (13 km; 5 hours), which follows the Kloof Trail in the opposite direction.

The Moepel Trail (8 km; 3 hours), named after the fine specimens of Transvaal red milkwood (moepel in Afrikaans) seen along the trail, is another option. Other highlights include a section of indigenous forest, splendid views of the Waterberg and interesting rock formations.

41. TAAIBOS HIKING TRAILS
Vaalwater

Trails: 2 walks; 2 to 3 hours; circular.

Bookings: Anvie Ventures, tel: (044) 696 6585, email: info@anvieventures.co.za, web: www.anvieventures.co.za.
Maps: Trails are clearly marked.
Facilities/Activities: Bush camp with four thatched chalets with beds, equipped kitchen, flush toilets, braai place; River Cabin for 6 people; Maroela Hut sleeping four; camp site with power points, braai places, communal hot-water ablutions; cliff swing, river rafting, abseiling, ziplining, 4x4 trails.

Taaibos Adventures and Safaris is situated in the heart of the Waterberg, where the Mokolo River, one of the main rivers flowing into the Limpopo River, meanders through the range. The vegetation is typical bushveld, with water pear, water berry, buffalo thorn, karee, wild olive and river bushwillow among the trees to be seen along the Taaibosspruit.

Hikers have a choice of two short routes: the Kudu and Leopard trails (both 5 km; 2 to 3 hours; circular) that wind through spectacular rock formations, past cliffs and along the Taaibosspruit, which is crossed several times. Rising on the northern slopes of the Waterberg, the Taaibosspruit is a tributary of the Mokolo River. Highlights along the trails include a termite mound that has displaced a massive 500 kg boulder as the mound grew taller, spectacular views across the valley and a large panel of rock paintings that can be seen on the Kudu Trail. The dam where the trails end was built by Italian prisoners of war during World War II.

42. LINDANI HIKING TRAILS
Vaalwater

Trails: 4 walks; 7.3 km to 11.2 km; 2 to 4 hours; circular.
Bookings: Cell: 083 631 5579 or 083 809 4291, email: info@lindani.co.za, web: www.lindani.co.za.
Maps: Colour map available.

Facilities/Activities: Various accommodation options; self-drive and guided game-viewing; guided walks; mountain biking.
Pertinent Information: Day visitors must make prior arrangements two days before arrival.

Lindani, a private 3,000-ha game farm, lies close to the eastern Escarpment of the Waterberg amid magnificent scenery dominated by spectacular sandstone cliffs. White seringa, milkplum, red seringa, weeping faurea, red ivory and bushwillow are among the many typical bushveld tree species to be seen.

Antelope that occur here include eland, kudu, waterbuck, blue wildebeest and red hartebeest. Other mammals to be on the lookout for are giraffe, Burchell's zebra and warthog. Birdlife is prolific and over 230 bird species have been recorded to date.

1. Melkrivier Trail owes its name to the Melk River. It is graded as moderately difficult. **11.2 km; 4 hours; circular.**

2. Mountain Trail is moderately difficult. **10.1 km; 3 hours; circular.**

3. Koperspruit Trail is an easy route and partly follows the Koperspruit. **7.6 km; 2 to 3 hours; circular.**

4. Kloof Trail is graded as easy. **7.3 km; 2 to 3 hours; circular.**

43. RHENOSTERPOORT HIKING TRAIL
Alma

Trails: 2 day walks; 8 and 12 km; 4 and 6 hours; network from base camp.
Bookings: Anvie Ventures, tel: (044) 696 6585, fax: 086 652 3288, email: anvie@iburst.co.za.
Maps: Sketch map.

Facilities/Activities: Two thatched bush camps with fully equipped kitchens and bathrooms; angling; 4x4 trail.

This trail can be started at either Dassie Camp or Bosbok Camp. The first day's trail (12 km; 6 hours) initially ascends steeply and follows the contours above Donkerkloof to a vantage point with spectacular views of the Waterberg.

The trail then descends, and at the halfway point an optional 4-km loop splits off to the right. Continuing on the direct route you will reach a delightful picnic place alongside a river with natural pools. From here the trail follows the contours above the river to Dassie Camp and onwards, to the highlight of the trail: a waterfall plunging into a magnificent pool.

The second day's hike of 8 km is completed in about four hours at quite a relaxed pace. More than 100 trees have been marked along the trail, which provides an ideal opportunity to get to know the trees found in the area. The trail also offers some good birding possibilities. **20 km; 2 days; network from base camp.**

44. MARAKELE NATIONAL PARK
Thabazimbi

Trails: Guided morning and sunset walks from Bontle and Tlopi camps; 3 hours.
Permits: Conservation fee. Book for guided walks at park reception.
Maps: General map of park.
Facilities/Activities: Tlopi Tented Camp; Bontle Rest Camp with tents and camping sites; picnic site, bird hide, viewing point accessible in a sedan vehicle; morning and sunset guided drives; 2-night 4x4 eco-trail.
Pertinent information: Visitors must be self-sufficient in terms of food and fuel, as there isn't a shop or filling station in the park.

Situated at the southwestern end of the Waterberg range, Marakele fittingly means 'place of sanctuary'

in Tswana. It is a wilderness of sheer cliffs, buttresses, cool forested kloofs and deep valleys and streams.

The historic 16,000-ha core of the park was proclaimed as the Kransberg National Park in 1988. After further land acquisitions, the park was proclaimed as the Marakele National Park. It has since been enlarged by the incorporation of several private properties by way of contractual agreements with adjoining landowners and covers over 67,000 ha.

Situated in a transitional zone between the moist east and the dry west, the flora and fauna are representative of both regions. The park is a sanctuary for over 91 mammal species, including the Big Five and rare antelope such as roan, sable and tsessebe. Other species roaming the bushveld and grasslands include giraffe, eland, kudu, impala, nyala, red hartebeest and plains zebra. The carnivores are represented by lion, leopard, cheetah, wild dog, brown and spotted hyaenas, aardwolf and 16 other smaller species.

With over 410 bird species to tick off, birding in the park is rewarding. The world's largest colony of Cape vultures roosts and breeds on the cliffs on the park's southern boundary. White-backed and lappet-faced vultures, martial eagle, Verreaux's eagle and peregrine falcon are among the 35 other raptor species recorded to date. Meyer's parrot, crimson-breasted shrike and pied babbler are among the vocal species to be seen, while the striking African green pigeon also occurs. Other species to be on the lookout for include the orange-breasted bushshrike, southern white-crowned shrike, red-crested korhaan and Gurney's sugarbird.

To date, some 765 plant species have been recorded, including the Waterberg cycad, which is endemic to the Waterberg and is classified as endangered. The vegetation varies from mixed bushveld dominated by silver clusterleaf, sicklebush, round-leaved teak and various thorn tree species on the lower elevations to mountain bushveld at higher elevations. Characteristic species of the mountain bushveld include Transvaal beechwood, the common sugarbush and Transvaal milkplum (stamvrug).

Guided morning and sunset walks, lasting about three hours, are conducted by experienced and armed rangers, who will also interpret the environment.

45. WEILAND BUSH TRAILS

Thabazimbi

Trails: 2 day walks; 7 and 10 km; 3 and 5 hours; circular.
Bookings: Cell: 082 375 6708, fax: 086 605 5814, email: info@weiland.co.za.
Maps: Colour map.
Facilities/Activities: Base camp with five wooden sleeping platforms, communal tent, kitchen, braai area, flush toilets and hot showers; mountain biking.
Pertinent Information: Tap water is supplied from the river and is not drinkable. Drinking water is supplied from boreholes and is available from plastic dispensers at the camp.

The Weiland Bush Trails are situated on 1,200 ha of wilderness in the Waterberg. They are laid out in the aptly named Lost Valley, a pristine mountain valley surrounded by the Boshoff Cliffs.

Hikers are rewarded with spectacular views of the surrounding countryside, which is characterised by a rich diversity of bushveld trees, some of which have been marked with name tags. Birdlife abounds in the area and hikers are also likely to encounter kudu, blue wildebeest, klipspringer, steenbok and mountain rhebok. Hiking is especially rewarding from September to April when the natural rock pools in the Blinkwaterspruit provide relief from the summer heat. Hikers can walk the 4 km from the parking area to the base camp (which is only accessible by 4x4 vehicle) or opt to be transported with their kit.

46. MAPUNGUBWE NATIONAL PARK

60 km west of Musina

Trails: Guided morning walks; 3 hours.
Permits: Conservation fee. Book for walks at park reception.
Maps: General map of park.

Facilities/Activities: Main Camp with self-catering accommodation, swimming pool and braai area; luxury lodge with swimming pool; tented camp with kitchen and shower; Vhembu Wilderness Camp with self-catering accommodation, bathroom, communal kitchen and lapa; camp site; heritage tours; guided drives; self-drive 4x4 trail; no shop, restaurant or filling station.

Situated at the confluence of the Limpopo and Shashe rivers, Mapungubwe National Park protects a rich diversity of fauna, flora as well as southern Africa's most important archaeological sites.

The park lies at the centre of southern Africa's earliest major kingdom, which began developing in 900 AD. The kingdom flourished between 1220 and 1270 AD, and at the height of its power it was ruled from Mapungubwe Hill. Research has provided compelling evidence of extensive trade links with settlements on the East African coast. Artefacts include imported glass beads and Chinese porcelain, while spindle whorls indicate that cotton was produced at Mapungubwe. But the most treasured artefact is a magnificent gold-plated rhino statue recovered from a royal grave on Mapungubwe Hill. Changing climatic conditions eventually led to Mapungubwe's demise and new states developed around Great Zimbabwe and Khami.

The significance of the site was recognised when the Mapungubwe Cultural Landscape was inscribed as a UNESCO World Heritage Site on 5 July 2003.

Mapungubwe National Park was officially opened in September 2004. The park lies at the centre of the planned Limpopo-Shashe Transfrontier Park – an agreement signed between the governments of South Africa, Botswana and Zimbabwe in June 2006. This park will also include the Northern Tuli Game Reserve, which is a sanctuary to Africa's largest elephant population.

Large mammal species include elephant, giraffe and white rhino, while antelope are represented by eland, kudu, gemsbok, waterbuck, blue wildebeest and impala. Predators include leopard, cheetah, lion and spotted and brown hyaena.

With some 400 species known to occur in the area, birdlife is prolific. Meves's starling, rocket-tailed roller and tropical boubou are specials to look out for. Verreaux's eagle, Dickinson's kestrel and augur buzzard count among the raptors.

The diverse habitat types support a wealth of trees and shrubs, among them acacias, marulas, stands of fever trees, mopane scrubveld, fig and ana trees. Enormous baobabs add to the scenic beauty of the landscape.

The park protects a magnificent tract of riparian forest along the Limpopo River, and the elevated boardwalk to the Treetop Hide is one of the highlights of a visit to Mapungubwe.

Other attractions include the viewpoint that overlooks the confluence of the Shashe and Limpopo rivers, where the boundaries of South Africa, Botswana and Zimbabwe meet, and the Pinnacles viewpoint, which overlooks a valley with 85 fossilised termite mounds. The Maloutswa Hide, in the western section of the park, offers good game-viewing during the dry winter months and excellent birding in the summer.

Guided Morning Walks are conducted by highly experienced and fully armed rangers. Walks depart from the main gate and last about three hours.

The forest plantations of Mpumalanga are an enchanting fairytale setting.

GAUTENG & NORTH WEST

Despite being South Africa's most densely populated province, Gauteng provides a surprising number of outdoor opportunities for those wanting to escape the pressures of city life, as does the adjoining North West province. These provinces offer everything from short walks in botanical gardens and overnight trails in nature reserves to guided walks in conservation areas such as Pilanesberg National Park — all within easy reach of the Johannesburg and Pretoria (Tshwane) metropolitan areas.

Over a large part of southern Gauteng and the Highveld areas of North West province the altitude ranges between 1,200 and 1,800 m. The vegetation here is characterised by extensive, almost pure grassland, with hardly any trees on the open plains. Woodlands are confined to river valleys, and patches of woodland and shrubland, known as Bankenveld, occur on the quartzite ridges of Gauteng.

To the north of the Magaliesberg, the vegetation of the two provinces is characterised by vast areas of bushveld. Trees found here include weeping wattle, marula, large-fruited and red bushwillows, silver cluster leaf, wild seringa and common wild pear.

Birding is especially rewarding in summer and among the species to look for are grey-winged and red-winged francolins, blue crane, white-bellied korhaan, several lark and pipit species, African grass owl and cisticolas. Species of the more arid west include crimson-breasted shrike, Marico flycatcher, Burchell's courser and Kalahari scrub robin.

Among the typical game species of the Highveld plains are blesbok, red hartebeest, black wildebeest, eland and Burchell's zebra. Although the large herds that once used to roam the Highveld plains have long since disappeared, game has been reintroduced into several nature reserves, national parks and farms in the two provinces. In small conservation areas such as the Kgaswane Mountain Reserve and the Suikerbosrand Nature Reserve there are good game-viewing and birding opportunities for outdoor enthusiasts doing self-guided hiking trails and walks.

In Borakalalo National Park visitors have a choice of a self-guided walk and guided walks. Among the big game species that may be seen on foot are white rhino, hippo, buffalo, giraffe, roan and tsessebe.

Pilanesberg National Park is a Big Five (elephant, rhino, buffalo, lion, leopard) park and can, therefore, only be explored with a guided walk, for safety reasons. Established in 1979 on severely degraded land, the park was restocked with game in what was one of the biggest game translocation projects ever undertaken. Known as Operation Genesis, the project involved the translocation of over 7,000 animals of 20 different species into the park.

The Pilanesberg itself is of great geological interest as it is one of the three largest alkaline volcanoes (formed by a distinct type of molten matter, known as alkaline magma, as opposed to acid magma) in the world. The volcano was active some 1,200 million years ago, but has been eroded down to its roots over time. Measuring about 25 km in diameter, the original volcanic centre is now surrounded by concentric hills.

There are several other important geological features in the two provinces that lend themselves to exploration on foot. Best known of the three quartzite ridges that dominate the landscape of Gauteng and the east of North West province is the Magaliesberg. Rising on average 330 m above the surrounding landscape, the range extends eastwards from Zeerust, past Hartbeespoort Dam, and continues through Pretoria to its eastern suburbs. It forms a natural boundary between the Highveld to the south and the bushveld to the north.

The vegetation of Gauteng's quartzite ridges is dominated by Bankenveld, a term referring to vegetation of the low, bench-like hills and ridges occurring in the area. Almost pure stands of grasslands occur on the crests of the hills and ridges, their cool southern slopes and on low-lying plains, while trees and shrubs grow on northern slopes, rocky outcrops and in sheltered valleys. Typical trees include common sugarbush, oldwood, sagewood, tree fuchsia, white stinkwood, mountain cabbage tree and cheesewood.

The quartzite ridges are the habitat of numerous bird species. Noteworthy ones include the Cape vulture, lanner and peregrine falcons, ground woodpecker and short-toed rock-thrush. The ridges also form natural wildlife corridors for a variety of mammals such as the brown hyaena, as well as reptiles and smaller creatures like beetles, colourful butterflies and many insects.

In the past, Gauteng's quartzite ridges also played an important role in the search for gold. The old mines in the Kloofendal Nature Reserve provide an interesting perspective on the frantic search that preceded the discovery of the Main Reef in 1886 and the development of Johannesburg.

Rising like an island above the surrounding urbanised landscape, most of the Magaliesberg was safeguarded against uncontrolled development when it was declared a Natural Area in 1977 and a Protected Natural Environment in 1993. Hiking opportunities in the Magaliesberg range from overnight hikes and day walks in the Kgaswane Mountain Reserve to walks and trails on private land.

At Tswaing Crater, about 40 km northwest of Pretoria, trailists can explore one of the best preserved and most accessible meteorite impact craters in the world. The almost circular crater, with a diameter of just over 1 km, was formed when a meteorite crashed into the earth some 200,000 years ago. Tswaing Crater is a natural heritage site.

In the southwestern corner of North West province lies another geological curiosity, which extends into the Free State: the Vredefort Dome. Its origin is the subject of two theories, one of which attributes it to an upwelling of granite and subsequent geological processes and pressures, and the other to the impact of a huge meteorite. This structure was declared a UNESCO World Heritage Site in 2005.

Frost is common on the Highveld in winter, when minimum temperatures can drop to below freezing point. Daytime temperatures are generally mild, but can be low. In the bushveld, winter temperatures are not as extreme and seldom drop to below zero. Summer on the Highveld is warm during the day and pleasant in the evenings. In the western parts of North West province, however, maximum temperatures are several degrees higher than on the Highveld.

The rainy season is during the summer months and is characterised by heavy mid-afternoon thunderstorms and lightning. Rainfall varies from 350 mm in the west to 750 mm on the eastern margins of the Gauteng Highveld. The highest rainfall is generally recorded between the months of October/ November and March, with very little rainfall in the winter months. A major attraction for visitors to the two provinces is that they are free of malaria.

IMPORTANT INFORMATION

➤ Pack sufficient warm clothing and a good-quality sleeping bag when hiking in the Gauteng Highveld and high mountain areas of North West province during winter.

➤ In summer, thunderstorms occur frequently and lightning can be extremely dangerous. An early start is recommended to ensure that you reach your destination before a thunderstorm sets in, usually during mid-afternoon.

➤ In the Highveld grassland the risk of fire is very high during winter. Extreme caution must be exercised when making fires and smokers must refrain from smoking while they are walking.

➤ Ticks can be a problem, so it is advisable to apply a repellent and to wear long trousers. It is also a good idea to inspect yourself thoroughly for ticks at the end of each day's hike.

➤ The grasslands of the Highveld offer virtually no overhead cover, so you should always wear a wide-brimmed hat and apply sunscreen regularly.

➤ During the winter months, most streams are likely to be dry. Never set off without at least 2 litres of water and use it sparingly until you can refill your water bottle. On overnight hikes, consult the trail map, or check with the trail authority whether water is available along the trail.

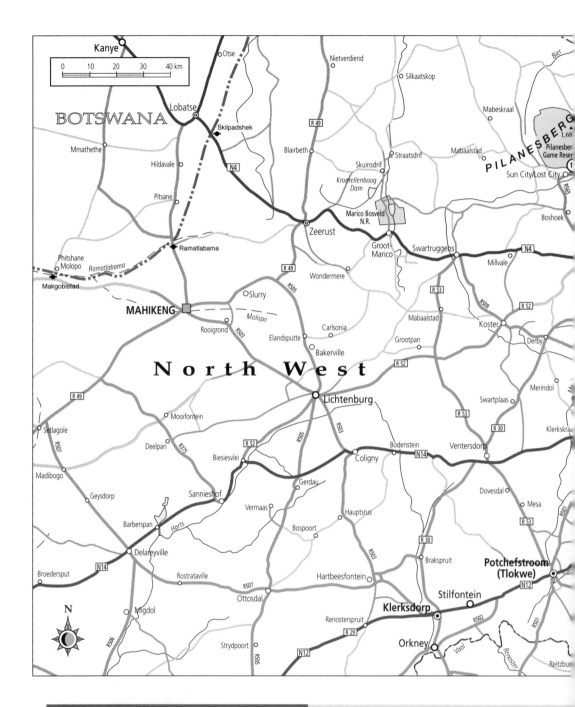

HIKING TRAILS

1 Suikerbosrand Hiking Trail p. 260
2 Suikerbosrand Nature Reserve p. 261
3 Klipkraal Hiking Trails p. 262
4 Walter Sisulu National Botanical Garden p. 262
5 Kloofendal Nature Reserve p. 262
6 Rietvlei Nature Reserve p. 263
7 Pretoria National Botanical Garden p. 264
8 Tswaing Crater Trail p. 264
9 Windy Brow Hiking Trail p. 265
10 Borakalalo Game Reserve p. 265
11 Uitkyk Hiking Trail p. 266
12 Hennops Hiking Trail p. 267

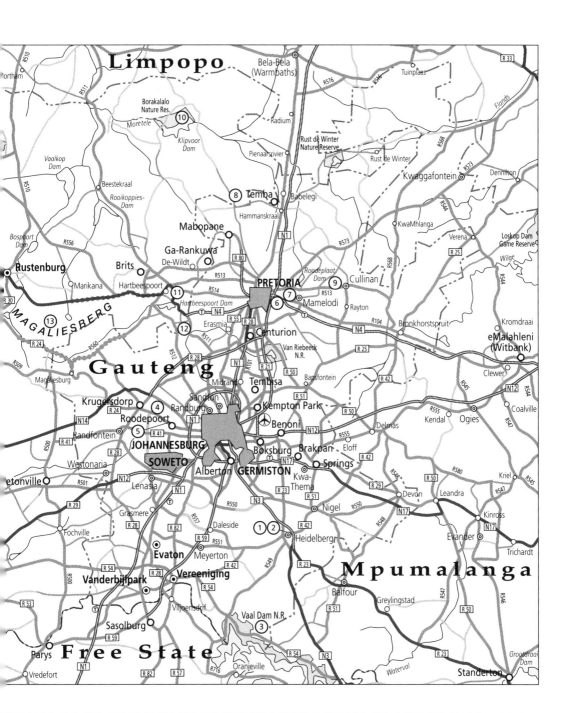

1. SUIKERBOSRAND HIKING TRAIL

Suikerbosrand Nature Reserve, Heidelberg

See no. 2 (p. 261) for walks.

Trail: Self-guided trail; 63.2 km (in total, depending on trailists' selected route); 2 to 7 days; circular.
Permits: Suikerbosrand Nature Reserve, Private Bag H616, Heidelberg 1436, tel: (011) 439 6300, cell: 079 439 0532.
Maps: Colour nature reserve and trail map.
Facilities/Activities: Four overnight huts with bunks, mattresses, enviro toilet, cold-water showers, braai, kettle, pots and firewood. Visitors' Centre; Diepkloof Farm Museum; two group camps; self-drive game-viewing; picnic site; guided game drives; horse trails; mountain biking.
Pertinent information: Hikers can plan their own route but may not stay in the same hut for more than one night. There is no electricity at the overnight huts. Due to regular maintenance, sections of the trail as well as overnight huts may be closed from time time. Enquire at reception for details ahead of your visit. Group size is limited; the trail caters for a minimum of 2 and a maximum of 10 people. Although the route is well marked, care should be taken at intersections because of the large number of options. A visit to the Visitors' Centre will enhance your enjoyment of the hike.

Dominated by the Suikerbosrand (meaning 'sugarbush ridge' in Afrikaans), a quartzite ridge that owes its name to the abundance of common sugarbushes in the area, this reserve covers 13,337 ha of false grassveld (a vegetation type consisting of grass, shrubs and trees, as opposed to pure grassveld), patches of woodland and shrubland. Over 1,000 plant and tree species have been identified in the reserve, including 115 grass species, 61 tree and 3 aloe species. Tree species include oldwood, sagewood, karee, tree fuchsia, white stinkwood, cheesewood, cabbage, wild olive and acacias. Aloes are represented by the mountain aloe (*Aloe marlothii*), the grass aloe (*Aloe greatheadii*) and the Transvaal aloe (*Aloe transvaalensis*), while a variety of flowering plants brightens up the grasslands in spring.

Large antelope roaming the reserve include eland, kudu, red hartebeest, black wildebeest, grey rhebok, blesbok, mountain reedbuck, reedbuck and springbok, while common duiker, steenbok and oribi also occur here. Among the other mammals you may see are Burchell's zebra, cheetah, brown hyaena, black-backed jackal and baboon.

With a bird checklist of some 250 species, birding here can be rewarding. Species you might tick include Verreaux's, African hawk and martial eagles, grey-winged francolin, ant-eating chat, mountain wheatear, Cape longclaw, and Cape robin-chat.

Situated within easy reach of Johannesburg, the Suikerbosrand Hiking Trail provides the perfect escape for those needing a break from city life. The short distances between trail huts (averaging under 10 km) and the relatively easy terrain make this an ideal trail for beginners and families.

Various trail options are available, allowing you to plan a hike to suit your personal needs. The trail network winds through contrasting flora, from aloe veld in the west to proteaveld in the east, and offers excellent game-viewing and birding opportunities.

A typical four-day trail (suitable for beginners and families with small children) is described here. The route can, however, be done fairly easily in two days or extended by three days by incorporating the eastern section of the reserve into your hike.

The first day's trail (6.3 km; 2.5 hours), from the Visitors' Centre to Springbok Hut, can easily be hiked after lunch. It ascends gently but steadily along the eastern slopes of Baboon Ridge and, just before crossing the tarred game-viewing road, passes a wall built by one of the early farmers to divert water trapped by a dolerite dyke into a side valley. About 1 km on you will find yourself at the Rantjies Lookout, the highest point of the day's hike. From here the trail skirts Kiepersolkloof as it descends to the hut, which is tucked away in a dense patch of kloof forest.

On day two (12.2 km; 5 hours) the trail follows the densely wooded Koedoekloof for a short distance and then climbs to grassland interspersed with aloes. At Blind Man's Corner the trail swings sharply westwards before descending gently along Doringbos Road, named for the profusion of acacias (doringbos in Afrikaans) dominating the valley. After crossing the tarred road to Kareekloof Resort the trail leads through the Aloe Forest, with its tall specimens of mountain aloes. The trail then continues its ascent as it makes its way up to the summit of Perdekop, before winding down to Eland Hut.

Day three's hike offers two options: a short, direct route (6.5 km; 2.5 hours) or a longer option (14.6 km; 6 hours) to Blesbok Hut. From the hut the trail ascends a kloof and heads across Springbokvlakte, where herds of springbok, black wildebeest and Burchell's zebra are likely to be seen. At Swaeltjieshoek the direct route to Blesbok Hut continues straight, while the longer option via Steenbok Hut (described here) branches off to the right. After a short, steep descent the trail levels out below Feeskrans to reach Steenbok Hut 7 km from the start. The hut is a good place to stop for brunch or tea, if it is not occupied by other hikers. About 2 km beyond Steenbok Hut the trail to Hartebees Hut branches off to the right, but you continue straight, and a short way on you will look down onto Hartebeesvlakte. The trail ascends the steep Hyaenakloof before dropping down to Blesbok Hut, which is situated 400 m off the main trail.

On the final day's hike (5 km; 2 hours) you backtrack along the last 400 m of the previous day's trail and then ascend the northern slopes of Kwaggakop, before dropping down to Jagluiperdbossie. Further along, the trail passes the remains of an old Iron Age settlement, winds downhill, and then follows the lower slopes of Baboon Ridge back to the start. **30 or 38.1 km; 4 days; circular.**

2. SUIKERBOSRAND NATURE RESERVE
Heidelberg

See no. 1 (p. 260) for hiking trail.

Trails: 3 walks; 1 to 7 hours; circular.
Permits: Entrance fee. No permit required for walks. Tel: (011) 439 6300.
Maps: Trail brochure with sketch map.

Facilities/Activities: Visitors' Centre; Diepkloof Farm Museum; two group camps; toilet facilities along Bokmakierie Nature Trail; self-drive game-viewing; picnic site; guided game drives; horse trails; mountain biking.
Pertinent information: Hikers must carry their own water, as there are no water sources along the trail.

1. Toktokkie Accessible Trail This short interpretative trail, accessible for people in wheelchairs, provides an ideal introduction to various ecological aspects of the reserve. Along the trail there are 14 points of interest, which are explained in the trail booklet. These range from herbs, food chains and climatology to various tree species, the adaptations of succulent plants and the Diepkloof Farm Museum. Trees along the trail include karee, white stinkwood and bluebush. **1 km; 1 hour; circular.**

2. Cheetah Trail focuses on several prominent features in the reserve, particularly its prehistory and ecology, the impact of erosion and pollution, as well as common trees, shrubs and aloes. Of cultural and historical interest are the stone-walled Iron Age sites along the trail, built by the ancestors of the Sotho and Tswana people. It is estimated that the area was first settled between 600 and 700 years ago. There are 13 marked points of interest along the trail, explained in the trail brochure. **4 km; 2 hours; circular.**

3. Bokmakierie Nature Trail is named after the bokmakierie, an attractive bird with a conspicuous black collar around a yellow throat. The trail can be walked as either a 10-km or an 11.5-km route, splitting to the right (indicated by green footprints) and the left (identified by yellow footprints) after about 6 km from the start. The trail follows a slightly undulating course through the northwestern corner of the reserve and passes six marked points of interest, which are explained in the trail brochure. Among these are the importance of surface water in a nature reserve, especially with regard to waterholes for animals, the succession of veld types, indigenous trees, Iron Age sites and food chains. **10 or 11.5 km; 3.5 to 4 hours; circular.**

3. KLIPKRAAL HIKING TRAILS
Heidelberg

Trails: 2 day walks; 11 and 13 km; 4 hours; network from base camp.
Bookings: Fagala Voet, cell: 082 776 5540, 081 894 9802, email: bookings@fagalavoet.co.za, web: fagalavoet.co.za.
Maps: Colour map with trail information.
Facilities/Activities: Accommodation options range from restored milk sheds with electricity, hot-water showers, kitchen and braai facilities and cooking utensils to fully equipped self-catering cottage and guesthouse. Canoeing on dam.
Pertinent information: Bring your own firewood/charcoal.

The Klipkraal Hiking Trails traverse three farms in the Heidelberg district and offer an interesting combination of farm life, natural habitat, and historical and archaeological sites. The vegetation is typical of the Highveld, with grassveld interspersed with shrubs and trees. Black wildebeest, blesbok, springbok, Burchell's zebra and grey rhebok count among the larger game species to be seen.

1. Panorama Route Starting from the Habitat Base Camp, the Panorama Route passes through a game camp and then meanders across grasslands. Further on, the trail makes its way up and down several hills and passes through shrubveld. There are expansive views of the Vaal Dam and the surrounding farms from the hill summits. **13 km; 4 hours; network.**

2. Kraal Route owes its name to Late Iron Age settlements established here between 1600 and 1700. A 5-km-long stone wall, built to capture game, and the Grootklip, which is revered as a sacred place, are other points of interest along the way. There are several ascents, and you will be rewarded with expansive views. **11 km; 4 hours; network.**

Both trails offer the option of a shortcut, reducing the distances of both the Panorama and Kraal routes to 7 km.

4. WALTER SISULU NATIONAL BOTANICAL GARDEN
Roodepoort

Trails: Network covering several kilometres.
Permits: Entrance fee. No permit required.
Maps: Available at entrance gate.
Facilities/Activities: Picnic area; cafeteria; book and gift shop; bird hide; indigenous plant nursery.

Set against the backdrop of the Roodekrans Ridge, the focal point of the 225-ha Walter Sisulu National Botanical Garden is the spectacular Witpoortjie Waterfall, where the Crocodile River cascades over a 70-m-high cliff.

The garden protects one of the few remaining patches of Bankenveld vegetation in Gauteng. This vegetation type consists of almost pure grassveld on the crests of Gauteng's characteristic quartzite ridges, their southern slopes and low-lying plains, while the northern slopes support trees and shrubs.

Best known among the more than 230 bird species recorded in this botanical garden is a breeding pair of Verreaux's eagles nesting against the cliffs near the waterfall. Other birds to be seen include arrow-marked babbler, black-headed oriole, Cape rock-thrush, fairy flycatcher and Acacia pied barbet.

Parts of the garden have been developed around particular plants and habitats. There are cycad, succulent, wild flower and water-wise gardens, while the remaining area has been left in its natural state.

The garden is criss-crossed by a network of trails, ranging from walks along the quartzite ridges, from where there are fine views over the garden and its surroundings, to walks along the Crocodile River, with its riverine forest.

5. KLOOFENDAL NATURE RESERVE
Roodepoort

Trails: Various guided walks; up to 3 hours; circular.

Situated in the centre of Roodepoort, Kloofendal Nature Reserve covers 150 ha of quartzite ridges, characterised by cliffs and unspoilt kloofs, while the Wilgespruit flows through the reserve. The vegetation is typical Bankenveld, with patches of common hook thorn, sagewood, common sugarbush, white stinkwood and tree fuchsia.

Birding is prolific and among the species you might tick are black-shouldered kite, rock kestrel, wailing cisticola, African pipit and bokmakierie. Also look out for Cape robin-chat and black-collared barbet.

Of historical interest is the Confidence Reef, where Fred Strubens discovered the first economically viable occurrence of gold on 18 September 1884. Initial optimism about the discovery prompted Fred and his brother Harry to develop the reef, and the first crushing plant on the Witwatersrand, a five-stamp battery (a machine for crushing ore), came into operation in December of the following year. .

6. RIETVLEI NATURE RESERVE
Pretoria

Covering 3,800 ha of undulating grassy hills, 20 km to the southeast of Pretoria, the Rietvlei Nature Reserve lies in the catchment area of the Rietvlei Dam. The reserve was established to ensure the supply of clean water to Pretoria; the reserve's dam (built in 1934), six fountains and one borehole supply approximately 15 per cent of the city's water requirements.

The reserve is home to a variety of Highveld game species. In addition to blesbok, the most abundant of the various antelope species, the reserve has also been stocked with black wildebeest, eland, red hartebeest, waterbuck, springbok, reedbuck, mountain reedbuck and oribi. Also to be seen are white rhino, hippo, buffalo and Burchell's zebra, as well as a variety of smaller mammals such as vlei rat, spring hare, suricate, slender mongoose and scrub hare.

About 270 bird species have been recorded and among the wetland birds to look out for are black-crowned night heron, greater flamingo, white-faced and knob-billed ducks, African finfoot and African wattled lapwing. Other species you may tick include African fish eagle, blue crane, Burchell's coucal, red-billed wood-hoopoe, and Cape longclaw.

1. Overnight Hiking Trail Groups are met at 17:00 on Friday afternoons at the reserve's main gate, from where it is a 2-km walk to the overnight hut.

On Saturday a 14-km hike is undertaken to the second overnight hut. Along the way, the guide will give you an insight into the ecology of the area you are hiking through and there will also be stops for game-viewing and birding. Although it is relatively flat, you should be walking fit as you have to carry your backpack. On Sunday morning a 6-km walk takes you back to the start. **22 km; 2 days; circular.**

2. Day Walks start at 08:00 at the reserve's main gate. In addition to game-viewing and birding, trailists will also gain a better understanding of the reserve's ecology. **10 km; 4 hours; circular.**

7. PRETORIA NATIONAL BOTANICAL GARDEN
Pretoria

Trails: Network of footpaths, including the Dassie Trail; 3 to 6 km; 1 to 2 hours; circular.
Permits: Entrance fee. No permit required.
Maps: Available at entrance gate.
Facilities/Activities: Restaurant; guided walks (on request).

Situated on the western outskirts of Pretoria on Silverton Ridge, a mere 8 km from the city centre, this garden was established in 1946 in the grounds of South Africa's National Herbarium, and is one of South Africa's ten national botanical gardens.

Covering 75 ha, the vegetation is characterised by Bankenveld trees and over 500 species of flowering plants. In the cultivated section there are gardens with succulents, fynbos, cycads, aloes and forest. The Desmond Cole Collection of *Lithops* (meaning 'stone-like') and the Hardy Collection of plants from Namaqualand, Namibia and Madagascar contain some of its most important plants.

A network of paved walkways winds through the various plant collections, and the **Dassie Trail** (3 to 6 km; 1 to 2 hours) makes its way along a quartzite ridge through natural Bankenveld vegetation.

8. TSWAING CRATER TRAIL
Pretoria

Trail: 7.2 km; 3 hours; circular.
Permits: Entrance fee. No permit required.
Maps: Available at office.
Facilities/Activities: Guided tours; kiosk; braai facilities; traditional African meals; accommodation for groups visiting for environmental education purposes.

Situated approximately 30 km north of Onderstepoort, the Tswaing Meteorite Crater is one of the best preserved meteorite impact craters in the world. It was formed some 220,000 years ago when a meteorite, estimated to be 60 m in diameter, collided with the earth. The impact created a crater with a diameter of 1.1 km and a depth of 120 m.

The name Tswaing means 'place of salt' in Setswana and refers to the brine lake that lies at the centre of the crater. The salt was mined for centuries by the Tswana, Sotho and Ndebele, who occupied the area at various periods, and during the early 1900s a soda factory was established at Tswaing.

The Tswaing Meteorite Crater is one of several museums managed by the Northern Flagship Institution and was established in 1992 as the first environmental museum in South Africa.

The vegetation is dominated by bushwillow and acacia species. Among the nearly 300 bird species found here that you may tick are Wahlberg's eagle, crested francolin, cardinal woodpecker, crimson-breasted shrike and groundscraper thrush.

The 7.2-km self-guided **Crater Trail** is probably the only one of its kind in the world. It starts at the Tswaing Meteorite Crater reception and heads north, to the southern crater rim, and then swings east to run along the crest of the southern and eastern crater rim. From here trailists are rewarded with superb views of the crater. A zigzag route down the wooded crater slopes leads to the crater floor and the peninsula extending into the crater lake. The return leg follows an old wagon route out of the crater and the trail then meanders past the old soda factory back to the reception area. Trees and other points of interest along the route have been marked, among them the site of the borehole that provided conclusive evidence that the crater was formed by a meteorite impact and not as a result of volcanic activity. Rock from the borehole showed a deformation of minerals that could only have been produced by pressures resulting from the impact of a meteorite.

9. WINDY BROW HIKING TRAIL
Cullinan

Trails: 3 day walks; 3.2 to 5.9 km; 1.5 to 6 hours; circular. Network from base camp.
Bookings: Fagala Voet, cell: 082 776 5540, 081 894 9802, email: bookings@fagalavoet.co.za, web: fagalavoet.co.za.
Maps: Trail pamphlet with map.
Facilities/Activities: Base camp: two dormitories with bunks, mattresses, gas cooker, pots, kettles, braai facilities, hot showers and toilets. Ndaba Camp: beds/bunks with mattresses, kitchen with stove, fridge, pots, pans, kettles, braai facilities, showers and toilets. Giraffe Barn: environmental education centre for groups, with bunks, braai facilities, showers and toilets. Camp sites: you need to supply your own tents and equipment; toilets.

This network of trails traverses the farm Elandsfontein, which once formed part of the farm Elandshoek, where the Premier Mine came into operation in 1902. The world's largest diamond, the famous 3,106-carat Cullinan diamond, was found here in 1905.

The vegetation is characterised by sourish, mixed bushveld, and among the 45 common tree species found here are mountain aloe, Transvaal beech, common sugarbush, Transvaal milkplum, Magalies plane, velvet rock alder and mountain silver oak.

Large game species you may encounter include giraffe, kudu, gemsbok, red hartebeest, blesbok and nyala. There is also an abundance of birdlife for birding enthusiasts.

1. Geological Route From the base camp, the trail ascends through grass savanna to the crest of a koppie with an extensive view over the Premier Diamond Mine. The route then traverses the northwestern slopes of the koppie, composed of Magaliesberg quartzite, and descends to Gemsbok Corner, where you can link up with the Ecology Route. After walking down through a saddle, followed by a steep climb to the crest of a hill, you make a sharp descent to the base camp. **3.2 km; 1.5 hours; circular.**

2. Archaeological Route wanders past trees and through grass and open plains in the western section of Elandsfontein. After about 1 km the Giraffe Loop, which links up with the Ecology Route, splits off to the left, and the Archaeological Route continues to the right. A short way on are the remains of a stone-walled Iron Age site, most likely used mainly as a livestock post, rather than a large-scale settlement. After a gentle descent on open plains, the trail ascends gradually to the start. **3.5 km; 2 hours; circular.**

3. Ecology Route follows the Archaeological Route for 1 km and then continues along the Giraffe Loop, passing through grass savanna interspersed with common sugarbush, cabbage and sour plum trees. A short, steep climb to a rocky outcrop is rewarded with splendid views of the surrounding landscape, and the outcrop provides an excellent vantage point from which to look out for giraffe, nyala and kudu. The trail then descends along Gemsbok Loop, passing a clump of common hook thorn, and crosses two marshy areas, the second of which has a bubbling stream after rains. From the junction of the Gemsbok Loop with the Geological Route you follow the latter for 1.7 km back to the base camp. . **5.9 km; 6 hours; circular.**

10. BORAKALALO GAME RESERVE
Jericho

Trails: Self-guided; 5 km; 2.5 hours; out-and-return.

Borakalalo means 'the place where people relax' in Setswana. Situated 90 km to the northwest of Pretoria, the Borakalalo National Park covers 14,000 ha of bushveld, riverine forest and grasslands around the Klipvoor Dam, which forms the focal point of the park. The 800-ha Klipvoor Dam impounds the water of the Moretele (Pienaars) River for over 10 km behind the dam wall. Various freshwater angling species, including kurper (bream) and carp, can be caught, and the dam is one of the finest inland fishing spots in South Africa.

The park has been stocked with over 30 large mammal species, including white rhino, hippo, giraffe, Burchell's zebra and a variety of antelope. Among these are buffalo, roan, tsessebe, red hartebeest, kudu, gemsbok, blue wildebeest, waterbuck, impala and springbok. Also found here are warthog, black-backed jackal, vervet monkey and a variety of other small mammal species.

Birding in Borakalalo is excellent and to date some 350 species have been recorded. The Klipvoor Dam and a nearby seasonal wetland attract a rich diversity of waterbirds, including the elusive African finfoot, greater and lesser flamingoes, black-crowned night and green-backed herons, white-faced whistling duck and various kingfisher species. Also seen in the park are white-throated robin-chat, Kalahari scrub robin, Kurrichane thrush, Meyer's parrot and arrow-marked babbler. Raptors that occur here include Wahlberg's eagle, lanner falcon and African harrier-hawk.

Self-guided Walk Starting at Moretele Camp, this walk wanders through riverine woodland, dry acacia thornveld and thicket along the Moretele River. The river forms a natural boundary between the northern and southern sections of the game reserve below the Klipvoor Dam, which was built in 1969 for mainly irrigation purposes. It is a popular walk, especially with birders, as it offers excellent birding opportunities along the walk. The Ga Dinonyane bird hides overlooking a seasonal wetland attract a variety of waterbirds, including green-backed and purple heron, kingfishers and white-faced duck. **5 km; 2.5 hours; out-and-return.**

11. UITKYK HIKING TRAIL
Hartbeespoort Dam, Magaliesberg

Stretching from Zeerust, eastwards, to Pretoria's eastern suburbs and rising on average 330 m above the surrounding landscape, the Magaliesberg forms a natural boundary between the bushveld to the north and the Highveld to the south.

The cliffs at Skeerpoort, to the southwest of the Hartbeespoort Dam, are an important breeding site for the Cape vulture, which can often be seen soaring over the area. Other bird species to look out for include Verreaux's eagle, short-toed rock-thrush, long-billed pipit and black-faced waxbill.

Laid out on the northern slopes of the Magaliesberg, the trail alternates between open woodlands, forested kloofs and grass-covered mountain slopes. The name Uitkyk means 'lookout' in Afrikaans, and along the routes there are spectacular views of the Magaliesberg and its surroundings.

The trail to the Magaliesberg summit descends from the start to a tunnel underneath the R513 and then continues to a kloof carved between two prominent mountain peaks. From here, trailists ascend the 1,517-m-high eastern peak. Along the way there are views of the winding Crocodile River and, once the summit of the Magaliesberg is reached, hikers are rewarded with stunning views. Looking west, you can see the range extending towards Rustenburg, while to the east the Magaliesberg cableway station is clearly visible. To the south the scenery is dominated by the Hartbeespoort Dam, and the Johannesburg skyline further south, while the vistas to the north extend as far as the Waterberg on clear days. The climb to the summit involves an altitude gain of 337 m.

12. HENNOPS HIKING TRAIL
Hartbeespoort Dam, Magaliesberg

Trails: 2 day walks; 6.1 and 11.3 km; 3 and 5 hours; network from base camp.
Bookings: Cell: 082 825 9205, email: info@hennops.co.za, web: www.hennopstrails.co.za.
Maps: Trail pamphlet with map.
Facilities/Activities: Loerie Camp: rondavels with bunks, mattresses, kitchen with two-plate stove, fridge, pots, pans, kettle, showers and toilets. Hadeda Camp: farmhouse and rondavel with swimming pool and the same facilities as Loerie Camp; braai facilities for day hikers.

This trail network traverses the 1,000-ha farm Skurweberg, 16 km southeast of Hartbeespoort Dam. In addition to spectacular views and the possibility of seeing game on foot, there are also several interesting historical sites here.

1. Zebra Route traverses the game camp in the north of the farm where hikers may spot blesbok and Burchell's zebra. The outward leg winds steadily up the mountain slopes and passes through several clumps of trees. On reaching the summit of a koppie the trail descends back to the start. **6.1 km; 3 hours; network.**

2. Krokodilberg Route initially meanders along the Hennops River and then leads to an overhang where the Boers set up a field hospital during the South African War (1899–1902) to treat their wounded. A short way on you cross the Hennops River by means of a suspension bridge and then come to Hardekraal, where the remains of a stone-walled settlement can be seen. A steady ascent leads to two viewpoints and, after following the contours, the path descends past an old dolomite mine and a lime oven. From here it is an undemanding walk to the Hennops River, which you can cross by means of a pulley-operated cable car to get back to the Loerie and Hadeda camps. **11.3 km; 5 hours; network.**

13. EAGLE COVE HIKING TRAIL
Rustenburg, Magaliesberg

Trails: 3 day walks; 5 to 12 km; 2.5 to 6 hours; circular.
Bookings: Anvie Ventures, tel: (044) 696 6585, email: info@anvieventures.co.za, web: www.anvieventures.co.za.
Maps: Sketch map.
Facilities/Activities: Base camp: two huts with bunks, mattresses, freezer, pots, pans, braai facilities, firewood, hot showers and toilets.
Pertinent information: Vehicles must be left at the parking area, 2 km from the hut. The descent into Hamerkop Kloof is not recommended for those with a fear of heights.

The northern slopes of the Magaliesberg provide the setting for this trail network, situated about 30 km southeast of Rustenburg.

1. Route 1 meanders gently up the slopes of the Magaliesberg, gaining some 100 m in altitude, and then descends along Hamerkop Kloof. **5 km; 2.5 hours; circular.**

2. Route 2 (also known as the Kloof Route) leads past Rotsboom Kloof and, after traversing the slopes above Hamerkop Kloof for a short way, the path comes to a ladder, which takes trailists down into the kloof. From here the trail ascends the kloof and then winds gradually downhill along the outward leg of Route 1. **6 km; 3 hours; circular.**

3. Route 3 follows Route 1 until its split to Hamerkop Kloof. Further along, the path crosses the Hamerkop Stream and then gradually ascends to the crest of the Magaliesberg, where trailists can enjoy stunning views of the mountain range and the surrounding landscape. The trail then descends gently along a stream and loops back to join its outward leg. After retracing your steps for a short way you can either follow the return leg of the Kloof Route or that of Route 1. **12 km; 6 hours; circular; shorter option of 9 km; 4.5 hour; circular.**

14. RUSTENBURG HIKING TRAIL
Kgaswane Mountain Reserve, Rustenburg, Magaliesberg

See no. 15 (p. 269) for walk.

Trails: 2 trails; 19.5 and 25.3 km; 2 days; circular.
Permits: Kgaswane Mountain Reserve, tel: (014) 533 2050/0808, email: kgaswaneadmin@nwpb.org.za, web: www.northwestparks.org.za.
Maps: Colour trail map.
Facilities/Activities: Overnight huts at Explorers', Avon More, Witkruiskrans and Naga camps, with bunks, mattresses, braai facilities, firewood, bucket showers and toilets.

Covering 4,257 ha on the eastern slopes of the Magaliesberg, the vegetation of the Kgaswane Mountain Reserve is a mosaic of grasslands, kloof forests, thornveld and woodland with open savannah. Proteaveld is found on the plateau and the middle slopes of the Waterkloofspruit Basin and contains common sugarbush and honey-scented proteas. Conspicuous among the rocky ridges and cliffs is the Transvaal milkplum. The red-hot poker aloe (*Aloe peglerae*) and a small succulent, elephant's feet (*Frithia pulchra* – its common name referring to

the appearance of its leaf tips), are two Magaliesberg endemics that occur in the reserve.

The reserve is home to 84 mammal species and among the antelope you might encounter are sable, black wildebeest, blesbok, impala, red hartebeest, springbok, kudu, reedbuck and oribi. Carnivores found in the reserve include leopard, brown hyaena, aardwolf, caracal and black-backed jackal, while the primates are represented by baboon, vervet monkey and lesser bushbaby.

With a bird checklist of over 300 species, birding can be rewarding. Among the species you might tick are Meyer's parrot, lilac-breasted roller, crimson-breasted shrike, African paradise flycatcher, arrow-marked babbler and black-headed oriole. Raptors include Cape vulture, Verreaux's eagle, African hawk eagle, jackal buzzard and lanner falcon. Eleven thrush and chat species have been recorded, among them Cape and short-toed rock-thrushes.

1. Baviaanskloof Route can be started at either Explorers' or Avon More camps. Soon after leaving Explorers' Camp on the first day (10.4 km; 5 hours), you follow the trail as it ascends a steep hill and then follows a gently undulating course to the Zebra Plains. Further along, the trail winds past fascinating rocky outcrops, leads down into the Waterkloofspruit Valley and then climbs Langkloof-rug before winding down to the overnight hut.

The second day's hike (9.1 km; 5 hours) begins with an ascent to the Garden of Memory and then continues its upward trend to the Tierkloof Cascades and the spectacular Tierkloof Waterfall, which plunges in several steps into a deep gorge. The pools above the falls are irresistible and a perfect spot for tea or lunch. Further on, the trail winds up Bakenkop and then descends steeply to cross Bobbejaanskloof, shortly before reaching the start.

2. Summit Route can be started at either Witkruiskrans or Naga camps. From Witkruiskrans Camp the first day's trail (11 km; 5 hours) gradually ascends to Bakenkop and then winds down to Tierkloof Pools. From here the trail climbs steadily, gaining some 200 m in altitude before traversing the slopes below Swartwildebeesrug. After this the trail makes its way past interesting quartzite rock formations to reach Naga Camp a short way beyond Civet Rock Arch.

Day two (14.3 km; 7 hours) crosses Secretary Bird Flats and then climbs gradually to the Mushroom Rocks, weathered quartzite rocks resembling giant mushrooms, before reaching a vantage point on the edge of the vertical western cliffs of the Magaliesberg. The trail now leads to the 1,690-m-high Hoogstepunt and after winding past Zebra Dam begins a long, steady descent along the eastern slopes of the Magaliesberg, back to the start.

15. KGASWANE MOUNTAIN RESERVE
Rustenburg, Magaliesberg

See no. 14 (p. 268) for hiking trails.

Trail: 5 km; 2 hours; circular.
Permits: Entrance fee. No permit required.
Maps: Trail booklet and sketch map.
Facilities/Activities: Visitors' Centre; picnic facilities; group camp.

Peglerae Interpretative Trail is named after the red-hot poker aloe (*Aloe peglerae*), which is endemic to the Magaliesberg and Witwatersberg. This aloe is particularly striking, with a stunted appearance, and is especially attractive in July and August when its dull red to pale greenish-yellow flowers brighten the grassveld.

Starting at the Visitors' Centre, the trail winds in a northwesterly direction along the slopes above Waterkloof. A trail booklet provides information about marked points of interest along the way. Among these are the eroded quartzite rocks seen along the trail, trees such as the Transvaal milkplum and the wild apricot, the red-hot poker aloe and a Magaliesberg endemic succulent, elephant's feet (*Frithia pulchra*).

16. PILANESBERG NATIONAL PARK
Sun City

Trails: Guided walks; distances variable, 4 to 6 km; 2 to 3 hours; circular.

Permits: Entrance fee. Guided trails, led by accredited trail guides, can be booked with Mankwe Gametrackers at the Welcome Centre, Sun City Resort, tel: (014) 552 5020, email: info@mankwegametrackers.co.za
Maps: Tourist map of park.
Facilities/Activities: A variety of accommodation options is available here, ranging from upmarket lodges (Bakubung, Kwa Maritane and Tshukudu) to tented safari camps and camp sites; self-drive game-viewing; self-drive Geology Trail; guided game and night drives; balloon safaris; Manyane indigenous 'walk-in' bird aviary; bird- and game-viewing hides; picnic sites.
Pertinent information: Guided walks are conducted for groups of a minimum of 6 people. Children under the age of 12 years are not allowed for safety reasons.

Situated 50 km northeast of Rustenburg, the 58,000-ha Pilanesberg National Park is enclosed by four concentric rings of hills, the roots of an ancient volcano that was active some 1,200 million years ago. The Pilanesberg Complex is one of the three largest alkaline volcanoes in the world (the other two are situated in Greenland and Russia), and has the most clearly defined ring structure. Rising some 300 m above the surrounding bushveld plains, the landscape of the Pilanesberg ranges from impressive mountain peaks and rolling plains to deep wooded valleys and ravines. At the centre of the crater floor is a dam, built by the park authorities.

The varied topography and geology of the area have resulted in a rich diversity of vegetation types. Typical tree species found here include Transvaal beech, common wild pear, wild olive, karee and a variety of acacia species. Of special interest is the Transvaal red balloon tree, which is endemic to Pilanesberg.

In addition to being a sanctuary for the Big Five (elephant, black and white rhino, buffalo, lion and leopard), Pilanesberg is home to numerous other species, as it lies in the transitional zone between the dry Kalahari and the wetter Lowveld vegetation. Among the antelope are kudu, gemsbok, red hartebeest, blue wildebeest, mountain reedbuck, impala and springbok. Other species to be seen include giraffe, hippo, Burchell's zebra, warthog and brown hyaena.

With a bird checklist of over 330 species, birding can be rewarding. There are no fewer than 32 raptor species here, including Cape and white-backed vultures, black-chested snake eagle and lanner falcon. Among the other species you may tick are lilac-breasted roller, black-headed

The hides in the Pilanesberg National Park offer good game-viewing possibilites.

oriole, short-toed rock-thrush, Cape longclaw, crimson-breasted shrike and violet-backed starling. Look out for Kalahari scrub robin and southern pied babbler.

Guided walks enable trailists to explore the park on foot under the guidance of an experienced and knowledgeable guide. In addition to tracking game on foot, trailists also learn more about the trees and the environment through which they walk. The walks are conducted in the morning, when the predators are less active. **4 to 6 km; 2 to 3 hours; circular.**

GREAT KAROO, NAMAQUALAND & KALAHARI

The Great Karoo and Namaqualand are characterised by vast tracts of arid land, wide open spaces and solitude, and the Kalahari is known as a thirstland. Together these regions cover nearly 50 per cent of South Africa's surface and their landscapes range from endless grassy plains and typical Karoo koppies to the imposing granite domes of Namaqualand and the orange dunes and stately camel thorn trees of the Kalahari.

The Great Karoo is bounded in the south by the Great Escarpment and in the north by the Orange River. It extends from the Eastern Cape Midlands, westwards, to the western Escarpment where it gives way to the plains, sandveld and the Namaqualand Klipkoppe. From the Orange River the Kalahari stretches northwards to the furthest reaches of the Northern Cape and into Botswana.

The apparent bleakness of the landscape belies the rich diversity of flora and fauna that have managed to adapt to survive in these seemingly inhospitable surroundings. Another major attraction of the Karoo is its beautiful scenery: vast open plains that melt into the horizon, conical dolerite koppies and table-top mountains.

Some 280 million years ago much of southern Africa lay in a shallow basin, which was filled during various periods by sand, mud, pebbles and boulders from the surrounding highlands. When temperatures increased after an ice age, around 250 million years ago, ferns, early conifers, horsetails, club mosses and large trees such as *Dadoxylon* began to flourish in the Karoo Basin, while dinosaurs roamed the swamps, shallow lakes and floodplains. The reign of the dinosaurs lasted for 50 million years, from 240 to 190 million years ago, when they became extinct, possibly as a result of drastic climate changes.

The Karoo is world renowned for its fossils, especially those of therapsid (mammal-like) reptiles. These relics from the distant past formed when the bodies of the therapsids were entombed in mud and the calcium of their bones replaced by silica from the surrounding sediments. The mud then hardened into rock, which was later subjected to millions of years of erosion, exposing the fossils.

The Karoo's characteristic cone-shaped koppies and table-top mountains were created during the middle-Jurassic period when magma was forced along cracks and fissures in the earth's crust, forming dolerite when it cooled down. The less resistant sedimentary rocks under the protective dolerite caps were then eroded to form the typical Karoo koppies and ridges.

Despite its harsh climate the Karoo is home to an estimated 7,000 plant species, including grasses, succulents, a variety of annuals and a wealth of dwarf shrubs, which are dominant over much of the Karoo. Commonly referred to as Karoo *bossies* (bushes), the shrublands are composed of species with colourful names, such as ankerkaroo (*Pentzia incana*), kapokbos (*Eriocephalus ericoides*), swartganna (*Salsola calluna*), koggelmandervoetkaroo (*Limeum aethiopicum*), perdekaroo (*Rosenia humilis*) and silver Karoo (*Plinthus karooicus*). Other typical trees and shrubs found here include sweet thorn, yellow pomegranate, common spike thorn, cancer bush (*Sutherlandia frutescens*), broom karee and Karoo cross berry (*Grewia robusta*).

Dutch farmers first settled in the Karoo in the 1750s, and soon exterminated the vast herds of game here. Fortunately, game numbers are again increasing in conservation areas and on many farms. Visitors may encounter game while hiking through the Karoo, Doornkloof and Rolfontein nature reserves and the Karoo National Park. Often overlooked, though, is the wide variety of smaller mammals that still occur here naturally. Among these are bat-eared fox, black-backed jackal, caracal, Cape clawless otter, badger, mongoose, hare and a host of nocturnal animals.

These regions, compared with others, have little diversity of bird species. Typical birds found here include Karoo korhaan, Ludwig's and kori bustards, spike-heeled and Karoo larks, tractrac, sickle-winged and Karoo chats, black-eared sparrow-lark, Karoo eremomela and Namaqua warbler.

There are many opportunities to explore on foot, from short day walks to overnight hiking trails. You can enjoy wide open spaces, smell the aromatic Karoo bushes and enjoy extensive views. Early mornings and late afternoons are especially beautiful, as the changing light on the landscape creates a kaleidoscope of colour.

Heading the list of attractions is the Augrabies Falls National Park. The park has as its focal point the Augrabies Falls, said to be one of the world's best examples of a cataract-type waterfall and of the weathering of granite by water.

At Graaff-Reinet titanic forces deep beneath the earth and subsequent erosion combined to create the spectacular Valley of Desolation, with its imposing dolerite pillars. The site falls within the Camdeboo National Park, which nearly encircles the town of Graaff-Reinet. The park offers several day walks.

The Karoo National Park, on the outskirts of Beaufort West, lies in the heart of the Great Karoo. Dominated by the Nuweveld Mountains, the park's landscape ranges from plains to Karoo koppies and sheer dolerite cliffs. Game species that used to roam the Karoo plains in their hundreds of thousands have been reintroduced here and the vegetation is slowly making a recovery.

Namaqualand is renowned for its succulents and its spectacular, colourful annual spring flower display, which can usually be seen from early August to mid-September, but depends entirely on good winter rains and well-spaced follow-up rains. The floral carpets are composed of annuals with names such as gansogies (*Cotula barbata*), sambreeltjies (*Felicia merxmuelleri*), gousblomme (*Osteospermum, Arctotis, Ursinia*), beetle daisies (*Gorteria diffusa* subsp. *diffusa*) and botterblom (*Gazania*).

Conspicuous among the Namaqualand succulents and the broken veld along the Orange River is the quiver tree, which favours the northern slopes of hills and granite outcrops. It is especially eye-catching in July, with its bright yellow flower spikes.

The prolific herds of game encountered by the early travellers through Namaqualand and the explorers searching for the fabulous wealth of the southern African empire of Monomotapa have sadly long since disappeared. Except in the Goegap Nature Reserve, where large mammals have been reintroduced, mammals throughout the two regions are limited to species that have been able to survive mainly because of their small size.

The climate of the three regions is one of extremes. Summer temperatures are excessively high, often exceeding 35 °C in the middle of the season. In winter, temperatures plunge to 5 °C and below, and the high mountain peaks of Sneeuberg north of Graaff-Reinet and the Nuweveld range at Beaufort West are frequently covered by a blanket of snow in the middle of winter.

Namaqualand and the western edge of the Great Karoo fall in the winter rainfall area and get 50 to 300 mm of rain, increasing from north to south and from the coast eastwards. In the Great Karoo rainfall ranges from 50 mm in the northwest to 500 mm in the east, falling mainly in late summer and early autumn, while the Kalahari's varies from 100 mm in the southwest to 450 mm in the northeast. Rainfall is, however, highly variable and annual evaporation often exceeds average rainfall.

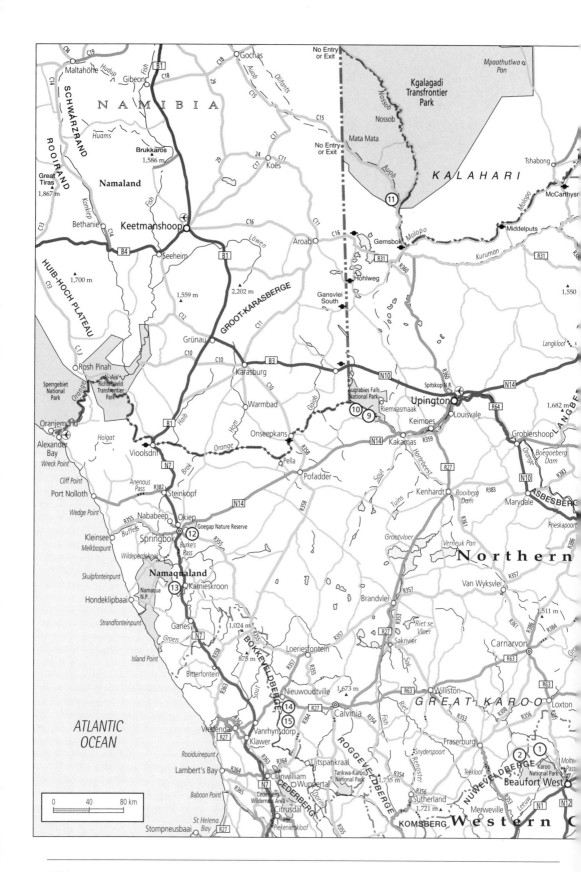

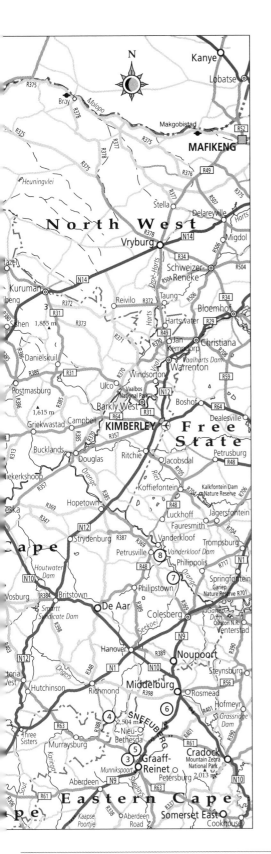

1. KAROO NATIONAL PARK
Beaufort West

Trails: 1 walk; guided walks.
Permits: Conservation fee. Book for guided walks at park reception.
Maps: Full-colour park map.
Facilities/Activities: Rest camp with fully equipped self-catering cottages; camp site with hot showers and toilets; restaurant; shop; swimming pool; self-drive game-viewing; 4x4 trails.

The Karoo National Park was proclaimed in 1979 to conserve a representative part of the Karoo. It covers 88,000 ha of plains, koppies and mountainous terrain, overlooked by the Nuweveld Mountains.

Animals found in the park include Cape mountain zebra (the park has the highest population of this species in the world), eland, kudu, gemsbok, red hartebeest, springbok, mountain reedbuck, grey rhebok, klipspringer, steenbok, common duiker and baboon. Black rhino and a small herd of buffalo have been reintroduced, while a group of eight lions were released in the park in late 2010. The riverine rabbit, South Africa's most endangered mammal, also occurs here. The park is host to a herd of Burchell's zebra that are part of the Quagga Project, a unique experiment to bring back the quagga from extinction through selective breeding with zebras with 'quagga-like' characteristics.

To date more than 200 bird species have been recorded in the park, including Karoo korhaan, Ludwig's bustard, spike-heeled and Cape long-billed larks, Karoo chat, Layard's tit-babbler, Namaqua sandgrouse and ground woodpecker. Some 20 raptors have been recorded, among them booted and martial eagles, peregrine falcon, African harrier-hawk and jackal buzzard. The Nuweberg Escarpment's Verreaux's eagle population is the largest in South Africa and the largest in the world after that found in the Matopo Hills in Zimbabwe.

Other attractions of the park are its typical Karoo landscape of koppies, mountains and wide open plains, and the treasure trove of fossilised reptiles, some of them with clear mammal-like features, entombed in the rocks of the Beaufort Group.

1. Fossil Trail provides a fascinating insight into the geological forces that shaped the Karoo, and several fossil specimens are displayed in glass cases along the trail. Some of the fossils have been partially reconstructed, while others are displayed as they were found. Numbered signs indicate points of interest that are explained in a trail pamphlet. Railway-sleeper seats provided along the trail are suitable for wheelchairs. Although this walk is under an hour, it is a highlight of the park and the main attraction for most visitors. **400 m; 45 minutes; circular.**

2. Guided Walks Following the reintroduction of lion, black rhino and buffalo, the two self-guided trails (Bossie Trail and Pointer Trail) have been closed. Visitors can, however, still explore the park and its fascainating plant life on foot on guided walks (subject to the availability of guards).

2. KAROO ERDVARK TRAILS
Beaufort West

Trails: 13 day walks: 2 to 18.9 km; 1 to 9 hours; network; circular and out-and-return. Hiking trail: 67.7 km; 5 days. A slackpacking option is also available.
Bookings: Marge Vivier, tel: (023) 412 1669, fax: 086 219 3491, email: flip.marge.vivier@gmail.com.
Maps: Colour topographical maps with GPS coordinates.
Facilities/Activities: Boplaas and Middelplaas: self-contained farmhouses. Boplaas: shed for groups. Grootdroom: mountain chalet. Camping sites at Boplaas (hot-water ablutions) and at Rietvlei (bush toilet only). Mountain biking; 4x4 trails; horse-riding.
Pertinent information: Hikers staying at the shed at Boplaas must provide their own bedding and towels. No water at Rietvlei. Amenities at Arendsnes are limited to drinking water and a lean-to. Avoid the summer months when temperatures can reach 40° C. Be prepared for cold weather in winter when snow can blanket the mountains. Carry enough water on walks and trails.

An integrated network of trails make up the Karoo Erdvark Trails on Rooiheuwel, a 13,000-ha sheep and guest farm in the Nuweveld Mountains, about 80 km west of Beaufort West. The Karoo Erdvark Trail was the first trail in the Great Karoo to be accredited as a Green Flag trail. The trail network offers hikers the opportunity to explore the Karoo on foot and to get close-up views of the rich diversity of Karoo plants.

Hikers may spot a variety of small mammals but are unlikely to see the elusive nocturnal erdvark (aardvark), after which the trail has been named.

Birding is excellent, with typical Karoo species, such as Ludwig's bustard, Karoo korhaan, Namaqua sandgrouse and several lark species, as well as Verreaux's eagle and rock kestrel occurring here.

The various trails can be hiked as day walks or combined as overnight hikes, ranging from two to seven days. The terrain alternates between usually dry riverbeds, deep kloofs, rolling hills, plains and mountain plateaus.

Day Walks

The two popular trail heads for day walks are Boplaas and Grootdroom. Hikers using Boplaas as a base have a choice of four day trails, ranging from a 6.2-km route to Piekniekval to a 13.3-km route to Tafelkop and back. The **Tafelkop Trail** (13.3 km; 6 hours), a fairly demanding hike that involves a sustained climb, gains over 550 m in altitude before hikers make their way back to Boplaas past Piekniekval. Six day trails radiate from Grootdroom, ranging from the short **Knoffelfontein Trail** (2 km; 1 hour) to the **Tafelkop Trail** (18.9 km; 8 to 9 hours), with shorter options of 14.4 km (6.5 hours) and 17.4 km (8.5 hours) available. The Tafelkop Trail takes you to a beacon at 1,456 m, where you will be met with breathtaking views of the Koekemoer River Valley to the west and Boplaas to the southeast.

Overnight Trails

Depending on your preference you can put together overnight hikes ranging from two to seven days. Boplaas is a popular start for a five-day hike, taking you to Middelplaas on day one (12.9 km). From Middelplaas the second day's trail (9.8 km) starts with an easy 3.5-km walk across the Karoo plains before making its way up a kloof to a plateau. The overnight stop at Arendsnes is limited to a lean-to shelter and water. Day three (15.4 km), the longest leg of the trail, starts with a steady ascent for the first 3 km to Donkerhoek and, after a short descent, follows the 1,300-m contour on the eastern side of Tierhoekberg. The trail then descends to the Wilderness Camp from where it is a 2.7-km walk to the Rietvlei camp site. The fourth day's hike to Grootdroom (15.3 km) follows a valley carved by the usually dry Koekemoers River. Day five (14.3 km, with a shorter 12.8 km option) is the most demanding leg of the trail. From Grootdroom the trail ascends to the 1,456-m summit of Tafelkop, a typical Karoo koppie, before descending to the valley in which Boplaas is situated.

A shorter, four-day alternative is to hike from Boplaas to Middelplaas and Arendsnes and to follow the trail from Donkerhoek past Donkerhoekfontein to Grootdroom, from where you continue to Boplaas.

3. CAMDEBOO NATIONAL PARK
Graaff-Reinet

Trails: 2 walks; 1.5 to 14 km; 1 to 7 hours; circular and out-and-return.
Permits: Conservation fee. Permits obtainable at the entrance gate, or the Camdeboo National Park headquarters, 4 km out of town on the N9 to Middelburg.
Maps: Colour map of reserve.
Facilities/Activities: Picnic sites; self-drive game-viewing; angling (permit required) and water sports on Nqweba Dam; Camdeboo Environmental Education Centre.

Covering 19,200 ha of typical Karoo plains, koppies and mountains, the Camdeboo National Park almost entirely surrounds the historic town of Graaff-Reinet. The park was established in 1979 to preserve an example of the Karoo eco-system. The acquisition of the land was made possible by a fund-raising campaign spearheaded by the late Dr Anton Rupert of the South African Nature Foundation (now WWF South Africa). The reserve was proclaimed a national park in October 2005 and renamed the Camdeboo National Park.

The focal point of the park is the towering dolerite pillars of the Valley of Desolation, set against a backdrop of Karoo plains. The origin of these rock pillars can be traced back some 180 to 200 million years, when molten magma intruded along cracks and fissures into the overlying sediments of the Karoo Supergroup. As the magma

cooled down and contracted, it solidified into vertical seams of dolerite rock. Over millions of years the softer surrounding Karoo sediments were eroded, exposing the dolerite columns, which rise to heights of 90 to 120 m.

Animals occurring in this section of the reserve include mountain reedbuck, Cape mountain zebra, rock dassie and Smith's red rock rabbit.

1. Crag Lizard Trail starts at the Valley of Desolation parking area and is an extension of a short circuit to two viewpoints overlooking the valley. From here the trail meanders westwards along the cliff edge to reveal spectacular views of the rock pillars and the distant plains far below. On reaching a beacon on the 1,400-m-high westernmost point of the mountain, the trail loops back to the start. Look out for the East Cape crag lizard. **1.5 km; 1 hour; circular.**

2. Eerstefontein Day Walk starts at Spandaukop Gate and offers options of 5, 11 and 14 km. The trail meanders through the southwestern section of the park, dominated by Spandaukop (1,316 m), a good example of a Karoo koppie. Eerstefontein and Agterstefontein are two picnic spots along the trail, offering good opportunities to see springbok, kudu, common duiker and steenbok. **5 km; 2 hours; out-and-return (or 11 km; 5 hours; circular, or 14 km; 7 hours; circular).**

4. GROENVLEI FARM
Graaff-Reinet

Trails: 11 walks; 1 to 8 hours; circular.
Bookings: Johnny Minnaar, cell: 082 876 5069, email: bookkeeping. groenvlei@gmail.com.
Maps: Sketch maps.
Facilities/Activities: Fully equipped self-catering guesthouse; four-bedroomed house; two- and one-bedroomed cottages; cycling.

Situated in the Sneeuberg Mountains, north of Graaff-Reinet, Groenvlei is a working merino stud farm with a guesthouse. In addition to the scenic beauty of the area, Groenvlei has other attractions such as 200-million-year-old fossils, Stone Age sites that were inhabited 150,000 years ago and rock art.

To date 205 bird species have been identified. Birds you may tick include ostrich, Verreaux's and booted eagles, peregrine falcon, Denham's and Ludwig's bustards, Namaqua sandgrouse, Cape rock-thrush and Karoo scrub robin. Eight lark and three pipit species have been recorded, while a variety of water birds are attracted to springs and dams on the farm.

The 11 trails range from the 1-hour-long **Bossie Trail**, with 50 typical Karoo plant species marked along the route, to the 20-km-long **Grootklip Route**. There are relatively easy hikes across flat plains and up gentle kloofs, as well as more challenging ones, such as an ascent of the 2,000-m-high Aasvoëlberg. The trails have been graded according to their degree of difficulty and hikers can choose routes to suit their personal level of fitness.

5. KAROO 3 PEAKS CHALLENGE
Graaff-Reinet

Trails: 3 day routes; 6 to 25 km; 4.5 to 10 hours; guided; out-and-return.
Bookings: Cell: 083 538 2865, email dawid@toerboer.co.za.
Maps: Not required as the trails are guided.
Facilities/Activities: Hikers can overnight at own cost at Toerboer Cottages in Graaff-Reinet before the start of the challenge. Various accommodation options are available in Nieu-Bethesda, where the challenge ends.
Pertinent information: The challenge is physically demanding and should only be attempted by fit hikers. Groups are limited to a maximum of 10 hikers. Participants must drive between starting points with their own vehicles. The Karoo 3 Peaks Challenge is conducted on set departure dates, but exception can be made for group bookings of 6 or more hikers. The trail package includes 2 nights' accommodation, 2 dinners, 2 breakfasts, 1 lunch packet, rum tasting at the Afrikanis Rum Tasting Room in Graaff-Reinet and entrance fees.

The Karoo 3 Peaks Challenge offers hikers an opportunity to ascend three well-known peaks in the Sneeuberg mountain range to the north, east and west of Graaff-Reinet, where this unique experience starts. Situated in the horseshoe bend of the Sunday's River, Graaff-Reinet is renowned for its many well-preserved historical buildings and the spectacular Valley of Desolation. The main attraction of the settlement of Nieu-Bethesda is the Owl House where artist Helen Martins lived until her death in 1976.

The three peaks are hiked on three consecutive days and hikers are rewarded with spectacular views of the Karoo landscape. The first challenge, Toorberg (2,106 m), is the easiest, an 8-km hike with an altitude gain of 773 m. The second day's hike of 25 km takes hikers to the summit of Nardouwsberg (2,420 m), an altitude gain of 1,266 m. From the summit, hikers will enjoy far-reaching vistas of the Tandjiesberg, which owes its Afrikaans name to the sharply toothed appearance of the peaks, as well as the Plains of the Camdeboo. These plains, south of Graaff-Reinet, were immortalized in the classic book by the botanist and writer Eve Palmer. Hikers then depart for Nieu-Bethesda after conquering Nardouwsberg. Although the third day's hike is only 6 km, the ascent of Compassberg (2,502 m) involves an elevation gain of 936 m. It is not only the highest peak in the Karoo, but also the second highest peak in the Eastern Cape. It has been suggested that the peak was named by R. J. Gordon in 1778 because streams could be seen flowing in all directions from its summit.

6. TRANSKAROO ADVENTURES
Noupoort

Trails: 21 or 40 km; 2 or 3 days; circular. Day walk; 10 km; 5 hours; circular.

This trail traverses a 10,500-ha farm in the Upper Karoo and affords hikers an opportunity to discover the scenic beauty and rich diversity of Karoo plants. Among the other attractions are imposing rock formations and rock paintings.

Trees you may find along the course of the trail include wild peach and dogwood, as well as a variety of succulents and Karoo shrub vegetation. Typical species include ghombos, bloublommetjie, kriedoring, jakkalsbos, waterharpuis and basterkaree.

Antelope you may see include springbok, grey rhebok, mountain reedbuck and steenbok. The predators are well represented by a number of species, among which are Cape and bat-eared foxes, caracal (depicted on the trail emblem), African wild cat and black-backed jackal. Baboon, vervet monkey, aardwolf, ground squirrel and suricate also occur.

Birds to keep an eye out for include Verreaux's and martial eagles, blue korhaan, ground woodpecker, Acacia pied barbet, Cape clapper lark, ant-eating chat, Karoo prinia and bokmakierie.

1. Day Walk This is a pleasant walk for visitors who do not have the time or energy to do an overnight trail. From Wilgerfontein the outward leg ascends along a jeep track and then heads in a northeasterly direction to join the Rooivoetpad, which is hiked on the third day of the three-day trail. **10 km; 5 hours; circular.**

2. Two-day Trail The first day's hike (12 km; 6 hours) heads along a jeep track and then gradually ascends Visserskloof, past dolerite pillars, before reaching an inviting rock pool. On leaving the kloof the trail traverses the Stone Desert and then reaches a viewpoint with wonderful vistas of

Kompasberg, 30 km to the south. From here you follow a ridge to Uitsig Camp. On day two (9 km; 4 hours) this hike joins up with the three-day trail route for a short while and then heads in a northeasterly direction to join the Rooivoetpad, which takes you back to the base camp. **21 km; 2 days; circular.**

3. Three-day Trail This option follows the same route to Uitsig Camp as the two-day trail. On the second day (19 km; 9 hours) the trail leads past oxwagon grooves worn into the sandstone rock and then ascends Beacon Hill, with its 360-degree views. The trail then descends steadily to a windmill and, after passing farm ruins and large pepper trees at Veeplaas, reaches Kanferkloof. The poplar grove is an ideal lunch stop, and a swimming hole on the last stretch of the hike to Wilgerfontein is especially welcome on a hot day. Day three's hike (9 km; 4 hours) passes rock paintings and then follows the Rooivoetpad through the Lichen Paradise, with its rich diversity of lichens. After descending along a kloof the trail climbs to a ridge overlooking Wilgerfontein, where the trail ends. **40 km; 3 days; circular.**

7. BOKMAKIERIE HIKING TRAIL
Doornkloof Nature Reserve, Colesberg

Covering 10,000 ha, the Doornkloof Nature Reserve has as its focal points the Seekoei River, which flows for 10 km through the reserve to its confluence with the Orange River and the Vanderkloof Dam.

The landscape is dominated by dolerite outcrops, interspersed with wooded kloofs and grassy plains, sheer cliffs and the shoreline of the Vanderkloof Dam. The reserve is situated in the transitional zone between Karoo and grassland vegetation.

Game animals include buffalo, gemsbok, kudu, eland, red hartebeest, mountain reedbuck, steenbok and common duiker. Also found here are brown hyaena, black-backed jackal, caracal, warthog, baboon and vervet monkey.

Considering the arid surroundings, the birdlife is rich and includes numerous waterbirds, raptors such as Verreaux's and African fish eagle and a variety of Karoo terrestrial birds. Among these are Karoo, large-billed and Cape clapper larks, tractrac and Karoo chats, Karoo korhaan and Ludwig's bustard.

The trail will appeal to those with a sense of adventure. Fortunately, it is difficult to get lost, because of the nature of the terrain – all the kloofs drain into the Vanderkloof Dam, which can be seen from part of the trail. This hike also offers the opportunity to view game on foot; remember, though, that you may encounter potentially dangerous species like buffalo.

This hike meanders along densely wooded kloofs and around and up koppies, with great views of the dam. On the first night you sleep in a hut with mattresses, a hot shower and toilets. The second overnight stop is at the ruins of an old stone kraal, with no facilities whatsoever. Fill up your water bottles before the overnight stop, as the next water point is 2 km along the third day's route.

8. ROLFONTEIN NATURE RESERVE
Petrusville

Trails: 4 km; 2 hours; circular. Guided morning walks for organised groups (these must be arranged in advance). Trailists are free to blaze their own trails in the reserve.
Permits: The Manager, Rolfontein Nature Reserve, P O Box 23, Vanderkloof 8771, tel: (053) 664 0900.
Maps: Sketch map of reserve.

Facilities/Activities: Two hikers' huts with basic facilities; tent camp for educational groups; picnic sites; night drives for groups; freshwater angling; watersports.

Covering 6,250 ha, Rolfontein Nature Reserve lies on the banks of the Vanderkloof Dam in the Orange River. The landscape is characterised by grassy plains, interspersed with many dolerite hills.

The vegetation alternates between False Upper Karoo Veld and Orange River Broken Veld. To date, more than 40 grass species have been identified, while a rich diversity of typical Karoo bushes also occurs here. Tree species in the densely wooded kloofs include wild olive, sweet thorn and karee, while cabbage trees, black thorn and wild camphor bush dominate the rocky hills and ridges.

Mammals roaming the reserve include white rhino, Burchell's zebra and warthog. Among the many antelope species to be seen are eland, gemsbok, black wildebeest, red hartebeest, mountain reedbuck, springbok and impala.

Waterbird species seen at the dam include African fish eagle, South African shelduck, yellow-billed duck and spur-winged goose. The koppies and plains are home to several Karoo bird species.

Pied Barbet Trail follows an easy route to several marked points of interest that are explained in a trail pamphlet, and some trees along the trail have also been labelled. **4 km; 2 hours; circular.**

9. KLIPSPRINGER HIKING TRAIL
Augrabies Falls National Park, Kakamas

Trail: 39.5 km; 3 days; circular.
Permits: SANParks, P O Box 787, Pretoria 0001, tel: (012) 428 9111, fax: (012) 343 0905, email: reservations@ sanparks.org.
Maps: Sketch map.
Facilities/Activities: Two overnight huts with bunks, mattresses, drinking

The spectacular Augrabies Falls, the Orange River Gorge and the weathered gneiss rock outcrops of the plains to the south of the river provide the setting for the three-day Klipspringer Hiking Trail.

The focal point of the park is the Main Falls, where the Orange River plunges 56 m into a pool. There are several secondary falls, among them the Bridal Veil Falls. The noise created by the falls prompted the early Khoikhoi inhabitants of the area to name them *Aukoerebis*, meaning 'place of the great noise'.

The Augrabies Falls are one of the world's best examples of weathering of granite by water. Originally the falls were at the lower end of the gorge but over the millennia have gradually eroded their way to the present position. Although the erosion is continuing, it has been slowed down by the prevailing relatively drier climatic period.

Downstream of the Main Falls, the Orange River flows through a narrow 18-km-long gorge with an average depth of 240 m. The river's average volume is 45 m^3 a second, but during the 1988 floods this increased to an incredible 7,800 m^3 a second.

The vegetation is characterised by Orange River Broken Veld, consisting of common species such as camel thorn, sheperd's tree, blue neat's foot, Namaqua porkbush, stink bush, honey bush and jacket plum. Among the other species here are sweet thorn, buffalo-thorn, white karee, ebony tree and wild tamarisk. The quiver tree is especially abundant in the vicinity of the Swartrante.

Animals you may see along the trail include klipspringer, springbok, gemsbok, rock dassie and baboon. Aardwolf and leopard are also found here, but owing to their retiring and nocturnal habits they are seldom seen.

To date some 195 bird species have been recorded here. Among these are Verreaux's eagle, African fish eagle, rosy-faced lovebird, Ludwig's bustard, Acacia pied barbet, dusky sunbird and black-chested prinia. The broken veld is the habitat of species such as sabota, Karoo long-billed and spike-heeled larks, as well as grey-backed cisticola. Also represented are the chats, including tractrac, Karoo and ant-eating chats.

The first day's hike (14 km; 6 hours) stays fairly close to the edge of the Orange River Gorge as it makes its way to Arrow Point, from where there are magnificent views over the gorge and the Twin Falls. It then meanders through pink gneiss formations, with the dome-shaped Moon Rock dominating the scenery to the south. After passing through four fairly deep river valleys you reach the Ararat Viewpoint and once again are rewarded with awesome views of the gorge. About 30 minutes on you will come to Oranjekom, a picnic site on the edge of the gorge; from here it is a short walk to the Fish Eagle Hut (Visarendhut) at the northern edge of the Swartrante.

The second day's hike (13.5 km; 6 hours) descends to the Orange River, which you follow downstream for about 7 km (2.5 to 4 hours), past Echo Corner to Arendkrans. The rocky terrain along the river later gives way to stretches of sand, making the going more difficult. At Arendkrans the trail leaves the river to wander down Diepkloof, a dry river course with smooth rock banks. The trail then swings east, following a drainage line for about 30 minutes before heading south along another drainage line that leads you to the Mountain Hut (Berghut), located among a jumble of rocks.

On day three (12 km; 5 hours) the trail steadily ascends the Swartrante's slopes and, after winding down the eastern slopes, crosses a grassy plain dotted with quiver trees. The trail then joins the main tourist road, which takes you to the Moon Rock, a large dome-shaped outcrop that is an excellent example of exfoliation (a weathering process whereby layers of rock flake off). From its summit there are 360-degree views of the park surroundings. The last 3 km of the trail passes mainly through sandy veld.

10. AUGRABIES FALLS NATIONAL PARK
Kakamas

See no. 9 (p. 281) for hiking trail.

Trail: 5 km; 3 hours; circular.
Permits: Conservation fee.
Maps: Map with information about places of interest along the trail available at camp reception.
Facilities/Activities: Rest camp with fully equipped self-catering cottages and bungalows; camp sites with communal kitchen and ablutions; swimming pools; picnic sites; restaurant; bar; shop; night drives; self-drive game-viewing; 4x4 trails; Gariep 3-in-1 Adventure (combination of hiking, canoeing and mountain biking).

Dassie Nature Trail From the rest camp the trail meanders along the Orange River Gorge to Arrow Point with its awe-inspiring views. You continue to the Potholes, which have been gouged into the rock by pebbles and rocks swirled around by water. The trail then makes its way to a large, weathered dome-shaped outcrop called Moon Rock. The flaking layers of rock on its surface have been created by an erosion process known as exfoliation. Along the way you might spot the rock dassie, after which the trail has been named, and klipspringer, as well as a variety of birds. From Moon Rock the trail doubles back to the rest camp. **5 km; 3 hours; circular.**

11. !XERRY WILDERNESS TRAIL
Kgalagadi Transfrontier Park

Trail: Morning and afternoon walks; no set distances.
Permits: Tel: (054) 561 2050, fax: (054) 561 2005.
Maps: General park map.
Facilities/Activities: Rustic base camp with a boma, long-drop toilet, braai and food preparation area, and bush shower. Chalets, family cottages and camp sites are available at Nossob Camp. Accommodation is also available at Mata Mata and Twee Rivieren.
Pertinent information: Trails run from 1 April to 31 October, departing from Nossob Camp at 11:30 on Wednesdays and returning at 12:00 on Fridays. Groups are limited to a minimum of 3 and a maximum of 8 people. The minimum age is 16 years. Hikers must provide their own food, water, tents, sleeping bags, daypack and braai wood, and should pack as lightly as possible.

The Kgalagadi Transfrontier Park provides the setting for this truly unique wilderness trail. The cross-border park was created in May 2000 when South Africa's Kalahari Gemsbok Park and the adjacent Gemsbok National Park in Botswana were amalgamated to create Africa's first transfrontier park.

The trail owes its name to the San name for the steenbok. Trailists meet at Nossob Camp from where they are transported to a rustic camp that will serve as the base for morning and afternoon walks under the guidance of an armed trail guide.

The trail gives hikers the opportunity to explore the Kalahari and to experience the solitude and wide open spaces of this fascinating tract of land. While there is always the anticipation of perhaps seeing a black-maned Kalahari lion, a cheetah, or herds of gemsbok, springbok or blue wildebeest, there are many other species such as suricate, ground squirrel, bat-eared fox and even brown hyaena to be seen. The Kalahari is also one of the best places to see the honey badger, which covers vast distances in search of food.

Trailists will also be able to enjoy birding. Kori bustard (the largest flying bird in the world), ostrich, secretarybird, sociable weaver, northern black and red-crested korhaan and several lark species are among the more than 200 bird species that have been recorded to date. The park is also renowned for its excellent viewing of raptors: bateleur, red-necked falcon, lappet-faced and white-backed vultures and pygmy falcon are some of the species you might spot.

The trail is, like other wilderness trails, not only about seeing game on foot, but understanding the complexities of nature and gaining new insights into the behaviour of animals.

12. GOEGAP NATURE RESERVE
Springbok

Trails: 3 walks; 2 to 3 hours; circular.
Permits: Entrance fee. No permit required.
Maps: Reserve map.
Facilities/Activities: Picnic sites; information centre; mountain biking; horse-riding (you need to bring your own horse); 17-km self-drive route; guided tours during flower season.

Dominated by the 1,342-m-high Carolusberg, the Goegap Nature Reserve covers 15,000 ha of sandy plains and granite hills, which are referred to locally as the Namaqualand Klipkoppe. Centred on the 4,600-ha Hester Malan Wildflower Garden (established in 1960), the reserve was enlarged in 1990 when the adjoining farm, Goegap, was acquired. The Khoikhoi name *goegap* means 'waterhole'.

Some 581 plant species have been recorded in the reserve, which has a spectacular seasonal display of spring flowers. Among these are a profusion of daisies (*Gorteria*), gousblomme (*Arctotis*, *Osteospermum*, *Ursinia*), gazanias and a diversity of Aizoaceae vygies that create a blaze of dense colour, usually from early August to mid-September. The world-renowned, magificent spring flower displays of Namaqualand are seen at their best between 11:00 and 16:00 on windless, sunny days and with the sun behind your back.

Animals found in the reserve include Hartmann's mountain zebra, springbok, gemsbok, klipspringer, steenbok and baboon. Among the reserve's 94 bird species are ostrich, Verreaux's eagle, Karoo korhaan, Karoo thrush, ground woodpecker and Acacia pied barbet.

Ian Myers Nature Walks This network of trails in the southwestern corner of the reserve is named after a keen naturalist, Ian Myers, who led groups of visitors in Namaqualand for 30 years. It consists of two loops, with a shorter option, and allows trailists to explore the fascinating Namaqualand Klipkoppe on foot. In addition to the flora and birds, there is also a wealth of smaller creatures to be seen, such as lizards and tortoises. **4 to 7 km; 2 to 3 hours; circular.**

13. NAMAQUA NATIONAL PARK
Kamieskroon and Namaqualand coast

Trails: 3; 1 to 3 hours; circular and open-ended.
Permits: Conservation fee. No permits for walks required.
Maps: Skilpad and Korhaan trail maps available at Skilpad office.
Facilities/Activities: Chalets, picnic sites and ablutions in Skilpad section; camp sites with basic facilities in Groenrivier section, accessible by 4x4 only; Caracal 4x4 Eco-Route; mountain biking.

The historic core of the Namaqua National Park was acquired when the South African Nature Foundation (now WWF–SA) bought a 930-ha portion of the farm Skilpad and established the Skilpad Wildflower Reserve in 1988 to protect the unique flora of Namaqualand. Additional land acquisitions and the incorporation of the contractual coastal area between the Groen and Spoeg rivers increased the park's size to some 150,000 ha since its proclamation in June 2002.

1. Skilpad Trail is popular during the flower season, when the landscape is transformed into a mass display of orange daisies. The trail starts and ends at the Skilpad office. The carpet of flowers at Skilpad grows on abandoned wheat fields which are dominated by a single species, the glossy-eyed parachute daisy (*Ursinia cakilefolia*). **5 km; 2 hours; circular.**

2. Korhaan Trail is named after the korhaan, of which two species occur in the area, the Karoo korhaan and the southern black korhaan. From the Skilpad office, the trail meanders in a southeasterly direction past an old predator trap and the graveyard of the Van Wyk family who farmed in the area in the late 1800s. The vegetation is varied, with trees, shrubs, perennial plants, geophytes and a great diversity of spring flowers. **3 km; 1 hour; circular.**

3. Heaviside Trail starts at the Abjoel viewing deck,

about 15km north of Groen River office, where a boardwalk down a dune leads to the coast. The trail follows the rocky coastline for about 2 km and then continues along a long white beach. It is named after the Heaviside's dolphin, which is endemic to the west coast of southern Africa. Humpback whales can be seen off the coast between June and November. The African black oystercatcher, which favours rocky areas, is among the variety of seabirds to be seen. Plan your walk to coincide with low tide so that you can explore the rock pools. It is also easier to walk on the firm sand at low tide. As this is a one-way trail, you can either make arrangement to be picked up at the end of the trail or retrace your tracks. **6 km; 3 hours; open-ended.**

14. OORLOGSKLOOF NATURE RESERVE
Nieuwoudtville

Trails: 4 trails; 15.5 to 52.3 km; 8 hours to 7 days; circular.
Permits: Oorlogskloof Nature Reserve, P O Box 142, Nieuwoudtville 8180, tel: (027) 218 1159 – call between 08:00 and 09:00 on weekdays, email: oorlogskloof@gmail.com.
Maps: Colour trail map.
Facilities/Activities: Accommodation throughout the reserve ranges from caves, stone kraals and clearings under trees to basic camps with tents and mattresses. Basic camps are available on both overnight routes. Groot Tuin: thatched hut with braai facilities, toilet for hikers, picnic sites and parking.
Pertinent information: Distances may be short, but the rugged terrain is physically very demanding.

The Oorlogskloof Nature Reserve covers 4,776 ha of wilderness in the Bokkeveld Mountains, south of Nieuwoudtville. A focal point of this tract of wild land is the Oorlogskloof River, flowing through a spectacular 500-m-wide and up to 200-m-deep gorge, which forms the reserve's eastern boundary.

The name Oorlogskloof (which means war gorge) recalls the violent clashes when the Dutch colonists fought the Khoikhoi and San here in the 1700s. Reminders of the early inhabitants of the area include rock paintings and ruins of structures built either by the Khoikhoi and San or farmers who settled in the area during the Great Depression (1929–34).

Since the reserve lies in the transition zone of fynbos, mountain renosterveld and Karoo flora, an interesting variety of plants occurs here. Among the proteas to be seen are Clanwilliam, laurel, wagon tree and real sugarbushes, as well as other representatives of the protea family. The reserve is home to a rich diversity of geophytes, while the sprawling mitre aloe (*Aloe mitriformis*) and the botterboom (*Tylecodon paniculatus*) are among the conspicuous succulents. Of special interest is a reddish clivia, which was discovered only recently and appropriately named *Clivia mirabilis* (*mirabilis* being Latin for 'wonderful' or 'extraordinary').

Antelope you may see are common duiker, klipspringer, steenbok, grysbok and grey rhebok. Leopard occur in the area, and the smaller predators are represented by caracal, aardwolf, African wild and small-spotted cats. Bat-eared and Cape foxes, black-backed jackal, Cape clawless otter, baboon and rock dassie also occur here.

Among the nearly 100 bird species recorded in the reserve to date are Verreaux's and booted eagles, Cape robin-chat, southern boubou, bokmakierie, Cape sugarbird and malachite, orange-breasted and southern double-collared sunbirds. Also to be seen are speckled, African olive and rameron pigeons, after which the two overnight trails are named. A variety of waterbirds are attracted to the Oorlogskloof River.

Adding to the allure of the reserve is the dramatic scenery of the Oorlogskloof River Gorge, with its sheer cliffs and the spectacular valley carved by the Rietvlei River. There are also fascinating sandstone formations, rock arches, rock tunnels and stunning views to be enjoyed.

1. Leopard Trap Day Hike winds from Groot Tuin down to Saaikloof and, after worming its way through a tunnel and up a chimney, where there is a ladder to assist hikers, it emerges onto the plateau. A short way on, you pass an old stone leopard trap, and the trail then traverses easy terrain above the valley created by the Rietvlei River. Further along it ascends steeply to a viewpoint on the Escarpment edge, with extensive views of the Knersvlakte. From here the trail descends steadily to Saaikloof and then climbs back to the plateau, past a cave that has been partly enclosed with a stone wall. After a 15-minute walk along the plateau edge the trail links up with the outward route you took at the start, along which you backtrack for 1.3 km to Groot Tuin. **15.5 km; 8 hours; circular.**

2. Rietvlei Day Hike From Groot Tuin the trail follows the Oorlogskloof River to Brakwater, where you join a jeep track that leads to the Kareebos turn-off, where you turn right. The trail then follows the magnificent valley through which the Rietvlei River runs, to take the Kleinheideveldvoetpad and climb sharply up a kloof to the Escarpment edge and the Knersvlakte Viewpoint. From here the trail follows the same route as the Leopard Trap Day Hike back to Groot Tuin. **17.9 km; 9 hours; circular.**

3. Rock Pigeon Route Although the short distances on the first two days might suggest that they can both be hiked in one day, the demanding terrain makes this inadvisable.

The first day's hike (4 km; 2 hours) descends into Saaikloof and, after climbing out, follows the kloof edge before descending to Brakwater Camp.

On day two (8.5 km; 6 hours) you follow a jeep track across the Oorlogskloof River, and the trail then ascends to the base of the cliffs. Further on you come to a ladder and rope to help you up to the plateau, which you traverse for a short while before descending steeply to the Oorlogskloof River. You follow the river for a few kilometres before once again climbing to the base of the cliffs. After passing through a long tunnel behind the Driefontein Waterfall, you join the outward leg of the third day's hike. A last steep uphill section leads to Driefontein, on the plateau above the Oorlogskloof River Gorge.

The third day's hike (12 km; 7 hours) descends steeply to the Oorlogskloof River, which is easily crossed if it is not in flood, and Kameel se Gat Camp. From here the trail climbs out of the gorge to the base of the cliffs, where two ropes in a rock chimney assist hikers on the ascent to the plateau.

Here the Rameron Pigeon Route splits off to the right. Further along, the trail passes through impressive stands of proteas and then skirts the edge of Saaikloof before swinging north to reach the turn-off to Suikerbosfontein Camp. About 1 km on, the trail gently descends and makes its way down a valley to Doltuin Camp.

On day 4 (17 km; 8 hours) the trail wanders to the head of the Doltuin Valley and, about 3.5 km from the start, passes through the first of the 10 rock arches you will encounter on the day's hike. The trail follows the edge of the plateau, past interesting sandstone sculptures, and, about 6 km after setting off, hikers are forced to crawl through a narrow passage. Still further on a signboard indicates a 2.6-km detour to the highest point of the trail, the 915-m-high Arrie se Punt, from where the Gifberg and Vanrhynsdorp can be seen on a clear day. From the start of the detour, the trail descends to Kouekloof and then returns to the plateau edge, which offers wonderful views of the plains some 600 m below. At Waboombult the trail passes through two caves and, after winding around Pramkoppie, descends steeply to the Rietvlei River and Pramkoppie Camp.

On day 5 (10.7 km; 6 hours) you initially walk along a jeep track, but after 10 minutes link up with the Kleinheideveldvoetpad and ascend a steep forested kloof to the top of the plateau and the Knersvlakte Viewpoint. For the next few kilometres the trail traverses the plateau, with the Rietvlei River Valley constantly in view, before swinging away to Spelonkkop, where you pass an old stone leopard trap. A short way on is a ladder to assist hikers in the climb down a rock chimney, and the trail then winds around and past a jumble of enormous boulders before reaching the junction with the first day's hike. Turn left here and retrace your tracks of the first day for 3.6 km, back to Groot Tuin. **52.2 km; 5 days; circular.**

4. Rameron Pigeon Route This is a circular route, totalling 52.3 km, and can be done as a four-, five-, six- or seven-day hike. The same route is followed irrespective of the number of days over which the trail is hiked, but for the four-, five- or six-day options correspondingly longer distances are covered each day to cover the whole route in time. The seven-day option is described below.

The first day's hike (5.9 km; 3 hours) follows the Rock Pigeon Route to Brakwater Camp, then continues along a jeep track to the Kareebos Camp turn-off. The camp, on the banks of Oorlogskloof River, is named after the karee tree, common to the area.

The second day's hike (7.9 km; 7 hours) follows the western bank of the Oorlogskloof River, then joins up with day two of the Rock Pigeon Route, which you follow to the turn-off for Kameel se Gat (meaning 'Kameel's hollow'), named for a farmer who lived here in the late 1800s and early 1900s.

On day three (4.6 km; 3 hours) the trail takes the Rock Pigeon Route (day two of the Rock Pigeon Route if you are hiking the four-day option of the Rameron Pigeon Route, or day three if you are hiking the five-, six- or seven-day option) for the first kilometre, making a steep ascent to the base of the cliffs and the turn-off to the Rameron Pigeon Route. You reach a large cave after crawling through narrow cracks in the cliffs of the Oorlogkloof River Gorge, and the route then follows another gorge to a turn-off to rock paintings. Climbing gradually, the trail reaches a crevice, where there is a rope to assist hikers in clambering down, and a short way on you reach Suikerbosfontein.

The fourth day's hike (6.4 km; 3 hours) descends Dwarskloof and then gradually climbs to Draaikraal, from where the route returns to the river. After crossing the river a steady ascent leads to the plateau, where rock paintings and an old stone used for grinding wheat serve as reminders of Oorlogskloof's early inhabitants. Of interest near Swartkliphuis Camp are a caracal trap and another rock painting site.

Day 5 (8.1 km; 4 hours) meanders across the plateau to the Donkiestasie (donkey station), named after the pack donkeys that were kept here during the Great Depression (1929–34) when the farmers used them to carry the rooibos tea collected in the mountains. Further on, you follow the cliffs above Doltuin Valley and, after climbing down a ladder, continue to Ghelling se Tenk and two caves with rock paintings. En route to Bo-kloof Camp you will pass another rock painting site.

On day 6 (7.4 km; 4 hours) the trail ascends gently, passing two rock painting sites, as it climbs to the head of Kouekloof and then descends to a viewsite overlooking the Knersvlakte, Pramkoppie Camp and the De Vondeling Valley. The trail then winds along the cliffs above the gorge carved by the Rietvlei River. Shortly before Olienhoutbos Camp, there is a ladder to help you climb through a hole in a rock.

The final day's hike (12 km; 6 hours) follows a jeep track to the Groot Tuin turn-off. From here you follow the return leg of the Rietvlei Day Hike to the Knersvlakte viewpoint with its expansive views of the plains below. The trail then follows the upper reaches of Saaikloof back to the start.

15. PAPKUILSFONTEIN TRAIL
Nieuwoudtville

Trail: 12 km; 6 hours; circular.
Permits: Mr & Mrs W van Wyk, P O Box 46, Nieuwoudtville 8180, tel. and fax: (027) 218 1246, email: info@papkuilsfontein.com
Maps: Sketch map.
Facilities/Activities: De Hoop and Gert Boom guest cottages: sleep 4 and 6 people. Fully equipped, or you may have breakfast and dinner at the main house.

The trail traverses the farm Papkuilsfontein, which borders on the Oorlogskloof Nature Reserve.

The vegetation ranges from fynbos and mountain renosterveld to succulent Karoo flora. A diversity of geophytes (plants with bulbs) also occurs in the area. Klipspringer, common duiker, steenbok, baboon, rock dassie and the elusive Cape clawless otter are among the mammals to be seen. Some 145 bird species have been recorded at Papkuilsfontein to date. Keep an eye out for the Cape sugarbird and sunbirds in the fynbos. Raptors include Verreaux's and martial eagles, rock kestrel and black harrier.

Starting at the historic De Hoop Cottage, the trail makes its way through interesting sandstone rock formations to a 90-m-high waterfall on the De Hoop River, a tributary of the Oorlogskloof River. From here the trail winds in a northwesterly direction to the boundary with the Oorlogskloof Nature Reserve, and then loops back to the start.

The Klipspringer Trail starts at the awe-inspiring Augrabies Falls.

PERSONAL TRAIL RECORD

This section is for you to record the hikes you have been on and the noteworthy birds, animals and sights you encountered along the way.

NAME OF HIKING TRAIL: _____

_____

BIRDS SEEN: _____

_____

_____

ANIMALS ENCOUNTERED: _____

_____

_____

HIGHLIGHTS OF THE TRAIL: _____

_____

_____

_____

_____

_____

PROBLEMS ALONG THE WAY: _____

_____

_____

_____

_____

_____

ADDITIONAL NOTES: _____

_____

_____

_____

_____

_____

NAME OF HIKING TRAIL:

BIRDS SEEN:

ANIMALS ENCOUNTERED:

HIGHLIGHTS OF THE TRAIL:

PROBLEMS ALONG THE WAY:

ADDITIONAL NOTES:

NAME OF HIKING TRAIL: _____

BIRDS SEEN: _____
_____
_____

ANIMALS ENCOUNTERED: _____
_____
_____

HIGHLIGHTS OF THE TRAIL: _____
_____
_____
_____
_____
_____
_____
_____

PROBLEMS ALONG THE WAY: _____
_____
_____
_____
_____

ADDITIONAL NOTES: _____
_____
_____
_____
_____

NAME OF HIKING TRAIL: _____

_____

BIRDS SEEN: _____

_____

_____

ANIMALS ENCOUNTERED: _____

_____

_____

HIGHLIGHTS OF THE TRAIL: _____

_____

_____

_____

_____

_____

_____

PROBLEMS ALONG THE WAY: _____

_____

_____

_____

_____

ADDITIONAL NOTES: _____

_____

_____

_____

_____

_____

GLOSSARY

ENVIRONMENTAL AND GEOLOGICAL TERMS

Basalt – a fine-grained igneous rock

Bushveld – vegetation typical of the northeast of North West, northern Mpumalanga and Limpopo

Carnivore – flesh-eating animals; can be predators or scavengers

Dolerite – a coarse-grained, light-coloured rock of volcanic origin occurring in dykes and sills and containing quartz and feldspar (see below)

Drift – a ford; usually natural, but could be artificial

Dyke – a vertical or steeply inclined wall-like sheet of dolerite that is only exposed during subsequent erosion

Endemic – a plant or animal that is restricted to a particular area

Estuary – a river mouth where fresh and sea water mix

Fault – a fracture along which the rocks on one side have been displaced relative to those opposite

Feldspar – a white or pink crystalline mineral found in rocks

Fynbos – the richly varied fine-leaved bush vegetation of the southwestern Cape, which is characterised by ericas, proteas, reeds and rushes

Gneiss – white-and-black-banded rock containing the same minerals as granite, which have undergone a metamorphosis by heat and pressure

Granite – a common, hard and coarse-grained igneous rock, consisting mainly of quartz and feldspar; it is exposed when the overlying rocks are worn away, and its colour ranges from pink to grey, according to the colour of the feldspar

Highveld – the high-lying area of South Africa, half of which lies above 1,600 m and is largely characterised by treeless grassveld

Igneous rock – formed from molten material, either on the earth's surface from lava becoming volcanic rocks, or underground magma forming plutonic rocks

Indigenous – occurring naturally in a particular area, but not necessarily restricted to that area.

Lagoon – an area of water partly or completely separated from the sea by a sand spit or sand bar

Lava – molten material forced to the surface by volcanic eruptions and cooling to form basalt

Magma – molten material that does not reach the earth's surface during a volcanic eruption, but is sometimes subsequently exposed through erosion

Metamorphic rocks – igneous or sedimentary rock that have undergone a metamorphosis because of temperature, pressure and chemical reactions

Nocturnal – active mainly by night

Palaearctic migrant – birds that migrate seasonally from the northern to the southern hemispheres

Predator – an animal that kills and feeds on other animals

Quartzite – a sedimentary, metamorphic rock formed from silica and sandstone

Raptor – diurnal bird of prey, i.e. one that hunts and feeds during the day

Sandstone – the second most common, but most familiar sedimentary rock, forming about one-third of the sedimentary rocks exposed on the earth's surface. It consists of rounded grains of sand and usually quartz cemented together; the colour varies according to the mineral make-up

Savannah – grassland containing scattered trees, shrubs and scrub vegetation

Scree – loose fragments of rock covering a slope

Sedimentary rocks – eroded material transported either by wind or water and deposited with the sediments, accumulating eventually to form firm rock after a cementation process has taken place

Tarn – small lake surrounded by mountains

Wader – collective name for nine bird families of the suborder Charadrii, including plovers and sandpipers. However, the term is often used very generally to refer to all wading birds, i.e. birds that wade in search of food

Woodland – vegetation type characterised by trees with a well-developed, but not completely closed canopy

AFRIKAANS WORDS

Baai – bay
Berg – mountain
Bos – bush
Fontein – fountain or spring
Gat – hole
Klip – stone
Kloof – gorge, ravine, or narrow gully
Koppie – hillock
Kraal – traditional African homestead, or enclosure for farm animals
Krans – cliff
Mond – river mouth
Nek – saddle between two high points
Poort – a narrow passage through a range of hills or a mountain
Rant – ridge

Rug – ridge
Sloot – ditch or furrow
Sneeu – snow; often used to refer to mountains that are frequently snow-capped in winter (e.g. Sneeuberg)
Spoor – tracks of animals, including scent, droppings and urine
Spruit – a stream that is often almost dry, except after rains
Stroom – stream
Tafel – table; used to refer to flat-topped mountains
Veld – open country with natural vegetation
Vlakte – plain
Vlei – a low-lying area into which water drains during the rainy season; usually smaller than a lake

RECOMMENDED READING AND BIBLIOGRAPHY

A practical and comprehensive guide – to tracking wildlife, identifying trees, insects, birds, mammals and reptiles, and on what to do in the event of a snakebite – can be very useful when you're out on the trail. The following is a selection of Penguin Random House's top titles, and all of these recommended books are small enough for you to take along in your backpack:

- *A Field Guide to Insects of South Africa*, by Mike Picker, Charles Griffiths & Alan Weaving
- *A Field Guide to Tracks & Signs of Southern & Eastern African Wildlife*, by Chris & Tilde Stuart
- *Mammals of Southern Africa*, by Chris & Tilde Stuart
- *Sasol Birds of Southern Africa*, Fifth Edition (2020), by Ian Sinclair, Phil Hockey, Warwick Tarboton, Niall Perrins, Dominic Rollinson & Peter Ryan
- *Snakes and Other Reptiles of Southern Africa*, by Bill Branch
- *Snakes & Snakebite in Southern Africa*, by Johan Marais
- *The Wildlife of Southern Africa – A Field Guide*, by Vincent Carruthers
- *Trees of Southern Africa*, by Braam Van Wyk
- *Wild Flowers of South Africa*, by John Rourke

The following sources have been consulted by the author in the course of writing this book, and will prove useful if you wish to obtain more detailed information. Titles in bold are especially recommended.

Acocks, J.H.P. (1988) *Veld Types of South Africa*. Memoirs of the Botanical Survey of South Africa, 57.

Barnes, K. (ed) (1998) *The Important Bird Areas of Southern Africa*. Johannesburg: BirdLife South Africa.

Berutti, A. & Sinclair, J.C. (1983) *Where to Watch Birds in Southern Africa*. Cape Town: Penguin Random House.

Bristow, D. (2010) *Best Walks of the Drakensberg*. Cape Town: Struik Travel & Heritage.

Brooke, R.K. (1984) *South African Red Data Book – Birds*. South African Scientific Programmes Report 97. Pretoria: CSIR.

Cameron, T. & Spies, S.B. (eds) (1986) *An Illustrated History of South Africa*. Johannesburg: Jonathan Ball Publishers.

Chittenden, H. (1992) *Top Birding Spots in Southern Africa*. Johannesburg: Southern Book Publishers.

Coates Palgrave, K. (2002) **Trees of Southern Africa**. Cape Town: Struik Nature.

Greyling, T. & Huntley, B.J. (eds) (1984) *Directory of Southern African Conservation Areas*. South African National Scientific Programmes Report 98. Pretoria: CSIR.

Irwin, D. & Irwin, P. (1992) *A Field Guide to the Natal Drakensberg*. Grahamstown: Rhodes University.

Low, A.B. & Rebelo, G. (eds) (1998) *Vegetation of South Africa, Lesotho and Swaziland*. Pretoria: Department of Environmental Affairs.

Maclean, G.L. (2005) **Roberts Birds of Southern Africa**. Johannesburg: Jacana Media.

Mountain, E.D. (1968) *Geology of Southern Africa*. Cape Town: Books of Africa.

Newman, K. (2010) **Newman's Birds of Southern Africa**. Cape Town: Struik Nature.

Olivier, W. (2010) *Hiking Trails of Southern Africa*. Cape Town: Struik Travel & Heritage.

Paterson-Jones, C. (1991) *Table Mountain Walks*. Cape Town: Struik Travel & Heritage.

Paterson-Jones, C (1999) **Best Walks of the Garden Route**. Cape Town: Struik Travel & Heritage.

Raper, P.E. (1972) *Streekname in Suid-Afrika en Suidwes*. Kaapstad: Tafelberg.

Raper, P.E. (1978) *Directory of Southern African Place Names*. Johannesburg: Lowry Publishers.

Raper, P.E. (2004) *New Dictionary of South African Place Names*. Jeppestown: Jonathan Ball Publishers.

Sinclair, I., Hockey, P., Tarboton, W., Perrins, N., Rollinson, D. & Ryan, P. (2020) **Sasol Birds of Southern Africa**. Cape Town: Struik Nature.

Skinner, J.D. & Smithers, R.H.N. (1990) *The Mammals of the Southern African Subregion*. Pretoria: University of Pretoria.

Viljoen, M.J. & Reimold, W.U. (1999) *An Introduction to South Africa's Geological and Mining Heritage*. Randburg: MINTEK.

Von Breitenbach, F. (1974) *Southern Cape Forests and Trees*. Pretoria: Government Printer.

Von Breitenbach, F. (1986) *National List of Indigenous Trees*. Pretoria: Dendrological Foundation.

Von Breitenbach, F. (1989) *National List of Introduced Trees*. Pretoria: Dendrological Foundation.

Wilcox, A.R. (1976) *Southern Land – The Prehistory and History of Southern Africa*. Cape Town: Purnell & Sons.